WHITE POISON

A BLACK CHRISTIAN IS A TRAITOR TO THE MEMORY OF HIS ANCESTORS

Kayemb "Uriël" Nawej

AFRICA WAKE UP !

ISBN: 2-9600478-0-X

WHITE POISON

Contents

WHITE POISON

Dedication

I dedicate this book on a purely posthumous basis to Giordano Bruno, monk, Dominican priest and philosopher scholar, of Naples, Italy... from where he fled in 1576, the Catholic Inquisition seeking him.

Giordano Bruno preached a strong and accurate thesis: the Universe is infinite and there is in this infinite universe an infinity of worlds that are inhabited by intelligent civilizations.

He was imprisoned in Rome in 1592. After having undergone eight years of interrogations and tortures, he refused repentance and was so declared "heretic". As such, in the year 1600 he was burned alive publicly in Rome under the order of the "Holy Inquisition" of the Roman Catholic Church.

A recent point of view of the Vatican specifies: "The judgment for heresy of Giordano Bruno, independently of the judgment which one wants to carry on the capital punishment which was imposed to him, was fully justified". On February 3, 2000, Cardinal Poupard – responsible for the "pontificam consilium cultura" (Vatican Institution that rehabilitated Jan Hus and Galileo) – confirmed that Bruno would never be rehabilitated.

I declare Giordano Bruno entirely gifted of a "healthy spirit". My deepest and most sincere thoughts of sympathy are dedicated to him. If I had lived at his time, I too would have been burned alive by the Christian Church of Rome!

On the other hand, I declare "idiot and stupid" Cardinal Bellarmin who instructed the trial of Giordano Bruno and Galileo and who nevertheless was canonized in 1930 by the Vatican. But this fact will not surprise all those who, like me, assign this organization a particular talent: able to lull ones mind to sleep

WHITE POISON

1. Introduction

This book is not at all an incitement to racial hatred or to vengeance regarding the crimes that the white race may have committed towards the black race, not at all. The white race has already paid the price for its crimes: it has lost its purity, its innocence and this is due to the crimes that it has committed. A people that is responsible for and guilty of such crimes becomes embittered and its level of civilization fades away bit by bit. But there are many among the white race that is ashamed of this vile part of their history and they work to restore or dream of a just equilibrium. Those people will recognize themselves in this work. The whole of Africa salutes them and will always keep a special place for them in its heart.

Because Africa has kept its purity, it has never looked for revenge towards white man. This Africa, despite all the cruelty it suffered, has never wanted to call for an interracial war of blacks against whites. This is what makes the greatness of the African people, and it is surely the reason why this nation is so much appreciated by those "from the sky" who gaze toward our humanity with deep affection and love. This generous and just attitude of Africa must remain unchanged.

Today, it is not up to Africa to tell the white race to examine itself. It is especially up to herself to do its own self-examination. It has to forgive once and for all, to stop blaming whites and decrying their misdeeds and the causes of their actual misfortune. It must dare to look itself directly into its own eyes, see things as they are today in its own house, amongst Africans themselves, and have the courage to say and recognize what they see in this house.

How many times have we heard an African official or a "black authority" saying, "We blacks, we are cursed, it is as if we were destined to remain inferior, retarded, to remain Negroes! Yes, we are cursed, we will never develop as the Asians or the whites do, we are not capable, mentally or intellectually, we are condemned to remain Negroes forever, always behind the others, cursed"! I have heard similar words coming from the mouth of ministers, ambassadors, African diplomats, some expressing themselves in front of their young children, who drank their words. What an example! Where is the hope they offer to the young African generations? But, let us forgive them, they don't know what they are saying and consequently "they don't know what they are doing"!

But, where does this mentality of eternal colonized and eternal slave come from, this mentality obviously nourished by an enormous, terrible and permanent inferiority complex? The root of this profound evil must come from somewhere. It cannot be simply due to "hazard" or chance. If a community as vast as the African population can be contaminated as a whole by such a complex, the injection of this poison in its body must have been well planned, perfectly orchestrated. This complex could only have been perpetrated at very specific moments in its history and realized by certain actors whose goal was to parasite, weaken, paralyse and sicken it by this poison so that this body would develop only slowly or not at all. This fact is apparent and obvious, otherwise such a discomfort would never have occurred in such a body.

This evil is deep in Africa and if it affects us profoundly because this continent has been completely assimilated at all levels: religiously, politically, economically and socially. No other nation on earth has lived such an assimilation, none! From this fact it is interesting to make a detailed analysis of the ills inhabiting this body and to destroy once and for all the deadly germs responsible for this state of being.

It is the essential goal of this book.

Consequently, the purpose of this work is to look as closely as possible at the great elements responsible for this African evil. First of all, let us begin by studying the religious assimilation of Africa because it opened the doors for all the other assimilations: political, economical and social. In fact, the religious assimilation has been the ideal instrument of all others. It has served - during slavery as well as during colonization - to engender the loss of a very large part of the authentic cultural heritage of Africa. It has aroused continuous racism towards the black race, instituted the status of inferiority of the blacks in the present society and, in general, all the prejudices against the black people.

The study of the past is only interesting in order to find out where we are situated today...precisely because of that past, and to find out which measures are to be taken today to reach a real decolonisation. Because the state of being "colonized" is above all a mental state, and in this, we can also say "spiritual" and\or "religious". The economical and political colonization can only become possible if we are ultimately "mentally" colonized.

As written recently by the 1986 Literature Nobel prize winner, Wole

SOYINKA (English language Nigerian writer) – in the "Courrier Internatio-nal" N° 433 of February 18-24 1999, "Africa cannot allow another century to go by, continuing to satisfy the West without managing to discipline its own leaders. It cannot go through another century gently sliding from the known "truth" to a very convenient "reconciliation", without self-exami-nation in a more rigorous way and to stand up more energetically against its ancient colonial masters". Who were they, those ancient colonial mas-ters: they were, above all, missionaries...mostly Christian Catholics, and in a lesser way, Protestants. The true decolonisation will consist, in fact, in restoring Africa to the state it was before colonization polluted it political-ly and religiously, to allow it to rediscover its roots – the authentic African traditions – and to look at them today under the light of future technolo-gies, under the light of science. Let us concentrate on the assimilation of the black continent by Christianity as it is clearly very interesting.

One of the best things that can happen to Africa is a progressive de-chris-tianisation of its populations, because Christianity has been used as an instrument to enslave the conquered African nations, ensuring that they lose their identity.

By taking this fact into account, it is quite disgusting to have had Chris-tian, and consequently, mentally "colonized" Presidents in Africa; for example: Mr. Houphouët-Boigny from Ivory Coast who built in the middle of the savannah a perfect replica – and even larger – of St. Peter's Basilica in Rome! Cost: 10 Billion US dollars, with filtered air and air conditioning, the largest windows in the world, the deepest carpets in the world, gold, etc. It is situated in the centre of a "French style" garden of several hec-tares wide and surrounded by fences covered with fine gold. This opulent basilica is encircled by villages comprised of poor Africans living in huts without running water, without electricity and without sewers, in which are crammed families without revenues, gnawed by parasites and illnesses undermining their health.

The fundamental question that we need to ask ourselves is: "How did we get to that point in Africa?" In other words, how is it possible for some Africans to accept such things, or to let such scandals happen? How is it possible that a vast majority accepts this as normal? How is it possible that Africa has so easily let itself be "auto-colonized" by its own leaders...them-selves mentally "colonized?" How is it possible that such things, realized in the name of the religion of the colonizer, were and still are accepted?

This work will try to answer these questions, hoping that Africans will one day free themselves completely and that they will finally be totally deco-lonised, prove their intent by transforming that Basilica into a superb se-cular University where our African youth will be offered access to science and knowledge. This space could be filled with computers linked to the Internet, one of many tools to awaken the minds, instead of putting them to asleep as is the case now inside that huge "Christian" building

One fundamental question remains in my mind: Why and how did the wes-tern Christian religion become somehow an essential escape in a society that on the other hand remained so deeply "African?"

2. Religious assimilation

« When Whites came to Africa, we had the land and they had the Bible. They taught us to pray with our eyes closed: when we opened them, the Whites had our lands and we had the Bible... »

JOMO KENYATTA (former and first President of Kenya)

This type of Assimilation is probably the main cause of this inferiority complex towards Whites that Blacks often have or show, without really realizing it (at least the vast majority of them). And the fact that the majority of them are unaware of this is the proof that this trap was well devised and, alas, has worked tremendously well.

Any sincere specialist in politics can confirm it easily: in order to completely assimilate a people, like a dog, to lead it to submission, to remove all its own dignity, to foster obedience to its master without question, to make it adore the master and take him as the absolute model and reference, find him great and beautiful, to consider him as the intermediate or the go between with «God,» seeing him as almost equal to «God» himself. All of these things, to dominate a people in such a way and to be able to exploit it fully, to treat it as little children who admire their ''colonial'' father and obey him without hesitation, it is simple, the one who wants to attain this goal must start by religiously assimilating such a people, or in other words, ensure that their authentic religion(s) are removed and abandoned, and that you can impose them your own religion! And this pernicious stratagem succeeded particularly well in Africa.

Once this assimilation is carried out, the people in question are under the wishes of their master and this absolute master, whoever he is, can do what he wishes with them. In a manner of speaking, this becomes the middleman between «God» and that people. The colonial master and the missionary can then model their subjects as they wish, and this from the president(s) in place to the last servant.

Once the religious assimilation is complete, thanks to the missionaries for whom this is precisely their mission (and nothing else!). The word «mission-ary» is really well chosen indeed. The door is wide open for the economic and political assimilation, or, in more concrete terms, for economic exploitation and political domination, as the exploitation of the wealth and the natural resources is the only real objective of that religious assimilation. It was entirely orchestrated to open the door to the fruitful economic exploitation and its easy and inevitable corollary: political domination of the colonized. All the people that have undergone such assimilation are like dumb sleepwalkers, without identity, like a tree without roots. And this is much more so in the case of people where spirituality always played a vital role within the cogwheels of its social organization.

We can easily say that Africans remain today the most «colonized» people in the world, that they are «the» archetype of a colonized person at all levels. It is absolutely obvious because if the vast majority of Africans are still today faithful to the religion of their colonizers - essentially Christianity - consequently one has not to be surprised that the West still manages to dominate and exploit Africa by the means of what we call today «neo-colonialism.»

The best illustrations of the role played by the religious assimilation, in order to successfully colonize and exploit economically a people, are probably the speeches of the Belgian Ministry of Colonies and above all the speech given by Belgian King Leopold II in 1883 before the missionaries departing for Africa. Those speeches allow us to grasp the real mission of the colonizer and of the Catholic Church in Africa. Particularly this speech delivered by Leopold II, in perfect agreement with the Church, two hands together on one big belly, deserves to be known because until today it is still current; nothing has really changed. Here is this oppressive speech: Speech of Leopold II, King of the Belgians, in 1883:

«Reverend Fathers and Dear Compatriots:

The task entrusted to you is very delicate to fulfill and requires some tact.Priests, you will go of course to evangelize, but your evangelization must be inspired above all by the interests of Belgium.

The main goal of your mission in Congo is therefore not to teach the Negroes to know God, because they know him already.They speak about and submit themselves to a MUNDI, A MUNGU, A DIAKOMBA, and what else I don't know. They know that to kill, to rob, to sleep with someone else's wife, to slander and to insult is bad.Let us have the courage to admit it. You are not going to teach them what they already know.
Your essential role is to facilitate the task of our Administrators and industrialists.This means you will interpret the Gospel in the way it will serve and protect our interests in that part of the world. For that

purpose, you will make sure among other things that our savages lose interest in the overflowing wealth of their soil, in order to avoid that they get interested in it, compete to death with us and dream one day to dislodge us.

Your knowledge of the Gospel will allow you to find easily texts recommending the faithful to love poverty such as, for example: «BLESSED ARE THE POOR BECAUSE THE KINGDOM OF HEAVEN IS THEIRS. IT IS DIFFICULT FOR A RICH PERSON TO ENTER HEAVEN». You will do everything so that Negroes are afraid of to get rich in order to deserve heaven. [...] You must detach them from that and make them despise everything that could give them the courage to confront us. I refer here mainly to their war fetishes. Do not let them claim they are not renouncing them. And you will do everything to ensure that they disappear.

Your action will be directed essentially towards the youth so that they won't revolt. If the Father's commandment is contradictory to their parents' teachings, the children have to learn to obey to what the missionary, who is the father of their soul, recommends them. You must particularly insist on their submission and obedience. Avoid developing critical minds in your schools. Teach pupils to believe and not to reason.

There, Dear Compatriots, are some of the principles that you must apply. You will find many more in the books that will be given to you at the end of this meeting. Evangelize Negroes the African way, so that they stay forever in submission to white colonialists, so that they never rebel against the injustices they will have to suffer from us. Do them meditate every day «BLESSED ARE THOSE WHO WEEP BECAUSE THE KINGDOM OF HEAVEN IS THEIRS,» Always convert Blacks by using the whip.

Keep their women for nine months into submission and have them working freely for you. Then force them to pay you as a gesture of gratitude - goats, chickens or eggs - every time you visit their villages. Do make sure that Blacks never become rich.

Sing every day that it is impossible for the rich to enter heaven. Make them pay a tax each week at the Sunday mass. Then use this money normally destined for the poor and transfer your missions into flourishing commercial centres. Institute for them a confessional system allowing you to be good detectives to denounce to the Authorities with power of decision any Black who has a sudden awakening of consciousness.

(From: Afric-Nature, No. 005),
(Oct. 1994, journal camerounais,in «le réformateur chrétien» No. 004, page 11)

Do not think that this kind of speech is unique. Not at all! There has been a multitude of them. For example, we could quote an extract from the chatter of the Minister of colonies of Belgium, Mr. Jules Renquin, addressed in 1920 to catholic missionaries going to the Belgian Kongo (source: Avenir Colonial Belge, 30 October 1921, Brussels). In this chatter the directives given to the missionaries are divided in several points. After the brilliance of the speech of Leopold II above I would like nevertheless to give you some excerpts from this talk as icing on the cake.

The chatter in question starts like this: «Welcome to our second homeland, Belgian Congo.» and here are some elements I would not like to deprive you from:

*"Tell to the Blacks that their statuettes are the work of Satan. Confiscate them and go and fill our museums with them: from Tervuren (in Brussels), of the Vatican. **Make the Blacks forget their ancestors**.*
Regard all Blacks as little children that you have to deceive. Require that they all call you «my father.»

Teach them a doctrine whose principles you will not put into practice yourself. And if they asked why you behave contrary to what you preach, answer them: «you Blacks follow what we say and not what we do". And if they reply making you notice that a faith without practice is a dead faith, get angry and answer: «happy those who believe without protesting».

And here is how this chatter ends:

«So that, Reverend Fathers, this is what I was asked to let you know today. Hand in hand let us work for the greatness of our dear Homeland, long live the Sovereign, long live Belgium.»

No surprise that the Belgian Dynasty and the Catholic Church are still on very good terms today!

14

But let us return to the words of Leopold II for a simple and concrete example of how the contents of his speech and the one of the Belgian colonial Authorities were enforced in the daily life of a Congolese woman at that time. Here is an excerpt from the book «Abo, a woman of Kongo» from Ludo Martens, EPO edition; Brussels, 1995 (page 68):

«Our ancestors were free and independent in their country. One day Whites came to colonize them. From village to village, they distributed salt and salted fish in order to buy them off. But our ancestors refused. Then Whites used guns. Before entering a village they fired a cannon shot in the middle of the huts. Blacks found with a bow or a spear in their hand were shot on the spot. Whites forced us to pay taxes and to execute hard labour. Then they sent us priests with the mission to convince us to work voluntarily for Whites. We didn't even want to listen to them. Then they grabbed small children from their mothers on the pretext that they were orphans. These children worked hard in farms in order to learn the religion of the Whites!

Little by little they imposed their religion on us. What is it telling us? It teaches us that we must not love money; we must love the good Lord. But them, don't they love money? Their companies like the Oil Mills of Belgian Congo are earning tens of millions thanks to our sweat. Not loving money is accepting a slave job for a starvation salary.

They also forbid us to kill. But them, don't they kill? Here in Kilamba in 1931 they massacred over one thousand villagers. They (their priests) forbid us to kill only to prevent us from fighting the occupying forces. Priests also forbid us to steal. But them, they stole from us our country, our lands, all our wealth, our palm groves. When a Black man steals, he has to tell it at the confession to the priest. Then the priest runs to inform the White boss and the authorities and the Black man is expelled from his job and put in prison.»

Everything has been well orchestrated as I said above! I love making Africans and especially Kongolese think about this! How can you be Catholic or Christian today? How can you embrace the religion of those who deliberately hurt you so much? How can you make yours the religion of those who whipped, tortured, humiliated, persecuted and killed your ancestors? How can you do it? I consider that today all Catholic Christian Africans are traitors to their conquered, persecuted, tortured and murdered ancestors. Nowadays all Catholic Christian Africans are the symbol of success of the policy presented above and instituted by settlers with the help of the Church. They are living examples or the proof that it worked successfully.

As already mentioned, one of the goals of this Religious Assimilation was to make the Blacks forget their ancestors...and results are there...and numerous! It worked wonderfully well in Kongo and elsewhere in Africa. How many poor Africans fell into this trap full of venom? Judging by the impressive number of Catholics and Christians in Africa, it is about the great majority of people that we are talking! A majority that betrayed its ancestors! If somewhere in heaven we have African ancestors who can look down to Earth, they must be very angry or filled with sadness to see their descendants embracing the religion of their colonizers. They must curse these descendants who became Catholics and Christians.

I consider that today an African can embrace any religion possible. You can be Kimbaguist, Muslim, Buddhist, anything you wish, except Catholic or Christian because this choice is a terrible insult towards your ancestors. Africa is still today being «colonized» and therefore «dominated,» still and always mentally a «slave» of the neo-colonialist powers aided by their principal ally, I named the Roman Catholic Church, this usurper and invading organism. Yes, you can chose all that you want, all...except to be a member of this Church, to belong to this religion. It is this religion that did so much harm to Africa, bringing so many injuries and scars to the people of our noble African continent.

When the Catholic, Protestant, Adventist, Baptist Churches and other «Salvation Armies» where created by the European «looters.» there were no African Africans in these churches! It is sad and even distressing to see today «Kongolese,» Angolan,» «Cameroonian,» «Ghanaian» people and others, citizens of various countries of Africa, taking everywhere they go the «Holy Bible» of Jerusalem or the King James version with them...even to the toilets or lavatories! Have they forgotten so quickly that this «Bible» was the Number 1 instrument of the spiritual and material oppression of their ancestors and by which the Westerners are keeping them prisoners today!

In Europe, in Canada, in the USA and above all in Black Africa, the Christian religion has become the foremost refuge of Blacks who even manage to be the top "founding fathers" of «Prayer Groups!» These groups in no way solve all the serious and numerous problems the Black continent has faced for 500 years already. (Yes, it has endured for five centuries)! The verses of Genesis, Exodus, Apocalypse, the 150 psalms of David and any other excerpt from the Bible recited day after night, do not manage, and will never manage to put an end to the descent toward hell of our different African countries. This has been a programmed downfall completely created by the Western invaders (who purposely gathered on the subject in Germany during the Berlin Conference of 1885, and this of course against the will of our African Ancestors) orchestrated in order to colonize us spiritually, economically, and politically. And the primary tool used to achieve this all was the Christian Religion! When will Blacks at last understand this reality, accept it and start to act in a reformative way with a wholesale denouncement of the religion of the colonizer?

Originally, in old times, the inner garden of individuals was completely virgin at the spiritual level, anywhere on the Earth. The right question to ask now is: «How was it built and why was its construction pushed into a certain direction?» Let us accept - just for a moment - the concept of a «God» in order to understand what happened: the caveman at the prehistoric time and his successors after him had to be able to give themselves an explanation of the universe. For that they needed a magical notion that could explain to them the order of the universe and the "why" of things, especially when they were feeling lost at night facing all those stars. Then two magic thoughts developed, one telling: we have a «protective dad» living in the stars (we speak in that case of «God the Father»), the other one telling: we have «several protective dads,» so several Gods, in the plural. From then on developed in the mind of our primitive ancestors numerous Gods: the god of rain, of sun, of mountain, of river, of fire, etc.

Everywhere in the world man has known this form of supra-ocular belief, with divinities everywhere to explain or sponsor the elements of nature, for example. Then developed a more organized thinking that was helped by an institution saying: «the gods you have are not good gods»... «We have the «good» god and we will systematically suppress all the beliefs in these «bad» gods and, if necessary, we will go as far as killing those who believe in these «bad» gods! It is in this way that monotheism originated and rushed into this mission, spreading everywhere, dwelling upon some aphorisms like: «suffer... and pray the good lord» and other vague precepts. But these are only principles that always have been fabrications of the mind, deliberately dealt with in order to remove the responsibility of men in the face of actual things and events.

There is only one ancient Religion that managed to escape from that; «Buddhism.» It was actually very amusing to see the Dalai Lama saying on CNN that in Buddhism there is no immaterial and almighty «God.» This deeply disturbed the program host who then tried to lead the Dalai Lama to avoid discussion of «God.» But he continued saying «a unique God,» omnipotent and immaterial, does not exist in Buddhism. This considerably disturbed the Americans; they have the word «God» mentioned on their currency («In God we trust»)!

Our African ancestors, were they uncultured barbarians compared to Whites? Not at all; however many Blacks think so and this is very unfortunate! Many Blacks are ashamed of the spirituality of their ancestors, but why? Doesn't the white spirituality based on a «unique, immaterial and all-powerful God» only relate to pure and simple «belief» and even a belief that pertains rather to the supra-ocular?

Our ancestors in Africa were polytheists. They believed not only in «Gods» by necessity to have «protecting fathers» in the sky or to be able to explain the universe; it went much further. They believed in celestial and cosmic beings, beings made of flesh and blood, really «physical» beings who came from the sky. They believed also in Humanized Gods, «angels» from heaven or, to use another term, «messengers» arriving from the sky, cosmic visitors coming from the deep end of space. Moreover they always believed in many beings populating the sky. They named them with different names according to their different languages or according to the specific characteristic traits of these celestial beings, whose strange apparitions were, at different ages, physically observed by them and by the Black Prophets of ancient times who guided their people.

How did we manage to lose our authenticity in such a way? How did we manage to such an extent to let us be dominated and colonized at all levels? Answer: because of the religious assimilation, based on total humiliation, completely lowering the Black race, based on a systematic denigration. Let us have a look to this closely.

WHITE POISON

3. The systematic denigration perpetrated by those in high positions inside the Church

Black people have been the object of a systematic conditioning, repeated many times over. Daily they have heard or seen examples chosen to prove to them that "the negro" was an "inferior being". Children have seen and heard their parents and grandparents accept...and swallow this. All this conditioning has been well orchestrated using all means available. Nevertheless, it has been essentially the work of missionaries and other people in "high positions" inside the Church.

In my native area, Shaba-Katanga, Jean-Felix de Hemptinne, apostolic vicar of Katanga (the representative of the Pope in this region) was known for his visceral racism, the lot of all the missionaries working for the Belgian colonial policy. He wrote in 1931, at the time of the Elizabethville International Exposition (presently Lubumbashi), a study published in a paper called the « Rise of Kongo » (Essor du Congo), a study that was dedicated to this event. This study was titled: «Social and political perspectives». Here is an excerpt:

"... The conflict of the races, perhaps one will object, is part of the logical and inescapable order of events". The conquest of a people upon another, and stepping on the rights of others are never definitive. History is made of this ebb and flow of human waves. This law is true everywhere there is a violent conquest of a man by another man. Two civilizations, two energies, two currents of ideologies and interests can oppose each other, fight and triumph in turn, but nevertheless without arriving to the point to destroy one another. The thought is a phoenix that is always reborn from its own ashes. Ancient Egypt, which we thought had died, comes out alive from Tutankhamen's tomb and asserts its independence.

But it is a very rare case and without doubt unique inside human history, where the general law that we have just stated, does not seem to find its application. A certain portion of humanity has remained without civilization, without energies, without ideas, without interests to defend. In Europe, intellectuals take pleasure in trying to define and celebrate the beauties of the Bantu civilization; in certain rooms, we swoon in front of black art. This kind of entertainment does not give any answers. The black race has nothing behind it. A people wi-

thout written language, a people without history, without philosophy, without any sort of consistency!

That's why the primitive person is not exposed to the reviviscences of a past that does not exist; that's why this new born can grow without knowing the reactions which would be unavoidable in an adult that we might have conquered and subjugated. In Paris or in London, in full European civilization, we can find Arab princes or Indian Maharajas grandiosely dressed, proud of themselves and conscious of what they represent on the world scene; Mr. Diagne, secretary of State for the Colonies, does not have the least remembrance of his ancestral loincloth...

Black Zionism is one of our own findings, of communist, ideological or political origin, whichever, this movement is factitious... The absolute perfectibility of the native is not shown yet. Experience reveals the existence of a certain barrier which the black genius has difficulty crossing. Abstraction is not one of his strengths... Otherwise the natives will always have something to learn from us and will never catch up to us. In other words, the lead in progress in higher mathematics, and in science if not in virtue ,is not for Negroes and will remain within the white man's head... ours. The weight which mysteriously accumulates along the centuries on a man's head remains a threat, even when one becomes unaware of it. This is the poet's lesson: chase away what's natural and it will return at full gallop".

Jean-Felix de Hemptinne is not alone in saying out loud that which Belgium, the colonizer, and the Church have expressed with a more or less muffled voice. Another colleague of Hemptinne, a Benedictine like himself, whose thoughts are well known in Katanga as well, has also developed the same idea. This Benedictine is Dom Guibert. All the elders in Saint Boni or from Kongo's Official University know him. In an article published in the review of the CEPSI, titled « Tribal Languages and Civilization », he wrote, among other things, the following:

"Those who take care of making notes of the Bantu languages, with or without phonetic instruments and complicated alphabets, and use them to build grammar and dictionaries, make a point of being called descriptive linguists, oh dear: "sit pro ratione voluntas". However, I prefer to call it glossography to avoid misunderstandings, because they do not always bother to include the distinctive epithet... Finally and above everything, those alleged tribal languages, once equipped with a manageable orthography, a grammar and a dictionary, become

22

a cultural vehicle through this simple treatment? That, I have to say, is false. What the population of central Africa is lacking is precisely this culture, that is: not the technical training - which they also lack - but this general human refinement, the whole complex that we refer to as a spiritual civilization. And this spiritual civilization, which is lacking in the Bantus, will not be provided to them through their languages, since they do not convey it. In a Western Humanities class, we can comment on Homer or Virgil, or Molière and Racine, or Shakespeare or Goethe. In India, we can comment on the Bhagavad-Gita, the Mahabharata, or the Ramayana, and in China Confucius or Lao-Tse, and through those comments we have better tools to furnish and educate rather than simply inform the illiterate or barbarian young brains and hearts, than with their native cultural productions such as the fable of the hare and the guinea fowl, or the hare and the frog of central Africa..".

This statement is laughable, because pre-colonial Africa knew at least seven different writing systems: the Arako scriptures (the Yorubas), the Giscandi (in Kenya), the Nsibidi (in Nigeria), the Mende (in Sierra Leone), the Vai scriptures, the Loma and Bamum...and within each of these scriptures there are magnificent books and writings...touching all the sciences, poetry, the arts, etc.

This statement is more than laughable. When we look at Herodotus and examine the sources coming from Greece as an example, or the writings of another Greek historian, Diodorus of Sicily, a contemporary of Julius Caesar, they reveal that the Hellenic writing (Greek) which gave birth to the Roman and Latin writing, was taught to the Hellenes by a black man from ancient Egypt by the name of "Cadmos" (in Chapter 29 we will develop this in detail with all the necessary references).

We can simply refer to the two quotes above as they demonstrate the characteristic and systematic daily denigration that the Black culture has had to bear in a repetitive and incessant manner for a long time...for centuries! What a beautiful colonizing Church, which has not ceased lying, humiliating and denigrating us! To all Africans and people spiritually colonized by Christianization, I would like to ask the following questions:

Do you know that Christians - and in particular the Pope - have supported slavery, the trading of black people and their deportation?

Do you know that the Christians - and in particular the Pope...allegedly "infallible" - proclaimed for a long time that black people did not have a soul?

Do you know that your ancestors were converted to Christianity by force, violence, and torture in a real genocide?
How do you think your ancestors must be feeling when they look at you from above, or from heaven if you believe there is one, when they see that you have adopted the religion of the colonizers who tortured and massacred them?

Do you know that to apostatize, to abjure Christianity - and in particular the Catholic religion - is very easy to do? You just need to sign a document, an "act of apostasy", and simply send it to your church or diocese.

In 1655, Father Pelleprat described... "The priceless happiness of the slaves enjoying the freedom of the children of God"... In 1764, the Catholic theologian Jean Bellon of Saint-Quentin added: "This possession and this service are not contrary to natural laws, nor to Divine laws, nor to the laws of the Gospel", and he adds without attempting to be comical that "the worst misfortune for Africans would be the suspension of this trade" (he referred to the trading of Africans, reduced to the status of slaves, nothing less!)

For a long time, 15,000,000 Africans, men, women and children, have been treated like beasts of burden, with the complete blessing of the "high authorities" of the Christian Catholic Religion...the one that preaches so highly and passionately, "love thy neighbour". To the best of my knowledge, the fact that one of the three Wise Men who came to acknowledge Jesus' birth, Melchior, Gaspar and Balthasar, all three of great renown and the third a black man, never perturbed any Pope...again, to the best of my knowledge!!

To properly understand the evolution of the Christian faith that originated in a message of love by a Jewish Prophet, Rabbi Jesus, "King of the Jews" and resulted in the exorbitant power of a Vatican crumbling under its riches, it is necessary to remember a few important historical facts:

- *the cult of Mary did not exist at the time of the first Christians. It is only after the year 431 that it became official;*
- *the worship of saints and angels became official in the year 609;*
- *the worship of the images and relics in the year 787;*

- *the festival of all saints ("All Saints' Day") was instituted in the year 835;*
- *obligatory celibacy was imposed to priests from the year 1074 (the apostles were all married, except for John and Paul)*
- *the crown of Christ and the prayer beads were introduced into the rites in 1090;*
- *the "sacrament of Penitence" (the confession) was created in 1213;*
- *the conversion of the wafer into the body of Christ was declared "truth" in 1215;*
- *the conversion of wine into the blood of Christ was proclaimed "truth" in 1415;*
- *the "Indulgences" (to pay off sins through money) in 1500*
- *the "Corpus Christi" was institutionalized in 1519;*
- *the dogma of the "Trans-substantiation" (the transformation of bread and wine into the body and blood of Christ) was solemnly affirmed during the Council of Trent in 1551;*
- *the dogma of the "Immaculate Conception" (of the "Virgin" Mary) was promulgated in 1854; and then infallibility of the Pope, was decreed by the 1st Council of the Vatican in 1870.*

What a diversity of human inventions during the lapse of time of almost 2,000 years! The Prophet Jesus, who never instituted such things, must be horrified to see how things are in the present, all those things implanted after him and claiming to be "in his name".

WHITE POISON

4. Assimilation through Christian names

It is funny nowadays to hear that Africans use "Christian" first names, to hear that Africans use first names of the "Christian" West! It is extraordinary funny! We can understand that they could have used – during colonization or during slavery – such first names because, in those times, they were obligated to use Catholic names, they had to, they were forced to. But today Africans continue to use those same names, to give western "Christian" first names to their children, thus to name them and call them, many times a day, by names coming from the religion of those who colonized and took them as slaves, harassed, whipped, tortured and killed their ancestors.

Using « Christian » first names is one of the extraordinary proofs that black people still stay "colonized" and to what point they are.

I lived two years in Burundi, a very Catholic country, and there I noticed the most unusual first names. Unbelievable...the vast majority of Burundians use first names referring to the West, to old colonizing Europe or to the religion of the colonizer.

How many girls there use first names like "Immaculée" (Immaculate), "Marie", "Gertrude", "Ruth", "Madeleine", etc.? And for the boys first names, like "Dieudonné", and "Jean de Dieu", "Célestin", "Bonaventure", "Perfectuose", "Pontien", "Donatien", "Jean", "Gabriel", "Jean-Baptiste", "Pierre", and so on. I even met a "Bonaparte" in Burundi...to celebrate, I suppose, "Napoléon Bonaparte", this bloodthirsty tyrant who reinstated the slave trade and slavery in France in 1802, abolished a short time before he took office! It's funny, frankly hilarious...but it is at the same time a bit ridiculous, demonstrating to what point someone can still remain "colonized" in his mind.

On Mauritius Island, a large number of girls attach to their first name the prefix "Marie :" "Marie-Ketty", "Marie-Josée", "Marie-Chantale", "Marie-Christine", "Marie-Paule", "Marie-France", "Marie-Louise", etc! As far as we know, does the Mary of the so-called "Immaculate Conception" protect them more particularly against the specific fates still today reserved to "black girls?" To be sure, I haven't noticed anything at all!

What's even more amusing...there are African girls who use as first name the name of the colonizing country "France", or in the English speaking countries of Africa, the first name of Queen "Elisabeth"! I know girls in Ivory Coast who have as their first name "France" or "Marie-France"!

There are even Kongolese who use the first name of "Leopold" in honour, perhaps, of the king of Belgium "Leopold II", the person responsible for the worst atrocities in Belgian Kongo, having exterminated, according to estimations, between 8 and 10 million Kongolese during his bloody reign. We actually talk about the "gulags" of Leopold II in Kongo! Conscious of all that, how can a Kongolese call his son "Leopold?" I don't understand! It's like a Jew naming and calling his child "Adolf" (in honor of Adolf Hitler), like a Chilean, whose grand-father would has suffered from Pinochet's fascist dictatorship, giving the first name "Pinochet" to his son, the same for an Inca who would choose the name of "Cortes" for his son, or a Japanese who would give to his child the first name of the President of The United States who gave the order to drop the atomic bomb on Hiroshima, or, even, a Tibetan whose parents have suffered from Chinese repression and would call his son "Mao"! Only one sentence comes into my mind when, so often, I come close to that reality: "Poor colonized Kongolese and Africans"!

Another element to crown it all: how many black Africans give to their daughter the first name of "Blanche" (white)! Could you imagine one moment white parents giving to their daughter the first name of "Noire" (black) while she is obviously white?

Can you imagine just a moment that, all of a sudden, the large majority of Belgians are going to give to their children genuine African first names? Moreover, could you imagine for a moment that white parents, French, Belgian, or English, are going to give to their child the first name of a leader or of a king of black Africa, such as "Mobutu", "Eyadema?" Or give to their child as first name "Kongo", "Togo", or "Gabon?" Never in your life! Then how could it be that we give to our children names like "France", " Blanche", "Leopold", "Elisabeth", "Winston" (from Winston Churchill)? Have you ever heard about a westerner giving to his child the name of "Lumumba", "Nkrumah", "Sankara", "Tshombe?" Never! So, why does it happen for us to make such decisions?

Would you like to know the unique answer to this set of questions? Here it is: it is simply (...if I dare say!) because we are still "poor colonized people" spiritually. Whether you like it or not, we are still and always "colonized people". And as long as we will continue to serve the Colonizers' religion, "Christianity", it will remain so, and as long as it will last, Africa will remain a continent behind the others.

28

If Africa wants to decolonise itself, it ought to proceed by giving up completely Christian first names and other names referring to the colonizers or to their religion. It should go back to using its genuine African first names, linked to its own cultural heritage and to its genuine maternal languages.

But it's not only about the first names given to our children, there are also names given to boulevards, to bridges, to large squares, to some streets. Let us simply look, for example, in a country like Ivory Coast we find one of the biggest boulevards named "Giscard d'Estaing Boulevard" and a big bridge named "Charles de Gaulle Bridge"! Honestly, what did Giscard d'Estaing do that is so "precious" or simply "good" for Ivory Coast or for Africa in general to deserve having a boulevard named after him...according to him maybe...but according to you? Tell me! It's too funny, and it shows, once more, at which point Africans remain in this mentality of "colonization?" How is it possible that Ivorians, and above all, the Ivorian youth, can still accept that today? Frankly, that is beyond my comprehension! With all the damage that the neo-colonizing France has done in Ivory Coast, with the only purpose being to preserve the interests of the great French companies!

When will the Ivorian youth finally require the withdrawal of these names assigned without a legitimate reason to their boulevards, squares, etc? Even, if necessary, by changing them by themselves, without the permission of their leaders but in a great outburst of civil disobedience. It is a quick thing to do, we remove the ancient names and replace them, for example, with "Simon Kimbangu Boulevard", "Nelson Mandela Bridge", " Kimpa Vita Square", " Fela Anikulapo Kuti Street", "Haïlé Sélassié Roundabout" (who had the merit to preserve his country from colonization in fighting the Italian fascist Mussolini), "Patrice Lumumba Avenue" (or Thomas Sankara), etc. It would definitely be more beautiful and just.

5. A Black Code

In order for the black race to be religiously assimilated by the colonist's religion – and therefore by the colonist himself – to the point where it is today, certain tools had to be used, specific tools. Utilizing some precise laws as well as very precise codes, used in a simple and easy way, it all becomes firmly rooted, as deeply as it is now, in the contemporary black generation. How much did their ancestors have to undergo so that it lead to this generation of today, completely lost...because it is lost, everywhere, wherever it is, whether in Africa or in the black diaspora?

Let's have a closer look at "the Black Code". It was supposed to be the first legal protection for the slaves. It was established in March 1685, by an ordinance of Louis XIV, King of France, and it showed very clearly the barbarity of the French at that time; it is a perfect testimony of the importance of the religious assimilation necessary for the domination of the black slaves.

This "Black Code" is composed of 60 articles. Here, we will consider only the ones we are interested in the most[(*)]:

> **First Article.** *We wish and intend that the edict by the late King of glorious memory our very honoured lord and father of 23 April 1615 be enforced in our islands, by this we charge all our officers to evict from our Islands all the Jews who have established their residence there, to whom, as to the declared enemies of the* **Christian** *name, we order to have left within three months from the day of the publication of these present [edicts], or face confiscation of body and property.*

> **Article 2.** *All the slaves who will be in our Islands will be baptized and instructed in the* **Catholic, Apostolic, and Roman religion.** *We charge the planters who will buy newly arrived negroes to inform the Governor and Intendant of the said islands within a week at the latest or face a discretionary fine, these [officials] will give the necessary orders to have them instructed and baptized within an appropriate*

time.

Article 3. *We forbid any public exercise of any religion other than* **the Catholic, Apostolic, and Roman;** *we wish that the offenders be punished as rebels and disobedient to our orders. We prohibit all congregations for this end, which we declare illicit and seditious, subject to the same penalty which will be levied even against masters who allow or tolerate them among their slaves.*
Article 4. *No overseers will be given charge of negroes who do not profess* **the Catholic, Apostolic, and Roman religion,** *on pain of confiscation of the said negroes from the masters who had given this charge to them and of discretionary punishment of the overseers who accepted the said charge.*

Article 8. *We declare our subjects who are not of* **the Catholic, Apostolic, and Roman religion** *incapable in the future of contracting a valid marriage. We declare bastards the children born of such unions which we desire to be held and considered, we hold and we consider, as real cohabitation.*

Article 38. *The fugitive slave who has been on the run for one month from the day his master reported him to the police, shall have his ears cut off and shall be branded with a "fleur de lys" (mark of France) on one shoulder. If he commits the same infraction for another month, again counting from the day he is reported, he shall have his hamstring cut and be branded with a " fleur de lys " on the other shoulder. The third time, he shall be put to death.*

Article 44. *We declare slaves to be charges, and as such enter into community property. They are not to be mortgaged, and shall be shared equally between the co-inheritors...*

Being informed about this all, in the light of all this, how could Creoles in the islands, like Maurice Island, Martinique, Guadeloupe, Haiti during an official visit of the Pope, walk through the streets on their knees and ask him for forgiveness? How could they? They should rather be walking through the streets standing up and demanding public apologies from the

Pope usurper of Rome and should apostatize, abjure this institution that continues to hold them as mental slaves!

Isn't it funny to see Creoles from Maurice Island pushing beds on their streets with sick and disabled people during a Pope's visit to have him, by the Catholic Church supreme authority, perform "miracles" in front of his congregation! None of the Vatican's Popes since the beginning of the Papacy ever performed, none!

The Vatican has never been commissioned by any prophet whomever, neither Moses, nor Jesus, and therefore it has no ability whatsoever to speak in their name. It never received either by Yahvelohim a mandate to speak in his name! The Roman Catholic Church has never been commissioned to be an intermediary between Heaven and the Men and Women of the Earth, never! The leaders of this usurper's Church created this institution with no foundation 3 centuries after Jesus' Death...yes, 300 years after Jesus' death, so 15 generations after his death!

How could it be possible that descendants of slaves and Africans could give credit to this institution that has no heavenly mandate, when it has done so much harm already and still continues to do so? Because these human beings, from generation to generation, have been the object of an education which raised them. From the very beginning, conditioned to the degree they were, they have lived without asking themselves the right questions, without ever questioning what they were being taught. Instead, they behaved like bleating sheep herd that only follows the rest of the herd. It is like that and it has always been like that, maintaining a collective sleepwalk well orchestrated by the Church that puts spirits to sleep, because putting people to sleep has always been this institution's strategy and speciality, with the obvious goal of staying in power...by keeping everybody away from the truth.

To illustrate these last words, here is a good proof of the Church's strategy. We can find it in a document written in 1550 by cardinals reunited to elect Pope GUILLO III; through this text these prelates give advice to the Pope on what they consider being indispensable for the management of the affairs of the Vatican. This document is preserved at the National Library of Paris. Here is a particularly revealing excerpt:

"The Gospel and Bible reading must be allowed as little as possible

especially in modern languages and only in countries under our authority.

The little that is being read, and generally during mass, should be enough and it should be forbidden to anyone to read more.

As long as people will be content with this little, your interests will prosper, but as soon as they will want to read more your interests will start to suffer.

Here is the book [the bible] that, more than any other, provokes against us rebellion, storms, that are risky for us.

For that reason, if someone examines carefully the Bible's teachings and its comparison of dates with our church, contradictions will be found very quickly and our teaching will be seen, often as, wandering from the bible's, and even more frequently in opposition with it.

If the people find this out, they will provoke without rest, until everything will be revealed, and then we will become the object of derision and universal hate.

So, it is necessary that the Bible be taken away and removed from the people's hands, however very carefully, not to cause a commotion".

It is not possible to be clearer than that! Power before anything else, and even before the truth, is always the Christian Catholic Church's Doctrine. This is why, among other reasons, the Great Prophet Simon Kimbangu said to his people:

"Keep on reading the Bible. Through its scripture, in between the lines, you will start to discern the acts of those who brought you this book and the moral principles included in this book. A thief has to be caught with the object he has stolen"!

But what did they actually steal? You will find the answer to this question in Chapter 20: "The Polytheism of our African ancestors: Source of Truth".

(*): In the Bibliography [chapter 36] you will find a website offering the complete text of the "Black Code's" 60 articles.

WHITE POISON

6. The Church, Christianity and slavery

We've already seen in this book that Christians and in particular the Pope of Rome supported slavery, slave trade and the massive deportation of black people, and that the Pope, presumably infallible, has for a long time proclaimed that blacks did not have a soul.

You also read that Catholic kings, like Louis XIV of France, established «black codes» in which it is stipulated that the conversion of the slaves into the Roman Catholic Apostolic Religion - by force, if necessary - is an obligation, it is an order, an imperative law...punishable by the sanctions of the time, which could go as far as the «death penalty.»

But the responsibility of the Church goes much further. The Vatican is, to some extent, at the origin of the triangular modern slave trade on a large scale.

The "modern" trade of black slaves began half a century before Christopher Columbus crossed the Atlantic Ocean in 1492. In 1441, a Portuguese sailor named Antam Gonçalvez brought the first Europeans to the West coast of Africa, close to Cape Bajador in the south of the Sahara.

Once there, Gonçalvez discovered "a commodity" which he thought could please his King. His decision was made at once: he captured 10 black people and transported them to Lisbon. Portugal was then controlled by Henri the Navigator, Prince and member of the Christian Catholic Portuguese dynasty, under the orders of Rome. Gonçalvez offered him his "those commodities" as a gift.

This treasure - the 10 captured black people - pleased Prince Henri so much that he decided to donate them to Pope Eugene IV. In return, the Pope gave to Prince Henri the title (rights) of all the properties to be discovered to the East of Blanco Cape, a point located on the West coast about 300 miles above Senegal!

Consequently, a new era started in the history of humanity, the era of the massive triangular slave trade!

The discovery of the enormous commercial potential offered by the trade of «Negroes» was an opportunity which the new religious anthropology of Rome could not let escape from its fingers...because the papacy, that had just tasted a great rise of its wealth due to the crusades, became increasingly demanding on the level of its accumulation of money. Those crusades had just established, accordingly, that wars led in and for the interests of the Holy See were always right and that the fruits of these wars were good, and consequently that all these enterprises were «holy!» Thus, according to the mentality of the crusades - and that of the crusaders - the colonial religious anthropology of the Catholic Church, like all the Christian anthropology of the time, was by no means opposed, neither to slavery nor to the trade of the blacks. Quite to the contrary, it preached that it was a «Holy» enterprise, that it had to be carried out in the name of Jesus Christ, the Lord and Saviour!

At that time there was on the Earth, in the eyes of the Church, only two kinds of people, more precisely: the Christians, and the pagans. Any non-Christian person was pagan. Moreover, European Christians were «holy» and «civilized,» while blacks were only «pagans,» «savages» without a soul, possessed by the demons, by the devil. To kill one of them was equivalent to putting down a wild beast.

Two years after the fall of Constantinople in 1453, Pope Nicolas V officially authorized the king of Portugal to capture and take into slavery all the «black» Saracens (thus «pagans») and to seize their lands, and to give the same treatment to all the enemies of Christ!

In the 15th century things will get worse. A new form of slavery will be born, supported by religious motivations: a religious ideology that pretends to claim that the humanity of somebody depends directly on his religion. At the same time, the religious motivations of colonial expansion will be animated with a search for power and wealth, accompanied by open racism.

Let us see an extract of what Pope Nicolas V formulated in a «bull» especially devoted to this subject:

> *"...favours and special graces on the Catholic kings and princes, who... not only restrain the savage excesses of the Saracens(Blacks) and other infidels... but also for the defense and increase of the faith, they must vanquish them and their kingdoms and habitations, even though they may be situated in remote areas unknown to us..."*
>
> (Romanus Pontifex bull, page 21)

Further, to achieve this masterpiece of propagation of the Christian faith, the same Nicolas V gives king Alfonso of Portugal:

> " *among other things, free and full power is given to the aforesaid King Alfonso -- to invade, search out, capture, vanquish, and subdue all Saracens (Blacks) and pagans whosoever, and other enemies of Christ anywhere, and to destroy or take possession of their kingdoms, dukedoms, principalities, dominions, possessions, and all movable and immovable goods whatsoever held and possessed by them and to reduce their persons to perpetual slavery, and to appropriate to himself and his successors those kingdoms, dukedoms, counties, principalities, dominions, possessions, and goods, and to convert them to his and their use and profit* "

(Romanus Pontifex bull page 23)

Thus, this papal decree, for the expansion of the Christian faith, was ordering the Christians of the old world to meet people of other worlds, to dominate them and reduce their person to perpetual slavery. Bravo! A beautiful way of obeying the principal command of the Jewish rabbi «Jesus,» «Love thy neighbour as thyself.»

So you, black Christian living today, will you remain Christian...still and always, after becoming aware of all that you have just read? If so, where is your self esteem, where is your self-confidence, where is your self love, where is your dignity, where is your courage, where is your consciousness and your intelligence?

To be a black «Christian» today is a total aberration. I will not stop saying it, repeating it to my last breath. It is quite simply a shame in respect to oneself and in respect to the whole of Africa!!

Let us note, by the way, that these same catholic Portuguese, under the direction of the Portuguese Catholic crown, as early as their arrival on the coasts of the Kongo Kingdom in 1482, had been confronted with great resistance by a faction of the leading class of the Kingdom (Essikongo), faction that rose against the plundering of the national resources, slavery and the alienation of the Kongo country. The outcome was a war of these Kongos against the Portuguese; it became a disaster for Kongos. Also let us note that in 1665, during the battle of Ambuila, the Portuguese overcame the Kongos and they literally decapitated all the elite of the country. We counted at once three hundred noble and a hundred Kongo leaders, with their head cut.

All this in the name of Christendom and with papal blessing...»urbi et orbi» (for the city and for the world) of course! It is not by chance that the Prophetess Kimpa Vita was born a few years later, in 1684. All the Prophets and all the Prophetesses of the great celestial plan are born in a nation battling with a particular context, this in order to bring it reform, opposition, revolt, revolution. It is for that that the majority of them were persecuted, mistreated and very often killed.

The cause of the great decline of Africa at a given time in its history is more than likely slavery. Ah, yes! There was a time when the civilization of «black» Africa was much more advanced than the one of Europe and at that time the one of the current United States did not even exist yet. At that time, Europeans were probably «savages» compared to the civiliza-tion of Africa. Be conscious of this! But Africa will be able to find back a glorious state – in the image of a certain time in its past - only if it is able to release itself today from the claws of the West, and especially of the spiritual claws of the West.

For example, the Aoukar Empire (in Ghana) thrived for about a thousand years. Ghana knew 44 kings before the 25th Egyptian dynasty. It is only towards 1240 that this great empire fell. It is said that emperor Tenkami-nen (1065) could assemble in a minimum of time a troop of 200,000 armed warriors.

In 1311, the emperor Abubakari II was famous for sending ships, naval fleets, stocked with water, food and presents, sailing towards other worlds. And, it is precisely from this era that evidence and signs of con-tacts appear between West Africa on the one hand, Mexico and Colombia on the other. It is from the exchanges that took place between them at these times, that rises an incredible number of parallels between the two cultures (in arts, food, etc.), that exchanges really took place seems the only plausible explanation for it.

Well before Christopher Columbus - let us recall that for him it was in 1492 - blacks had already made the crossing toward the Americas and they tra-ded with the inhabitants of those lands...without ever seeking to colonize or invade the people that they found on the other side of the Atlantic. The pre-Columbian history contains much convincing evidence on this subject and various passages of its writings show that the «historical dogma» im-posed on all and making the point that Christopher Columbus would have discovered the Americas in 1492 is only one pure lie...inculcated in the West because that was very convenient for the old Christian Europe.

In 1324, Mansa Musa the emperor of Mali carried out a pilgrimage to Mecca, his entourage including 60,000 people and 12,000 servants. Five hundred of the latter preceded him and each one with a bar of pure gold weighing «six pounds.» Twelve years after his passage to Mecca, songs in memory of his visit were still sung there.

One of the greatest developments of the civilization of Africa certainly occurred at the time of the Songhai Empire during the 15th century. The Songhai Empire produced an incredible number of doctors, judges, priests, scientists (they were the responsibility of the emperor), and knew exceptional credit and mutual banking systems. In this empire, there were four great intellectual centers (universities), that is: Gao, Walata, Tombouctou (the university called Sankoré and of which the diploma was called «adjaga») and Jenne.

We could continue a very long history lesson but let us simply recall that Africa had already reached a high level of civilization many centuries before the birth of Jesus-Christ. At the time of its architectural miracles: Pyramids, the Sphinx, the Luxor Palace. Africa was advanced on all levels: medicine, transport, agriculture, aestheticism, mathematics, and so on.

What made all that disappear? It is that the development of Africa was brutally stopped around the 14th century by a rational organization of brutality: this heinous institution that was the slave trade. For a period of 400 years spanning 20 generations, the best of its inhabitants are stolen from Africa, men, women, and young people, constrained by «the force of the weapons» (fire guns) and taken along to the slave markets in the Americas and in Europe.

UNESCO stipulates in its estimates that the trade of the Blacks will have cost Africa about 210 million human beings. This figure includes blacks who died at the time of their capture, at the time of their transport towards the coasts, and at the time of the crossing of the Ocean, during which, quite often, as many as fifty percent died in the holds of the ships. The slave trade will be the greatest displacement of men of all times. The devastations that it caused in Africa are inestimable: it pitted a considerable number of tribes against each other, causing many wars, devastations, plundering and violence. The loss of men will dramatically slow the development of the African countries on all levels: production, agriculture, craft activities, etc.

The importation of European manufactured goods exchanged against the slaves will force many traditional crafts and craftsmen into obscurity, a whole series of trades will therefore disappear. For 20 generations, families, clans will have to take refuge in the forests, in deep bushes, to escape from being captured. Throughout these generations, the former social organization is completely dissolved. There is no longer education such as had existed previously. There is practically no more transmission of knowledge, no more schooling for the young people. There is permanent fear, nothing but one concern: to avoid being captured!

There will be during these 400 years an extraordinary loss for all Africans. Model men and women, professors, teachers, scientists will all be removed from Africa and parents will be also removed from their own children. It is a total decline of knowledge and education for all the African civilization.

This miserable slave trade generated more revenue to those who executed it than any other commercial venture in history. Oh, yes, you were unaware of this? Well, read attentively what follows: In the British parliamentary debates one finds, in full letters entered into the agenda, the following sentence: «one claims that a slave bought for 4 pounds on the African coast can in these days be sold in Brazil for 80 pounds.» This shameless trade pays big, very big...up to a profit of 2 000%! Yes, yes, you read well: 2 000%!

Therefore to become an economic power, the United States fed themselves with the blood of tens of millions of African slaves and their descendants and this over many generations. But English industrialization also benefited from it: cities like London, Liverpool, Manchester, and Bristol purely and simply built their wealth on the trade of black slaves. And let us not forget that France, with such large harboured cities like Nantes and Bordeaux, are superb emblematic examples. But also Amsterdam in the Netherlands and Antwerp in the Belgian Flanders! The list is long among all those who profited without scruple from this trade...the most revolting!!

But worse still, the trade of the black slaves has terrible remainders, in particular the racist theories, some of which still prevail today. Therefore, to justify the continuation of their trade toward an increasingly abolitionist movement, proslavery people will resort to the discriminatory theories generating racism. Several writings will appear which will analyze the characteristics of the Black people based on a theory that its propagandists dared to call «scientific.» It compares the skeletons and craniums of Blacks to those of monkeys, and concludes the inferiority of Blacks. Among these writings are those of the Dutchman Camper (1771) and of White (1799). These theories will still be detailed in the United States during the middle of the 19th century by certain authors like Morton, Nott and Cartwright who proclaim high and strong the inequality of the races. Darwinism will also strongly be fed by these theses. Europe imposed itself as an intellectual guide to the world and succeeded very well in this aspect with regard to Africa. But is time to set the record straight. We have an identity, a personality! Our strength was our great oral African culture, in this Africa where the verb is sovereign, that really helped colonizing Europe to carry out its plan of assimilation of the African populations. Acting on what Africa underwent during this entire long period, one can really speak about a «cultural genocide!»

It is necessary to remember of this dark period of its History that Africa has known a decline, a rupture with its boost of progress, of development, because of slavery. During these 400 years, Africa will have been plundered, it will have been robbed of its great forces, its human capital, of its brains able to transmit knowledge, able to educate.

But, if Africa had to realize this incredible deceleration of its progress, one should not forget that it also knew, at another given moment of this same and long History, an extraordinary explosion of science as it was the case in the Old Egypt.

But how sad to see Africa embracing with such enthusiasm this dishonest and usurping Christian religion, whereas it is not hers!

Let us look as a sad example of these African bishops of the Catholic Church, gathered together in 2003 in Senegal within the context of the triennial assembly of their organization. In Gorea - island symbol of the slave trade - they asked forgiveness in the name of Africa « for the responsibility of the African people in the Trade of the slaves.» No but? Who are they making fun of? It seems to me that a certain passage in the Gospel speaks of the straw in your brother's eye but pays no attention to the plank in your own eye! The Gospels should be the bedside reading of all these «Lordships.» Unfortunately, the application of the «true» commandments of their Master Jesus is not one of their strongest features!

But in our era, now in 2003-2004, it is particularly amusing to look at the way in which some events came to pass. Being at the same place and always within the same context of their triennial assembly, those same African Christian bishops asked...and always to the same Africans...

whether they be willing to forgive the Church for its responsibility, its participation, its involvement long ago in the slave trade! It is really an upside down world! It is rather Africa that should have things to ask and demand to the Church!

The «request for forgiveness» of the Catholic Church with regard to the support that it brought to slavery in the past is certainly well intentioned but it is still not sufficient.

The Vatican accumulated outrageous wealth by scandalously stealing it from the African countries. Consequently, the sincerity of this «request for forgiveness» will be proven only when it will redistribute a great part of this wealth by substantial financial compensation. This must be done morally and materially, and this, in «currency sounding and stumbling» to...

- on the one hand, those same African countries from which the slaves were taken away, and which are now the most destitute nations of the planet because they were deprived of their strongest forces and that their development was seriously impaired for centuries by the wound of this scandal named "slavery"

- on the other hand, to the descendants of the slaves who, because of the crimes perpetrated for 5 centuries under the initial orders of many successive "Papacies", live in disadvantage today, sometimes "famished" in comparison with the countries known as "modern" such as the United States or Italy, but especially towards this tiny state which is perhaps the wealthiest of the world or which is more than probable, not far from it...I named "the State of the Vatican" itself... their debtor for more than 500 years!

Even if such an action were to ruin the Catholic Church, by acting this way it would only conform to its own "official" tradition of poverty and it would help countries and people who did not take a vow of poverty themselves but are legitimately impatient to finally reach a decent social and economic standing.

If the Vatican and Western Christendom were sincere, they should evaluate with an international committee of experts the colossal sums that enriched them from this crime and give back to the victims referred above the totality of these sums with appropriate interest. Germany is doing it for the families of the exterminated Jews and for Israel. We are probably speaking of billions of dollars in these cases, an amount in great excess of the so-called "debt" of the Third World. In fact, it is the rich world that has a colossal debt toward the rest of the world, the African continent... among others!

As long as this compensation is not made it is necessary to encourage all Catholic and Christian Africans to apostatize: that they abjure the religion that has been responsible for the triangular slave trade and the humiliation of their ancestors for 5 centuries. To be Catholic or Christian for an African is to be a traitor to the memory of his ancestors and to seriously lack respect toward them.

Our African ancestors who were once subjected to slavery, wherever they may be, must look with horror at their descendants who agree to be baptized and to become Christians and Catholics. They must definitely feel betrayed and offended and surely disavow their descendants as traitors to their memory and the sufferings that they had to endure.

Forgiveness is possible only if there is compensation as painful to pay as the crime was for the victims...even if it is not violent but only of financial nature. This is not about going back to «the law of retaliation» (an eye for an eye, a tooth for a tooth) but monetary compensation is legitimate by today's standard for all serious faults.

It is undeniable that the ancestors ask their descendants to apostatize immediately, to leave this Catholic Church that tortured, uprooted and converted them by violence, and to return to their African traditional religions that actually were a worship of the Ancestors.

From the sky they look at their treacherous descendants and curse them until they divert themselves away from the religion of their torturers.

Imagine yourself to be recreated after your death in a paradise called the «Planet of the Eternals» and to see your descendants on Earth continuing to belong - even having the freedom to leave it - to the religion that chained and sold you like cattle. What would you think of it? Africans, find your dignity and by respect for your ancestors who look at you from the sky, apostatize, abjure this catholic church, apostatize yourself from the Christian religion, denouncing any entity that makes you feel guilty, since this religion itself recognizes its crimes, and find the religions of our ancestors who are the essence of our dignity.

We have endured obtained «political» decolonisation through sweat and suffering. We still have to gain the «spiritual» decolonization. And this conquest, you will see, will be much easier because no army will prevent you from leaving this religion, to change it if you wish. It will be much more important however, because it will enable you to stand up straight in front of the white Man - that you know only as colonizer and exploiter - and to finally look at him as an equal to yourself. The «Universal Declaration of Human rights,» accepted by an ever-increasing number of countries, affirms that «All the men are equal.»

You will no longer have to submit yourself to his white and superior God but you will be able to show proudly our traditional religions and the human "gods" venerated by our black ancestors. The de-Christianization of Africa is a priority for any African who wants to find his or her dignity and to help his black brothers and sisters to find it, to look at the rest of the world with pride, all the time being more proud of their negritude.

Because, let us not be misled, when one studies the history of the Negro slave trade, one realizes this: the Church, Christendom close behind and omnipresent has always been the catalyst of the slave system. Thus the Asiento Treaty concluded on March 26, 1713, allowed England for a period of thirty consecutive years to hold a gigantic monopoly on certain markets of slaves. However, this treaty stipulated that the ships were obligatorily to be French or Spanish and specified, moreover, that the crews could be composed of people of all nationalities, under the express condition that they all be Catholic (Article 8)!

In the royal palace of Benin, in the town of Abomey, old capital of this kingdom, one can appreciate a low-relief representing a slave ship; on the higher bridge one can see lounging a «man of God»...holding the cross. Slavery in the name of the Christian cross, here is what reality was, what the truth is!

I happily dedicate this chapter to the inhabitants of Haiti, the country on the open sea of the Caribbean. The marvellous Haitian people are composed of an enormous majority of black skinned people who deserve our full respect. We were delighted that they could celebrate the bicentennial of their independence on January 1st, 2004. Indeed, it is Haiti that achieved from 1791 to 1803, under the initial impulse of Toussaint Louverture, the first successful revolt of black slaves that the world has known. And from this, their independence was gained on January 1st, 1804, thanks to this revolt movement, giving birth to the first black, or Negro, republic of the world. In addition, this very young Haitian State quickly assisted

Simon Bolivar in freeing Venezuela from Spanish domination in 1811, thus continuing its battle for the abolition of slavery in all Latin America! What a formidable population these black people of Haiti. I truly carry them in my heart.

7. The systematic assassination of black Prophets by the Church and their elimination from history.

«How long shall they kill our Prophets, while we stand aside and look?»

(Redemption song by Robert Nesta Marley)

Another idea I find amusing is the fact that black Africans do not really ask themselves the question as to whether there were certain Black Prophets during the course of humanity. The great majority of black Africans pray to "Jesus" on Sunday in "white" churches, receiving once again a good collective conditioning to adore the «Jesus» of the Whites, the «Jesus» of the slave colonizers' religion.

On a visit to Ghana in 2003 I was astonished to note that the coast of this country was lined with a great number of fortresses from where slaves departed, bound for the Americas and human markets all over the world. I also noted that Ghana is one of the cradles of pan-Africanism, the large majority of the people are kept asleep by Christian Churches of all kinds. Everywhere along the road are signs of their devotion to "Jesus;" «Jesus loves you,» «Jesus will save you,» «Jesus is your guide,» «Jesus will provide,» etc. Radio stations broadcast speeches of Christian preachers continually. In almost every taxi we see stickers, small posters, key-holders with reference to Jesus, and in still others we hear songs that speak of Jesus!

Where are the roots of all these Ghanaians today? Where is their attachment to ancestral traditions, to the pride of their ancestors? Where is the pride in their own history, the pride of their great past, equally glorious. Where? I felt an enormous sense of pity for them!

I would like also for us Africans to ponder on this important fact: Everywhere on Earth, people have had, at any given moment in their history, their own indigenous Prophets. The Asians have Asian Prophets, such as Buddha, Krishna, Lao-Tzu, Confucius, etc; the Arab and Jewish Semites have Prophets of the Middle-East, such as Moses, Mohamed, Bab, Zoroaster, etc; the Americans, whose civilization is rather recent, nevertheless have an American Prophet, Joseph Smith, initiator of the Mormons; Europeans have had, for the last 2000 years their Prophet, «Jesus.» How is it that we, blacks of Africa, do not have our own black African Prophets? Does a reason exist for the blacks not having had their own Prophets in the same way and at the same level as other people? Is there a single explainable motive for the Heavens to discriminate against the black people with respect to «Prophets?» The answer is in the question itself, it is plainly NO!

Then, how is it that black Africans do not know, or do not know anymore, their Prophets? Why did they forget them? Why don't they venerate them or don't venerate them anymore or not enough? Why do we never speak about them in the schools, in the Religion courses in the West? Yes, for what reason(s)?

First of all, the «colonized black» mentality imbues Africans with a complex of inferiority, and this complex makes them wrongly feel ashamed of their history and everything that comes from their homeland. Their «colonized» state of mind has caused them to view all things "white" as inevitably the best, just, most valid, as beautiful and good, as «civilized»... blacks still being, in their minds «savages.»

It should not be forgotten that the white missionary, the white priest, were mediums for their parents, their grandparents, their great-grandparents, (one can look back 25 generations!) between "God" and the «colonized» black people. The divine word came to the black through the white missionary and so the white man ultimately received the status of "superior" being in all the minds of the blacks converted to Christianity. This education continued on, generation after generation, without question and with ignorant imitation. Progressively, little by little, this shaped the «spiritually colonized» people that Africa and its Diaspora comprise today.

Then there was the Inquisition of the Roman Catholic Church in Africa. It is funny to note today what Africans think and say when they hear the word «Inquisition.» For them, this is part of Europe's history; it is a history that occurred between Europeans during the Middle Age. This connection of the word Inquisition with only Europe is yet another example, which proves to what extent, the Africans are lost and to what extent they are unaware of their very own history. We can easily understand how this happened as it was all part of the orchestration to force them to forget their own history!

It is mainly the Church that undertook the arduous task of numbing the brains: it did all it could so that blacks forget their authentic Prophets and their Religions. Indeed the Inquisition of the Roman Catholic Church, one can even say the Inquisition of «Christianity,» also prevailed in Africa.

Here are some examples of black Prophets:

a. Osiris: The Great Negro Black Prophet

Since we will speak about the African Prophets, it is only logical for me to begin with the famous Osiris, the most senior of the black Prophets, whom we call also the ancestor of the great Pharaohs of Egypt. It is with Osiris that we approach the oldest prophet in history, that of «Ancient Egypt». His tomb was discovered by a Frenchman, Emile Amelineau, professor of History of Religions. (1850-1915). What do we know about Osiris? He was designated as the son of Geb (the Earth) and Nout (the sky); he was thus the fruit of an interbreeding between somebody from the Earth and somebody from the sky! Apparently he was someone who could also say «my father who is in Heaven!»

Osiris was the embodiment of good; the writings say that he was sent to triumph over evil. The name «Un-nefer,» is translated as "eternally good Being" in Ancient Egyptian. He gives food and all forms of nourishment to the entire country that he traverses to teach wisdom, agriculture, the rejection of cannibalism, the culture of the vine, the use and the conservation of wine. He indicates which ones are the good fruits to be harvested from the trees and the usefulness of many other products of the Earth (cereals, corn). Thus the ancient Africans showed him love as they saw in him an envoy of the heavens...which is who he actually was.

He was also called «USR» or «Usir» which means «the great one,» «the powerful one.» He said amongst other things:

> «I am the lord of Maât (truth-justice)»
> «I am the Master of Eternity»
> «I am» the one who is»
> «I am on Earth the first of the Amentiu
> (resuscitated among the dead).»

Osiris is represented in the documents of the Pyramids and old monuments as a «black» of large size. Let us emphasize in support that the Greek Plutarch, later in Antiquity, would write about Osiris and his wife. The "Treaty of Isis and Osiris" would stipulate very clearly the physical characteristics of Osiris. Volume 2 of the historical encyclopaedia carried out under the name of «General History of Africa» also informs us, according to their sacred texts, the Egyptians called Osiris «Great Black:» «KEM-WR» (KEM =

51

black and WR = large) and that his wife was named Isis, which is translated as "black woman!»

Here again, a text drawn from the teachings of the wise Merikare (2070-2050 BC):

>*«Act for RA (the supreme god) (...) do all these things for him, so that in return he provides for men. For «Ra» made the heavens and the Earth for their well-being, he calmed for them the greed of water, he made the air to give the breath to their nostrils, he created them in his own image.»*

There was indeed already a genesis in Africa where Ancient Egypt was called by its inhabitants «KEMET,» not referring to the color of the ground, but to mean that it is a civilized land, quite simply inhabited by black men, because «KEMET» means «ground (or city) of the black man's science.» Moreover the determinative Nwt (Niout) is often used after the word «Kemet,» indicating a city that is administered: a civilized city.

>*However, the examination of the religious texts and the accounts of the ancients show that it is also for spiritual reasons related to Osiris (representing good) and of Seth (representing evil) that the first Pharaohs chose the North-East of Egypt to build their first large city: Memphis. Thus, the Greek historian, Diodorus of Sicily, already referred to above (in Chapter 3), will write later that Osiris would have led his people from the south towards the valley of the Nile (cf. Diodorus of Sicily, Book III).*

When Egyptians portray Divinities in their symbolic function, their color changes. For example, Osiris is painted in green to symbolize vegetation, the vegetating Osiris. In other cases, the divinities, and in particular goddesses, are represented in gold color. Gold is indeed the flesh of the Gods for the Africans.

The Great Black Prophet Osiris was venerated in all of Egypt (Abydos, Heliopolis, Athribis, etc). The account of his life is the center of the religious texts of Kemet (ancient Egypt). Towards 1985 B.C., a theatrical school in Abydos existed which gave representations of the mysteries of Osiris.

Thereafter Osiris became Dionysus in the Greek tradition. In turn, Dionysus became Bacchus in the Roman tradition. The Greek writer Plutarch (50-125 A.D.), in his «Treaty on Isis and Osiris» about Clea confirms for us this Greek tradition:

> *«Let Osiris become one with Dionysus, who could know this better than you Clea, you the mother superior of the Delphian Thyades (priestesses of Dionysus), who was consecrated by your father and mother to the Osirian rites?*

What do we learn again from the Greek historian Diodorus of Sicily? That the mission of Osiris reported in the Egyptian sacred Texts was, among others, of traversing the inhabited Earth to civilize humanity and to force humanity to give up cannibalism definitively and discover the divine virtues:

> *«He left Egypt with his whole army for his expedition, with at his sides his brother whom the Greeks call Apollo. As they say, it is he who discovered the laurel and all men particularly crown this God with it. He attributes the discovery of ivy to Osiris and consecrates it to this God-Prophet, just as the Greeks for Dionysus (...) Specialists in agriculture also accompanied Osiris (...) He traveled to other people and went to Europe by crossing Hellespont (...) In Thrace he killed the king of the Barbarians, Lycourgus, who was opposed to his actions, there he left Maron who was then old, to watch over the plantations that he had made in this country and made him the founder of the city that bears his name and that he named Maroneia. He also left Macedon as king of the country that was called after his name Macedonia.»*

We could understand by this that the ancient Africans, answering a divine call from the heavens through Osiris, traveled the Earth to share their knowledge with men. We also find there the origin of the laurel crown as carried thereafter by the Roman emperors. Lastly, ancient archaeology shows that the temples built at that time have the same astral orientation as the temples of Nubia, of ancient Egypt.

Thus one finds sitting on the first «divine» throne in the history of the religions as «Prophet» sent by the Heavens on Earth, Osiris a black, and a Negro...Osiris Kem-Our, in ancient Egyptian, «Osiris the Great Black.» Details on this subject are in «the Book of the Dead» of Nebqued (1320 B.C.). (See the illustration on Page I of the central booklet.)

Let us specify that the ancient Egyptians, that is, the distant ancestors of the black African, were polytheists. They venerated creator-gods (in the plural), people who came from the sky in «solar discs» (flying saucers).

b. The Prophetess Kimpa Vita: burnt alive by the Church.

Kimpa Vita was the founder of a religion called the "Antonians" or "Kimpa-si", a religion that agitated the entire Kingdom of Kongo at the beginning of the 18th century. At that time, slavery was in full force; it was the first commercial activity in the Kingdom.

Kimpa Vita, it is said, was the first to rebel against the foreign domination. It was possible for her to do so as a woman because, at that time, the society of the Kingdom of Kongo was a matriarchal society: the filiations of individuals were made through the female lineage. The power only appeared to be in the hands of men; at the head of the Kingdom of Kongo was a man, the king, but women had essential attributions as much in politics as in religion.

Her parents gave her the African name of "Kimpa Vita", Kimpa meaning "craftiness" and Vita meaning "war" or "guerrilla". Her Christian name is Dona Beatrice. She was born in 1684. In Kikongo, language of the lower Kongo, her religious movement took the name of "Kimpasi".

Kimpa Vita was a girl born into the noble society of the Kongo people. When she was very young, she learned of an old lady named Matuffa who criss-crossed the countryside and villages announcing the coming of a young black prophetess, claiming that "black angels" from the heavens appeared to her, among whom was "St-Antoine" (patron of the humble and destitute).

Kimpa Vita and Matuffa meet and the former enthroned as "Prophetess". In turn Kimpa Vita encounters the angel (from the Greek "angelus", etymologically "messenger coming from the sky") St-Antoine who dictates to her the mission to be accomplished.

Kimpa Vita with her disciples called "angels" preached throughout the Kingdom of Kongo by saying, among other things: "the missionaries whiten God for their profit...that is how they blessed the black slaves' boats" or also, "in the heavens, on the eternals' planet in paradise...there are blacks, there are Kongos".

Kimpa Vita performed healing in the same manner as Jesus, Kimbangu, and others. It is said that with a simple touch, for example, the young woman rendered sterile wombs fertile.

She called on the people of Kongo to establish a more humane society, without luxury and misery, without master and without slaves, similar to the society where their ancestors live on their celestial planet.

It is said that during the Antonians' prayer sessions, the Gods were invoked with "obscene" and sexual gestures, and that during their ceremonies the participants were engaging in sensual and carnal relations. This precipitated the Catholic Church's perception of Kimpa Vita as a lowly woman of, possessed by the Devil, this moreso since she lived with two men. It is also said that she was taught women to be fearless, neither to fear tomorrow from the day after tomorrow, to free themselves from men's control and to take their well deserved place in society. It should be said that at the time, the official position of the Catholic Church was simple: woman did not have a soul (no more than animals!). However, the messages of Kimpa Vita were extremely revolutionary and gathered huge success.

She started her preaching and teachings in 1702. She then became the head of the movement for national recovery of her time. She taught eminently subversive ideology. It is reported that while the black slave trade had developed a declared racism from the whites, she advocated with an exceptional power of conviction the absolute equality between blacks and whites. The number of her followers increased by great proportions. Historian Bernado do Gallo reports that almost the whole kingdom adhered to the Kimpasi movement of Kimpa Vita, and she was only twenty years old! In doing so, she not only endangered the missionaries and the two competing kings of the time but also threatened the flourishing and highly lucrative slave trade.

In 1704, the Catholic Church accused her of "witchcraft". She was first arrested by the missionaries but soon released under pressure from the people. In 1706, she bore a child with one of her men. The Catholic Church then orchestrated a large campaign of slander against the "false saint", the "so called black virgin", proclaiming that she was an envoy of the devil. She was once again arrested, but her trial, worthy of the Inquisition's tribunals, this time divided the kingdom with no one wishing to assume the responsibility for her execution, not even King Pedro IV. It is finally the Catholic Church itself that pronounced the sentence by forcing the Royal Council to follow it. The sentence imposed was that reserved for witches: death by fire.

She was arrested on orders of the Italian missionaries (at the service of the Vatican) led by two Capuchins fathers, Lorenzo da Luca and Bernardo do

Gallo. It is these same two men who pillaged villages in Kongo with Portuguese troops at their service to capture the Kongos and force them to the Christian Catholic baptism.

During her trial, the Capuchin father Bernardo do Gallo asked the following question:

> *"Tell me if in heaven there are blacks from Kongo and are they present there with their black color?"* *Kimpa Vita answered:* *"In the heavens, there are blacks from Kongo and adults that observed the law of Nzambi (Yahweh); but they don't have the color of Negro nor the white, for in the heavens there is no color".*

Kimpa Vita was burnt alive publicly with many of her followers on Sunday July 2, 1706, executed by Capuchin missionary monks. But in the only four years of preaching, before she herself was burnt, her ideas were able to set the whole kingdom afire. Before she died, she announced the coming of another prophet that would come to finish her work, a black Christ who would come to show the black people the path to follow toward its liberation; she was thus announcing the coming of the prophet Simon Kimbangu.

While being burnt alive at the stake alongside many of her disciples and her own son, Kimpa Vita repeated that the heavens would send another prophet to be born to stop slavery and save the black man. It is normal or easy to "understand" why the history books of the West do not mention her.

c. The Prophet Simon Kimbangu: jailed, condemned, tortured to death by the Church and its valets of the Belgium dynasty.

The people of the Kongo kingdom, with unrelenting mistreatment by the European missionaries, felt deeply abused. The decline of the kingdom was absolute and the distress of its inhabitants was at its highest. Above all, the colonial powers that had gathered for a conference in Berlin (1884-1885) shamefully split among them all of Africa by drawing and creating arbitrary borders. These artificial borders, lines drawn on a map, took nothing into account with regard to the homogenous social groups of population, nor the natural frontiers of kingdoms, empires and existing sultanates. The Gods in the sky, contemplating this disaster, then decided to have another Prophet born.

And so Simon Kimbangu, whose name means, "The one who reveals hidden things", was born in Nkamba, a small village in central Kongo, on September 12, 1887.

From 1910, Simon Kimbangu began to hear the call of Yahweh's spirit that asks him to "cater to his flock". Numerous times, Kimbangu refuses to obey the call by explaining that he was not up to such a high and important mission. He even took refuge in Leopoldville (Kinshasa) to escape the "Voice" and finds work in the oil mills there. He worked without pay, and returns home disillusioned to Nkamba where, on April 6, 1921, in the hamlet of Ngombe Kinsuka, the spirit of Yahweh gives him the order to resuscitate a young girl, Nkiatundo, who had just died.

This first "miracle" by Kimbangu would begin what historians called the "effervescent semester" (from April 6 to September 12, 1921), an intense period of preaching and miracles that will shake the Belgium colonial empire, Angola and even French Kongo.

From the month of June 1921, following the colonial persecutions mainly orchestrated by the Catholic and Protestant missionaries, the Church begins to see a sharp decline in its followers. It is at this time that the Great Prophet Kimbangu enters clandestinely and sojourns notably in Mbanza-Nsanda where he will fulfill the terrible prophecy about which you can read an excerpt at the end of this short biography of Simon Kimbangu.

On September 12, 1921, the Great Prophet Kimbangu is arrested and transferred to Thysville (Mbanza-Ngungu) where he is summarily judged and condemned to death. But shortly after, the king of Belgium, Albert 1st, commutes his capital punishment to a life sentence. The Great Prophet Kimbangu is promptly taken to Elizabethville (Lubumbashi), in Katanga where he will spend thirty years in a minuscule cell of .80 by 1.2 meter without aeration and proper hygiene conditions. His bed was a mere slab of concrete. Every morning Kimbangu was dipped in a deep well containing cold and salty water, this in order to accelerate his death.

Two days prior to his death, on October 10, 1951, the Great Prophet Kimbangu announced to his co-detainees that his detention would end and that he would die two days later: on Friday October 12, 1951 at precisely 3 pm!

Indeed, on October 12, 1951, after saying goodbye to his guards and co-detainees, the Great Prophet Kimbangu hit himself three times with his fists on the right and left ribs. Lying down on his blanket on the floor, he died peacefully but not without having first prophesized terrible ordeals for Belgium and the West in the future to come.

In his preaching, the Great Prophet Kimbangu often announced the soon to be liberation of Africa and "Kongo" from the colonial domination, first and of the West's domination in general later on. This liberation should, according to the Prophet, occur in 3 steps.

Before his death, the Prophet Kimbangu created a powerful spiritual movement that he called "Kintuadi" (Union, Unity, Community), devoted to the total liberation of the black man. He presented himself as the saviour of the black race that he asserted solemnly during his trial in Thysville (Mbanza-Ngungu) in front of Mr. De Rossi, president of the War Council instituted for the occasion. This the Catholic and Protestant missionaries did not accept, no more than their eternal allies: black pastors, abbots, bishops and other African religious dignitaries of the neo-colonialist system.

The members of the Kintuadi movement of the Prophet Kimbangu were the object of numerous persecutions and deportations from their native central Kongo towards many equatorial localities of the higher Kongo and Katanga like Ekafela, Ubundu, Lowa, and Elizabethville. The number of faithful of the Prophet Kimbangu that were deported from 1921 to 1959 was in excess of 150,000! Many of them never came back to central Kongo and died in exile, in hard labour, under the whiplash and relentless beating!

The Great Prophet Kimbangu never made any compromise with, nor ever had any complacency for, the white colonizers whom he treated as invaders and usurpers.

Here is the famous speech given by the Prophet Simon Kimbangu, on Saturday September 10, 1921, at the very beginning of the morning service, around 9 am. (;) As he entered (as he was entering) the enclosed palm area, his face grim, but with a keen look, he addressed the crowd in these words:

"My brothers, the Spirit came to reveal to me that the time to give myself up to the authorities has come. Keep this in mind: with my arrest, a period will begin of inexpressible persecutions, for me and a great number of people. We will have to hold on strong, for the spirit of Nzambi all mighty (Yahweh) will never abandon us. He never aban-

doned whoever confides into him".

"The government authorities (colonial) will impose to my physical person a very long silence, but they will never be able to destroy the work I have accomplished, for it comes from Nzambi (Yahweh) the father. Indeed, my physical person will be submitted to humiliation and suffering, but my spiritual person will fight against injustices sowed by the people of the nether world who came to colonize us".

"For I was sent to liberate the people of Kongo (Cula minkangu mai Kongo) and the world black race (Zindombe zazo). The black man will become white and the white man will become black. For spiritual and moral foundations, as we know them today, will be profoundly shaken. Wars will persist throughout the world. Kongo will be free and Africa also".

"But the decades following the liberation of Africa (the nominal independences of the sixties) will be awful and atrocious. For all the first rulers of free Africa will work for the benefit of whites. A great spiritual and material disorder will take place. The rulers (Minyadi) of Africa will take along, on counsel from the whites, their respective populations in murderous wars where they will kill each other. Misery will be in place. Many youths will leave Africa hoping to find happiness in the white countries. They will all speak the whites' languages. Among them, many will be seduced by the material lifestyle of the whites. Thus, they will become prey for the whites (Nkuta Mindele). There will be high mortality among them, and some will never see their parents again".

"It will take a long period for the black man to acquire his spiritual maturity. This will enable him to acquire his material independence. Then the third step will be accomplished. During this period, a great divine king will be born (Nkua Tulendo). He will come with his 3 powers: Spiritual Power (Kinzambi), Scientific Power (Kimazayu) and Political Power (Kimayala).

"I myself will be the representative of this king. I will eliminate the humiliation that, since past time, was always inflicted to blacks. For among all the Earth's races, none has been as mistreated and humiliated as the black race.

«Continue to read the Bible. Through its writings, you will be able to *distinguish the acts of those who came to bring you this book and the writings or moral principles contained in this book. The robber must be caught with the object that he stole!*

«We will have our own Sacred Book, in which will be written things hidden from the Black Race and the People of Kongo. An Instructor-teacher (Nlongi) will come before my return to write this Book and prepare for the arrival of the Great Divine King, the Nkua Tulendo. He will be fought by the generation of his time, but gradually, most of the people will understand and follow his teaching. For the arrival of the King will be without forgiveness. Then, it is necessary for the People of Kongo to be informed before this event.

«You do not know yet what a spiritual war is like. When the Kongo People start to liberate themselves, any country that will dare attack Kongo will be engulfed under water. You do not know yet the power of those who are sent by Nzambi (Yahweh) the Almighty. «The Kongo generation will lose everything. It will be muddled by teachings and perverse moral principles coming from the European world (Mavanga my bisi Mputu). It will not know any more the marital principles of its ancestors. It will ignore its mother tongue. So I exhort you to not neglect nor scorn your mother tongues. They should be taught to your children and your little children... for a time will come when the languages of the Whites will be forgotten. Nzambi gave to each human group (Nkangu wa bantu) a language, which he uses as an «alliance of communication» (Nsinga wa Mbila)...»

(Excerpt from the "Prophecy of the Great Prophet Simon KIMBANGU",
Saturday, September 10, 1921 in Mbanza-Nsanda, Kongo-Exchange).

Then the Prophet Kimbangu invited everyone to pray with the following words, translated from Kikongo (excerpt):

«Prayer to You all Angels of the Celestial Throne, source of our existence! Prayer to You the Seven Angels who sit at the Court of Nzambi (Yahweh)!
Prayer where the sun rises and where the sun sets!
Prayer to the East and to the West!
Prayer to You Nzambi (Yahweh) Solar Creator (Mbumba Lowa)!
Prayer to You Governors of Humanity (Mpina Nza)!
Prayer to You all Angels of the Earth and the Air!
Prayer to You all the Angels who manage Water and Fire!

Prayer to You the Great Spirit of Kongo!
Prayer to You all the Angels of War who control the center of Kongo!
Prayer to You all the Angels of Victory (Mbasi za Lunungu) who fight in
the four corners of the Heavens and the Earth!

In the name of the work that you entrusted to me in front of the
Heavens and the Earth, I repeat it three times: Make so that your
holy benediction can fill the hearts of those who will rise to help the
people of Kongo!

I repeat it to you three more times and I address myself to those who
will despise my work by ignorance: I will beg Nzambi (Yahweh) so
that he forgives them and that he opens the Way of Comprehension
to them!

I swear in the name of all the Envoys who were killed in Kongo, in
Africa, in Asia, in America and Europe: may their spirits curse these
horrid individuals who will have caused death and desolation to the
people of Kongo, be they Whites or Blacks! May they be destroyed and
sent to the Spiritual Prisons of the Heavens.

I repeat it three more times before the Heavens and the Earth: Bewa-
re to those who continue to seek desolation in the four corners of the
world!

Come! Oh! Nzambi (Yahweh), come! I call you as well as all the Angels
of the War (Mbasi za Mvita), in order to lead a combat against this
world of darkness (Nsi ya bubu)!

Beware to those who continue to reinforce the Slave system and the
Colonization of the Black people! Nzambi, you are a Living God. I
unceasingly beg you (Ngieti ku fiogonena) in the name of the blood
poured by all your Envoys, and their humiliations, I ask it to you, and
I recommend it to you, oh! Nzambi of love: come with the Angels from
the Heavens and the Earth to destroy this humanity of darkness that
continues to make fun of Your Majestic Love!

May Your Alliance be sanctified and bless the Kongo People and the
Black Race of all humanity! AMEN (so be it)»

We will see further in this work who these Angels of the Court of Nzambi
(Yahweh) that Kimbangu prayed to are, and who is really Nzambi, this «li-

ving» god, therefore physical, in flesh and bone. We can say already that they are nothing other than Humanized Gods, physical beings, of flesh and blood, that all the ancient ones of Africa prayed to before the religious colonization by Christianity.

Let us be well aware that this arrival in Africa of Christianity by way of its European missionaries had as its essential goal to avail itself to those whose final program was the exploitation and the unrestrained plundering of the wealth of Africa. Do not think that the real goal of the missionaries was to bring us the Gospel, not at all! Moreover, let us be reminded that etymologically «Gospel» means «good news,» so to bring the Gospel would be thus «to bring the good news.»

What good news did they bring? We see none! What we only see is that they brought slavery, humiliation, racism, tears, blood, and death.

Did they bring noble values, spirituality, a link with the heavens and the universe? No. Moreover, we already possessed those values in a beautiful, healthy, pure and noble way. The works of our Prophetess and Prophets such as Kimpa Vita and Simon Kimbangu are testaments to this.

On September 12, 1921, the Prophet Kimbangu was arrested by the Belgian colonial authority in Nkamba. Eighteen years later in September of 1939, the Second World War began in Europe, as Kimbangu had announced. After this second international conflict, beginning in the 50s, the wind of Independence started to blow on all of Africa, also as Prophet Kimbangu foretold. One another, the European colonies of this continent started to break the chains of humiliation and servitude. But, as announced by Kimbangu, the true African «leaders» were assassinated and replaced by black dictators, African themselves. But only concerned with their personal interests, they were treacherously at the service of «neo-colonialism.»

The word of the Prophet Kimbangu was profound and while he was alive the roads of Nkamba were always full of people coming from everywhere to meet him!

It should be noted that when the Prophet Simon Kimbangu speaks about the Kongo People or Kongo, he speaks about the ancient Kingdom Kongo (Kongo Dia Ntotila) which extends today in the D.R.C (Democratic Republic of Kongo, or Kongo-Kinshasa), in Angola, in Kongo Brazzaville, Kongo Gabon, but also includes all the Bantu people of Africa.

62

Also note: the Prophet Kimbangu was arrested and imprisoned in a villainous way and was judged in Mbanza-Ngungu (ex Thysville) in the same manner of a true Inquisition trial, led by Italian Commander Rossi. This exceptional court sat from September 29 to October 3, 1921, without re-presentation for the Prophet or his disciples who were likewise charged with him. It is not surprising that Rome (the Catholic Church) pulled the strings behind closed doors so that an Italian chaired this court, a common practice in Europe at the time of these Inquisition courts! It is still one of its beautiful traditions...of which it undoubtedly likes to glorify itself in the Roman living rooms!

Simon Kimbangu was also called «the Black Samson» because of the many tortures he endured and the numerous assassination attempts made on his life. For example, on December 3, 1921, Simon Kimbangu was transferred to Leopoldville by soldiers and a Belgian officer. But the colonial Adminis-tration that was not satisfied with keeping Kimbangu in hard labour for life (it estimated that, alive, Kimbangu would always remain dangerous) wished to get rid of him. From Kinshasa he was transferred to Kintambo, then to Lutendele at the edge of the Kongo River, and there he was placed in a barrel containing asphyxiating products. Welded closed, the barrel was then thrown into the Kongo River. To their great astonishment, all those present witnessed Kimbangu emerge...safe and sound! It was then decided to shoot him at once, but there too, to the great surprise of the shooters, Kimbangu did not die! He was then tied to a large stone and thrown once again into the waters of the Kongo River only to emerge peacefully and unharmed a short time later.

Later, on December 6, 1921, Kimbangu was taken along to the prison of Kasombo in Lubumbashi, in Katanga. It is there that he died in 1951 after many years of detention during which, besides his daily immersion in the salted cold water, he regularly received whiplashes intended to systema-tically weakening him.

Moreover, during these thirty years of imprisonment, there were several times when Simon Kimbangu appeared in various places, all while he was supposed to be locked up in his cell in Lubumbashi! On this topic, the two sinister accomplices (the Belgian authorities and the Catholic Church) continue to maintain a very opaque secrecy despite numerous documents attesting to these facts. It is absolutely necessary for the «true» Kimban-guists to continue requiring firmly that these documents be released from the safes of the Church or the State.

In prison in Lubumbashi, Kimbangu announced the date and the precise hour of his death, claiming that he would die on October 12, 1951 at 3pm precisely. Indeed, on that day and at the announced time, he died peacefully. The colonial authorities (and the Church) immediately ordered his autopsy and to the great amazement of all those who witnessed it, no vital organ was found inside his body! The legendary mystery of the Prophet Kimbangu Father continued...to the great dismay of the Belgian colonizer and the Christian Catholic Church of Rome. The body of the Prophet Kimbangu was buried in Lubumbashi; soldiers and guards of the Colonial Authority were posted at once to guard his tomb permanently.

The announcement of Kimbangu's death and burial found the Colonial Authorities of the capital Leopoldville in a state of festival and of jubilation such that a dinner was organized to celebrate...what these people undoubtedly hoped to be the end of their nightmare. However, during the meal, Simon Kimbangu appeared physically in front of the assembled guests that led to a general panic and to the fleeing of many among those present. The only Kongolese attending this dinner – thus the only one originating from the country having seen this extraordinary event - was sent at once to Belgium with his entire family. The authorities did their maximum to maintain this secrecy; this fact is more than unsettling!

Special signs related to Simon Kimbangu were revealed in great numbers: like Jesus he performed «miracles,» returned the sight to blind men, healed cripples, calmed and healed mental patients, and resurrected the dead. One of these resurrections, particularly spectacular, was that of a girl named Dina. She was then 15 years old, she had died and her body was already in decomposition (like that of «Lazarus» resuscitated by Jesus). Through a prayer, Kimbangu brought her back to life.

As briefly mentioned above, Father Simon Kimbangu did not cease appearing physically here and there, living and eating with his faithful or humans in distress everywhere on the planet, while he was at the same time physically in his cell at the prison of Kasombo in Lubumbashi in Katanga. Apparitions of the Prophet Kimbangu were observed in Efonda (Ecuador), in Befale (Ecuador), in Boma (Lower-Kongo) in 1942, in Makanga, Lowa from July 29 to August 5. In April 1942, the Prophet Kimbangu appeared physically in Lubumbashi in five different places but at the same time! Five Simon Kimbangu were arrested in Lubumbashi in five distinct places. These five Simon Kimbangu arrested were even gathered in Lubumbashi! The population of Kongo Brazzaville was also witness to physical appearances of Simon Kimbangu during this period. But he also appeared in Angola, in Nigeria, and in Europe! Yes, in Europe too!

One day, in his cell in Lubumbashi, Kimbangu decided to take a long journey. He required of the Belgian priest present then to simply touch his clothing, which he did. Kimbangu pronounced a few words and they were at once transported in a «cloud» and visited thousands of families throughout the whole planet, including that of the Belgian priest. They then landed in Rome, at the Vatican, and there they saw many things. And then they returned to Lubumbashi…in prison. The Belgian priest, after reporting the journey to his superiors, was immediately and definitively repatriated to Belgium! Finally, although extradited, this priest continued to share his testimony far and wide for to have lived this moment of omnipresence on the planet was stronger than he, proving that the truth cannot be hidden indefinitely.

On July 29, 1952, nine months after his death, the Prophet Kimbangu appeared physically in Lowa in front of his faithful. He remained among them for eight days, eating and drinking like them, and preaching to them. Then his faithful and all people present could witness after that the majestic rise of Kimbangu going up into the heavens. In the middle of the night, in an indescribable bliss for all, the Prophet Kimbangu was sucked up in the cloud of a ball of fire.

Before closing this sub-chapter concerning the Prophet Simon Kimbangu, let us look a bit more closely at the most important prophecies that he announced between 1921 and 1951, in chronological order:

> - *The liberation of Africans through the first nominal independences of the Sixties, which will only be false independences, an illusion of independence;*
> - *The coming to power of dictators in Africa who will serve their own interests and those of the former colonial Masters (West);*
> - *The rise of deadly wars (civil wars) everywhere in Africa shortly after nominal independences of the Sixties;*
> - *The exodus of many young Africans towards the countries of the Westerners to flee oppression and misery;*
> - *Then, finally, the hard and heroic conquest of a second «true» Independence for all Africa "Dipanda Dianzole", which will be led by the arrival of a Prophet, "Nkua Tulendo", whose role will be at the same time Religious, Scientific and Political. This great Leader will be a*

King (House of David, house of Israel) and Prophet; he will restore the broken link between Nzambi (Yahweh) and the black people; he will restore true Peace and Harmony in Africa. He will come to lead a real spiritual, economic and political decolonization of Black Africa. He will come to restore the Kingdom of Kongo. He will come to restore the natural African borders prior to the era of colonization (of before the conference of Berlin in 1884). He will come with a powerful message in a Book; this book will be rejected initially, but will finally be accepted by all. One of his instructor-teachers ('nlongi' in Kikongo) will come to announce him to the black people, will come to present him to the black people, will come to explain verbally and in writing who he is.

d. The Prophet Simao Toko

Another case of the arrival of a Prophet on the African continent is perhaps the advent of Simao Toko in the North of Angola. This part of Angola formed part of the Kongo Kingdom before the arbitrary splitting of Africa at the time of the Conference of Berlin. I do not know if Simao Toko was truly a Prophet among the Great Prophets sent by Yahweh Elohim, but he deserves nevertheless a place in this chapter. Nowadays the religion of the colonizer, «Christian Catholicism,» is a social force in Angola, where the language of the colonizer «Portuguese» reigns as an absolute mistress.

Practically no authentic African languages are heard there as it is the case in other nearby countries, and it is logical: the country is 97 % Catholic, therefore 97 % under the influence of the religion of the colonizer, and consequently also the language of this colonizer. Many young people in the large cities only speak Portuguese!

The Angolan Government approved the Kimbanguist Church there officially only after its members accepted, under pressure of this government, to stop their ceremonies against the Vatican. Kimbanguists should never have accepted this renouncement; they should have continued their anti-Vatican celebrations to remain in the line of their Prophet Founder.

But, there is also in Angola, many «Tokoists» (approximately 3 million of them). In truth, we can only say "numerous" to describe them as no accurate records exist. The authorities do not really want the correct figure of this section of population be known, because the life, the works, the words of Simao Toko highly disturbed the colonial authorities and their Angolan servants...as well as the Vatican, obviously.

Who is this famous Simao Toko? He was born at the beginning of the century, in February 1918, in the north of Angola, in Kisadi Kibango. At a very young age, he rebels against the colonial teaching and calls for the restoration of the black history of Angola. The Movement of which he will take the head is called «Kitawala» and his followers will be pursued by the Belgian colonial power in Belgian Kongo.

Simao Toko will be arrested and thrown in prison. But the man nevertheless had time to create his Religious Movement that already extended from Kongo to Angola. His imprisonment will not curtail the survival of this very structured and extremely solid Movement. Moreover, Kitawala regularly organized actions of resistance, strikes, and civil disobedience in the North of Angola.

In prison in Belgian Kongo in 1950, Simao Toko and his followers were often mistreated and insulted. During one of these waves of insults, (the Belgian prison chief, Pirote, was very familiar with the work of Simao Toko, Simao Toko raised his hands and asked the Belgians to count his fingers (ten fingers) and told them it is exactly the number of years that remain for you to stay here; giving them ten more years, no less, no more, to leave this country, ten years! He added that his army would fly over them then.

This history is well known everywhere in Central Africa. That is easy to understand for thousands of people were witness to an exceptional thing on January 4, 1959 (the 10th "finger" of the announcement of Simao Toko!). This day the thousands of citizens of the commune of Leopoldville - and many of them are still alive today - saw something so splendid that today still, the date of January 4 is still recognized as a public holiday in Kinshasa to commemorate this event. Here is what occurred: the Kinois people (inhabitants of Kinshasa) at this time were in full rebellion against the Belgian colonial authorities. But this day remains memorable, because... thousands of Kinois saw «Cherubs» appearing in front of the Belgian colonial army. Thousands of citizens of Kinshasa saw an army of approximately a thousand very small beings, the size of a child or dwarf, having very imposing bodies, very muscular. These small beings, with human appearance although very small, were endowed with an exceptional force; witnesses saw some of them raising 5 ton trucks with an arm!

The Belgian colonial army opened fire on these Cherubs, but without results! Terrified, the Belgian colonial army fled, and at once, the small beings disappeared as they had appeared! This day, January 4, 1959 is called in Kinshasa «the day of Cherubs and Seraphim!»

And a few months after this incredible event, June 30, 1960, Belgian Kongo reached independence.

That is thus exactly ten years after the prediction made, in 1950, by Simao Toko, that the Belgians were driven out and forced to leave Belgian Kongo, in 1960!

Is this unique? Not really! After the Six Day War of Israel, there were many testimonies from Israeli soldiers, saying that they had been assisted on the frontline by small beings, by spacecrafts coming from elsewhere, also by surprising phenomena, to overcome the Arab forces! In Nkamba, the native village of the Prophet Simon Kimbangu, there where the large temple of the Kimbanguist Church is located, called «the new Jerusalem,» there is a building that they call the "city of the Kings", built at the precise place where a "mysterious" spacecraft would have landed and from which the Prophet would have descended. At the entrance of each floor of this building, there is a portrait of a small black cherub, a small black being, of more or less 1m20, with stretched eyes in the shape of almonds, carrying around his waist a large and broad green belt with shiny adornments on it. And the Kimbanguists will tell you that it is with these individual belts that the angels of Armageddon (the fight of good against evil) can move in the air, and they will tell you that these are the small beings who came to assist the Prophet while he was alive, that these are the small beings who came to help drive out the Belgian colonial army and to help the Kongo people to acquire their independence. We will discover later in this work exactly who these small beings are that came from the sky?

Upon his release from prison, Simao Toko took again his pilgrim stick to continue his mission in Angola. From there on, the life of Simao Toko will primarily consist of avoiding assassination attempts. He will be imprisoned in Angola from where the Portuguese authorities will deport him nine times in all; he will thus spend 12 years of his life in nine different prisons! The Portuguese decided to put a price on his head. They sent Simao Toko to hard labour and offered a reward for anyone who could and would dare kill him.

As with the Prophet Simon Kimbangu, there are many accounts and testimonies that attest to the numerous attempts to kill Simao Toko, but without success. Each time he came back to life, just like Jesus or Simon Kimbangu. Testimonies of this abound in Angola.

During the period when he was deported for the ninth time, during his stay in Luanda, Pope John XXIII dispatched from the Vatican to Luanda two emissaries to meet Simao Toko and to deliver a personal message to him. One of the two emissaries fell sick while arriving at Luanda and had to be hospitalized; the other was welcomed by Simao Toko, and he told him:

> «I am an emissary of the Pope John XXIII who personally mandated me to ask you only one question: 'Who are you?'»

We are then in 1962 (two years after the deadline when the Vatican should have revealed the third secret of Fatima).

Simao Toko answered as follows:

> «I am surprised that a person as high up as the Pope is interested by my person to the point of having you travel 8,000 kilometres, just to meet me. The answer that you should give to your Master is found in the Bible, in Matthew XI, 2-6».

Let us examine this passage of Matthew:

> "Now when John had heard in the prison the works of Christ, he sent two of his disciples, and said unto him, Art thou he that should come, or do we look for another?"

Jesus answered them:

> « Go and show John again those things which ye do hear and see: The blind receive their sight, and the lame walk, the lepers are cleansed, and the deaf hear, the dead are raised up, and the poor have the gospel preached to them. And blessed is he, whosoever shall not be offended in me".
>
> (The Bible, New Testament - Library of the Pleiades, Matt. XI, 2-6)

Indeed, Simao Toko, knowing that the Pope was called "John,» quite simply put himself in the place of Jesus answering John... in the place of the Prophet who answers a man. And, John, who had heard about the works of the Prophet from his prison, becomes here, Pope John XXIII, the usurper, who, from his prison «the Vatican» had heard about this black Prophet. Interesting, isn't this?

Following this exchange, the Pope contacted the Portuguese dictator Antonio de Salazar and again on July 18 Simao Toko was deported, this time not to an isolated corner of Angola, but to Portugal where the agents of the Catholic dictator were not able to kill Simao Toko! Thus, Simao Toko became in Portugal «an exiled political prisoner.»

Simao Toko was released and announced before re-entering Angola that the reign of the colonizer was finished. He re-entered Angola on August 31, 1974, and a year later, November 11, 1975 Angola gained its Independence from Portugal.

During the night of December 31, 1983 to January 1, 1984, the Angolan media announced the death of Simao Toko. A man, a strong man of the entourage of the President of the Republic of Angola, Neto, a man who had fiercely fought the Portuguese for 14 years, was then the commanding officer Paiva. After having heard that Simao Toko was deceased, he ran towards the place where the body was laid out for the public to see. Pushing through a crowd of tens of thousands of people, he arrived near the body and asked to speak. "It is not true that Simao Toko died, because he is invulnerable"! This same officer had received orders some seven years earlier to eliminate Simao Toko permanently.

He testified at this time in front of the crowd that before he had kidnapped Simao Toko with his men he had taken him to a secret place. Here they had methodologically tortured him to death, descending on him as a butcher would on a carcass. He testified that they had severely damaged his head, then his arms and his legs, then spread his chest from his abdomen and placed his body in a large bag. They sealed the bag and hid it in a non-disclosed place. He further testified that they returned three days later to dispose of the body, what remained of it, into the ocean for the sharks. But the bag had disappeared. Suddenly they heard, overpowering their voices, a noise like that of rushing waters and then a voice spoke to them saying, «Who are you looking for? I am here.» It was Simao Toko, in the flesh and bone, alive. At the sight of him they fled at once while saying, «He is God, this man is God.»

On the day of Simao Toko's death, the commandant Paiva was there in front of the body of Simao Toko, exposed to the public, and he refused to believe that now he had really died. This occurred in 1984, therefore not so long ago. Many people, still living today, testify to having killed Simao Toko and to have seen him alive afterwards.

Were Kimpa Vita, Simon Kimbangu, and perhaps also Simao Toko, Prophets of the same order as Moses, Jesus, Buddha, Mohamed, Joseph Smith (of the Mormons), Krishna, and others? Of course, yes! There were many Prophets who came in past times; all these Prophets are one, both indivisible and complementary. They are each one a link of the same chain, and are one in their main orientation...each one having come to end or complete the work of another or to announce the arrival of the one who will succeed him.

Each Prophet came on Earth to bring a message adapted to his time and his environment. The message of each one of them always corresponded to the needs of each different local population to which the prophet or the prophetess addressed himself or herself. Thus, for the African blacks - as for others – the message that was intended for them was adapted to the needs of the time and the environment that was theirs; Kimpa Vita and Simon Kimbangu have thus each brought a message perfectly suited for the needs of the black people among whom they lived.

They are our own Prophets, whether the «colonized» blacks accept this or not, and their messages are still always present for us, because of the fact that the great mass of blacks "is still mentally and spiritually colonized!» The proof is that the number of «Christian» blacks is terribly high around the world! All our black Prophets came to fight the colonization, which is above all spiritual; they came to fight slavery, colonization, the pro-slavery Church, and the colonizing and usurping Church of Rome. We will see later in this work that our creator-gods in the plural assisted them to achieve certain "scientific" miracles.

I already hear certain blacks saying, after reading what precedes: «Yes, it is right that Osiris, Kimpa Vita and Simon Kimbangu, Simao Toko were African Black Prophets, but it is not the same thing as Jesus who is «the son of God,» «the Messiah,» «the Saviour,» therefore the one on which all rests".

Frankly they make me laugh. Lacking knowledge on this matter, they quite simply have swallowed raw and in a large dose the false teachings dispensed on this subject by "their white fathers". How gullible can they be on that level! Please, may these colonized blacks stop using their lack of culture as an argument?

Lies, trickery...Jesus is not at all «the Messiah.» Sorry for you, all the Christian Blacks, you will have to wake up and accept that he is not «the Messiah,» accept that you were led astray, that you were lied to voluntarily on this subject. You will find the explanation of what I affirm here in the next chapter.

8. The announced Messiah was not Jesus

If we work with the logic that all the Great Prophets of the history of mankind are one and indivisible, that they are one in their main orientation, that they are all one link of a same chain, it is then as logical to deduce that there will be an identical «Messiah» announced by the different branches lead by these various Prophets.

Each Prophet at the inception of one or several branches would have to announce, from that point forward, the same last messenger, the last of the Prophets, the same shepherd of the shepherds, that is to say «the Messiah,» the one who will be the last to come, the one who will bring the «final Revelation» while raising the veil of «God's» mystery, as it is written in the holy books.

It is very funny to see today the Christian «colonized» blacks praying to Jesus, regarding him as «the Messiah,» the «announced Saviour!» It is false, and it proves to what point these blacks became spiritually stupid. This stupidity is so deep at home that one can understand the use of the term «spiritual war» used by Simon Kimbangu to describe the spiritual revolution that the black people should undergo...and ultimately to win, if it wants to decolonize itself and to completely free itself. To believe that Jesus is «the Messiah» is pure and simple ignorance for these blacks. «Every man is brutish in his knowledge... due to a lack of science,» as it is also written (in the Bible, Old Testament, Jeremiah X, 14).

But let us have a closer look at this by reviewing the various most predominant current religions.

"THE PEOPLE OF THE BOOK", the Hebrew Jewish people, await the Messiah, **the Machia'h,** for these coming days. In the Jewish tradition, Jesus was a Prophet...no more than that, but by no means «the Messiah.» The awaited Messiah will arrive the night of Erev, on the seventh day that corresponds to the current epoch, according to the actual Hebrew calendar. When he will arrive, the Messiah should be announced by the sound of the «Shofar Gadol» in Jerusalem, at the universally known Wailing Wall, and he should build the Third Temple close to Jerusalem to welcome the return of yhwhelohim in company of all the Ancients Prophets. The Jewish faith does not acknowledge the New Testament and this is understandable. According to Judaism the Machia'h will then drive the whole world to the state of perfection and will bring all men to serve Elohim together with one heart.

According to **THE PAGAN TRADITION,** which calculates the eras according to the precessions of spring equinoxes, according to the zodiac signs, the times will come when mankind will have entered the era of Aquarius. This era of knowledge is symbolized by water pouring knowledge and revelation on mankind, of all things unknown prior to this age. Jesus' era was the era of Pisces, preceding the era of Aquarius that began in 1945 according to the calculation of the precession of spring equinoxes, coinciding with the explosion of the atomic bomb in Hiroshima, or in other words, the entry of mankind into the era of scientific knowledge to the level of universes as particles.

According to **BUDDHISM,** the New Western Buddha, called the **"Maitreya"** (also called **"Mirokou"** in the Japanese branch taught by the Shingon school), will appear in a country ruled by the king of the roosters 3,000 years after Buddha's death. It is clear throughout history that France is the country of the rooster. For Buddhism, «the Messiah» will therefore be born in France. The weathervanes in the shape of a rooster were invented in France. For a long time, the French were referred to as "Gauls;" (Gallis) and in Latin, dominant language of the time, the word for rooster is «Gallus.» The rooster is the symbol of France, appearing again on the medals of honour given by the French government. The mascot of the soccer World Cup for France was the rooster, and the French players and sportsmen of national teams bear the rooster on their shirts.

Therefore, for Buddhism the «Messiah» or «Maitreya» must be born in France, and he must arrive at this time. Also in France there was a Chief of state named «De Gaulle» (his name is even closer to «gallus,» the Latin translation of the word «rooster»). With respect to his memory, we can recall that this general, President of the French Republic, was proud like a rooster and considered himself as «the king of the French» after having led his troops to victory against the Nazis. In August of 1944, De Gaulle became the Chief of the first French Government after World War II (!).

In summary, for Buddhism the period of the Messiah's advent is now. He must have been born in France and one could say that the Messiah's conception should have taken place around 1945, after the "king" of the roosters, Charles de Gaulle. While interpreting the monument of King Asoka, according to the Buddhist branch of North Korea and according to its calendar, year 2003 (for the world calendar...Christian) is Buddhist year 3030, already 30 years beyond the 3000th anniversary of Buddha's death. Therefore, the "Messiah" or "Maitreya" should be here now, in flesh, physically present on our planet...and of French origin.

The Buddhist teaching says that the Truth about the past, present and future «will be revealed» then. According to the tradition of a Buddhist branch, the year 3000 of Buddhism must correspond to year 1973; therefore that year should be an important year in this Messiah's mission! Here is a beautiful example of the announcement of the Maitreya in Buddhism:

> «*And the Blessed One said to Ananda: 'I am not the first Buddha who came upon this earth, nor shall I be the last. In due time another Buddha will arise in the world, a Holy One, a supremely enlightened One, endowed with wisdom in conduct, auspicious knowing the universe, an incomparable leader of men, a Master of angels and mortals. He will reveal to you the same eternal truth which I have taught you. He will preach to you His religion, glorious in its origin, glorious at the climax and glorious at the goal, in spirit and in the letter. He will proclaim a religious life, wholly perfect and pure, such as I now proclaim.' His disciples will number many thousands, while mine number many hundreds'. Ananda asked: 'How shall we know him?' The Blessed One replied: 'He will be known as Maitreya'.* »

Now let's take **ISLAM** (the Religion of the Muslim) where the "**MADHI**" is awaited, named also **IMAN MADHI**,» the imam of the Imams. His era will arrive when man will have walked on the moon, which was done in 1969 by astronaut Neil Armstrong. The Koran even comes to «remind» the Jewish and the Christians that began to distort the teachings of Yahweh through Moses and Jesus. So the Koran and Muhammad come to bring some corrections, warnings as reminder to the Jewish and the Christian, telling the Christian for example: «Jesus was only a Prophet and not 'the Messiah,'» or: «Mary was only a girl of the earth,» or "There is no Holy Trinity of the Father, the Son and the Holy Ghost - it is only an invention of men". As the Muslim calendar begins in 622, the Koran rightly recognizes that the Jewish people possess the writings about creation, or the genesis, which means that it recognizes «the Old Testament» but not «the New Testament,» the one of the Christians (of which we will discuss further)

The Koran is the source of the faith of the Moslem. There Muhammad announces the arrival of the Mahdi:

The family of Imran

> «*3.81*»: « *And when Allah made a covenant through the prophets: Certainly what I have given you of Book and wisdom -- then an apostle comes to you verifying that which is with you, you must believe in*

him, and you must aid him. He said: Do you affirm and accept My compact in this (matter)? They said: We do affirm. He said: Then bear witness, and I (too) am of the bearers of witness with you. »

According to Ibn Majjah and Al Hakim, the Prophet highly recommended:

"If you see him, give him your allegiance, even if you have to crawl over ice, because surely he is the Caliph of Allah, Al Mahdi".

Ibn Mass'Oud reports this hadith where the Prophet is saying:

« If only one day in life remains, Allah will send a man from the Family of my House. He will fill the earth with justice just as it has been filled by injustice. »

SIMON KIMBANGU announced the arrival for these days, of a Great King, whose role will be spiritual, scientific and political. He will come with an instructor and a «new» book, a new "Bible" for the black people. In this book all will be revealed, and thanks to this Book the black people will understand the secrets hidden in the Bible by the white people so that he may free himself and decolonise once and for all. In other words, it will be a Book that will make him abandon the religion of the colonizers: Christianity and/or Catholicism.

HINDUISM also has important writings about the Kalki Avatar. They too announce a man's arrival, reincarnation of Vishnu, with the mission to lead the world toward a better age: **THE KALKI AVATAR.**

The Srimad-Bhagavatam, verse 25:

« Thereafter, at the conjunction of the two yugas, the Lord of creation will take His birth as the Kalki incarnation and become the son of Visnu Yasa. At this time the rulers of the earth will have degenerated into plunderers. »

Bhagavad-Gita, (Chapter 4), Verse 7:

« So in the Kali Yuga [our era: the age of iron], the decline won't stop intensifying until the human race approaches its extinction. When the end of Dark Age will be next, a part of this divine essence that exists in /its own spiritual nature, Kalki Avatar will descend on the earth, endowed with the eight supernatural qualities. He will re-establish

righteousness in the world. When the sun, the moon, Tishya and the planet Jupiter will be together in the same house, the age of Krita or Satya: [the golden age] will be back. »

Verse 8:

« But every time that there is laxness in the observation of the Divine Law, upsurge of profanity in all places, then I appear millennium after millennium, for the protection of the devotees and the annihilation of the miscreants, and to fully establish righteousness. »

Mahâbhârata, (Chapter 3), verse 189:

«A Brahmin named Kalki «Glory of Vishnu», under the impulse of the time, will arise with a great war strength, courage and wisdom. [...] Surrounded of Brahmans, he will wipe out the miserable troops of barbarians who had invaded everywhere. «

The «Kalki Avatar» is mentioned again in many other works: the Brahma Purâna (chap. 213), the Purâna Agni (chap. 16), the Vâyu Purâna (chap. 98 and 104), the Varâha Purâna (chap. 15) and many others. But it is important to note that a whole book is dedicated to the description of the coming of Kalki down on Earth: the Kalki Purâna. It is said there that his final incarnation will come from the west.

I pity all Christian blacks on this globe as today the most practiced religions on the planet agree on the fact that someone must come again to accomplish things. Therefore, the Jesus of white colonizers, of the ashamed Vatican, of your missionary father, is not the announced «Messiah,» «the Saviour,» «the Last of the Prophets,» the one that will bring the Revelation. Not at all! They should stop letting themselves be deceived by lies, blinded and manipulated by Christian, Apostolic, Roman, Adventist, Baptist, Pentecostal Churches and other institutional trickeries of white colonizers.

Additionally, aside from major religions, there are many less widespread religions still hoping today for the arrival of the one that they announce; for the Persian he is called **"Saoshyant"**, for the **HOPI INDIANS, "Pahana", "Quetzalcoalt"** for the **INDIANS FROM MEXICO.**

For example, even though the **BAHÀ'I** faith is not awaiting the arrival of a specific prophet, the writings of the Bab announce that others will follow him. Besides, the Bahà'is celebrate May 23rd, anniversary of the announcement, made in 1844 by the Bab (word meaning: the door), of the future arrival of a universal divine messenger.

Another example in **ZOROASTRISM**: this religion was founded, in Persia around the year 500 B.C. by Zoroaster in order to reform Mazdeism. Mazdeism is essentially a dualist religion: two principles share the world: one good, Ahura-Mazdâ (Ormuzd); the other bad, Ahriman (Angra-Mainyu). Man should fight for good and against bad; he must be the adversary of lie and error and must devote himself to the service of the truth. The soul of the righteous reaches the «better world» whereas the miscreant go to «the home of pain". Those whose good and bad actions balance each other out stay in the «Hammistagân.» The Mazdeans, in any case, expect the arrival of this **"Saoshyant"** quoted before. For them, he is «the saviour;» they also wait for the last judgment. The world will be purified by the melted metal and, following the victory of good on evil, a new universe will be built. It is foreseen by them that «The Saoshyant» will be there for the twelfth Zoroastrian millennium (around year 2000).

The **HOPI PEOPLE (**Indians established in Arizona) await, as I mentioned earlier, the arrival of «**Pahana,**» the white brother of truth who will come from the West (therefore from the Occident). He will come to sow wisdom in our hearts. Pahana must come and bring the hope for harmony and peace between nations and to maintain the precarious stability of the planet. Otherwise, the Purifier could all very well destroy the whole Earth on which we live.

The **NOMADS OF CENTRAL ASIA**'s Messiah is called «**the white Burkhan.**» He will arrive when the peoples of the steppes will have abandoned their Ancient Gods. He will come to offer them, as well as to the whole humanity, a spiritual rebirth.

The SUFIS's Messiah is called «**Khidr.**» He is the mysterious guide and he will come toward the end of Islam when man will have walked on the soil of the moon.

Of **the Messiah of the INUITS**, it is said that he will come from the East, that he will have a white beard and long hair, and that he will speak in the name of people with olive skin.

The **Messiah SHIITE** is called «**the twelfth Imam.**» He will be the last religious leader of the Shiite sect of Islam. He will appear to Jesus' side on the Day of Judgment in order to accomplish the Holy Koran.

The **Messiah of the MAORIS** in Polynesia is **still awaited**.

The **Messiah of Japanese SHINTOISM** is also still awaited; **he must appear after August 8, 1988** [08/08/88].

The Messiah of the **ORTHODOX SUNNITE** is called «**Muntazar.**» He is Muhammad's successor and, to «the end of times» he will unify all races of the world through «understanding» (this «understanding» in fact is science and, with it, spirituality based on science).

Practiced by men that, in these ancient times, had no means of communicating from one continent to another, as varied, as they are, they share one common point: they all predict the arrival of a man whose mission is to save mankind from its own destruction.

Of course, I already hear the voices of some blacks, «colonized» to the spinal cord, saying: «Yes, but everything here is about Christ. He is the one announced!" Once again, I must apologize, among these many religions there are those that appeared after Christ and Jesus himself announced the arrival of someone who will come after him to complete and accomplish his mission. Let us look closer.

Let's just look at the example of **JESUS, HIMSELF.** Didn't he say, before dying, that he would ask his father to send a **New Paraclet**? Let us not forget that Christianity emerged totally from Judaism; Christianity recognizes the Torah and completes it with other books gathered under the name of the Old Testament.

Although Christians unfairly see «the Messiah» in Christ, the New Testament mentions the arrival after him of the «Paraclet» (term of old Greek meaning: Counsellor, intercessor, defender, lawyer, assistant).
John XIV, 16 « *And I will pray the Father, and he shall give you another Comforter [Paraclet] that he may abide with you for ever.* »

John XIV, 26 « *But the Comforter [Paraclet], which is the Holy Ghost, whom the Father will send in my name, he shall teach you all things, and bring all things to your remembrance, whatsoever I have said unto you.* »

John XV, 26 « *But when the Comforter [Paraclet] is come, whom I will send unto you from the Father, even the Spirit of truth, which proceedeth from the Father, he shall testify of me. »*

John XVI, 7 « *Nevertheless I tell you the truth; It is expedient for you that I go away: for if I go not away, the Comforter [Paraclet] will not come unto you; but if I depart, I will send him unto you. »*

John XVI, 13 « *Howbeit when he, the Spirit of truth, is come, he will guide you into all truth: for he shall not speak of himself; but whatsoever he shall hear, that shall he speak: and he will shew you things to come. »*

It is therefore about time that the blacks stop praying to the Christ of the white colonizer, as «the Saviour,» as «the Messiah,» and that they recover their traditions under the light of the sciences of today and tomorrow. Yes, it is time that science becomes their Religion and that they accept that the physical «humanized Gods" coming from the sky - those whom their ancestors prayed to - decided to send another Prophet, as «the last of the Prophets» as «the Messiah,» as the last Messenger. It is time also that they recognize that this «Messiah» is announced by all traditions and religions and that he will come for all these religions because their source is common, their source is one and indivisible. And finally it is time that they realize that this «Messiah» who is going to federate men is not Christ, on no account, but another Great Prophet who is foreseen for these days and whose role will be religious, political and especially scientific. Of course they made us, Africans, believe something else...but it was for a very precise goal: to colonize us and to exploit us until the end, through an absolute and unequivocal religious assimilation.

9. A black "Christian" betrays his ancestors and the black Prophets!

After the death of the Great Prophet Kimbangu in Elisabethville (actually Lubumbashi) in 1951, his junior son, Joseph Diangienda Kuntima, (former Secretary of the Colonial Governor of the Province of "Kongo-Kasaï", Mr. Peigneux) establishes, December 24, 1959 a Church of Christian inspiration that he baptizes, CHURCH OF JESUS-CHRIST ON THE EARTH BY THE PROPHET SIMON KIMBANGU (CJCSK).

This Church will become in 1969 a full member of the World Council of Churches, whose main office is in Geneva, thus turning its back on the historical combat - open without any compromise - of the KINTUADI Militant Movement established by the Prophet Kimbangu and turning its back, at the same time, on the politico-spiritual program of the latter, a program which aimed to the total and unconditional rehabilitation of the black Man in the whole world! Kimbanguists should have maintained the name of "KINTUADI", this name that the Prophet himself had given to the movement that he created, more especially as this name translated the vocation correctly, the range of the mission of the Prophet Kimbangu. Let us recall that an essential part of this mission was the liberation of the Kongo people and all the other people of Africa...whereas Christianity had come to bring only colonization at all levels, humiliation, slavery, whip and bloodshed.

It is indeed more than surprising - and it is extremely sad - to see such a serious compromise with the World Power station of the Colonial Churches, that one which had precisely called for the death of the Great Prophet Simon KIMBANGU in 1921, and who wished so much that catholic and protestant missionaries such as "Reverend Pastors" Jennings, Hilliard, Frederickson, Vikterlof, and the "Very Reverend Fathers" Van Cleemput, Jodogne had personally written to Belgian King Albert 1st in 1921 to ensure that the death penalty taken against Kimbangu be maintained!!! They are also the same catholic and protestant missionaries who will try to assassinate the Great Prophet Kimbangu in Lutendele, not far from Kinshasa, by drowning him - although in vain - in the waters of the Kongo river!!!

How can one betray to this point the Prophet Kimbangu, whose mission was precisely to fight until the end Christianity, Catholicism, in other words, to fight the Religion of the usurping colonizer and invader? How could Kimbanguists have accepted, in the name of Simon Kimbangu, the

adhesion to the World Council of Churches of the colonizer, decision maker of the final elimination of their Prophet? How could this be possible? I
don't understand!

Not only is it treason of the original teaching of the Prophet but more still,
it is their Prophet himself whom they betray. All true Kimbanguists should
require the withdrawal of the Kimbanguist Church from this Ecumenical
Council and to require that the pure and hard combat against the presence
of the Religion of the colonizer in Africa be continued, as asked for and required by the Great Prophet Simon Kimbangu. In all logic, while following
the teachings of Simon Kimbangu, all the "true" Kimbanguists should take
a great action through the whole of Africa, such as an action of "Apostasy", inviting all the catholic African blacks and/or Christians to forswear
the catholic and/or Christian faith, and this, by evoking the teachings and
prophecies of the Prophet Simon Kimbangu.

As Kimbanguist, one cannot be member of a Church of Christian inspiration? It is to destroy all the efforts, to go contrary to the entire mission
carried out by the Prophet Kimbangu, who, from his place in the skies,
must dislike this mentality of perpetual "colonization".

It is obvious that Simon Kimbangu was born and also presented as a prophet, just like Moses, Jesus, Buddha, Muhammad, etc. He affirmed having
been contacted "directly" by the Supreme Being, by Yahweh the Eternal, the "Lord", without the aid of anyone. The voice of the lord who
asked Simon Kimbangu to start his mission, it was not Jesus, but Yahweh
the eternal, Jahwehelohim! The faithful ones and followers of the first
hour introduced the Prophet Kimbangu as "the prophet of the God of the
Negroes" as opposed to Jesus, "the prophet of the God of the Christian
missionaries" or to Muhammad, "the prophet of the Arabs". This must be
quite clear to be understood by all, because it is essential to seize all the
importance of this fundamental difference!

In addition to that, it is also clear that the prophet Simon Kimbangu was
provided with the power not only to comment on the Scriptures and to
testify on their matter but also to take initiatives and decisions in this
context, a gift only allotted to the Prophets. Even more important is the
fact that the religious teaching of Simon Kimbangu contained biblical elements re-examined from the anti-colonial political point of view. This specificity "to re-examine" the teachings brought by the sacred texts is the
characteristic of all the Great Prophets: they all came "to re-establish the
lines of communication", all came to put things in their right place and

82

they did it by using the Scriptures, which was also the case for Muhammad...to quote only this other prophet.

The colonial Council of war of Thysville (today Mbanza-Ngungu) that judged and condemned Kimbangu in what was still Belgian Kongo retained against him as principal objection the fact that "Simon Kimbangu established himself as redeemer and saver of the black race". This is why his trial and his condemnation were compared by his faithful ones to the appearance of Jesus before Pontius Pilate, and it is completely justified. Therefore, we can easily conclude from it that it was never a question of placing Jesus of Nazareth above or below Simon Kimbangu, that those brothers are prophets at the same level, and that they are consequently one and indivisible, i.e., they are both one link of the large chain of the Prophets and complementary in this.

Living in the middle of Africa, Simon Kimbangu said that if the first Christ had come only for the Whites, the time of salvation had now come for the Blacks. Or, in other words, Simon Kimbangu had announced himself as another Christ, but then a Christ whose mission was in a very different environment, that of the Black Africa at his time, and concerned a very different people than that of the contemporaries of Jesus. Another parallel, Jesus – who proclaimed himself as king of the Jews – said he was coming to save his people; Kimbangu, in prison, was conscious of dying to save his own people.

It is quite obvious that the Prophet Kimbangu invited his people to re-read the Scriptures, and this in a way autonomous and independent of the strategic doctrines of the Latin, Western Church, and also that he encouraged them to take account of the religious design of the Negro-African people. Better, he said that he was no longer Christian even though he based his teachings on the Bible and declared that his religious movement was now going to interpret the Scriptures according to the Negro-African canons and no longer according to the scale of interpretation of the "white Fathers of the Church". It is, without any doubt, the reason why his first faithful ones made signs with a highly provocative expression: placing Simon Kimbangu in the place of Jesus, they said, "In the name of the father, of Simon Kimbangu and Andre Matsoua, (*)" thus giving an extraordinary kick to the "Trinity" imposed by the Christian Catholic Church. It was not at all a naive gesture, but precisely it was indeed the assertion of a new Religion, in opposition with another religion of which many members, and especially the more "high placed", did nothing but bring the lie and the treason of the original Scriptures, i.e., Christianity to countless generations!

The worse that could happen to the Christian Church Catholic was to see being born in Central Africa a Religion that is "non-Christian" based on the Bible. I did say "non-Christian"! So Kintuadi, the religious movement of Kimbangu, was precisely that. It was thus needed, for the Church, at all costs and by all possible means – honest or not – to put an end to that, not that it wants to defend "the Truth", but quite rather to maintain its Power, the only thing which interests in all priority "the dignitaries" of this Institution...and besides today still: power before Truth! Such is their most concrete objective.

It is for this reason that the very influential catholic hierarchy, looking towards the colonial administration, entirely vested in its cause, encouraged it to act in a well defined direction: to eliminate Kimbangu and destroy his Movement.

But, how to destroy in a lasting way this famous movement created by the Prophet Kimbangu? Very simple: by making sure that it is later called "Church" (the Kimbanguist Church), and that this Church is indeed Christian, and called for example "CHURCH OF JESUS-CHRIST ON THE EARTH BY THE PROPHET SIMON KIMBANGU". And, alas, it is exactly what happened.

On April 6, 1960 – just a little before the independence of the Belgian Kongo – the Kimbanguist Church obtained civil personality. Before this, however, recognizing "the Church of Jesus-Christ on the earth by the prophet Simon Kimbangu", the colonial administration had taken an additional precaution in relation to their paramount objective specified above: Joseph Diangenda (son of Simon Kimbangu) had to sign a "solemn declaration" in which he renounced to any political concern, etc. The reference to Jesus-Christ or to Christianity in the official denomination of this Church and the renunciation to political activism of the founder made this solemn statement, in itself, a major treason of the essential options of Simon Kimbangu. One can easily speak here about a complete deviation from the mission, ideology and semantics of the Prophet Kimbangu; it is indeed a victory of the colonizer aiming at maintaining the spirits "colonized" for his only and single profit! It is necessary that Kimbanguists join again in political activism in order to carry out prophecies of the Prophet Kimbangu. These prophecies will not be carried out like that by themselves, or by magic; they will be carried out by the means of spiritual and political activism ...let us not be mislead!

From the skies above, the Prophet Kimbangu must be dismayed and crying bitter tears to see what has become of his original Kintuadi Movement. One could, in extreme cases, call his Movement quite simply today "Kimbanguist Church". It would have still been correct because "Church" means etymologically "assembly of people;" but to add to it "of Jesus Christ on the Earth by..." really is something to cry about! Kimbangu, who opened the way towards the "decolonization", sees his Movement today somewhere "colonized", losing its personality, to some extent decapitated, with this accepted return inside the trap tended by the colonizer and his usurping religion!

Kimbangu, who preached a return towards authenticity, our authentic traditions and roots, sees the Kimbanguist Church today, in a formal way, indenture itself with International Christendom. One could say it has offered itself to the claws of the white colonizer, who maintains in this 21st century, still and always, Black Africa into a "neocolonialism" that is strangling on all levels! From above, Kimbangu sees in the Africa of today persons in charge who allow themselves to be reclaimed by the most reactionary regimes put to the service of the Westerners supposedly "on his behalf"!

The rough-casting of the Kimbanguist Church of today to the rank of church of Christian obedience constitutes "de facto", a "de-prophetization" of its founder Simon Kimbangu. Note that black Africans, and you also, Kimbanguists, the founders of the other Christian Protestant branches, Calvin, Luther and others, were not "prophets". Moreover, they never declared themselves as such; they did not have, contrary to the Prophet Kimbangu, the Messianic prophetic seal. Whatever the importance of the role that they had to play, they were never a part of the chain link of the prophets. They were, quite simply, dissidents who, at their time, created a schism. The Prophet Simon Kimbangu did not make a schism at all; he received a mission directly from Yahweh the Eternal. It is extremely different and much more important, for Africa and even for the whole of humanity.

Moreover, Christianity being, in fact, engineered by the Apostle Paul, who was its true founder and who made a universal religion of it, it would be completely absurd that Simon Kimbangu came later to have to reveal Christianity again, like a kind of post-prophet for the same religion, Christianity...always Christianity! Not so; each Prophet founded his own religious movement very much distinct from the others, the work and the initiative of the Prophet Kimbangu is autonomous and is not related in any way to Jesus-Christ. Consequently, in my humble opinion, the name C.J.C.S.K (the Church of Jesus Christ on the Earth by the Prophet Simon Kimbangu) betrays the Prophet Simon Kimbangu, I am sure!

Today the Kimbanguist Church is run by Papa Simon Kimbangu Kiangani, one of the Prophet's grandsons, and there is reason to believe and hope that under his guidance Kimbanguism will definitively turn its back on the World Council of Churches, that it will give up the designation of being of "Christian" obedience and that it will become again a true politico-religious movement, revolutionist, aiming at the liberation and the de-colonization of the black man. I have confidence in Papa Simon Kimbangu Kiangani; I hope that he will follow the good way!

A black, nowadays, cannot be "Christian". A Kimbanguist cannot be of "Christian" obedience! A black can be all, except "Christian"! Christianity (, it) is the Religion of the colonizer, of the proslaver. Christianity, Catholicism, was not established by Jesus who was a "Jew", a "Jewish" rabbi, the "king of the Jews!" The mission that Jesus had on Earth on behalf of his father, the Eternal Yahweh, president of the planet of our creator-gods, was to spread to the world the Biblical Scriptures so that they would be used as proof when the era of science would explain everything to man, to all of humanity. And he accomplished his mission very well, but on the other hand, the mission of the Prophet Kimbangu was completely different!

Either one is Kimbanguist or one is Christian, but not both at the same time! And obviously, it is preferable to be just Kimbanguist because in this one does not betray his ancestors or our black Prophets, such as Kimpa Vita, Simao Toko and Simon Kimbangu, who were all persecuted, abused, tortured and sometimes killed by the colonizing and proslavery Christian Church Catholic!

History is moving; the African Rebirth is on the way. The Great Divine King (Nkua Tulendo), announced by the Prophet Kimbangu, is here. He has been living on the Earth among us for several years already. That those who have eyes see, and that those who have ears hear!

(*) regarded as a hero of the anti-colonial revolt within the Lari ethnic group of Kongo, in February 1941, André Matsoua was condemned to prison for life and imprisoned in Mayama a locality of the area of Pool in the south of Kongo-Brazzaville, he died in prison on January 3, 1942, and his body was buried clandestinely by the colonial administration, since, his remembrance remains almost intact and still influences the Lari people.

86

WHITE POISON

10. Jewish descent and ancestry in black Africa

If an African says that he's "Jewish", yes, it is understandable, but not that he's a Christian. This is something entirely different! Nowadays, Africa has faint reminders of the visit of those called "Elohim" by the Hebrews of the Old Testament. Africa also remembers the Prophets sent to them by "Elohim". However, many African people are carriers of DNA markers, like the Semite Jews, proving their prestigious "Jewish" ancestry dating back to the Biblical time of the Old Testament. There is ample proof!

It is undisputable that in Africa many homogeneous social groups have Semite Jewish roots. Let us look at a specific example, the "Lembas", a black people from South Africa. According to local tradition, it is said that the Lembas left Judea guided by a man named Buba. They practice male circumcision, observe Sabbath and do not eat pork or any similar animals, such as hippopotamus.

A team of geneticists noticed that many Lembas men have in their male chromosomes a series of DNA sequence that distinguishes and characterizes the "Cohanim" sequence. These are the descendant priests of Aaron. The genetic signature of the Cohanim priests among Jewish people is very specific and is strongly present among the Lembas men who belong to the senior of their 12 groups, known as the Buba clan.

This discovery is the result of joint but markedly different investigations. One project was developed by geneticists in the USA, Israel, and England. This team sought the truth about the following fact: the Jewish tradition says that the priests are the descendants of Aaron, Moses' elder brother. The other investigation was conducted by Dr. Tudor Parfitt, director of the "Center for Jewish Studies at the School of Oriental African Studies in London". For 10 years, he and his team of researchers worked diligently to learn more about the Lembas who claim to come from "Senna" thousands of years ago.

But the "genetic" part of this story began when Dr. Karl Skorecki, a medical expert specializing in 'kidneys' at the Technion-Israel Institute of Technology, was seated in a synagogue in Toronto. Skorecki, who is a "Cohen" priest, was wondering if another Cohen called to read the Torah in this synagogue could be genetically related to him, according to the tradition that warrants that all priests be descendants from the Aarons.

Skorecki then called Dr. Michael F. Hammer of the University of Arizona, a population genetics expert working with the Y male chromosome. Unlike the other chromosomes, the genetic material of this one, the Y, does not change from one generation to another, a change that blurs the line of descent of an individual. The Y chromosomes are saved intact, practically unchanged from father to son, except for a few occasional mutations. Those mutations help to rebuild an historical population because each human line of DNA has its own distinctive pattern of mutations. It is the study of the Y chromosome that confirmed this oral tradition known among the descendants of the slave Sally Hemmings and claiming that their ancestor was Thomas Jefferson, the third president of the American Nation.

In 1997, Hammer, Skorecki and their colleagues reported on their analysis of the Y chromosome of the Jewish priests (those priests of a hereditary caste are different from the Rabbis and the Levites). They found a specific pattern of DNA sequence in those priests that differentiates them from other Jews. This pattern is specific to the 'Cohanim,' 'Ashkenazi,' and 'Sephardic' priests, even if these branches of the Jewish population have been geographically separated for a long time.

Another researcher named Neil Bradman, a businessman and colleague of Hammer and Skorecki, is currently the president of the 'Center for Genetic Anthropology at the University College of London.' Bradman embarked on a mission to study the Jewish population around the world using the technique of the Y chromosome. An employee of Bradman's project, David B. Goldstein, was a population geneticist at the Oxford University in England. Goldstein improved Hammer's work in order to develop a better genetic signature of the Jewish populations; the problem encountered frequently is the mixing with other populations, phenomenon that obfuscates the file that goes back to a common ancestor.

Goldstein observed a pallet of three sites of Y chromosomes with stable genetic mutations and six sites where mutations occur frequently in order to get a mixing that is valid enough to give a good resolution between similar Y chromosomes during the historical periods. Since the mutations are all on sites existing outside the genes, they do not contribute to the physical "make up" of the individual.

In these nine sites, he found a special pallet of genetic mutations associated with the cast of Jewish priests but that are not as present in other Jews and quite rare in non-Jewish populations. Contrary to the DNA marks, each individual has its own personal specific mark. This genetic signature, associated to the name 'Cohen' is the most widely accepted method of verifying a person's ancestry.

Therefore, those researchers found that 45% of Ashkenazi priests and 56% of Sephardic priests have a 'Cohen' genetic signature, therefore "Cohanim", that is to say, of the Aaron descendants, while in the Jewish population this frequency is 3%.

Through the techniques he developed, Goldstein could determine when different carriers of the 'Cohen' genetic signature had had a common ancestor for the last time, and he could determine this for a time period of 3180 years.

Coincidentally, this matches the Jewish tradition saying that Moses assigned the priesthood to the male descendants of his brother Aaron after the exodus of Egypt, about 3000 years ago!

So, if we want to analyze the line of descent of priests from the Aaron line according to the genetic specificity of this line of descent, with the study of the Y chromosome we have the tool par excellence to know if a population is Jewish or not, according to the work published by Goldstein.

As part of Bradman's project on the relationship between the Jewish populations, Goldstein then tested the DNA samples of the Lembas. He reported that 10% of the Lembas men were carriers of the 'Cohen' genetic signature, and that 53% of the Lembas who claimed they belonged to the Buba clan carried a distinctive sequence. This proportion is completely similar to the one found in the major part of the Jewish population.

The fact that the "Cohen" genetic signature is very rare, not to say nonexistent in all non-Jewish populations, is a discovery that proves that the Lembas definitely have Jewish ancestors. These findings were published in the "American Journal of Human Genetics".

The Lembas live in South Africa and Zimbabwe. They have clan names like "Sadiqui" and "Hamisi" which are clearly "Semite". We can also find those names in Yemen, for example.

Additionally, according to the Jewish tradition, Simon Kimbangu was Jewish, because being Jewish is to recognize the messenger(s) of the Elohim and who follows his (or their) teachings, therefore any prophet sent or contacted by Yahweh Elohim is necessarily "Jewish". If today's Kimbanguist Church really wants to respect the Prophet Kimbangu and not betray him it should rather claim to be Jewish, but certainly not Christian! This church claiming to be Christian is insulting its own Prophet. And besides, Jesus was "Jewish" and not Christian; He was the "king of the Jews"!

Traces of the "Jewish" or "Semite" roots are widespread throughout Africa. We need simply to look at Ethiopia (the Judea of the Old Testament). This region gave its name to one of the twelve tribes of Israel, the tribe of Judea (Judah). The Ethiopian Orthodox Church is probably the oldest African Church still remaining today. There are good reasons to dream when looking at its history and the ancestry of the Ethiopian dynasty in olden times. The last sovereign of the dynasty was Negus, the Emperor Haile Selassie I, born Tafari Makonnen in 1892. He was the 111th emperor in the succession of the famous King Salomon of the Bible. One can only be Jewish when one is a descendent of the King Salomon...who could refute that?

And let us not forget the Falashas, the "black Jews of Ethiopia". The name 'Falasha' means, "foreigner" in Amharic. But the Falashas call themselves "Beta Isra'el" which means "house of Israel". The male priests of the Falasha were called "Kohanim", which rings a bell, doesn't it? In the original work of the Falashas, written in Ge'ez (which is also the sacred language of the Ethiopian Christians), there is the book of Abba Elijah, the Apocalypse of Gorgorios, the Apocalypse of Ezra, and the book of the Deaths of Moses. Of course, the Church and Christianity will never acknowledge those books or Gospels as being part of their canon, neither biblical nor Christian!

However, according to some traditions, the Falashas are the descendents of Menelek, the son of King Salomon and Queen of Sabah (Sheba), which, according to the Falashas' legend, would have taken the Arch of Alliance of Jerusalem to Judea, that is to say, to Ethiopia. They were persecuted by the Christian authorities of Ethiopia but nevertheless managed to keep their "Jewish" identity.

The Falashas were officially recognized as "Jewish" by the Chief Rabbi of the Sephardi in 1973 and in 1975 by the Chief Rabbi of the Ashkenazi.

The Tutsis of "Havilah" of the Ancient Empire "Hima-Tutsi" (Rwanda, Burundi, Ankole region (Uganda), of Buha (West Tanzania) Uvira, of Bukavu and other regions in the East of The Democratic Republic of Kongo, also claim the right to say that they are "Jewish".

They are the courageous of the great biblical Kushite empire of Abyssinia whose army (the Kush army) has been the spearhead of the Pharaonic army since the ancient time of the great Kushite-Tutsi conqueror, Menes-Horaha. Forty small statues carrying the Kush bow found in the tomb of Musigati (Mesehty in Upper Nubia) in 2040 B.C. indicate this. Several times, the Bible makes reference to this army of Kush composed of black Jews and lead by the great King Kushite-Tutsi, Mutabaruka Taharqa. It is this army that rushed to the aid of Jerusalem, besieged by the Assyrians around 701 B.C., among other accomplishments.

One should also know that the Ethiopian Kushite throne of Saba, which was an archetypal Jewish throne, stretched in the past over a vast territory. We just have to look at old maps of Africa from before the conference of Berlin in 1884, the maps that drew the old natural borders before the age of the Christian colonization, to realize that the Kushite Ethiopia once stretched in the north of the present day Ethiopia to the south to Shaba (Katanga) and Zambezi. That's right, on the old maps, Shaba and Katanga belonged to Ethiopia, or in other words, to the former southerner Abyssinia!

Therefore, for all times, the Batutsi-Bahimas were the guardians of the White Nile sources for the Throne of Ethiopian Kushite of Saba, of Jewish essence, which stretched to the south of Shaba (Katanga). No one on earth can deny or contradict the fact that the blacks of "Kush" are Jewish, that they are "black" Jews and that the Tutsis, who were the archers, the soldiers and the warriors defending the Kushite Empire of Ethiopia (of Abyssinia) on all fronts, and who nowadays are the guardians of the "Kush" memory, are not "Jewish".

All this has nothing to do with Christianity and the New Testament! We are rather of "Jewish" or "Semite" persuasion, of "Jewish" ancestry and of "Jewish" origin in Black Africa. And we must (like any Hebrew "Jewish" of Israel who rightly does not recognize the New Testament) as "Semite Jewish" of Africa, denounce this New Testament. We should be conscious that the New Testament, the Vatican and Christianity are not at all part of the teachings, recommendations or doctrines established by Yahweh Elohim and/or their Prophet Jesus. Not in the least! Jesus was the king of the "Jews" as he acknowledged himself before Pontius Pilate during the Praetorium, when the Prosecutor of Judea asked him: "Art thou the King of the Jews?" Jesus answered, "Sayest thou this thing of thyself (...)"
(Gospel according to John, XVIII, 33 and 37).

And let's look at the Kongo people of the old kingdom of Kongo which stretched at one time to the north of Angola, to Kongo-Brazzaville, to the south of Kongo Gabon, and also to the South-West of Kongo Kinshasa, with their sacred language the "kikongo". The first pro-slavers who arrived to the Kongo Kingdom in the 15th century found an advanced society with specific codes of ethics. They found an intelligent people, nice, dignified, wearing beautiful artistic clothes and who had beautiful avenues, pleasant buildings and a well-maintained agriculture. And above all, they found a population that used the old mosaic code that resembles very closely the Egyptian code and which sacred language, the Kikongo, has elements that can be found in the biblical old Hebrew! Many linguists have confirmed this particularity! But how could this Kongo People have observed the Law of Moses and have in their language elements of the old biblical Hebrew, all this, long before these elements appear in the European languages?

Well, to get an idea, let us briefly compare the history of the twelve tribes of Israel with the history of the Kongo people. This we will do in the following chapter.

94

10. Jewish descent and ancestry in black Africa

WHITE POISON

11. History of the Kongo People and their biblical Semite ancestry

We must not believe that Africa has lost all of its history, not at all! We gradually start to reconstitute it. Bit by bit, we are starting to write it again in order to spread it among the children of today's Africa, and this time nothing will be lost because all will be sealed on paper.

Significant recognition must be expressed towards the bards, troubadours (griots), monarchs, and the ancient and old chiefs of Black Africa. They are very often gifted archivists with an exceptional, even extraordinary, memory. They are fantastic genealogists, able sometimes to recite the list of dynasties and kings over a period of several centuries. They have been the memory of Africa...memory that is put nowadays preserved on paper for posterity, that history is known.

Throughout history in Black Africa, in the discourse presented to our primary and secondary schools, we very often heard the following expression pronounced and taught by the French and Belgian teachers: "our ancestors the Gauls"! Their very mention suggests that if a people had a history and a past and that the other did not have any, the latter consequently derived its history from the former. There was obviously an organized attempt here to encourage Black Africa to forget its history, a purposeful intent to deny the history of Black Africa. All of this is in the past, we have our history indeed, and it is now out of the question that they teach us the French revolution and other inane topics of this kind as being part of "our history"!

The Jews designated the blacks by the word "Kushim" and the current African continent by the word "Kush" (Isaie XIII, 1 and Jeremie 13, 23). It is interesting to note that a tribe of the Kongo people is still called today "Kush" and its members the "BaKush or Bakushu"! The scriptures also mention clearly that one of Moses' wives was "Kushite", therefore "black"! Certain Peul people (Bororos, Woodabe) in Africa actually say that they are descendants of Moses with this "Kushite" woman names Sephora or Tshipora.

We can also note that Chapter 10 of the Book of Genesis names three continents and calls the current African continent with the old name "KaM", the diminutive of KaMa. In Aramean "KaMa" and in Hebrew "KaM" mean Burned, Heat, Blackened. And Herodotus (History II, 22) says that heat turns Men Black. The word "KaM" is also reproduced on a canaanean ins-cription dated from the 10th century B.C. and indicates the current Afri-can continent (Stele of Paraiba, in Brazil).

Consequently, the right question that we can ask ourselves is the fol-lowing: is this word "KaMa" of African origin? Well, yes! And it is an ad-ditional proof that the original inhabitants of Ancient Egypt were Blacks and that the black people of Africa are directly related to the history of Ancient Egypt (and their Gods who descended from the sky in their solar discs). The Ancient Egyptians distinguished themselves in particular by the word "KaMtu", meaning "Blacks", because they were black (moreover in an African language, Mandjaku, "KeMatu" means completely black and/or burned). And the Ancient Egyptians also used the word KaMi and/or Kemet, meaning "Black" to indicate their land and the remainder of the continent.

The root of this word "KaMa" is omnipresent for a considerable number of people of central Africa, of West Africa, showing that their history dates back to Ancient Egypt. This root can be found in the following langua-ges: "KaMa" means black in Copte, "iKama" means blackened in Mbochi (Kongo-Brazzaville, Gabon, Cameroon), KaMi means burned and black in Bambara (Mali, Burkina Faso), "KeM" means burned in Wolof (Senegal), "KiM" means burned in Mossi (Burkina Faso, Niger).

Moreover, the Ancient Egyptian word "KaM" also referred to burned wood (coal). Thus one can find in many languages of black people (Kikongo, Teke, Lingala, Mbati, Zigoula, Swahili, etc.) the derivative "Kala" which means "coal", whose plural is "MaKala".

But let us look more closely at what degree the Bantu people and the Kongo Kingdom are linked to the history of Ancient Egypt and to Moses, to whom certain Peul people (Bororos, Woodabe) say they are direct des-cendants!

According to the tradition of the people of the Kongo Kingdom, here is the history and here is the origin of this marvelous Kongo, these people, this particular kingdom that was the cradle of three great known black pro-phets, i.e., Kimpa Vita, Simon Kimbangu, and Simao Toko. What follows is what ancient Kongo people tell concerning the origin, the foundation of the old Kongo Kingdom.

According to tradition certainly, but also according to the deep meaning of the sacred language of the Kongo Kingdom, the "Kikongo", this word "Kongo" means "Love". Moreover, today still, in certain corners of Lower Kongo to answer a call from her husband a woman answers by "kongo". And, as the god of Kongos was a god of Love, himself was often called "Kongo".

The history of the Kongo Kingdom tells that the ancestors of Kongos were in search of their promised land, that they called "Mbanza Koongo" or, in other words, "the core of all Kongos". The legend says that the supreme god, chief of all the gods, said to their ancestors:

> *"It is with my love that I created man and all living things, to you my beloved people who bear my name I say: to invoke my love, call me "Kongo Kalunga" [which means "omnipresent love"]. With Love, wisdom and intelligence the world and all its creatures were created; bear my name beloved people. "*

Thus, for Kongos their name is of celestial origin and also their various languages such as the "Kikongo". But let us study closely the history of these people, such as it is reported to us by tradition, according to the ancient ones and the descendants of various dynasties within the Kingdom, such as the Teke Dynasty, historically the most important.

Before the fish [the era of Pisces], about 4200 B.C., the Kongo people would have come from Judah [current Ethiopia] towards the Nile. They founded at this place a country that they named Ekipata [located in what is currently Egypt].

In 4000 before the era of Pisces, Ekipata belonged to an extremely developed area, in all disciplines, at the religious, scientific, and political levels, etc. From everywhere else one came here to learn, as well as to seek food. Then the area fell into a great disorder.

In the year 1300 before the era of Pisces, Kenatu [who would be, if one establishes the links with the history of Ancient Egypt, the famous Pharaoh "Akenaton"] decided he must hinder the collapse, to bring reforms, and to restore order. But following the death of Kenatu this period of disorder resumed. Kongos were again mistreated and decided to leave this area and to take refuge in Judah [Ethiopia].

Around the year 960 before the era of Pisces, it is told in tradition in the legends of the Kongo people of a queen named Makenda Sheba [all leads to believe that it is indeed "the queen of Sabah"], who married King Solomon. And, according to what Kongos say, this queen Makenda Sheba would have a bond with them.

In the year 220 before the era of Pisces, a messenger of the eternal, an angel, appeared to Mbemba Zulu asking him to become the leader of Kongos. Under the guidance of this Mbemba Zulu, Kongos left Judah [Ethiopia] for a promised land that they named Dizimba ["Sanctuary"]; it would be located inside current Zimbabwe. After the death of Mbemba Zulu, the replacement was ensured by Isanusi and then by a woman called Mbangala, who guided the Kongo people to the Kalahari Desert. According to tradition, Kongos mixed with Pygmies of the desert, which gave birth to Hereros, or baheleles of Namib, again according to legend.

In the year 320 of the era of Pisces (320 A.D.), someone named "Nsasukulu a Nkanda" directed Kongos and guided them into the conquest of the lands of Kuandu, Kubangu, Okavambu and Kunene; they are the lands that were later called "Kongo dia Mpangala".

In the year 424 of the same era, under Kodi Puanga, Kongos increased their territory with the lands of Kuangu, Luangu, Kuilu and Lulua. So their territory became then the "Kongo dia Kuimba".

In 529 of the era of Pisces still, under Tuti Dia Tiya they occupied the land of Nzaza Vumba and built the "Kongo dia Luangu" there.

Nearly two centuries later, around the year 690 and under Nimi A Lukeni, they occupied the lands of Kuanza, built the town of Mbanza-Koongo in the "Kongo dia Ntotila" (Mbanza means "city" or "large and wide agglomeration"). Currently this "great agglomeration", renamed by the Portuguese San Salvador, is located in Angola. It is what will become the great Kongo kingdom, where the following kings will succeed one another: Muabi Mayidi, Zananga Mowa, Ngongo Masaki, Mbala Lukeni, Kalunga Punu, Nzinga Sengele, Kkanga Malunda, Ngoyi Malanda, Nklu Kiangala and Ngungu Kisama. Then, from 1370 to 1481 several other kings succeeded one another. This Kingdom included the Northern areas of Angola, the areas in the South-west of Kongo-Kinshasa, the southern areas of Kongo-Brazzaville and the south of Gabon, with Mbanza-Koongo as capital. But let us now talk about the important facts that marked the remainder of the history of the Kongo people.

In 1457, the prophet Buela Muanda rose and announced the imminent arrival of Westerners on the Kongo land and specified what their (bad) intentions were.

On May 3rd 1491, King Nzinga Nkuvu was converted to Christianity and then baptized. All Kongos who accepted the entry of Jesus in their life gathered behind Mvemba Nzinga, son of King Nzinga Nkuvu, and those who defended the Kongo religion gathered behind Mpanzu a Nzinga, the other son of king Nzinga Nkuvu.

In 1518 in Rome, the pope Leon X consecrated the mukongo Lukeni lua Nzinga as the first catholic African Bishop. Lukeni lua Nzinga was the son of King Mvemba Nzinga.

From 1702 until 1706, the female Prophet Kimpa Vita accomplished her works in Kongo. She had succeeded in awakening all Kongos and in rebuilding the town of Mbanza-Koongo. She then began to fight the Western religion in all regions of the Kongo territory. The Portuguese soldiers, on order of the Catholic Church as well as Father Lorenzo da Lucca and the Father Bernado da Gallo then stopped the Prophet Kimpa Vita and had her burned alive on July 2,nd 1706.

It should be noted that the name of the Kongo Kingdom has nothing to do with the tribe "Kongo" of the same name, because indeed the Kongo tribe consists of the Kongo ethnic group. Certainly this ethnic group had a king; it formed within the large Kongo Kingdom, a sub-kingdom that, in fact, was a liege of the true tribe reigning on all the territory of the Large Kongo Kingdom, namely the Teke (Téké) tribe. This one was and is still currently the only tribe that is present on the totality of the territory of Kongo Brazzaville, that is also present in Kongo-Kinshasa, in Gabon (via the Mbéti tribe) and to the South of Cameroon.

Thus, the Great Kingdom was lead by the Makoko, which means "king" in Teke language, until today despite the physical disappearance of the Kingdom. The latter continues to exist in a virtual way because the usual authority of the Makoko is still recognized in the two Kongos, Gabon and Angola. This may explain why one can still find on the level of Kongo Brazzaville the heiress family of the Makoko throne, which is the AMPION family, whose name is in fact a title which means (in the Teke language) the tomb of the ancestors. This title was allotted to Ngansibi Leon, as well as to his cousin, because they were the last of the Makoko line (Queen Ngalefuru), nowadays the elder son; and heir to the throne is Ampion Willy Christian. The Tekes belong to the linguistic group Bantu with clear Hebraic bonds.

In 1880, a beleaguered King Teke Makoko Iloo, at the head of a country ruined, devastated, torn by the trade of the slaves, signs into practice a treaty known as a "protectorate". With this unfortunate passage, signed in Mbe on the plateau in the north of the current town of Brazzaville with Savorgnan de Brazza, Italian mercenary-explorer at the service of France, and due to the fact that he could neither read or write and could not understand the scope and reason for the treaty, virtually uninformed, he unwittingly and without desire yielded to France his rights to the Empire.

In 1885, the Westerners gathering together at the Berlin conference to share Africa like a large birthday cake, cut the Kongo kingdom in four pieces: Kongo Zaire, Kongo Brazza, Kongo Angola and Kongo Gabon.

In 1921, prophet KIMBANGU achieves his mission to awaken all Kongos. At that time, thanks to the message of the prophet Simon Kimbangu, Kongos were opposed to the Western religion.

On June 30th 1960, Kongo Kinshasa achieved independence under the presidency of Mbuta Kasa Vubu, child of the Kongo Kingdom.

On August 15th 1960, Kongo Brazza achieved independence.

On August 17th 1960, Kongo Gabon achieved independence.

In 1969, Kongos founded the religious and political organization "Bundu Dia Kongo" with the following objectives:

> to bring back the Kongo people towards "the Kongo Religion",
> to abandon the Churches of the colonizer
> to find their roots and traditions;
> to recognize their sacred language "Kikongo" and
> to restore it to Kongos, in place of the colonial language;
> to prepare Kongos for all that will occur during the era of Aquarius;
> to reconstitute the borders of the ancient Kongo Kingdom.

On November 11th 1975, Kongo Angola achieved independence.
The era of the predicted Spiritual War announced by the Prophet Simon Kimbangu begins now; the era of the arrival of Nkua Tulendo, Great Divine King whose verb will be spiritual, political and scientific is starting. The era of the liberation of the people of Central Africa and consequently of

the whole of Africa, is arriving. This era starts now and is heralded by a liberation, a spiritual decolonization coming from the abandonment of the Religion of the colonizer "Christianity", indispensable condition for the achievement of Prophecies of Kimpa Vita, Simon Kimbangu and Simao Toko and the total liberation of the black man under the guidance of "Nkua Tulendo" whose arrival was announced for this era by Simon Kimbangu.

This Nkua Tulendo will be from the house of Israel; he will be from the house of David; he will be blood of Yahweh; he will say "my father who is in the Skies". Not only will he reveal the secrets of our origins and will show the way to reach a splendid future thanks to science - because we will become ourselves gods, creators - but what's more he will also become involved in the current politics and do so especially in the countries which had to suffer more from the selfishness and the brutality of those who, for a short time in history had a minor temporary advancement over the oppressed. This is particularly the case with the "Christian" West who had guns at their disposal to dominate the people who did not have this weapon (the blacks, Indians). Thus his role as "the Messiah" will not be only spiritual, religious; it will be also political, without forgetting that he will be one of the greatest among the popularizers of Science.

"Jerusalem", "Jerusalem coming down from the sky" has a foot in Africa, an important foot in Africa!

If Africa is currently "behind" compared to rich countries on the technological level, it has on the other hand the privilege of being ahead spiritually, thanks to the fact that it does not suffer from the handicap of the complex of superiority of the catholic and Christian Whites, these "ex-colonizers" who continue to situate themselves in the center of the universe. Yes, "Jerusalem" with a foot in Africa. It is written somewhere that "the last will be the first", is it not? This will become a fact, you'll see, as soon as Africa manages to break the claws of the Religion of the colonizer, to leave this prison. This term is necessary so that Africa can open its arms and accommodate the one who is announced, "Nkua Tulendo", who will be without pity for the usurping Church which has spoken for 2,000 years in the name of Jesus and of Yahweh without ever having been mandated for that, neither by one nor by the other, nor by a third person doing it on their behalf.

WHITE POISON

12. Christianity in Africa: source of poverty

Just a quick glance at the world is all it takes to realize that the majority of Christian regions and mainly the Catholic ones are the poorest of all, contrary to those that are Jewish, for example, but also Protestant; these regions are indeed rich, some quite wealthy.

In Europe, the Catholic regions of Portugal, southern Italy, and Ireland are the poorest. The Catholic Latin America is poor! Catholic South America, poor! Catholic Africa, poor!

It is of an implacable logic, through its New Testament, that the Christian Catholic Church established an attitude, an ambivalent teaching about money and fortune, with passages such as:

"Yes, I tell you, it's hard for a rich man to enter the kingdom of heaven. Again I tell you, it is easier for a camel to go through the eye of a needle than for a rich man to enter the kingdom of God".(Matthew XIX, 23-24, taken up again in Luke XVIII, 25 and Mark X, 25), or: "Ye cannot serve God and Mammon. [Mammon: Aramaic word indicating wealth]" (Luke XVI, 13), and also: "[...] and having food and raiment let us be therewith content. But they that will be rich fall into temptation and a snare, and into many foolish and hurtful lusts, which drown men in destruction and perdition". (1-Timothy VI, 8-9), and still for example: "For the love of money is the root of all evil". (1-Timothy VI, 10)

Here is what the Church teaches. It teaches to its faithful the «holy» worship of poverty, and preaches that the kingdom of heaven belongs to the poor. If we are educated in this way, in disdain for money, we will not have any. If we think that money is dirty and bad, of course, we will not have any. It is a very simple law and completely logic. Somebody who thinks that «sex» is bad and evil, will have a miserable sexual life, or won't even have any at all. The principle is identical where it concerns money and the acquisition of fortune.

The teaching of the white "fathers" was very simple: "be happy to be poor, the kingdom of heaven will then be opened to you" which amounts to saying: "remain poor down here, you will have the right to paradise in heaven, and there, you will be happy; we, in order for you to remain poor, we will take care of your wealth, as good family "fathers"... we the "fathers" who are sent to you in the name of Jesus!"

Shame on this Church, on this Christian Religion, that Scriptures recommend that we not be called "Lord" but whose high executives are called "his lordship"!

Africa would have been better off in preserving its links with Judaism instead of allowing it to be converted to Christianity by force. It would have been better off by indoctrinating itself with "Jewish" teaching with regard to money; it would be most certainly richer today. To be sure! Not only would it be better off financially, but it would also be closer to the Truth, in all matters, because Christianity - with its New Testament - came to bring and teach some "whatever", including its worship of poverty, which is a large piece of its "whatever". It is pure silliness, but the African blacks swallowed it and accepted it, whereas it is absolutely not in the original teaching on this matter...neither of Moses, neither of Jesus, nor of any Prophet or Messenger sent by Yahweh. Let us look at briefly at what the original teaching about money is, about wealth. For an accurate teaching, let us turn towards the "Jewish" people, the people of the Book, such as they are also called in the Koran.

For Jews, fortune and wealth are good, respectable and noble objectives to strive for. But more than this, once that it is acquired, it is tragic to lose it. Judaism never regarded poverty as a virtue, and is right about that. The first Jews were not poor and money was regarded as something good. The founding fathers of Judaism, Abraham, Isaac and Jacob, were blessed with cattle in abundance. Asceticism and disavowal of oneself are not Jewish ideals. According to Jews, it is necessary to have one's financial house in good condition, to enable one to live fully and lead one's spiritual life:

"Where there is no corn, there is no Torah [Bible]". "The Mishna" (a collection of books that describes the detailed laws for the Jewish way of living on a daily basis), says, "poverty creates transgression". The Hassidic Jews as well as the Talmud [collection of rabbinical books of comments on the Old Testament] say: "poverty in the house of a man is worse than fifty plagues".

Which is the surest source, the Old Testament and Judaism, of which the Rabbi and the Prophet Jesus are part off, or Christianity and/or Catholicism, created three centuries after the death of Jesus and their New Testament which is only a collection of carefully selected pieces, an assembly of texts handled by Rome in order to seat its power? The answer is obvious: it is the Old Testament, of course.

106

Africa must denounce once and for all the faith, the Christian doctrine that does nothing but pull us downward in all manner and respect. Take, as an example, the "Jewish" people and the matter of money. As already shown in this work, in Black Africa we have Jewish descent and ascent in our genes. Jesus also was "Jewish" and he never taught this worship of poverty. It is merely an invention, an instrument of manipulation and domination at the hands of the Catholic and Roman Christian Church.

Thus let Africa be inspired by Judaism, in the matter of philosophy concerning money, wealth, and fortune. Undoubtedly, it will definitely be better off!

In the United State, Jews constitute only 2 % of the population yet they dominate all of the most important institutions: university teaching and research, politics, the media, liberal professions, industry, the field of culture and sciences. Further, 45 % of Jews live in the United States and 35 % in Israel. From the incredible success of the small group of Jews living and working in the US comes a considerable transfer of fortune and knowledge towards Israel.

Steven Spielberg, Ralph Lauren, Michael Eisner, Michael Dell. They are all successful; they are at the top of their art or their trade; they are all enormously rich; and they are all "Jewish". That's it! Today in the USA, the three main characteristics that are linked together are: success, fortune and Judaism. This is neither by chance nor by accident. If the Jewish people profit from such success, from such fortune, it is because of their religion, their culture and their collective historical experience. We, Black Africans, also have our culture, our collective historical experience (slavery, colonization, apartheid). But hear this, we do not have, or rather we no longer have "our" Religion! We have Christianity, but this is not "our" Religion. It was imposed on us by force and, moreover, it teaches us nonsense about money, wealth and fortune while claiming that this message – the one brought by the Christian West – is from Jesus and consequently from Yahweh. This is unmistakably false...shamefully false! And those who decide to bring it to us, to impose it on us, they know well that their message is distorted, but they also know to what extent it is beneficial for them that we adopt it!

Here, on this subject, some enlightening... statistics:

45 % of the top 40 of Forbes 400 (the 400 richest people in the USA) is "Jewish"!
33 % of the American multimillionaires are "Jewish"!
20 % of professors in the greatest universities in the USA are "Jews"!
40 % of partners in the most performing legal offices in the USA are "Jews"!
30 % of all the USA "Nobel Prize" winners in science are "Jews"!
25 % of all the USA "Nobel Prize" winners are "Jews"!

Whereas "Jews" only represent 2 % of the United States population!

The Jewish tradition says that there are 7 keys for success, the first being to understand that the way of making a fortune is transmittable; it is "knowledge;" and its transmission is carried out through the channel of education; it is learned by education and through Religion.

So the importance of asking ourselves: what do the Christian African blacks transmit to their children by the channel of education? Well, it is precisely the opposite: the children of the Christian blacks learn how to venerate the worship of poverty. And you don't have to wait for the result: poor they are, poor they will remain. And their future will consist, in various Christian Churches and other prayer groups, of asking each day for the Heaven to send them their daily bread! What incredible ignorance! "Incredible", yes...but especially for those who, at home, collect a fortune... in our place!

What does Christendom teach to the African children? It teaches them to say, "I cannot afford to buy this or to have that"! instead of teaching them to say, "How can I find a way to afford buying that?" Becoming rich individually or collectively as people or nation is not learned at school; it is learned through education and the placement of money in the spiritual concept that is part of education. The Christian concept teaches Africans to work at the service of money but does not teach Africans to put money at their service.

The project of de-Christianization of the African population is an invitation to throw a new glance on wealth, at the individual and collective levels.

All this "Christian" mentality, this lack of education, or worse, this pernicious Christian education about wealth and money made Africa fall - with great ease - inside the vicious churning carrousel of begging. And I could

108

easily explain it to a friend by saying to him: if you want to control so-mebody, teach him what he must do to never aspire to wealth. In fact, teach him the opposite, that he should be poor and to remain poor. Offer him financial assistance and institutionalize his home from begging. In this way, we will require to beg of you each time he is in need, falling deeper into this vicious cycle, becoming accustomed to this deplorable way of life without question. With this, you will have him at your disposal. We can say that you will inflict upon him, to some extent, a permanent "econo-mic occupation". You will make so that he consumes your products; you will transform him into "a Consumer" who only thinks of his immediate consumption...without ever thinking that he could produce himself that which he needs, or that he could not consume immediately the whole, but to invest a part of it in order to be able to benefit from the output tomorrow and the days that will follow. And I could add to my friend: look at what extent this plan succeeded bloody well in Africa!

When will there be a great „black" restaurant listed in the European Mi-chelin guide next to the other world specialties? Is the African cuisine less inviting than the other cuisines? Is it less refined? Not at all. It is only that blacks are entrenched in a dreadful complex of inferiority with respect to the whites that came to impose their "white Religion", that this one became now "the" Religion of the blacks. It is Christianity that imposed this "complex of inferiority" on us but it is extremely well anchored now in the head of Africans. And what does one note? The Christian black is some-body defeated, he is beaten, a loser who gave himself to his attacker. He voluntarily threw himself in the claws and the prisons of the colonizer and his religion. And together, this sinister tandem, neo-colonizer and Chris-tianity, repeat endlessly that blacks, fundamentally disadvantaged simply because they are black, will never know a restaurant of his "indigenous" cuisine in the Michelin Guide!

Which black can accept that? Not a sensible black...only a defeated black, beaten, dominated, colonized...the black who adopted the Religion of the one who walked beside him for hundreds of years with a whip on his belt and a "chicotte" in his hand.

It is high time that Africans, the blacks, understand that all is "economic war" on Earth, that all revolves around the conquest of "economic mar-kets". They should further understand that it is because of this that we should have "economic warriors" among us who possess a broad vision of money and wealth, who are impassioned by monetary gain, and who are scrupulous and careful in how they may distribute this wealth.

But to identify with this new type of "warrior", it is necessary to cast off any inferiority complex, for this kind of complex inevitably involves a lack of self-esteem, a lack of self-confidence that renders us disabled, removes our will to dare, and imposes limits on oneself. No, my African brothers and sisters! Give up this poison that you have accepted in your body. This poison is called „Christianity." Give it up and you will be relieved of all its side effects that are so harmful for you.

The Christian teaching brought by the former colonizing West and the neo-colonizer West of today never taught and still do not teach the "Christian" blacks to understand that true wealth is portable and reproducible anywhere, that those who are successful are so because they are entrepreneurs and competitors, that it is necessary to be impassioned by what one gains, and that it is necessary to be proud of one's individuality. Creativity should be encouraged especially since, psychologically, it is necessary to be fully justified; it is necessary to want to prove something in this field, because success is 5 % inspiration and 95 % perspiration.

Christianity inculcated to blacks is light years away from all that. All this deplorable "Christian" education concerning wealth and money made "colonized" blacks individuals who have a bad approach to "doing business". How many times are we not astonished, even flatly surprised by the way in which one is welcomed or treated in businesses owned by blacks? They display an attitude, composure, slowness, words, gestures, and a glance... all but a "commercial attitude", i.e., an attitude adapted to "business".

When we come face to face with such "proprietor", we have to ask ourselves: "does he really want to earn money?" He radiates so little enthusiasm while facing the very people who can bring him money; therefore we can only deduce that he is here against his will, as though a burden to earn his money. That surprises me each time, this lack of "commercial" touch or "feeling" to adopt a good attitude, to have good invigorating enthusiasm for business. Each time I find myself in a similar situation, I say to myself while looking at the person, "poor colonized", he submits without even knowing to the heavy consequences of centuries of "Christian" colonization where the black moved only on command from the white Master at the slapping of the whip and the blows of the "chicotte"!

Often we enter stores or other establishments owned by blacks and somehow feel unwelcome. Apparently, they ignore your presence and will come to serve you only when they are "ready" to do it...quite amusing!

They still and always behave like "slaves", "servants" who need to be whipped by the white "Christian" Master! This time it's not amusing any longer; it becomes really "very sad"!

These consequences of Christian colonization and this anti-science and anti-wealth "Christian" education was indeed very damaging to the spirits of the blacks, that only a total "spiritual decolonisation", as taught by our Great Prophet Simon Kimbangu, will be able to change. Anti-science Catholicism and Christianity are quite simply an invitation to intellectual idleness.

WHITE POISON

13. Christianity in Africa: source of non-progress

"The (Catholic) Religion and the clergy have been, and maybe will remain for a long time among the most important enemies of progress and liberty"

Khristo Bote, Bulgarian writer and patriot (1849-1876)

Not only is Catholicism a source of poverty, it is inevitably a source of non-progress. I will explain. But before that, I would like to share a brief thought for all the inventors of all times who had to bear condemnations, harassment and also contempt from the Roman Catholic Church. To all these clever people who suffered from short-sightedness, denial and irony from the anti-science, anti-progressive Christian culture, I dedicate a thought of sympathy; in the etymological meaning: I feel inside what they had felt.

The Catholic Church has always had an anti-science behaviour and position. It has always been opposed – and still nowadays- to scientific progress. There have always been papal condemnations to bar the progress of science.

Nevertheless, we have read in the Bible "Every man is stupefied for lack of science"! And we observe yet that the Church places its power on ignorance, on lack of scientific knowledge, on a truly scientific non-culture.

Today papal condemnations refer to biology, genetics, therapeutic cloning, and GMOs (genetically modified organisms). But papal condemnation also touched in the past, for example, aircrafts...the domain of the skies having to be reserved for God, the fork...the first people who ate with a fork were excommunicated because it was considered an obligation to touch God's food with one's hand, to pay tribute to him.

Condemned in the same way were also...wearing glasses, the belief in a plurality of worlds in the universe and the possibility of existence of other civilizations in the cosmos. For having insisted on the possibility of an extra-terrestrial life, a "Dominican" priest and very talented scientist, Giordano BRUNO, was burnt on a stake in public in Rome in 1600. To say that the earth is round was also cause for condemnation; and therefore Copernicus' condemnation. And then came Galileo's adjudication by the court of inquisition in 1633. Ironically, notice that Galileo realized a bit of luck and was restored by the papacy....in 1992, only 359 years later...with all things being relative, once "scientists" of the Vatican were able to understand quickly!

As we say, "It is better to quickly laugh about it...to avoid crying"! because the list of all the vile abuses of power is so long, much too long!

And nevertheless, in spite of this obstinate obstruction known yesterday and today, the Pope and his clergy travel now in aircrafts, eat with forks and wear glasses when they need them!

This does not prevent the Vatican from perpetually rising up against every progress and even the simple advances in science, arguing that it is forbidden for Men to "play god". Thus a Pope took the decision in the past to condemn the first surgical operations. Really! But here: today's Pope would have died by the time I wrote this, thanks to the many life-saving surgeries available to us today... and without "playing god", as was felt of surgeons in our past. But the wrong teaching that the Pope now spreads and has other people spread today all over the world causes probably millions of deaths...innocent victims of AIDS, to quote only this principal example! (Refer to a little further in this chapter and to Chapter 17 of this book).

Another side of the same problem, the present Pope still thriving at age 83 due to the help of dozens of physicians (at the time of this writing) rises up with all his forces against the progress of molecular biology and genetics, and consequently against all research on aging and regenerator stem cells, forgetting that one of his predecessors, Pope Pie XI, was regularly given injections of ewe's foetus in the rejuvenation clinic of Paul Niehaus in Switzerland.

Somewhere in all of this, try to find a bit of common sense, logic in these anti-progressive, anti-science positions taken by the Catholic Church. At every opportunity, its leaders oppose progress. They are systematically opposed to novelties...and yet later they will avail themselves of the (are going to use themselves the) benefit of these discoveries which they had condemned, sometimes criminalized, the "discoverers" at the time when they wanted to have humanity benefit from the result of their fertile research! And, as we can observe every day, their attitude is certainly not about to change.

Unfortunately, the incoherence of these officials has perverse effects. The stance they take influences every time a huge mass of people, who in turn, take a stand against science and curb and slow down progress. This in its way brings more misfortune to us who wish only for more happiness and a better quality of life.

Today, for example, the Church's stance, resounding on the great majority of Catholic politicians, ensures that there is a wholesale boycott, indeed a complete refusal of genetically modified food, since Africa greatly needs it, and soon, very soon. Africa is in dire need of genetically modified food in order to eliminate famine and malnutrition...so that its children do not die, do not die anymore, victims of this ancestral calamity, to which Science is capable of bringing an effective remedy. For the first time in history, GMO's represent for Africa a solution for its undernourished regions, the only possibility for them to envision how to feed their future populations.

But then, in the face of the application of this fantastic remedy, a huge hindrance rises up: the Pope is opposed, the Church is opposed! As always! The Clergy is opposed too – no matter whether his skin is white or black – because black Catholic people, Christians, whether they are "church goers" or not, are above all " dominated" and as well, they have an unfortunate tendency to bend in front of their "rulers". All the way to the highest level of decision there are black Catholics who follow this "middle-ages" Roman way of thinking, the source of the curb on progress and with it the decrease in well-being, health and prosperity for all.

We can easily say that this conservative mind is synonymous with "recurrent idiocy", to "collective somnambulism", to "intellectual constipation" and to the "moronic state of masses". This entire manner of thinking continues to disturb the condition of our lives more and more. And Africa does not need all that at all; it needs science, knowledge, new technologies, itself much more than other continents.

On this matter, we would prefer not to have to speak about the Church's firm and relentless position "against" wearing condoms. But AIDS strikes the African nations' life bloods with such force that we do not have the right to keep quiet. It is far (much) too serious. It is simply a "crime against humanity" to take such a stance and to hold so firmly, especially with the prevailing opposite advice of so many worldwide physicians, all more competent than another! Also arguable is the Church's position against the simple use of contraceptive means. This too we can even judge as "criminal" when we consider the increasing problem of overpopulation facing our planet. If nothing changes, this situation will worsen.

All that is being done openly and publicly, is it believable that Africans could still support such an institution and be its "faithful?" Because to be Christian means to serve the Vatican, directly or indirectly, because even if we are a part of a Christian Church that is not directly under the tutelage of the Vatican, in fact it is indirectly. The same idiocies are conveyed, the same moronic state is instilled, and after all is said and done, it is only strengthening the colonizer's religion in Africa and the dependency of Africa with regard to it. Result: Africa and Africans stay in a condition of beggary at all levels, material and spiritual, intellectual and emotional.

Africa, wake up, please! Wake up before it is too late. Get out of this spiritual coffin in which you were placed. You can pray in the colonizer's Christian Churches, as much as you like, as much as you can, but it is without any hope. It does not bring resolution at all. If you carry on with this way of life, you will see your situation getting degraded still further. Look around you! You die, you cry, beautiful Africa, and all these Catholic and Christian prayers of your children have never changed anything and will never change anything. You can know the Bible of the "white father" by heart, recite passages ten times a day; this will not change your misery even a little!

The skies, the gods and our ancient Prophets are waiting for something else from you. Have you not yet understood that they expect from you that you decolonize yourself at all levels, including the religious level. Wake up!

13. Christianity in Africa: source of non-progress

WHITE POISON

14 - The Church and the genocide in Rwanda: more than accomplice?

«Rwanda-Urundi constitutes the area where evangelization is the most advanced. The leaders are in majority Catholics, the local clergy abundant, especially in Rwanda. The whole offers us the jewel of Africa»

(Universal History of the Catholic Missions, t.4, Grund, Paris, 1958, page 167).

The images of this genocide are still strongly engraved in the memories of everyone. It began on April 6, 1994, and in 100 days culminated in the brutal extermination of at least 800,000 people, all of them belonging primarily to the Tutsi ethnic group. A horrible massacre that took place to the almost total indifference of those in charge in the international community!

It is very interesting to note that the first official list of presumed perpetrators of genocide enumerated some two thousand people, all of them responsible for the crime of genocide. Among those appeared eleven ecclesiastics of the Catholic Church. Here are their names, and their functions:

Rwamayanja, priest, of Ndusu
Munyeshyaka Wenceslas, abbot,
Gakuba reverend of the Ndera parish,
Gikomero Hitayezu Marcel, priest of the Mubuga parish,
Gishyita Maindron Gabriel (alias Muderere), abbot, reverend of the parish of the Kongo-Nil,
Rutsiro Ntamugabumwe Jean, priest, school principal of Murunda,
Rutsiro (personal friend of the abbot Maindron)
Seromba Athanase, priest of Nyange,
Kivumu (spiritual son of the abbot Maindron)
Twagirayesu Urbain, priest of the parish of the Kongo-Nil,
Rutsiro Bellomi Isaco Carlo, priest,
Rusumo Rusingizandekwe Thaddée, abbot, priest,
Kibeho Harmisidasi, abbot, priest, school principal, Nyabisindu, Nyanza!

Another important point to note is that among these eleven people there are two European missionaries, they are: the abbot Maindron Gabriel (of France) and the priest Bellomi Carlo (of Italy)!

The genocide in Rwanda is clearly linked to a global Catholic extremist ideology that was installed over a period of 30 years and now deserves to be seriously called into question.

In the analytical report of May 16, 1997, on the senate hearings of the Belgian parliamentary board of inquiry concerning the Rwandan network, one can read interesting testimonies directly blaming the Catholic Church and its network.

It is mentioned, as an example, the abbot Rukundo Emmanuel who is evidenced as having a responsibility in the genocide. Later when fleeing Rwanda, this abbot benefited from the services of the «Caritas Catholica,» the Vatican network "par excellence". This priest, with plenty of blood on his hands, found himself healthy and safe in the Vatican, where, henceforth, he quietly spent his time studying...the canon law, the Vatican's legal provisions. This is undoubtedly useful to him!

Caritas Catholica is not the only network available to the Vatican. There are also the networks of «Caritas International» and those of «the International Christian-Democrat» that have, it is said, close links with the Opus Dei, who for their part, allowed about fifty Rwandan priests to escape to Europe and Canada.

A white priest, Johan Pristil, who was a fervent supporter of Hutu-power, Hutu extremism - the Hutu are all mostly Catholic in Rwanda - was given the opportunity at one time to take part in the creation of a radio station in Rwanda. Once this station began broadcasting, he hosted meetings there, where he translated into Kinyarwanda nothing less than Hitler's «Mein Kampf» in order to incite hatred, not towards the Jews this time, but towards the Tutsis! The German Christian Democracy funded the creation of this radio station!

According to this same analytical report, as well as documents and testimonies collected, the NGAs (non governmental agencies) were numerous that financed the armament of the Hutu militia in Zaire (the current D.R.C.), in the refugee camps!

120

There are even testimonies claiming that Catholic priests during the genocide wore military attire to take an active part in this odious work!

Certain «good nuns» («good»...really?) were judged by Belgian tribunals, guilty of handing over people of the Tutsi ethnic group to the Hutu military leaders of the genocide operation, people who had come to seek refuge with the nuns. This took place in their respective convents... in particular, Consolata Mukangango (sister Gertrude), and Julienne Mikabutera (sister Maria Kisito).

But how are such horrors possible? How can the Church be implicated on such a level in genocide of such scale?

To fully grasp how such a killing madness can occur, let us take a look at the history of Rwanda. Around 1890 the first Catholic missionaries faced a great resistance to their full colonization and evangelization campaign from the Tutsi Kings (Imwamis). The Tutsi's did not wish to be converted. Thus, in all the country, it was only with the Hutus that the missionaries found «souls» to convert.

Then, in 1922, Rwanda and Burundi fell officially under Belgian administration. Later, Belgium shook hands with the Tutsi aristocracy that was opposed to the Tutsi King (Mwami), and in doing so lay destitute the Hutu chiefs. Stated differently, the Belgians stabbed their allies in the back at the first opportunity. The good converted Hutus took as allies the members of the Tutsi aristocracy who were in opposition with their own King.

One can say that it is the choice of a new political strategy: once all the Hutus converted to their Religion, the Belgians switched camps to the other ethnic group. They privileged the Tutsis and disadvantaged the Hutus. In any case, they were already converted. So it is the Tutsis that start to flow into the Catholic churches and schools.

Later, in 1931 exactly, the Church obtained from its partners, the Belgian authorities of course, the dismissal of Tutsi king "Musinga", accused by the Church of being opposed to the Christianization of the Tutsi people. The colonizer and the Church then put in place a puppet of theirs who they could manipulate. A successor who replaced this «treacherous» African king, whom they said was a traitor to them.

Thus, in 1946, the successor of Musinga was Mutara III, who hastened to officially devote Rwanda to the «Christ-King", simply a fortunate coincidence! The Vatican swore readily that it did not have anything to do with this, that it was a decision of the king the «true believer,» Mutara III. Well come on...all which remains is for us to be naive enough to believe it!

In fact, at that time, it was perfect for the Church and also for Belgians, two hands on another large belly, that of Albert 1st this time! The simple Hutus people were converted to Christianity, and there was a fantastic trinity: The throne of Tutsi king devoted to the Christ-King, the Church, and the Tutsi aristocracy! As one would say now, when all is so well: «It is the will of the people.» But at that time, for the people to have a will to express, that would have been really incongruous!

As everywhere in Africa, from the mid to late 1950s, a wind of reclamation of independence started to blow on the Tutsis. The Church, in partnership with Belgium, once again adjusted its political strategy, always in the direction of its usual interests, and once again it broke an alliance to create another one that it considered more advantageous.

The «independent» Tutsis were dropped and treated as «Communists», thus becoming an "atheist" people, "un-faithful"...what? The Hutus were once again, the privileged darlings. This attitude, always deliberately aggressive toward one or the other of these two ethnic groups - who hitherto, cohabited for centuries without any animosity, marrying between them, living as good neighbours - this attitude of the religious powers, as well as political, created in Rwanda society, a de facto division that only deepened until it became a total racial division.

In 1957, the Hutus close to the Rwanda apostolic vicariate wrote a manifesto. This manifesto and certain letters of the white apostolic vicars in Rwanda led the Tutsis to break away completely from the Church. Tutsis were then plunged into anti-colonialism and a burning nationalism, and began aloud to call for the end of the Belgian supervision on their country.

The scenario co-written by the Church and Belgium was clear: to be allies with the Hutus by favouring them on all levels, and to confront the Tutsis who had become anti-clericals and hostile to the colonizers. It was not difficult for Belgium, at this moment, to make a united front with the Church because the Christian parties constituted the Belgian political majority in power at this time, and in the Senate their majority was absolute! Thus, for 30 years the Church and Belgium supported the Hutu power in Rwanda and their President, Juvenal Habyarimana. It is easy to understand very well the then great friendship between the very Catholic Baudoin, king of the Belgians, and the very Catholic Juvenal Habyarimana, President of the Rwandans.

Consequently, a very good question to ask about this period is as follows: «What support, what links did the President Juvenal Habyarimana enjoy during all these years until the moment just preceding the beginning of the genocide, the moment where he found death in his aircraft that was shot in flight?»

Answer: He found this support and links within Catholicism and also the Charismatic Revival for which king Baudoin had himself great sympathy. Certain sources speak about the «Opus Dei» in which Habyarimana held a high position! Other witnesses go as far as to describe a great friendship between him and then Pope John-Paul II. To follow the path of these various supports it is necessary to leave the Belgian royal Palace, to go through the Belgium Christian political parties (especially the Flemish), to find the (secret) Office of «Opus Dei» and finally to go all the way to the Pope's apartments, at the Vatican!

One realizes that this Hutus President Habyarimana and his entourage wallowed in a bath of fundamental and extreme Catholicism and sought to re-Christianize the world by employing as a privileged mean, the penetration of this cogwheel of all the possible powers (political, economic, cultural and religious).

If one speaks about the «Opus Dei,» there are many clues that lead one to think that Mr. Leon Mugesera - the person who pronounced on November 22, 1992 in a speech considered as the «ambassador» speech of the genocidal thought in Rwanda - was a member of the Opus Dei. It is this same Leon Mugesera who introduced in 1977-1978, prayer groups within the University of Butare in Rwanda! «Opus Dei,» since its creation, had led a true crusade! (Work of God, in Latin). It was founded by Monsignor Escriva de Balaguer during the Spanish civil war, and it is purely and simply a secret Catholic brotherhood created to fight «atheistic» Communism, the anarchists and all other opponents of the Church. It is based on all the fascistic religious networks and after the Second World War, it settled in Rome. It ex-filtrated the most visible Nazi criminals to Latin America and took part in the establishment of various Catholic dictatorships (one can easily say that the Hutu dictatorship of Juvenal Habyarimana in Rwanda was a Catholic dictatorship).

In Europe «Opus Dei» infiltrated all the economic and political machines.

123

In Spain, for example, one could count up to 17 of its ministers as members of Opus Dei. Various sources say that it is Opus Dei, among other works (things) that are pushing civilization today toward a war against Islam.

Monsignor Escriva de Balaguer was a spiritual adviser, to Franco and Pinochet, these two Catholic sanguinary dictators. But Pope John-Paul II canonized him on October 6, 2002! This canonization was additional proof, without any doubt, of the total approval from the «Holy Father» of the action of this sad sire. To thus «fabricate» a «Saint» the Church conducts «trials in canonization» – that sometimes last centuries. The canonization of Monsignor Balaguer is worthy of being in the «Guinness Book of World Records,» having taken the shortest time in the last 2000 years of the Church's existence to be pronounced so soon after the death of the person concerned.

But let us return to Africa. In fact, with the assistance of puppets, black «traitors,» «colonized» blacks, «Catholic Christians» blacks, such as Habyarimana, the colonizer and Church succeeded in making of Rwanda the Catholic country that it is. It was, in their eyes, a model, not only for Africa itself, but for the whole world, i.e., a pious country, hard-working, peasant, virtuous, humble, of good morals and behaviour, and almost 100% Catholic! Also, with Juvenal Habyarimana as the great representative of God in Rwanda, it was perfect!

The death of Habyarimana and the threats of the Tutsi Rwanda Patriotic Front were the occasion for the Hutus to begin the genocide of Tutsis. We can see more clearly the role of the Church in this genocide by knowing the help that it brought to the genocidal killers, sanctioning them by means of its own networks, once their barbaric acts were accomplished. Moreover, numerous notorious genocidal killers today are still protected, lodged, nourished by the Church, and are neither prosecuted nor tried, for it is obvious to everyone – serious clues attest to it - that certain Belgian personalities close to the old Regime of President Habyarimana, also close to the Charismatic Catholic Movement and «Opus Dei» use their power and their relationships to prevent justice from doing its work. One can thus cite as examples notorious genocidal killers hidden and protected in convents, monasteries; a Wenceslas abbot in Evreux (in France), the abbot Gabriel Maindron in Fontenay-le-Comte (also in France), the abbot Martin Kabakira in Luchon, (always in France), the abbot Emmanuel Rekundo in Geneva (in Switzerland), the abbot Athaknase Serumbo in Florence (in Italy) and the abbot Daniel Nahimana (in Italy also).

Already in its history, the Catholic Church had shown that it could easily organize itself in such a way. It was not the first attempt for her, the creation of networks allowing persons responsible for crimes against humanity to flee and to be sheltered from prosecutions. Obviously it was necessary each time that these individuals were compulsorily Catholics and anticommunists and that they served with devotion the cause of Rome. One can thus quote the network of Ratlines that had allowed individuals like Ante Pavelic and Joseph Mengele to find refuge in Latin America. The leader of this network was the Father Draganovic, Croatian, personal friend of the Cardinal Montini, the future Paul VI.

Here one can perhaps speak of "colonized black Nazis", having done very well their job for their gig bosses in Rome! The Church did not evangelize in Rwanda but it indoctrinated and it conditioned. This was not only done in Rwanda, but rather everywhere in Africa, for to evangelize is to bring the good news. What good news did it bring? None, quite the contrary!

Informed of all of this, how can a Rwandan, a Burundian still nowadays be Catholic, whether he is Hutu or Tutsi? I do not understand! It exceeds my understanding completely. How can an African, knowing all this, still be Catholic today? It is so far beyond my understanding that I am filled with pity, compassion and forgiveness towards these Catholic Africans, Christians, who are unaware of the evil that they do to Africa by continuing to embrace the Religion of the colonizer, manipulator, usurper, attacker, plotter, killer!

In Rwanda, the colonial West and the Catholic Church divided two people that had lived in harmony together for centuries and centuries. This division was willed and programmed to the extent that in this country the ethnic group, either Hutu, or Tutsi, was noted on all identity cards! Only one nation on the African continent, South Africa has known, with Apartheid, such a serious racial division. But in Rwanda, this division was established between people of the same colour of skin and it was organized by the Western politicking Christian and orchestrated by the world strategy of the Catholic Church, itself helped to do so, by its agents, their branches and secret intelligence.

The Church and the Christian Western politic are both accomplices in the genocide perpetrated in Rwanda, both clearly prepared this massacre by inciting hatred towards the Tutsis considered in their separatist literature as "non-Christians", as "Communists", as "anti-white", as "intelligent sly ones" refusing to be enslaved at will, whereas the Hutu was known as a "good Christian", "friend of the white", "small Negro", "serf", "native", "flexible", and "hard-working".

When I think that there are still so many Tutsis who remain Catholic today who pray in Catholic and Christian Churches, whereas these same churches were chosen by the genocidal killers to trap them there in order to exterminate them. A trap that worked several times; Tutsis were called there and believed that they would be safe in these places of worship. They went there and were crammed in and then delivered to their genocidal killers. Such was the case in the Church Saint-Pierre of Kibuye where 4,000 Tutsis who thought they had found a refuge there were savagely killed. This also happened in the church of Nyange where 2,000 people, thinking they were safe, were all were massacred. And the same yet again in the cathedral of Nyundo!

Those who say that the genocide in Rwanda was a black affair, an ethnic quarrel of blacks between each other, make me laugh with sadness. It is too simple an explanation. There was very clearly a vast conspiracy behind this genocide. A global plan existed with meticulous orchestration from outside, with an ideology extremely similar to that of the Nazis of Europe in the Thirties and Forties who, it should be said, were also very good Christians. Those who have eyes and ears can easily see and feel behind all of this the actions of a Catholic Christian extreme right and apparently the hidden hand of the "Opus Dei" also somewhere in this affair.

In 1933 some White fathers came to establish in Rwanda the Catholic newspaper "Kinyamateka" to spread the ideology "Parmehutu" [Hutu extremism]. A Rwandan priest, the abbot André Sibomana, directed this newspaper at the time of the period preceding the genocide. The white Italian father Bérôme Carlisquia, also known as Carlo Bellomi, was accused by many witnesses as well as the current Rwandan authorities of being the brain behind the preparation and execution of the genocide against Tutsis in the area of Rusumo. He preached, according to many testimonies, hatred and violence towards Tutsis. He was regularly seen at various barriers, rifle in hand and accompanied by Hutu killers! He has taken refuge today in Brescia in Italy where he leads a quiet life.

Father Johan Pristill, a former German professor of dogma at the Great Seminar of Nyakibanda in Rwanda, translated Hitler's «Mein Kamf» into kinyarwanda, not only to broadcast it on his radio waves as mentioned above, but also to the attention of the Hutus extremist executives co-architects of the genocide, transforming along the way Hitler's master work so that it is no longer aimed any more at the «Jew» but at the «Tutsi» this time! When the genocide was over, this same Father Pristill used networks close to Caritas Internationalis to ex-filter some Rwandan priests, monks and nuns who took part in the genocide.

Thus, the countries that welcomed the ecclesiastics responsible for participating in an incentive to genocide are: Italy, France, Belgium and Switzerland. It would seem that to do what he did, Father Pristill would have narrowly collaborated with the Canadian Dominican Father Yvon Romerlau who was a close relation of former Hutu president Habyarimana; this Canadian Father is today in Rome. Coincidence or not the fact is that the parish of Nyumba, that of Father Pristill, was one of the places hardest hit by the massacres. Following the genocide, approximately 30,000 corpses were discovered there. From time immemorial and everywhere in the world, propaganda and the manipulation of minds has been very greatly efficient; all advertising agents know this, politicians and religious leaders too unfortunately!

Well before the genocide, at the time of its preparation, the Adenauer foundation in Germany, which took an active part in projects supported by the International Christian-Democrat, financed radio station RTLM (radio-TV of the Thousand Hills) that was called after the genocide «radio TV-Death.» Indeed every day and for many months, this radio incited to murder a whole series of people whose names and addresses were quoted daily!

Within this Conrad Adenauer foundation sat a certain professor, Doctor Peter Molt, who had published an analysis that presented Tutsis in an absolutely unfavourable light. His links, through the Christian-Democrat dominion, woven in Rwanda went all the way to our famous Father Pristill, already referred to twice above.

Most certainly one of the great missionary figures of the Catholic Church in Rwanda was the white priest Gabriel Maindron. He resided in Rwanda for more than thirty years! He was responsible in Rwanda for the Crete-Kongo-Nile parish. It should be noted that as soon as he arrived in this area of Rwanda in 1985, everything changed; nothing was the same. On arrival he began to create discord between Hutus and Tutsis, two ethnic groups who had lived in harmony until then. To carry out his mission the white priest, Maindron, relied on four Hutus extremist priests who he trained very well, namely: the abbots:

Jean-Baptist Ntamugabumwe,
Athanase Seromba,
Twagirayezu,
Balthazar Habimana.

Abbott Maindron was also a close relation of President Habyarimana. It is surely not by chance that this Father Maindron was the only European in his area to remain until the end of the genocide. He was always escorted by Hutu extremist militiamen who also served as his bodyguards. Maindron was directly present many times at killings during the genocide. Maindron was also a great friend of Lieutenant-Colonel Chollet, an all-powerful French military adviser of President Habyarimana; documents prove that Maindron had received some military intelligence in preparation of the genocide, and even during! He took part in practically all the political meetings of the Hutus extremists.

Survivors of the genocide testify about him in this way: «After the massacres in the church of Kibuye, I see, from the height of my hiding place in the bell-tower, Father Maindron and several people walking towards the church, among those there were the burgomaster and the Kahishema prefect, the great organizer of the genocide in the area". Perhaps could one think - and even say - that Father Maindron was part of an organization that orchestrated (organized) the genocide, and that this was his mission in Rwanda. One thing is certain; the West knew that the genocide was being prepared and the Church also knew it, and they did nothing to stop it. That is really the bare minimum that they can rightly be blamed for! Besides many documents prove the following things:

a. The secret service knew of the arms caches:
b. The UN authorities in New York had been alerted before the beginning of the genocide
c. Some secret services insisted on the gravity of the situation
d. The work of the Hutu militia, the RAF (Rwandan Armed Forces) and their presidential death squads, preparing the genocide, were already well analyzed and known by Western secret service
e. Western secret services already had lists of the Interhamwe Hutu in charge well before the beginning of the genocide.

The White Fathers in Rwanda were informed of the «Nazi» program of the

128

CDR, of the Interhamwe Hutus, three weeks before the genocide.

The Archbishop of Kigali [the capital of Rwanda], «Monsignor» Vincent Nsengiyumva, was a member of the unique party of the Hutu regime of Habyarimana. The presidential guard escorted him, he was an informant-adviser to the President, to his hard-core colonels and most extremists, such as colonel Elie Sagatwa. A document, found later in the presidential residence, shows that the Archbishop even played the middleman for promotions of officers and that he was working in intelligence!

You Africans who lived or who live in what is called the area of the Great Lakes, the one that was touched so much by the genocide of Rwanda, if you are still Catholic or Christian today, how could you? How can you, in the name of all those killed during this genocide, with the complicity of the Church, how can you remain in this Church which is responsible for your greatest misfortunes? Apostatize to pay homage to the dead, to remove Africa from the claws of this team of robbers, liars, usurpers, killers, hypocrites in cassocks, and disassociate from the unconscious valets that the African priests, cardinals and black bishops are...these domestic dogs, well tamed, well drilled, well stultified.

African, how can you still be Catholic, Christian? How can you be?

I cannot stop asking you this question! The whole of Africa is suffering and crying in pain because of you, when you pray in the Christian Churches. It will be necessary one day for you to become aware of it and quickly, please so that these unjust, useless and monstrous sufferings that Christianity has inflicted on humanity for so long may cease!

I have just addressed myself here to each «African,» but know, for you who are Tutsis, that I have for you a very particular thought. Why do I have a particular thought for you Tutsis? Because humans sometimes quickly forget! This genocide of 1994, during which approximately 800,000 Tutsis lost their life and about which the world now starts to ask questions, it was not the first genocide that Tutsis were submitted to, those of 1959 and 1963 had also preceded it! Was the Church already there...was it already involved during these first two genocides? Well, yes, it was already there during these two crimes, «Saint-Bartholomew» of Rwanda, which were baptized «the Red All Saints' day- of 1959» and «the Red Christmas of 1963!» Why? Well, quite simply because these two genocides took place - and it is not by chance - the day of these two Catholic and/or Christian holidays!

For all time the Rwandan pastor kings, these «Magi» of Rwanda, had assumed the direction of traditional institutions perfectly well organized where each one found its place and where everything functioned wonderfully, including on the religious level where the Imandwas (the Gods coming from the sky) were venerated and especially their chief, supreme God «Imana» (the equivalent of Yahweh). However, some time before these years when the first two genocides were to occur, the UN decided and proclaimed that Rwanda was to base its governmental regime on «modern» democratic elections and that destroyed all the existing traditional institutions and broke up the kingdom. It was inevitable, for in these kinds of elections only the numbers count, but the Tutsis (the Hamite monarchs) constituted only fifteen percent of the population in Rwanda, the Bantus (Hutus) constituting the remaining eighty-five percent!

The Church, at that time, very quickly understood that in order to make Rwanda its seat of power that it was necessary for the Hutu (85 %) mass to be on its side. It systematically fanaticized the Hutu masses by means of the Catholic Christian schools and of the Catholic seminars. It also multiplied, within organizations of Catholic activities, the training of Hutu abbots and seminarians and the instillation in all of these of hatred towards the Tutsis, after which it was inevitably easy for the Church to begin each of these genocides on these two precise dates. On these dates, All Saints' Day in 1959 and Christmas in 1963, (for,) during these two «red days,» the crowd present «was sufficiently conditioned!» Here, what is the true face of the Church: all for power...even at the price of a blood bath on Christmas if it is needed!

Once perpetrated, the first genocide of 1959, it was necessary to wait until October 1960 so that one recognizes the essential responsibility of the popular religious assemblies in the triggering of this massacre! This did not prevent the next genocide in 1963 or the escape, after the elections that followed, of the Tutsis chiefs who took refuge outside the Rwandan borders (for example in Uganda). Lastly, in 1994, the Church started again a new genocide and for a third time under the amazed eye of all the international community...which however remained mute and still remains so today at least with regard to an essential point: the undeniable responsibility of Christianity, of the Catholic/Christian Church in these 3 horrible massacres!

«Christian» Tutsi, it is to you all alone this time that I address myself: How is it possible for you to remain Christian? Apostatize and find «Imana» and the «Imandwas» in your prayers.

130

15. Christianity: cradle of racism and anti-Semitism

"Until the philosophy which holds one race superior and another inferior is finally and permanently discredited and abandoned; that until there is No longer any first-class and second-class citizens of any nation; that until the colour of man's skin is of no more significance than the colour of his eyes; that until the basic human rights are equally guaranteed to all, without regard to race

— until that day, the dreams of lasting peace and world citizenship and the rule of international morality will remain but a fleeting illusion, to be pursued but never attained [...] until all Africans stand and speak as free beings, equal in the eyes of all men as they are in Heaven

— until that day the African continent will not know peace. We Africans will fight, if necessary and we know that we shall win, as we are confident in the victory of good over evil. "

– EMPEROR HAILE SÉLASSIE I, Negus of Ethiopia,
speech of 28th of February 1968 –

The blacks in the past were considered by the Church and the Christians of Europe as people without hearts; thus like animals, "non-humans". It is an obvious fact that there was among European Christians, in times not so remote, a visceral racism towards blacks.

It is in this state of mind that the Christian colonizing whites came to colonize Africa. You'd better believe it. The proof: in certain European countries a white Christian could sponsor the Christian baptism of a small black in Africa; by giving an amount of money to the Church, he obtained for this black child a certificate being used as ticket for him to go only to the purgatory, rather than to hell, after his death! It was thus a highly noble and holy act to contribute to deliver from the devil the "demon" whom this small child inevitably was...since he was a black, and to make him, by sponsoring his baptism, a little bit "human"...to put him, to some extent, halfway between an animal and a man!

Among the many writers and Western philosophers who proposed, in far away times, their highly racist theories, the majority were "good Christians". And all these Christian currents of thoughts were constitutive

131

of the anti-Semitism and racism existing today. It should also be specified, Christianity is at the initial base of racism towards blacks as well
as anti-Semitism towards Jews. However, now, at the beginning of this
21st century, it is also against Muslim Semites that it launches into the
continuation of a new "war of religion".

Atheism in Europe has practically played no role in the rise of neither
Fascism nor Nazism which developed there during the 20th century; in
other words, it is not atheism that influenced the rise of racism: racism
was already very deeply anchored among Christians and in the Church before we talked about Mussolini or Hitler. These two rulers – actually both
"good Christians" – took as a starting point a racist Christian policy that
existed already indeed before their era. Neither the doctrines, nor the
practice were, alas, something new! It is also important to note that these
leaders could not have carried out all that they achieved without their
alliance with the Vatican. The great majority of German Christians were
enthusiastic supporters of the Nazi Reich and they continued to be…even
after evidence of the cruelties made by the fascistic troops and their allies
were reported. And it was not the case for Germany only. The same was
occurring elsewhere in other countries in Europe, where fascist movements were the fruit of the Christian culture and went hand in hand with
it. Thus there were, in addition to Hitler in Germany and Mussolini in Italy,
Franco in Spain, Pétain in France, Salazar in Portugal, Pinochet in Chile,
etc. Millions of white Christians were behind these manifestly fascist and
racist regimes. That's the truth!

The Nazi writers of the Laws of Nuremberg "For the protection of blood
and the German honor", quite simply paraphrased the ecclesiastical right.
It is also wise to note that the Church, therefore Christendom, by means
of its official press and this until the end of the 1920s, claimed, not only
that the Jews were "deicides", but that they belonged to an "inferior
race". This is without speaking about the Enquiry introduced in the 15th
century by the Holy Office, which affirmed that there were harmful and
transmissible characteristic features, physical and spiritual, which were
specific to the Jews!

To understand how we could arrive there, all we need to do is to examine
the history of Christianity. But, it is as necessary to know that, in fact, very
little, practically nothing has changed. In its hard core, Christianity and
the Church are currently, still and always, as basically fascist and racist as
ever. The place of the black remains an inferior place; you'd better believe it. They tolerate black cardinals and bishops, only to amuse the gallery,

as well behaved servants that became humans because they have chosen "the good" faith. Actually, they are there to better serve the missions and objectives of the Church and Christianity. But this latter point, deep down, still and always carries out a fight identical to that of the past. The Christian and Catholic blacks are, as a whole, more pleasant and beautiful trophies of victory than anything else; the Church has only privileged some of them to appear to conform to "the times".

Already at the very beginning of Christendom with the Apostle Paul, the man of lies and treason – the one who can be regarded as the builder of the Christianity of today – racism started, in particular towards the Jews, who will be passed off a little later as the people responsible for the crucifixion of Jesus, in place of the Romans. The rage of Christians towards the Jews will be further accentuated because of the refusal of Jews to convert or to be converted (by force!) to Christianity. History tells us that the first great extermination of Jews perpetrated by the Christians took place towards the year 414. All during history a good number of anti-Semite practices were carried out by Christians: the ghetto, the confiscation of Jewish goods and properties, prohibition for the Christians to marry Jews, etc. Martin Luther, the father of Protestantism, will even in 1543 issue a leaflet entitled "All about Jews and their lies"! Hitler was an admirer of Luther and one could even say that this leaflet of Luther inspired Hitler's "Mein Kampf".

During his council of 1870, the ultra conservative Pope Pie IX, will reaffirm the reactionary program of the Church which condemns modernity, democracy and Marxism. And in the development of this program, the Jew had a predicted and well-defined place: he was the source of judgment and hatred. This concept later,) will quite simply be imitated later by the Nazis. The Nazi ideology will become to some extent a natural prolongation of the thought of the Church, such as it existed soon after the Franco-German war of 1870-71.

Even "scientific" racism will be an instrument used by Christians to perpetrate their prejudicial cultural actions; it is not at all by chance if, at that time, the races considered as inferior by the Western Christian communities are the same as those also defined as inferior by "the sciences" of the time!

If we seek the precursors of anti-Semitism and Nazi racism, it is not in the atheistic environment that they should be sought, but within the European Christian environment. It is largely the Western Christian culture, deeply racist, often antidemocratic, and dangerous in many aspects that will be the fertile ground from which Nazism will be born later.

According to available biographies, all the principal Nazi leaders were baptized Christians. They grew up in very strict Christian homes where tolerance was unknown. Let us quote some of these unsavoury individuals: Adolf Hitler, Heinrich Himmler, Rienhard Heydrich, Joseph Goebbels, and Rudolf Hess. Not a single one of the top Nazi leaders had grown up in an atheistic family! Not a single one! They were all "Christians".

There are even authentic photographs where one sees top Nazi leaders placed near ecclesiastics of high stature doing the Nazi gesture with the raised right hand, at the time of ceremonies! One cannot be clearer!

Hitler regularly thanked the Christian "god" for his victories. In a repetitive way he often claimed that "god" was on the side of Nazism! Hitler even often condemned atheism. The Nazi constitution of the time evoked "God" legally. Hitler was clearly a racist Christian with deep Catholic roots, influenced by Martin Luther, by certain aspects of Darwinism and a little less by occultism.

The Nazis thus shared the same preserving values imposed by the Church and Christendom: the middle-class, the patriarchate, antifeminism, marriage, prohibition of the abortion, the condemnation of homosexuality, etc. Consequently, the Nazis were not at all "good friends" with the atheistic minority of the time, which Hitler specified and declared firmly in a speech that he held in 1933. Moreover, everyone knows the "Gott mit uns" [God with us] inscribed on the loop of the belt carried by all the Nazi soldiers...all Christians, too, as a matter of fact!

It is above all the German Catholics and the Roman Catholic Church who will contribute to the total and totalitarian power of the Nazis, thanks amongst other things to the "Catholic Zentrum Party" of the time. Incidentally, in 1928 a priest, Ludwig Kaas, became the first ecclesiastic at the head of this party!

The chancellor Franz von Papen, an enthusiastic racist Christian and as such greatly appreciated - besides after the war, at the famous Nuremberg Trial in 1946...he will be acquitted! - In 1933 it was nevertheless he who was the engine of the electoral victory of Hitler. One can even say that it was he (him) who took Hitler to victory. By yielding him his own place, he enabled him to become chancellor of the Third Reich in the following year, before he became the "Führer", chief responsible for the death of millions of people. Immediately the Church recognized and accepted Hitler's new regime! Normal, Christians and Catholics had taken Hitler to his position of chancellor. In fascist Germany and other countries, during these horrible Thirties and Forties, there was only a negligible minority of Christians who were "astonished" or "disgusted" by what was happening. They are the Christian Catholics who will, with their votes, give to the cabinet of Hitler an absolute majority so that this cabinet has an executive and legislative authority without needing the German Parliament. And all this will lead, in 1933, to a concordat between Nazism and the Vatican, which will bring to Hitler, as on a plate, an extraordinary legitimacy. With this intention, the Vatican quite simply did this based on a concordat signed beforehand in 1929 with the father of Fascism, a certain racist manifestly known and named...Mussolini!

As a result of this concordat with Nazism, the Church was largely rewarded. It accepted much in return: enormous tax revenues, the protection of privileges, that the prayer and the courses of catechism be obligatory in all the schools of Germany...and other countries under its boot, prohibition for whosoever to criticize the Church, etc.

All this was celebrated with pomp and circumstance in the cathedral of Berlin during a mass where Christian Catholic Nazis and high clergy of the Vatican stood shoulder to shoulder and hand in hand! Collaboration with Nazism was absolutely "without fail".Many contemporary Christians try to defend all that occurred at that dark time by saying that the Christians of that time did not have any choice. That is false: they had the choice and they made their choice!

But, let us reconsider a particular point, part of the History ignored by many: the fact that racism and anti-Semitism existed already indeed in those days and for a very long time and that moreover, both, were the perverse and extremely bitter fruits of Christendom. That can shock Christian Africans, but that is also the plain truth, and it is easily verifiable. Here are some bases of it:

As of 541 the council of Orleans in France prohibited the Jews "to appear in public for the period of Easter".

The Archbishop of Lyon, in France ("Primacy of Gaules") gathers in 828 all Jewish children, without requesting the permission of the parents and makes arrangements so that they are copiously terrorized so that they agree to convert to Christianity. A nice Prelate, isn't he? And not "sectarian" at all, of course not!

As of year 944, in Toulouse, a Jew, designated by his co-religionists, was to present himself in front of the cathedral of the Christians each Good Friday to be publicly slapped in remembrance of the death of Jesus. In the year 1018, the slap, administered by the chaplain of the Christian Viscount, Amery de Rochechouart, was so strong that the victim was killed by the blow. This Christian monstrosity was uprooted in France only from the 12th century!

In the year 1010, an excellent Christian...as his name indicates, King Robert le Pieux, ordered all Jews of France to choose between conversion and death. The refusal was general and a great massacre began.
The same year, in 1010, the very Christian town of Limoges – and thus filled with "good charitable hearts" – this high place known for its fine and delicate "Porcelain of Limoges", expelled, without fear of breakage and without exception, all the members of its Jewish community.

The king Louis VII, back from a Crusade carried out between 1147 and 1149, in the company of the "Great" Saint Bernard, with a single stroke, had 80 Jews executed on the pyre and this, "as an example" after he had himself launched the rumor pleading that the Jews devoted themselves to sacrifices of children.

At this same period, the bishop of Béziers exhorted "his population" each year, at the time of Palm Sunday, so that it avenges the death of Jesus by attacking the inhabitants of the Jewish district, but "only with stones" this "good Father said"! This wretched Christian habit was uprooted only in 1161...but not freely, needless to say, because in exchange the Jews were constrained to pay a heavy annual tax!

Some ten years later, in 1171, in Blois, the governor imprisoned all the Jews in a house that was set immediately on fire. Result: 32 dead.
A little later and undoubtedly to mark his reign with a flash, it is in 1182 that Christian King Philippe Auguste ordered all the Jews to leave France. It was the first time that a Christian country decided, in the name of Christendom, to get rid of all the Jews living on its territory; a precedent that was indeed going to mark its time and have influence because it will inspire later the fascist and Nazi regimes of Europe.

What very few people know – because it is rare that any mention of it is made – is that the obligation for the Jews by the Nazis to carry a yellow star was not the first measure of the sort. In fact, in 1940 the Nazis decided to follow themselves, in France and in the other countries where they imposed it, a decision of the 4th Council of the Latran, held in Rome in 1215 where the people in charge of the Catholic hierarchy issued the obligation for Jews to carry on their clothing a distinctive sign.

Finally, Christendom, Hitler, the Pope, the Kings of…France – "firstborn daughter of the Church" as its current President of the Republic recently recalled during his visit to Rome, – all that is: same spirit, same fight…only the dates change.

In 1269, the Christian King Louis IX specified what were to be the size and the color of the distinctive signs: the Jews were to sew on their clothing, on the chest and in the back a red circle of "four fingers of circumference and of a surface of a palm" which one called "the round slice".

In 1290, in Paris, a Jew named Jonathan was accused of having transpierced…a wafer! He was tortured with his wife, they were burned alive, their house was destroyed and the Christians built in its place a chapel for the Virgin Mary! Always the alliance of fire and the purity, strong symbols…to mark weak spirits! Concrete result: many Jews fled, they left Christian Western and racist Europe of that period; for France only, more than 100,000 Jews exiled themselves that way.

In Metz, in 1698, the Jews must wear a yellow hat at all times. During the same period, Strasbourg was a city prohibited to the Jews; they had to leave the city when the bells of the Christian churches started to sound before sunset! After the headgear, the curfew…they are well covered, for winter! What would they complain about?

In 1890, Edouard Drumont, a little journalist without talent, publishes in France a book in two volumes, "Jewish France", published at Marpon and Flammarion. This scathing attack will be an enormous popular success: more than 150,000 books sold (Half more than the number of Jews previously expelled, for those who can count). But this sales figure, for the time, (it) is a colossal figure! What could we ascribe this record to? During this period, the country undergoes an economic crisis (one more!). What solution does Mr. Drumont propose in his book to solve the problem of the moment? Well…the answer is quite simple: to seize all the Jews' goods; that's it!

Finally I find the list already too long so I will avoid detailing here the Dreyfus affair that shook France. At the time of the change of centuries that occurred before the last one, yet another odious affair that, for a long time, divided France in 2, but that affair is relatively well-known, thanks to the sensation article, "I Accuse", written by the courageous journalist and talented novelist, Emile Zola.

What remains necessary to know is that these examples are certainly not limited to France alone. It was general in Christian Western Europe, in France, yes, but also in Italy, in Spain, in Portugal, etc. Racism and anti-Semitism are two abominable and pernicious fruits falling from the tree of the Christian thought. Look at the extreme right nowadays, whether it be Le Pen in France, or the Vlaams Blok in Belgium Flanders, the extreme right in Austria and others, ask all these frightening politicians drawing the strings, which faith is theirs, you will receive in answer that they are "great" defenders of the Christian moral principles, that they are convinced and enthusiastic Christians/Catholics!

Do not think that that belongs only in the past, in the history, that all that is finished now. It would be a serious mistake. It is really not the time to fall asleep; one has "to react" for our children, for life!

Still in France, Paul Touvier, chief of the anti-Jewish militia of Lyon, will be hidden a long time by religious people. He had been pardoned by President George Pompidou in 1970. Sought again, he was arrested in Nice in a convent in 1989. To have been found "knowingly accessory to crimes against humanity", he was condemned to criminal imprisonment for life in 1994. He died in 1996 in Fresnes. It is just an example, but in this way, many racist Nazis and collaborator Nazis have been hidden in Christian catholic convents!

A last example, a recent one, in 1990, the president of the ADFI (Association of Defense of the Individuals and Families) in Switzerland – "anti-sect association" which is only a disguised ramification of fundamentalist Christians – the Catholic deacon, Paul Ranc, publishes anti-Semite remarks! Christendom spews always and still nowadays its racism, but it is now in a more camouflaged way, because it cannot do it anymore, at least not as easily as in the past, escorted by sounds of boots...and Rome really regrets it!

But all that is written above concerning anti-Semitism is quite as valid for racism towards blacks, through time and space.

138

The only difference that there is between Semite Jews of Europe and the African blacks, is that Jews did not disavow their faith. They remained Jewish despite all the historical atrocities which they had to undergo because of Christendom, from the Middle Ages until the Nazi era, while Africans, adopted this religion of the Christian colonizer. Africans let it happen and have become today the appetizer of this great trickery that is Christianity. Poor Africa! It is poor today, while the Jews who did not let themselves be converted are the rich people of this world, which is only a logical continuation of their distinct religious choice.

In 1675, the Christian Jacques Savary writes a book explaining the benefits of the wretched trade of black slaves, "Handbook of the perfect negotiator" one can read there that the fact of tearing off by force from Africa millions of black men, women and children to make of them slaves is: "to bring them spiritual and moral benefits like conversion to Christianity"! No comment, it's too despicable!

We could thus lengthen the list of facts by entire pages. It should be also known, because it is another aspect of reality, that the Holy See of Rome regards itself as a perfect system, at the image of any totalitarian State, lead by a dictator. Thus, for this state, labor laws do not exist. Also it does not accept the formation of trade unions although it employs many Italian nationals. Moreover, and it is not surprising, neither the Vatican City nor the Holy See are signatories of the "Universal Declaration of Human Rights". Since Pie VI, the popes condemn the principle of separation of the public sphere and the private sphere. They condemn the freedom of conscience as a failure of the States to preserve the people from error, and condemn the freedom of expression as being a freedom to propagate the error. This totalitarian philosophy did not prevent the Holy See from adhering to the UN, where the Church has a status of privileged observer. Which once again shows hypocrisy in the world and to what degree the UN is a puppet organization infiltrated by evil.

In addition, it is indeed necessary to also note that Aryan, racist Christendom, continues to exist today in the contemporary West, for example in groups such as "Christian Identity", "Aryan Nation", "White Power", the "Ku Klux Klan" and other extremist Christian groups who preach the supremacy of the white race while basing their values on the biblical scriptures.

This fact that the German Christian churches of the time of Nazism, neither rose against Nazism, nor even simply opposed it and especially opposed the racial persecutions that were undertaken. It is all the more disgusting considering that the Nazis feared the propaganda and the political power of the Christian churches. It was thus a certainty that during that period in Germany, the leaders of the Christian churches could have been easily opposed to racial persecution by Nazis, but the fact remains: they did not do it and it is not even because of fear or "cowardice"…no, it is because Hitler's and his Nazi assistants' way of thinking and acting tallied perfectly with "the Christian thought" and its way of being since the dawn of Christianity. Somber reality!

Moreover "scientific racism" can be regarded as the perfect instrument on which Christendom always rested to universally legitimate its cultural prejudices; in other words: to give the force of law to its visceral racism. Let us become aware also that is it not at all by chance if, during this same period, it was always about the same races, when they were talking about either the ones judged "inferior" by western Christianity, or about the ones whose "western Science" had "demonstrated" – at least so it claimed – that they only disposed of a "limited intelligence"!

Among the great godfathers of this racism, called "scientific", during the pre-Nazi era we can quote the three following people: Thomas Robert Malthus, Gobineau and Chamberlain. As an example– and this time we can use the expression in the first degree– it is enough to become convinced…to only look at "the title", precisely, of the work of the Count of Gobineau, diplomat and French writer: "Essay on the Inequity of Human Races"!

Later, "declared" racists like Nietzsche and Hitler will be inspired deeply by the theses of the Count of Gobineau. All these people considered "openly"…and "scientifically"– in their eyes already but also according to the opinion of much of their contemporaries– that blacks and Jews were genetically inferior races. We had the occasion to observe an entirely identical position among all first Popes of the Vatican, and this to Pope… (I leave it up to you dear reader to replace these three dots by the name of your choice!).

I hear already some Christian black people reply to me: "Yes, but all that is in the past"! Well, no, my dear brothers and sisters, the "Christian scientific racism" of the West…if it was vibrant in the 20th century, it is still indeed alive in the beginning of our 21st. (,) Would you like examples?

Until 1924 it is the IQ test [Intellectual Quotient] of Cyril Burt, a white Christian eugenist, who was used in the United States as scientific justification by the "U.S. Immigration Act" in order to keep out of the borders of the States of the Union the Africans whose entry was not desirable.

During the winter of 1969, the "Harvard Educational Review" (Teaching review of the universally famous Harvard University) published a treaty of 123 pages, signed by Professor Arthur R. Jensen entitled "How much can we boost IQ and Scholastic Achievement?" Jensen, being an enthusiastic admirer of Cyril Burt, claimed high and strong that blacks were genetically less intelligent than whites.

In March of 1969, an article in the famous English magazine "Newsweek" summarized his philosophy with a title thus entitled "Born stupid?" It is rather eloquent! Later Professor Jensen will once again try to defend his viewpoints, in 1973, in his book "Educability and Group Difference" in which he will claim that there is a biochemical bond between pigmentation of the skin and intelligence!

Professor Jensen's theses will also be echoed by other Professors like, for example, William Shockley, of Yale University and Richard Herrnstein, Professor and President of the Department of Psychology of Harvard University! In 1994, this Mr. Herrnstein will write, in the company of a joint author, Charles Murray, a book entitled "The Bell Curve" and in this work they will affirm that blacks are less intelligent than whites, quite simply...because they are "genetically unable" to be intelligent!

Another American "scientist", Paul Popenoe will publish a study called "Intelligence and Race: A Review of Some of the Results of the Army Intelligence Tests – The Negro". In this work he dares to claim that the few intelligent blacks existing in the USA must have, by the effect of some hereditary chance, a little white blood in their chromosomes because blacks are mentally inferior to whites and that this is irremediable since it is genetic!

We could ask ourselves: what is the purpose of such a bludgeoning of the minds? The answer is simple: these ideas, even if they are at the same time false and ridiculous, being insidiously and endlessly widespread in the public...it ends up accepting them and assimilating them without realizing it, simply because, in its eyes, they emanate from "high-ranking persons" that the population as a whole considers, according to their position in the company, as "eminent" and "respectable" beings and whom their "credibility" does not have to be disputed. Such is the case of Leaders, Faculty Professors, renowned scientists or perhaps Bishops, Priests and/or Missionaries of the great dominant religions, etc.

And it is in this way that, finally, we manage to make the "good people" concede the unspeakable.

Here is precisely another example – surely less well known than Nazism – but quite typical of a behavior that would be considered "unspeakable" by any normal mind...if it were not bludgeoned by these racist and nauseous ideas, erroneous and repugnant that are being imposed on him endlessly and that end up entering the head of "Mister everybody" without anybody becoming aware of it.

We are talking about psycho-surgical experiments undertaken by Robert Heath of the University of Tulane with the Australian psychiatrist Harry Bailey in the middle of the Fifties. To conclude the experiments in question, these two characters, as despicable as they are racist, had the nerve to implant electrodes in the brains of American prisoners...blacks, obviously! And that's not all: during a conference given to a class at Tulane twenty years later, therefore in the middle of the Seventies, they will openly venture to say, without any apparent remorse, that it cost them less to use Negroes than cats, because Negroes were everywhere and that it did not cost them anything.

This sadly "famous" Robert Heath will actually continue to use blacks as guinea-pigs for other experiments. This time it will be experiments about drugs, a "research" subsidized by the CIA. He will use for this work American blacks imprisoned in the "Louisiana State Penitentiary".

We would like to know what "the very Christian" current President of the USA, Mr. Bush, boss of the CIA, thinks of this use of human beings. Lately, he announced to his fellow-citizens that it was God Himself who had told him that he had to bombard Iraq! Perhaps this time "God Himself" will tell him just how much He is satisfied that the USA uses as guinea-pigs the "children of God" with black skin rather than to martyr poor kittens? It is true, since "his omnipresent God" knows all, He inevitably knows that among the multitude of "his children with black skin" there are so many of them in American prisons that it is..."what are we going to do with them", we might as well use them for experiments that will be useful for the "children of God" with white skin...those at least we have known for a long time that they have a soul!

We could thus lengthily continue and fill whole pages with cases of this kind, all more abominable the ones than the others.

But, in your opinion, of which religion are, in great majority, these people who preach "scientific racism?" Look and you will see: they are all "good Christians", "excellent Catholics"!

Any Christian black is a blind man, an ignorant, "moron for lack of science", i.e., for lack of knowledge. He is like a lamb that threw himself in the mouth of a wolf; worse, who settled in the digestive tract of the wolf. The wolf has nothing left to do except preserve this prey that surrendered to its predator, its persecutor. Perhaps it is without knowing that the lamb put himself in such a deplorable position. But for him, that changes nothing about the result! He will be eaten, where and when, I do not know, but undoubtedly he will.

What was the mark of Hitler's "Luftwaffe" [his Air Force]? The swastika accompanied by six Christian crosses! Same for the "Kreigsmarine" [his Naval Force] where the swastika was combined with the Christian cross! It is a historical fact that Hitler took part in public prayer meetings and religious services where the swastika and the Christian cross were exposed together, side-by-side.

When the Nazis published in various newspapers, with much pride, the articles on their "new concentration camps" with the support of photographs...the large majority of the German Christians who prayed to Jesus had no objections whatsoever. Even the high rate of legal executions reported in this same press left the majority of the German Christians completely indifferent, quite to the contrary, they approved this "progression".

Moreover, let us see a little what the great Catholic dictator of Spain, Franco, declared in relation to Hitler, undoubtedly enlightened by his "spiritual adviser" – you know the founder of "Opus Dei", the one that Jean-Paul II hastily "sanctified" soon after his death. Here are the words of Franco upon learning about the death of the German dictator: "Adolf Hitler, son of Catholicism, died defending Christendom.... With the palm of the martyr, God gave to Hitler the laurels of victory"! Franco undoubtedly had, him also, a "hot line" connection with "God the Father"...the supreme invention of the Catholic Christians and other monotheists!

Africans, I say it to you and I repeat it to you, Christendom takes a much greater responsibility in front of the Heavens than National-Socialism Nazi, the SS or the Gestapo!

In its root, in its heart, Christendom, the Catholicism of the West is racist, fascist and neo-Nazi. Which doesn't mean that there aren't many, perhaps even a lot of, Christian whites with good faith and who have a

143

"good heart". But they are, them too, ignorant and naive, who belong to an Institution that does not deserve them, and who them, in turn, do not deserve to have to support it, because this Institution, it is in its cellular core that it is racist and fascist. Understand it well; open your eyes and your ears! And let the neurons in your brain work: Think! Currently, for the life of the world...thus yours and that of all those who are dear to you, I do not hesitate to say it: nothing is more important than this reflection!

Yes, the Christian Catholic Church is the cradle of racism towards the Jews and the blacks. This Church is quite simply responsible to have conveyed and have maintained a famous spiritual swindle to justify its racism towards blacks. I speak here about the so-called curse of the descent of Ham, the black son of Noah! The Christian Catholic Church has quite likely falsified a passage of the Genesis, Chapter 9, Verses 20 to 27, to seat its racism, to defend its idea of the hierarchy of the races having justified slavery and the colonization of blacks. Let us be conscious, the Old Testament, such as we know it today, comprises racist elements, elements that have never been pronounced or dictated by Yahweh the eternal and his colleagues creators of his people, called "Elohim" of the original Bible in ancient Hebrew...never!

Here is this famous text of the Genesis, Chapter 9, Verses 20 to 27:

> "And Noah began to be an husbandman, and he planted a vineyard: And he drank of the wine, and was drunken; and he was uncovered within his tent. And Ham, the father of Canaan, saw the nakedness of his father, and told his two brethren without. And Shem and Japheth took a garment, and laid it upon both their shoulders, and went backward, and covered the nakedness of their father; and their faces were backward, and they saw not their father's nakedness. And Noah awoke from his wine, and knew what his younger son had done unto him. And he said, Cursed be Canaan; a servant of servants shall he be unto his brethren. God shall enlarge Japheth, and he shall dwell in the tents of Shem; and Canaan shall be his servant".

Now let us give very small short explanation for all this. We are thus at the period right after the flood, where the ground will be re-planted with life, among other things, through the line of descent of Noah. Noah had three sons: Shem (the ancestor of the Semites), Japheth and Ham (the black son of Noah). In these verses of the Old Testament we can thus read that Noah will curse the line of descent of Ham, more precisely Canaan, black grandson of Noah! Very funny all that and so incoherent!

First of all, it is not Yahweh (God) who pronounces this curse, but Noah, while this same Noah curses not Ham, the author of these so-called events, but Canaan, one of Ham's four sons, because Ham had four sons: Canaan, Put, Mizraim and Cush (Kush)! Frankly, very funny all that Canaan, who does not have anything to do with this, takes it in the face, becoming cursed like all his line of descent! Moreover, Noah, the drunkard would have ordered Yahweh (God) to curse Canaan! Does this make any sense? It does not hold; it is ridiculous and grotesque!

Thus, based on this passage, the Christian catholic ecclesiastics will claim that the black race was cursed by Yahweh (God)! There will be a whole europeocentrist approach of the fathers of the Church who will claim and maintain that, and this will later feed the famous fascist and Nazi "Aryan" within Christian Catholic Europe. Quite something isn't it! This thesis about the black race having been cursed and that it was consequently destined to become the slave of the others, developed from the 2nd and 4th century of our era, this, especially, with the fathers of the Church!

Of course Yahweh (God) never cursed the black race. Then why did the Christian Catholic Church deliberately lie on this subject? This leads us to believe that this passage of the Old Testament was adulterated!

This passage, such as it is currently presented to us, is only a bunch of inanities...how can we have faith in such inanities?!! The Church was always hypocritical with regard to the black race and continues to be...that's for sure! I hear already Christian blacks saying: "Yes, but this is not the way that we should interpret these things"!

They are wrong to say that or to think that! This is precisely where the major problem lies; the large majority of Christian blacks are naive, ignorant and continue to be mislead like little children, assimilated as they are by the harmful consequences of slavery and of spiritual colonization, making so that they do as if nothing, thus behaving like ostriches, the head buried in the ground and the butt up in the air, sodomized by the Religion of their usurping colonizers! They venerate and adore the biblical accounts but are hardly interested in the explanatory Christian catholic works of these same biblical accounts.

Too bad! Because, these works offer to us the beautiful bouquet of interpretation that the fathers and Doctors of the Church made this famous passage. It is in these explanatory works that a great number of theologians profuse their ignominies and their deeply racist comments!

On one side, they gave the Bible to the Blacks by taking good care to put to sleep and deaden the minds of Blacks with this same instrument, teaching Blacks how to read naively. And on another side they write texts and explanatory comments intended for the non-Negro mass. And in those texts, they destroy all the humanity of the black man, making him the symbol of the devil, all the evils!

Thus, certain theologians claim that by "he saw his naked father", it should be understood that Ham would have committed an act of homosexuality on his father while this last slept, or in other words, that Ham would have sodomized his father during his sleep! Others go even as far as saying that Ham would have mated with animals in Noah's Ark and that it is for this reason that he became black and cursed! Others will claim that Canaan would have emasculated his grandfather, Noah, with a cord under the tent and that Ham would have laughed when seeing that, while others say that that would have been Ham himself who would have proceeded with the emasculation! Whatever!

Let us look one moment at the encyclopedic dictionary of Judaism. What does it say? It says that Ham would have raped his mother and thus conceived Canaan! Nothing but inanities in all these comments, whether they be Christian or Judaic...comments where the black man is cursed for eternity...and I reassure you that eternity is long!

Thus fathers of the Church, such as Father Duterte, wrote (See "General History of the Antilles inhabited by the French"): "I do not know what this unhappy nation did to which God attached like a particular and hereditary curse, as well as the blackness and ugliness of the body, slavery and servitude. It is enough to be black, to be taken, sold and reduced to slavery for all the nations of the world".

Professor E. Lefebvre acknowledges in his work, "Ham and the Egyptian Adam", that the Hebrew authors of the Old Testament, had a certain aversion for the black race. He said the following about it: "They (Hebrew authors) gave it an origin inferior to that of the other races".

At the beginning of the 19th century, Montabert fingers the naked body of the ideological heart of the Christian Catholic Church. He writes: "The white is the symbol of the divinity or of God; the black is the symbol of the demon or evil spirit"!

There still exists, nowadays, prayer books that circulate in the West of

146

which some are entitled "Liberation and Delivery, to pray with the Holy Spirit with the Angels, the Saints and the Virgin Mary" (supplement to the Monthly Bulletin 'l'étoile Notre Dame, composed and directed at the Association Etoile Notre Dame - PO BOX 434 - 53104 Mayenne Cedex, France), who represent on their front cover a European Saint Micheal, blond with blue eyes, striking down an African black devil with a sword!

And, the majority of Christian blacks spiritually colonized, pretend to see nothing, or do not want to see! Their ancestors curse them! They are the proof that colonization continues and continues! Christian blacks have, once and for all, the courage and the goodwill to see and to understand the truth. You have been misled and manipulated!

But, let us finish this chapter in beauty. When we consult the manuscripts of the dead mother, also called the manuscripts of Qumran, which are regarded as an original of the Bible, what does this famous passage regarding the episode of the vine say about the intoxication of Noah and the curse of Ham and his line of descent (See texts of Qumran, translated and annotated, Letouzey and Ané editions, page 226)? It says the following: "... and I began me and all my sons to cultivate the earth and I planted a vine on Mount Lubar and in the fourth year, it made me wine... And I started to drink the first day of the fifth year... I called my sons and all our women and their daughters and we did a festive celebration... We had escaped destruction (the flood)".

So, what happened here, in this original manuscript, to this famous curse of the black race by Yahweh (God)? Not the least trace of all that! Nothing! The passage in the Old Testament was adulterated, added, to deliberately harm the black race...that's the truth! Because, what else does the original say? It says that Noah wanted to do a religious ritual with the wine, under the tent, to call upon Yahweh (God) and that Ham, his black son, intrigued, penetrated under the tent in the midst of the full ritual and saw Yahweh the eternal speaking to Noah. On that, his Noah father said to him: "My son you saw the truth in its nakedness. You are here thus in charge of the mission of guiding your brothers towards this truth"! That's where the truth lies...no question at all of a curse of the black race, but rather a role or a mission entrusted to the black descent of Noah to guide the others (Shem and Japheth) towards the truth!

And nowadays, that remains a current event, that the black race can find again the truth, that the black race can again join the broken bond with its creators, in the plural, with its gods ancestors, with the Elohim of

147

the original Bible in ancient Hebrew...because the white Christian Catholic Church lies and hides the truth, that the black race can again monopolize this mission and guide humanity towards the truth by destroying the myth and the mystery of God such as it was imposed to us by the white man.

And, it is not by chance that the Christian missionaries called and continue to call Tutsis "Hamites" (descendants of Ham)! Confronted that they were with the great resistance of Tutsis to conversion to Christianity, they have somewhere desired to make those "damn" Tutsis suffer from the curse of Ham through Noah! Those Tutsis who categorically refused the Christian baptism and assimilation, those Tutsis whose last great kings and chiefs like Mwezi, Mutaga, Maconco, Rwabugiri and Musinga fought the Christian evangelization until death for the majority of them...it is not by chance!

The Christian Catholic Church is the cradle of racism.

16. AFRICA: The Vatican's bordello

This chapter is written above all for those who will be shocked. I have a great pleasure in imagining those very people as this they will realize a beneficial awakening...I hope.

It is such a screaming truth. Are you surprised?

A great number of young girls from the third world and, in particular, young African girls are being used as sexual slaves by the ecclesiastic body. Oh, yes, it is the plain truth! It is also a very sad reality!

Numerous sources of information state nun prostitutes who are being sent from Bendash India to far away regions in Africa. They are duped into believing a promise of a great future and entry to heaven, to top it all off...but once on African soil, real hell awaits them.

There they will be used as sexual slaves, as sexual toys by the ecclesiasts. Celibacy for these gentlemen? Yes...chastity, not really! This is not surprising. It is only a logical consequence of the lies and hypocrisy characterizing this Catholic Church.

Certain historic sources even mention that this hypocritical practice, the sexual slavery of girls for the service of ecclesiasts, goes back eighteen centuries, and it would be where modern prostitution originated.

In those days, Church people would have been both customers as well as procurers of half the feminine population of Bendash. Rome, that pilgrimage city compulsory for all Bendash seminarians, would have been reduced to prostitution during various periods of its history. Fortunately there exists for certain periods, traces testifying those criminal activities: reports coming from doctor-nuns overwhelmed by those crimes. No use telling you that the reports sent to the Holy See were discarded or forgotten forever.

Reuters, the internationally well known press agency, has stated on the subject: "accused of maintaining a conspiracy of silence surrounding cases of sexual abuse in the convents, particularly in Africa, the Vatican has acknowledged the existence of a series of scandals".

A specific report mentions that some priests and missionaries have forced nuns to have sexual intercourse with them, by squarely raping them! Some of those priests have even forced some nuns to take birth control pills so they would not become pregnant! Other nuns who became pregnant were, of course, forced by those ecclesiasts responsible for their state to get an abortion.

A spokesman from the Vatican, Joaquin Navarro-Valls, declared that the "Holy See" was "aware of the problem" but that it was "limited to specific geographical zones" and he did not deign specify which ones.

So, what are those non-specified famous geographical zones? Well, it is first of all Africa, of course. But even if it is not, unfortunately, the only place where that clergy, disrespectful towards human beings, runs wild, just the same it is Africa that remains the great bordello of the Vatican. In Africa, when you are an ecclesiast, amongst the Negroes and with them, you can do whatever you like. "Those colonized blacks" must certainly say, those "cassock wearers" "they are under our spiritual domination, they have forgotten their authenticity and their ancestors, we can do wha-tever we want with them. Those are our well-trained dogs and bitches".

That's the kind of instruction transmitted by word of mouth in this Church that came to "evangelize"...that is to "bring the good news", right?

A few years back, a report was submitted to cardinal Martinez Solamo, prefect of the Congregation for the institutions of dedicated lives and the societies of apostolic lives. This report was written by Maura O'Donohue, a woman, a nun, and a doctor. Her report compiles cases of abuses in 23 distinct countries! Yes, you read correctly, 23 countries...only that! Those include USA, Italy and Ireland. But, where do you think, according to the report, on which continent are the majority of the countries where sexual violence was committed by priests and missionaries (and this is still going on today, don't forget)?

Answer: in Africa, the Vatican's Bordello where the "good" religious nuns are said to be exempt from the aids virus, the plague that is devastating the continent in a most disastrous way. (Considering the seriousness of the subject, we will dedicate the next chapter entirely to it: Chapter 17)

That report provides names, and even details the case of one priest, a chaplain at one of the convents, who impregnated a nun. As a result of the abortion she was forced to have, the woman died. And it is that same priest who celebrated the burial mass, in his "function" as chaplain of that convent... In his "function"! ("quality" in French). It is sometimes that the "proper French" forces us to use a contradictory word: who would dare to sustain that that chaplain is a "man of quality?" Yes, certain people would probably dare: a cardinal from the Vatican or even a pope, both unscrupulous. As has been the case throughout history, men like this chaplain were declared "saints" while in reality they were true monsters. (In this book we cite many who were attested through history as being criminals!)

As for the barbarity of certain priests sexually abusing nuns for such a long time, this with impunity, it is only now that the scandals raised by those moral issues begin to jump over the high walls of the convents of the "Holy" Church!

The same report from Dr Maura O'Donohue draws attention to a Catholic community where 29 Bendash religious nuns became pregnant almost simultaneously!

Meanwhile, the insane "Holy-See" remains mute! From one report to the next, it obstinately continues to stay mute...hypocritical and lying, as always. It also maintained the same blind stance with regard to a report compiled in 1998 by Mary McDonald, another nun. The title of this report, "Superior of the 'Missions de Notre Dame d'Afrique,'" speaks for itself and is a detailed account of "sexual abuses and rapes committed by priests and bishops from the Christian-Catholic clergy". In her report, Sister Mary McDonald, despite pressure against her, has firmly stated that she regretted "the lack of inspections and the conspiracy of silence".

During the synod of the Bishops of Oceania held in Rome in November of 1998, Monsignor Geoffrey Robinson, Bishop of Sydney, had also stated that the "sexual abuses coming from the priests and the monks have become the main obstacle to preaching the gospel in Oceania". Sexual abuses on who? Mainly on nuns...children...and women.... And all from aboriginal origins!

It is somewhat comforting to note that the European Parliament adopted on April 5th, 2001, a resolution concerning the responsibility of the Vatican in the violation of Human Rights by Catholic priests! Yes indeed, the Church in no way respects Human Rights. To confirm this, refer to the "Universal Declaration of Human Rights", to the "European Convention of Human Rights". There are also several European and International resolutions concerning "violence towards women" and also several reports published on the subject of which at least five were submitted to the Vatican since 1994 without any means being taken by the presumed "Holy" See it to help advance these situations in the right direction.

In Europe, churches are being deserted. And this is quite logical as people benefit from information and knowledge; with the lack of it, people abandon the churches, basilicas and other courses on catechism. Their young followers do not want to associate with that type of church any more, to practise a religion so unjust and retrograde. But in Africa, through a lack of information, a lack of knowledge about this subject as about many others, the black catholic Christians remain "dazed". Lulled by that religion, they become (or remain) enslaved.

Let us look at what the European Parliament has to say on this matter:

« *The European Parliament:*

1 - Condemns every violation of women's rights and every action of sexual violence, in particular against catholic nuns; expresses its solidarity towards the victims.

2 - Requests that the persons responsible for those crimes be arrested and remanded to authorities; asks the judicial authorities of the 23 countries cited in the reports to ensure that proper juridical action be taken in order to obtain the truth on the cases of violence against women.

3 - Requests the Holy See to record solemnly all the complaints stating sexual abuses, to cooperate with judicial authorities and to expel the guilty.

4 - Requests the Holy See to reinstate the female officials who were fired for bringing the abuses to the attention of their superiors and to bring the victims the proper protection and redress for all discrimination that may have resulted.

5 - Requests the publication of the uncut version of all 5 reports cited, (National Catholic Report).

6 - Gives its president the mandate to address this resolution to the Holy See, to the European Counsel, to the commission of the United Nations for Human Rights and to the governments of the 23 countries quoted »

What is the situation today? The Vatican has not lifted its small finger on that question anymore than on any other because its hypocritical institution is rotten to the core. But it should not forget that what is at the bottom always resurfaces...sooner or later. Dear Africans, this is the "good news" brought by the false Holy See. I am deeply disgusted by that religious institution and I do not understand my African brothers and sisters who continue to give credit to such a hypocritical especially so criminal institution.

Yes, the Church is a colonizing, enslaving, usurping, lying and criminal institution. That is the truth! And Africa is especially suffering in its flesh from this state of being. So, how can you be part of it, promote it, serve it, obey it foolishly? Yes, foolishly, because to obey that institution and serving it can only be done "foolishly", without thinking, without making use of a single atom of intelligence.

In the name of our ancestors, conquered, persecuted, tortured and killed, I vomit from my mouth that institution that deserves no respect, that will have to be removed from our land and returned to Rome, by leaving it completely, by apostatizing it, which is very simple to do, and would be so efficient! As long as it is done by a sufficiently large number of Africans, finally awakened from their nightmarish sleep and who decide to extract themselves from their lethargy, it can be most efficient.

WHITE POISON

17. AIDS: The Church accelerates and multiplies the action of the virus in Africa

In this coming chapter, before unraveling the long, much too long, list of the red pages of Christianity during its 20 centuries of existence, let us first address the red page of the emerging 21st century as this infamous page concerns us today and this terrible "AIDS virus" that touches Africa particularly.

From the start we can declare that Christianity deserves already the "red card" that means the immediate ousting from the field, i.e., of the African field.

Indeed, in this matter, I accuse the Catholic Church and Christendom. Yes, by these lines I accuse publicly this religion of non-assistance to people in danger; I accuse it of leading Africa to its death. I accuse it for the creation of rumors, the propagation of false news. I accuse it of conveying lies and of cultivating ignorance.

I accuse Christianity and in particular the cell responsible for the management of Catholic Christianity, the "Holy See" of the Vatican, of telling the African population, that if touched by the AIDS virus, that the condom does not preserve against this mortal virus, and that there is no use in using it.

How can cardinals, bishops, priests and nuns (or can they) claim and declare that the AIDS virus passes through condoms through small holes? Knowing, moreover, that these declarations from people in positions of authority in the Church come on the heals of reports stating that a young person between the ages of 15 and 24 is infected with the virus every 14 seconds, how can they maintain this stance? How can they? It could only be that it is a seriously criminal Institution for it to proceed like this.

It is a pure and simple lie! What they claim is strictly false: condoms are impermeable. Condoms are impermeable to all liquids (more impermeable still...if however it is possible (?) than the brains of the cardinals and Christian bishops are to the scientific truth, and even to science period!). A condom does not let through the tiniest drop of liquid. Nothing! Absolutely NOTHING!! We are facing the installation of a new form of genocide, very perverse, perpetrated by the Church...always, alas, with the complicity of these morons who are the catholic cardinals, bishops and priests with black skin. We are faced here with a new grotesque lie of the religion of the colonizer: he continues to kill, but in another way, a more camouflaged way, more subtle. We are faced here with a new crime of Christendom: a "crime against humanity" and in particular against Africa, the continent most touched by the AIDS virus.

Not only does the Vatican continue to be opposed to contraception, and therefore to the use of contraceptives, but it is now also claiming, by the mouth of its officers, "in-competent" and especially "irresponsible" people, that there is no use wearing condoms because the AIDS virus passes through! What a horrible and shameful lie!

That similar monstrous nonsense be claimed seems hardly believable. Here, therefore is an example of their statements: Cardinal Alfonso Lopez Trujillo categorically claims in an interview that the AIDS virus passes through condoms! Then he even specifies that "the AIDS virus is about 450 times smaller than the spermatozoon" [and that] "the spermatozoon itself can easily pass through the condom"! This Cardinal that I have just named is the President of the "Vatican Pontifical Council for the Family" and from the top of his pompous world functions, he recommends to the various governments of our planet to vigorously encourage their populations not to use condoms!

Already, on the whole of the Earth and according to the "United Nations Population Fund" nearly 6000 young people between 15 and 24 years are each day contaminated, infected by HIV, the AIDS virus. That represents more than half of all the new world contaminations and the great majority of the victims of this new plague reside in Third World countries, in underdeveloped countries and in particular in Africa where the Catholic religion has most recently and without any doubt recruited the greatest number of its new "faithful"!

We have also seen on the screen, in a TV program, a "good Christian sister" who advises an African affected with the AIDS virus not to use the condom in the relationship with his wife because the virus would pass through the condom!

More extreme yet, the Archbishop of Nairobi in Kenya, Raphaël Ndingi Nzeki, declared that the use of the condom helps to transmit the AIDS virus instead of stopping its transmission! Increasingly aberrant statements and more and more criminal, when one knows – and how could the Archbishop of the capital of the country be unaware of it – that in Kenya, one person in five is HIV positive!

How Christendom can convey such "crap" – forgive me, but it is really the only qualifier that is appropriate – yes, "crap" of such magnitude, such a terrible lie that leads directly to the death of thousands, perhaps of millions of young people (Africans and others)? Because now these young people are affected with AIDS, a fatal disease, we cannot repeat strongly enough, these claims by Christendom are entirely false. Simply due to the fact that the claims emanate from "their Church", all these young people (and with them adults too), accept them as truth and carry out great damage to their partners and themselves with these "imbecilic" acts. By accepting these false claims, they are forced to accomplish the same wretched assassinations as those in black vestments. Red or white, it does not matter the color of the mask-misery of these hypocrites. Yes, I even call them "despicable hypocrites" because they impose on the world morbid rules that they take good care not to apply to themselves (see – or re-examine – about their conducts, our preceding chapter, "Africa: brothel of the Vatican")!

Would you like a further example of the criminal color of the Catholic Church of Africa in this matter? Mr. Gordon Wambi, director of an AIDS screening program in Lwak, close to Lake Victoria, declared that it was impossible for him to distribute condoms because of a formal opposition of the Catholic Church! He even declares that he heard catholic priests say and claim that the condoms are contaminated with the virus and that they are thus at the origin of the transmission of the disease. That is completely false, it is a grotesque lie, and it is a misinformation of the populations that is absolutely contemptible!

We could thus continue to give other examples within these pages.

Of course, the scientific community condemns the Church – rightly and unanimously – for its standpoint vis-à-vis the condom. Latex condoms are impermeable and protect against the transmission of the virus and, of course, that they can by themselves transmit the virus because they are impregnated with it is a most delirious lying invention. Scientists are absolutely categorical on all these points.

John-Paul II, I address you directly and I say to you, fully conscious of what I advance: "You are a criminal, responsible for crimes against humanity". And to you, Catholic cardinals, bishops, priests, black monks and nuns, I say: "To spread this scurvy gossip makes you accessory, whether it be consciously or unconsciously, it does not matter...you are accessory to crimes on your own human brothers and sisters and in particular on those of Africa".

It is scientifically established that the use of the condom decreases the risk of contamination by 98%. The 2% remaining risk can be attributed only to 2 potential incidents: that the condom was badly worn and/or that it breaks, which there too would be attributable to a bad application or to misuse.

Given the dramatic present circumstances, the question that we must all ask ourselves is: Why? Why did the Church embark on the diffusion on a large scale of such a lie? It is impossible for it to be unaware that the ideas that it conveys are contrary to the truth. Then what is its aim? Is their concern to reduce the world population, in particular in Africa and in the remainder of the Third World, to solve, by the use of this genocidal means, the thorny problem of the imminent overpopulation of the Earth? Or is this its manner of trying to impose on the earth's inhabitants its concepts of virginity, fidelity, and chastity? Or because of its will to reserve the practice of the coitus to the needs for procreation with formal prohibition for all sexual practices that would have as the only goal the search for pleasure that we derive from them? Concerning the two last assumptions, let us recall again that this "way of life" it intends to impose on the rest of the world excludes its own clergy...in practice in any case: sad truths compel us to observe it each day!

Whatever its goal (unconfessed...as usual!) what it undertakes here is called committing "a crime against humanity". I repeat it and it is more particularly a crime against "African humanity" because, as everybody knows, Africa is the continent more affected by AIDS.

When will the time come when the African masses decide to give to the Church the red card that it has deserved for centuries? When will the referee of Africa - I speak here about its own conscience and those who should be carrying this African conscience - when will we see a responsible African draw from his/her pocket a red card and apply it to the Church while firmly asking it to leave the field and from this point on to shower and change in different locker rooms?

The Church came to Africa disguised but behind its mask of humane appearance there is a criminal institution, that never sincerely desired either the well being or the prosperity of Africa. Even if in its beautiful speeches it often claimed its good intentions, it was to lie already, and in any case it never carried out anything that was deeply beneficial for Africa.

160

The Church misleads Africa every day. It is white in its root and it will remain so; it is white in its veins and its heart. The few blacks that haunt its upper hierarchy are powder in the eyes thrown in the face of Africans. It lies; it misleads; it is wretched and despicable every day of its existence.

Do you remember the chapter "religious assimilation" at the very beginning of this work? I made mention there of an excerpt of the talk of the Minister for the Colonies in Belgium, Mr. Jules Renquin, October 30, 1921, in relation to the missionaries leaving for Belgian Kongo, at the moment when the Minister gave them, among others, the following directive:

> *"Teach them doctrines which you will not yourselves put the principles into practice. And if they ask you why you behave as opposed to what you preach, answer them that you blacks, follow what we say to you and not what we do. And if they replied while pointing out to you that a faith without practice is a dead faith, get angry and answer: happy those who believe without protesting".*

The application of this kind of directive is particularly topical now with regard to AIDS, the use of the condom, and sexuality. The Church is both manipulative and hypocritical on this matter. This will perhaps ire any Christian black, Catholic, reading this work, but the facts are there. AIDS caused in the United States, for example, the death of hundreds of Catholic priests since the middle of the Eighties! These facts were reported in many media including "The Star of Kansas City". This publication paid great attention to this question, revealing that many other causes of death were actually indicated on the death certificates for the majority of those priests who died from AIDS. One can also read in these media about the discussions with experts and doctors who attest that in addition to these hundreds of death, there are still other hundreds of catholic priests still alive, but carrying the HIV virus.

This means, according to these experts, that for catholic priests the death rate related to AIDS is at least four times superior to that of the general population. That's the reality of the Church!

(Source: The star - http://www.kcstar.com/projects/priests/)

Well, yes, and there is no reason to believe that in Africa it will not be the same. I would venture to say that this rate would inevitably be even higher! Everywhere in the world Catholic priests have died of AIDS, in silence. In its investigation into the matter "the Star" of Kansas City in the

USA claims that six priests out of ten know at least one priest who died of a disease related to AIDS, and that a third of the priests in the USA know a priest living and carrying HIV.

It is high time that the Church, that the Catholics, the Christians...and even the world population - because everyone is directly or indirectly concerned - recognizes and admits openly that a considerable number of Catholic priests are homosexual, therefore that they belong to a high-risk sexual orientation for the transmission of the virus. This is a logical succession of these antiquated opinions that are those of the Church on all matters relating to sexuality and/or sensuality.

It is high time that the Church takes care to provide to its clergy an education that is correct and balanced on these two basic human levels, distinct and complementary, that are sensuality and sexuality. We will not here go in details about the thousands of cases indexed in the world and relating only to Catholic priests condemned for sexual abuse, rapes of children, and many other pedophile acts. We will simply recall, with much affliction, that such practices are still current today and that it is as undeniable as unacceptable. To deny reality because it is unpleasant to see does not make it disappear. Except in the sand kingdom of ostriches, apparently!

What is the remedy for the death of Catholic priests due to AIDS? Very simple: the use of the condom...that the Church condemns and for which it claims untruthfully that there is no use using it, that the virus passes through! I will ask you once again this endless question: how can one manage to understand anything about this Church, about this Catholicism? It bathes in a mental confusion as disproportionate as its own crimes...what can we say?

"That those who have ears hear and that those who have eyes see"!

You have already heard this beautiful sentence somewhere, haven't you?

17. AIDS: The Church accelerates and multiplies the action of the virus in Africa

WHITE POISON

18. The red pages of Christianity

«Kill them all, because God will be able to recognize his own!»

- ARNAUD AMALRIC (1150-1225) abbot of Citaux, papal legate
- At the time of the capture of Béziers in 1209
(so we don't have to sort the «good Christians»)

Let us look closely at these red pages of Christianity. Moreover one always says «black» when it is a question of atrocities...why? Let us call them «red» pages rather to commemorate all the «blood» spilled and to think of the red card of the football matches, because it is really time for Africa to take out the red card for this false player, this bad player that Christianity is and ask it to leave the field of Africa, its field of predilection and definitively go shower elsewhere.

Thus let us look at these red pages of Christianity, period-by-period. Let us look at it chronologically by successive stages as there is so much to discover.

Period 50-70

The Christian religion is spreading. And, immediately at the dawn of Christianity, religious intolerance sees the day: from the very start, Christians openly aim at imposing a prohibition of polytheist worships (polytheism, extremely prevalent in previous times is, as you recall, is the belief in the existence of several gods). The Christians insist that what they claim is recognized as the only accepted view: there is only one and unique God, and obviously this "only existing God" is theirs. It begins very strongly!

Year 312

Christians seize power at the end of a civil war, a conquest carried out by Roman Emperor Constantine the Great. He himself converts officially to Christianity and establishes himself as being the 1st «Monarch of divine right,» a title that he inaugurates on his own initiative but that a multitude of successors will find quite useful to attribute to themselves as he had!

And so, as of this first «Monarch of divine right,» the freedom of worship is abolished. From this moment all that remains is to classify this invaluable freedom in the catalogue of pleasant memories...of «the good old days!» From then on, Atheism, Polytheism and/or any religion other than Christianity become objects of persecution. Thus in Europe a new kind of plague starts: «religious persecution.» But this epidemic is not caused by some unknown virus but the work of an alliance of new powerful allies in Rome: «the alliance of the sword and the aspergillum» as it will be called a little later on!

With time, as we will see, this deplorable disease will spread to the whole planet. And at the time I am writing these lines, in «the year of grace» 2004 of the «Christian era,» 1971 years after Jesus left the Earth by leaving to us this new command: «love one another,» a different command prevails, one directed to spite «the one that is different". This can be seen all over the world and, in spite of its scurvy and innumerable devastations, if we do not unite now to do what is necessary so that things change...definitively, one can despair from awaiting the end of this hateful pandemic.

Year 385

Theophilus is appointed patriarch of Alexandria (today this "Theophilus" has become "Holy Theophilus"...that ranks a man!). And what does this patriarch Theophilus do that is so prestigious? He starts at once after upon his nomination to undertake a systematic destruction of all non-Christian temples and sanctuaries and this, with the support of the Roman emperor Theodosius. He thus destroys in Alexandria the temples of Mythriade and Dionysius. This, in turn, leads to the destruction of the temple of Serapis and that of its sublime library in 39. But the stones are preserved to be used but as if by chance it will be...you guessed...for the profit of the new unique religion, Christianity.

Year 389

For the first time, a bishop dictates to an emperor the policy that he wants him to follow. The bishop of Callinicum on the Euphrates and his congregation had destroyed a synagogue and the emperor had then given the order to this bishop to rebuild the demolished building. In these circumstances and, inside the cathedral, Ambroise, bishop of Milan (the future «Saint Ambroise»...you suspected it already, I suppose), rises and making himself emperor, commands him to cancel the order of rebuilding that he had given to his colleague of Callinicum on the Euphrates. The Church has thus sanctioned, from its beginnings, the burners of synagogues, a course that it will continue to support without fail until its most known ending: that of the 1940s, years of the holocaust, which saw the Church and Nazism unite their efforts in preparation for the annihilation of the Jewish people... that these two horrible associates wished complete and final!

Beginning of the years 390

The emperor Theodosius, a very pious Christian, gradually prohibits all non-Christian worships. Little by little, all non-Christian temples are closed to their own worship and the "pagan" processions are prohibited. But this suppression of the freedom of religion to the exclusive profit of Christianity does not go without clashes; it sometimes even resulted in riots like those of 408 in Calama, Numidia. At this same time in Germany the first executions of heretics begin. It is the beginning of a "beautiful tradition," although highly criminal and that the Church unscrupulously develops with the Inquisition and will perpetuate until 1826...when the pyres are replaced by another form of murder!

Year 391

A crowd composed of Christians guided by (the future)"Saint Athanasius" and (the future)"Saint Theophilus" brings down the temple and the large statue of Serapis in Alexandria, two great masterpieces of antiquity. The literary collection of the temple is also completely destroyed.

Year 412

Cyrillius (who became «Saint,» one more...he too chosen according to his «virtuous merits!») is named bishop of Alexandria and succeeds his uncle Theophilus. He incites anti-Semitic feelings that already ruminated among Christians of the city and, with his followers, he sets fire to the synagogues of this large city, forcing the Jews to flee. He then encourages the Christians to seize the goods that Jews had to leave behind.

Year 415

Let us see the fate reserved to Hypathia. She will be the last great mathematician of the school of Alexandria. Although her father, Theon of Alexandria, was also famous as mathematician and astronomer, she could not avoid being killed by a crowd of Christian monks whose excitement was exacerbated by Cyrillius, the patriarch of Alexandria...and the Church, obviously, will canonize him later on! The motivation of the assassins of this brilliant mathematician, far from justifying their gesture, is clear: Hypathia, who brilliantly taught mathematical sciences, also taught the philosophy of Neo-Platonism, and from then on it appeared to the clergy of the time that she represented a threat for the diffusion of Christianity. The added fact that she was a woman and, additionally, both pretty and charismatic, made her existence completely unbearable to Christians. Moreover, her murder will mark a turning point in the history of the West. After her death, many researchers and philosophers will leave Alexandria for India and Persia, and so this city, as superb as it was famous, created seven centuries earlier by the great Greek emperor Alexander, will cease to be the centre of teaching and science of the ancient world. From now on, science will regress in the West, and it will not find a level comparable to the one it had at the time of the splendour of Alexandria...until the dawn of the industrial revolution of the 19th century.

The works of the school of Alexandria concerning mathematics, physics and astronomy will be preserved, in part at least, but they will be so only thanks to the Arabs, the Persians, to the Indians and even also to the Chinese.

From the consequences of the murder of this scientist, the whole West will plunge unrelentingly in obscurantism due to the «precious benefits» of Christianity and it will not be able to exit this lethargy - gift of the Catholic Church - after more than one millennium of stagnation!

On the other hand - and we will not be astonished by that - in recognition of his effective actions with regard to the persecution of the scientific community and the Jews of Alexandria and also, undoubtedly, to congratulate him on a purely posthumous basis on the destruction of a seven centuries old civilization, Cyrillius will be initially canonized, as we said. But apparently the reward was not sufficient, considering the so-called «excellence» of the character (!) as he will later be pronounced «Doctor of the Church» by the Pope Leon XIII 14 centuries later in 1882.

The life of a «Saint» is an ideal model that we should not neglect to present to all «good Christians,» is it not?

... Until the 15th century

We are in the «Christian Middle-Age.» Benefiting from the disappearance of the large Roman libraries and the almost total absence of editing activity in Europe, the Church obtains a monopoly in fact on all of the writings and, consequently, it is the Pope alone who reigns as a Master on information. The people are left voluntarily in ignorance, discouraged from reading the bible except in rare cases when one might find one in his possession.

We will yet have, some centuries later, in 1550 exactly, the material confirmation of the danger that people reading the Bible represents for the Church, and this thanks to the document compiled by the cardinals' college for the new pope GUILLO III (document which you have read an extract above in our Chapter 6).

Little by little, the Catholic Church thus inflicts on all of society the obligation of respecting its Catholic and Roman stamp.

The Inquisition...the celibacy of priests...the compulsory aspect of marriage before the least sexual intercourse...these are but only institutions and ways of life imposed by the Church to the populations of several consecutive epochs.

Concerning the celibacy to which priest and monks are compelled, one notes that this new obligation emerges at the time when the great land properties of the Church multiply, in particular the monasteries and the cathedrals. At this point in time at the top of the Church's hierarchy, one becomes aware that the problems of heritage would not fail to be born... as are born already numerous descendants from the members of the clergy. These problems would then cause serious financial prejudices to the Church, if its institution did not put quickly a stop to it, so that she could keep only to herself all its inheritance.

It is also at that time that develops what will become one of the richest (!) Christian traditions: «to burn alive» all opponents. Approximately 1 million «witches» will thus be burned during the Middle Ages. Cities compete to beat the record of the greatest number of witches burned in one year. The city having won this «honourable» (!) competition is Bamberg in Bavaria (Episcopal office and cathedral renowned for its sculptures). It «succeeded» in burning 600 witches in one year.

This record has not been surpassed, in this form at least, but amply exceeded by the «crematoriums» of Nazism of the 1940s, installed in Poland and Germany with financial and technical assistance coming for some from American industrialists.

Oh, yes, the Church always remains positioned against Science. This has never changed, but nevertheless it is well-known: «one does not stop progress»...insofar as one dares to be cynical enough to call «progress» the replacement of pyres by crematoriums...that burn a few thousand innocent people at once instead of a few dozen (only!).

And, in spite of their fertile friendship with the fascist parties, Nazis and similar numerous members of the ecclesiastical hierarchy in the Vatican must nevertheless be nostalgic today of the time when the Church held in hand more firmly than now the life of society, with its privileged allies, nominated over time...Constantine 1st, Charlemagne, Leopold II, Franco, Hitler, Mobutu and so many other bloodthirsty tyrants so often venerated by the crowds regardless of their skin colour.

Year 804

He is precisely recalled here in "our red list" this Christian Emperor Charlemagne whose monumental equestrian statue stands alone and proud on a vast square in the heart of old Paris, right in front of the main entrance of the Cathedral of Notre-Dame. His pride, he conquered it (... in the eyes of the Church at the very least!) by converting numerous Saxons with a very simple process: the choice for each one to transform himself into a Catholic or to be beheaded! And indeed several tens of thousands of heads fell...with the "Holy" blessing of the "sovereign pontiff" and his Church, the priests seldom objecting to taking part in the plays of the Emperor.

11th century

Schism of the Orient. The patriarch of Constantinople claims that bread with leaven is to be used for the Eucharist. The Pope, bishop of Rome, affirms that one needs unleavened bread. On this question of capital importance...as you can see, Christianity is divided, and the two patriarchs, of Rome and Constantinople excommunicate each other mutually. This schism will provoke an incalculable number of dead until the 1990s (example: recent civil wars in Yugoslavia between «Catholics» and «Orthodox»). And who suffers? They are always the same ones: the «little ones,» the «underlings,» as we say in the army!

11th-12th centuries

Facing the growth of the population in Europe, the Church proposes a natural method for the control of the world population, and so "effective:" the Crusades. The first call to the crusade is launched in 1095. In 1099 Jerusalem «is liberated.» The whole of its population – which includes primarily Jews and Moslems – is annihilated. One can say indeed, for them, that they «freed» them from their daily worries (!) but alas, not without having been able to escape once again from their very last torments, because the crusaders took care to rape their wives and children before cutting their throats or opening their bellies.

And in these grandiose operations «for the radiance of the Faith»...Christian, of course (and careful, it is forbidden to doubt it!) one discovers again all the services rendered to their Church by the people who «will be sanctified later on» by Rome. This is the case of the Abbot «Bernard» who will personally preach the 2nd crusade. What a beautiful example of Christian love on behalf of the founder of the abbey of Clairvaux, the one that we know as «Saint Bernard» (and «Doctor of the Church» also...might as well!).

Year 1204

The 4th crusade makes a pass through Constantinople. At that time, it is the largest city of Christianity. But the crusaders are completely able to do to Christians what they are accustomed to doing to "pagans:" Constantinople is sacked in an orgy of unnameable violence. As we see, if there is an idea that develops briskly thanks to - let us say rather because of - "Christianity", well it is this culture of "Holy" violence. "Holy," we do not understand very well what that means, but "violence"...alas, everyone knows!

Year 1208-1244

Albigenses Crusade: on the initiative of the pope Innocent III, a crusade is launched in the Albi area against the Cathars (or Albigenses). It is led by Simon IV le Fort, "Lord of Montfort." In 1209, "heretics" having succeeded in mixing with the population of Béziers, it will be the occasion for Simon de Montfort to transmit his name to posterity at the same time as he transmitted to his troops the command that the Pope himself had just given to him through his legate: «Kill them all, God will recognize his own.» All the population, men, women and children killed by the swords. That is a hefty price paid by so many innocent victims, to offer at the time of a «good word» fame to their Lord and Master...a very «sad Sire»!

Year 1252

Foundation of the dismally famous "Inquisition." During its long history, this frightening institution "will have succeeded in" primarily burning more than 1 million people (!) essentially: Jews and Moslems converted to Christianity, heretics and "witches." The last of the "witches" to be burned will be so in 1788. As for the last "heretic," his demise would come later in 1826. The "Holy Inquisition" and its Protestant imitators will also burn doctors and scientists...when the opportunity arises.

The Church will never disavow the "Inquisition" and will guarantee the historical continuity of the institution until our modern days. It will limit itself to modifying its name...and still, we'll have to wait for Pie X, in 1906, for the name of "Holy Office of the Inquisition" to be shortened to "Holy See." And in 1965, the aforementioned office is renamed "Congregation for the Doctrine of the Faith." Lastly, in 1997, the Pope opens the files of Holy See and some carefully selected historians are authorized to undertake certain research.

The estimates of the total number of victims of the Inquisition are then revised upwards. The consensus turns today around the million people executed to which it is necessary nevertheless to add innumerable tortured people whose goods have been seized.

1483

Tomás of Torquemada, Inquisitor of Castille, is named General Inquisitor for all of the Iberian Peninsula. This Dominican monk amply uses torture and seizure of his victims' goods. Beyond this physical and financial violence, an estimated 2,000 people were burned under his mandate.

1492

In Spain the «very Catholic» king and the «very Catholic» queen, (these titles are personally conferred by the Pope!) also use their authority for the expulsion of Jews. In fact, the Jews are faced with the choice between converting themselves to spare the wrath of the Inquisition (which will burn many of them), or leave Spain. More than 160,000 Jews thus leave Spain.

In spite of the frightening cruelty of such «a diktat»...or perhaps because of this cruelty (who knows?)...the Catholic hierarchy does not remain indifferent to this measure, so much so and even quite to the contrary. It approves it and the pope encourages other European monarchs to be inspired by the Spanish example. In perfect agreement with this decision, in all of Europe, the bishops mobilize themselves to push their respective governments to prevent the expelled Jews from entering their territory.

The Jews who chose to convert will thus be persecuted by the Inquisition as decided by the «very Catholic…Monarchs «(but not nice at all!), and that with impressive determination. Following is an example. Until the 18th century, the «pork test» will be used with the converted Jews and their descendants; the test consists of this: a salad with bacon is proposed to the «converted;» if it is noted that he sets aside the bacon while eating, he is burned as a «false convert".

For the same reasons and in the same way, the method will also be applied to converted Moslems and their descendants.

1499

It is during this year that the greatest "autodafé" in history took place. In only one of these horrible «autodafé» the inquisitor Diego Rodrigues Lucero burned alive in Cordova, Andalusia. No less than 107 Jews converted to Christianity.

When one thinks that «autodafé» is the translation of the Portuguese words «act of faith» one remains stunned about it…astounded, towards such nonsense. But in what could these poor people have faith in, those who witnessed their families treated like that? "Faith" in the existence of an alleged "God" of the Christians? "Faith" in «the divine charity» of this God in the name of who they were burned? Could they "believe" in the "Christian charity" of their inquisitors who deliberately dispossessed them of their goods and their life…under such atrocious conditions? All this can only appear, to the first comer, to the most «moron» of the «morons,» as nothing other than "pure madness" perpetrated by people of the lowest human principle!

16th century

The castratos' drama. The Church (the institution) prohibiting women from entering the chancel of the churches (buildings), a tragic problem arises: it would be a torture for the ears of the pious prelates of Christ, if one deprived them of hearing so important high voices in the chancel to praise the love of God. At the time, these pretty voices were undoubtedly requested from the Pope by God in person! - At all events, a solution will be found to solve this «serious problem»…a barbarian solution…to deprive of young boys of the sexual organ associated with these beautiful voices before it changes.

Thus the chancels of the Holy Roman and Catholic Church will never lack neither sopranos nor contraltos. It is supposed that, from up there where they placed him, this God of love, invented by the Christians, must be very satisfied!

These barbaric castrations will cease only in 1878 on order of the Pope Leon XIII. The practice still remained widespread during the 19th century, so much so that Rossini, when he composes his «Small solemn mass» writes...naturally...that all it takes to play this score «is a piano and a dozen singers of the 3 sexes, men, women and castratos.»

1503-1513

Pontificate of Jules II, Giuliano Della Rovere. Even if one can put to his credit the fact of having given work to certain eminent artists of his time like Michelangelo Buonarroti (Michael-Angelo), this pope was mainly a skilled military leader. It is reported that he even once wore the armour during mass, an insolent monk pointing out to him that this attire was not suitable. He replied: «When it is a question of conquering lands, God does not look at the dress, but the faith of his servant.» These few words found him his place in history. His «God» allowed him indeed to conquer Bologna, capital of the Italian area of Emilia, not without the assistance of his roughneck soldiers and, as one can suspect, this important city was immediately ransacked.

1506

Pogrom of Lisbon, capital of Portugal: 3,000 Jews killed by pious Catholics.

1521

Inspired, he will later say, by the «Holy Spirit" always invisible to the eyes of the common people (!)...apparently with nothing else to do, a German monk, «protesting» against the powers of the Pope, translates the «New Testament» in a few weeks. This man is Martin Luther.

The event could seem insignificant. Not at all, for it introduces the greatest schism of Christianity: in the centuries that will follow, Christians will massacre each other with even more enthusiasm than when they massacred and burned non-Christians, the heretics, the witches, the converted Jews and Moslems, and tutti quanti.

174

1527

Ransack of Rome: Protestant soldiers massacred the whole population of Rome, that is to say, approximately 40,000 people and the good old customs of the Catholic Christians having become also those of the Protestant Christians. The whole city will be plundered at their hand. The Pope was saved by his Swiss guards. He locks himself up with them in Castel Sant' Angelo while the population is massacred. He and his guards are the only ones to escape this frightful event.

With this, the Swiss gain a professional outlet abroad that still exists today.

1553

Calvin, leader of another branch of Protestantism, condemns the excesses of the Catholic Church... but he decapitates the free thinker and doctor Michel Servet, the one who had discovered blood circulation. His discovery, so useful for humanity, ultimately warranted death in the eyes of a Christian, whether a Catholic or Protestant. Servet was one of approximately 15 "heretics" who were executed during Calvin's dictatorial reign over Geneva.

Calvin plays a very active role in the arrest and death sentence of Michel Servet. He first exchanged letters with him, but when fleeing the Inquisition, Servet arrived in Geneva and Calvin had him arrested. Calvin had said to his friend the reformer Farel that if Michel Servet were to come to Geneva, he would not let him get out alive again. He thus holds his promise while intervening personally in his trial and by pleading for his execution. The only mercy he was willing to concede for Servet is for him to be decapitated instead of burnt.

1566-1572

The years of Pie V Pontificate who became «Saint» by the grace of one of his successors, this pope of the Catholic Church had bragged publicly and on several occasions to having lit more than 100 heretics' pyres that he himself had accused, confronted and condemned during his reign as General Inquisitor.

Not fearing any paradox, he had however not hesitated to publish in 1566 a new edition of the official catechism of the Church, the one elaborated at the Council of Trent and in which the love of fellow men and the mercy have, of course, found an important place.

1571

The invention of printing allowing a growing number of people to access information, the Church reacts by establishing the Index (Index Additus Librorum Prohibitorum). This institution regularly publishes a list of books whose reading is prohibited to any Catholic Christian, under penalty of «sin» of which the «confession» to a priest is compulsory, to be able «to be forgiven.» One will find in this list in 1616, as an example, the work of Copernicus describing the heliocentric system. The publication of the last issue of the Index will only happen in 1961.

1547-1593 - Wars of religion in France

The Christian sub-sects indulge in a merciless civil war interrupted by several temporary peace and truces. It is during one of those, however, that the massacre of 20,000 Protestants, men, women and children takes place in a single night (Night of the St. Bartholomew's Day Massacre, 1572). Of all slaughters due to these innumerable religious conflicts, this massacre - perhaps because the future King Henri IV, still very popular today in the mind of French, had to abjure Protestantism to accede the throne of France - is practically the only one to have remained in the collective memory of the majority of our contemporaries, as the symbol of religious intolerance. The numerous other misdeeds due to this intolerance seem to be have been quickly forgotten. It would, however, be quite useful for the health of the collective conscience that they be recalled.

Yeat 1600

Condemned for "heresy," Dominican priest and famous scientist Giordano Bruno was burnt alive in Rome in a public square. He had dared to define the universe as "infinite" and, more serious than this, dared to set forth the assumption that certain forms of life could perhaps exist beyond the Earth. This was too much for the Church to bear. After 8 years of trial, during which confessions were extorted by torture, Bruno is condemned to die as a "stubborn and impertinent heretic." His principal accuser, the Cardinal Bellarmin, later will be canonized and, in 1931, will be proclaimed "Doctor of the Church." It is insane and impressive the number of "Doctors" that this Church offered itself...and yet it is obviously still affected by serious and numerous diseases!

176

Year 1609 - Expulsion of the Moors from Spain.

After the expulsion of the Jews from Spain, the Inquisition, now lacking purpose in this beautiful country, undertook a different mission. It thus launches the hunt for the Moors, Arabs who had converted to Christianity. They are suspected of being false converts and executed, all those who refuse to drink wine or to eat pig, or who are too clean. Indeed, Islam, contrary to Christianity, prescribed periodic washings of the body. Cleanliness was never as dangerous as in 16th century in Spain! Lastly, in 1609, undoubtedly fearing to have missed some «false converts,» the Inquisition obtains from the king orders to expel the Moors to North Africa. The number of deported is unknown but the estimates vary between 300,000 and 3 million.

Year 1633

Galileo's trial. To have rallied the heliocentric system of Copernicus and thus to have doubted the geocentric theory of Ptolemy (who, by the way, was not Christian!), Galileo Galilei, known as Galileo, is forced by the Inquisition to retract, having been shown the instruments of torture that would be used if he persisted. Galileo's trial will be reopened for revision only by the Pope John in 1992 (Paul II and Galileo Galilei will nevertheless be rehabilitated). His works had already been listed in the Index in 1616 at the same time as those of his master Copernicus. He will spend the remainder of his life confined in his villa (house arrest). It is only his international reputation of scientist that will allow him to avoid even more severe punishment.

1618 to 1648

30 years War. The very Catholic Hapsburg Monarchs force to conversion their Protestant subjects of Bohemia, starting the largest war that the European continent knew hitherto. Germany's population is reduced by half. Many cities are devastated. Epidemics of plague decimate all of Central Europe from Lombardy to Prussia.

It is indeed a war of religion even if the churches tried thereafter to create the impression that it was a political conflict: the war is started because of a religious dissension after which foreign kings, like Gustav II of Sweden, intervene according to their religious convictions.

The case of Gustav II of Sweden is especially significant: he forces his soldiers to sing Christian canticles each evening. That does not prevent his warriors from being accomplished plunderers and the Swedish army will be awarded the title of «Schrecken of Krieges» (fright of war) by the German population. The latter knows, from experience alas, how «plundering» is done: an army enters a city, cuts the throat of the adult men, rapes women and children before also cutting the throat of all or part of the latter and setting fire to the city. However, Germans are still more afraid of the Swedish soldiers than those of the army of Hapsburg.

2nd half of the 18th century

Affair of the "reductions" in Paraguay. The case is particularly interesting because here the Catholics massacred and excommunicated each other. The Jesuits - members of the Society of Jesus, founded in 1539 to bring to the church «soldiers of God» - had established in Paraguay a small private empire made of «reductions», i.e., small villages reinforced in the forest where Indians converted to Catholicism lived. But a re-designation of the border put several of these "reductions" in the Portuguese territory.

However, Portugal, a Christian and Catholic country, perpetuating at the time the tradition of slavery, wanted to take from the Jesuits their Indians in order to sell them as slaves.

The pope intervened and excommunicated the Jesuits of the «reductions.» Then an army, whose canons and swords had been blessed by the priests on duty, attacked the "reductions", massacred the Jesuits and took the Indians as slaves. Un Te Deum, the usual song for thanking God, was then proclaimed loudly during the mass said to celebrate the victory...as it should be!

A little later in 1773, the pope Clement XIV will prohibit «the Society of Jesus,» guilty in his eyes of being too intelligent and rational. Today still, the Society having been restored by Pie VII, a priest entering the order undergoes 13 years of studies after his masters before becoming truly «Jesuit.»   In fact, Clement XIV especially reproached them for not having loyally served the Bourbon family enough, family of the kings of France and Spain, absolute monarchs and great friends of the Catholic Church... to which these reigning families were always very devoted!

Year 1788

In the canton of Glaris, in Switzerland, the last «witch» is burned. But this execution is not yet the last of the Inquisition that will continue to burn «heretics» until 1826.

Year 1793

Kant, professor of philosophy in Königsberg and international «star» of the modern philosophy since the publication of «Kritik DER reinen Vernunft» publishes «Die Religion innerhalb der Grenzen DER blossen Vernuft» («Religion within the limits of the only reason»), where he puts the Christian doctrines to the test of the reason and the «kategorische Imperativ» (categorical imperative). This is too much for the pious King of Prussia. Pressured by Protestant prelates, he intervenes and Kant is forced to retract publicly under penalty of immediate dismissal of his position at the University of Königsberg.

One by one, the other professors of the university must sign, also under penalty of immediate dismissal, a document where they commit themselves to cease quoting in their teachings the writings of Kant related to religion. As in the case of Galileo, the international fame of Kant saves him from more severe consequences. Kant will think about going into exile, but at this point in time, there are few lenient skies for the thinkers who dare to criticize...be it only some aspects of the Christian ideology. He will thus finish his life at Königsberg.

Year 1826

The last "heretic" is burnt alive by the Inquisition in Spain. A rich Christian tradition ends. It is proper to say that it dies out (... which should never have been ignited...nor of igniting the least human pyre!). And yet the Church did not fully quench its thirst for crimes. From then on, acting more subtly, it will have recourse to very subtle means to kill. It will prohibit, for example, to aid women who must get an abortion, it will sabotage the family planning in poor countries, it will be opposed, with all its weight (heavy, well too heavy!) to the use of the condom as means of damming up the AIDS epidemic. And this list is not exhaustive...unfortunate for humanity!

Year 1847

Sonderbund War: Switzerland, in turn, is torn by a war of religion. The Catholic cantons whose governments are strongly influenced by Jesuits advisers set up a special military alliance (Sonderbund). In this small country, divided into multiple "cantons," some are with the Catholic majority, others with a Protestant one.

The new alliance created for the occasion claims that the Protestant cantons are annexed to the Catholic cantons when the latter are located in areas mainly Catholic. They call the Catholic Monarchs of Austria to their rescue, and then engage in the hostilities. Only the quick victory of the federal troops, which are Protestants, allows avoiding an Austrian intervention, which is good, because if this intervention had taken place, it would have ultimately caused an extension of the conflict on a European scale.

But the Protestants, propelled by their impulse, indulge in ferocious "Hunts for the Catholics" in the Geneva countryside. The Jesuits, considered responsible for the war, are then expelled from Switzerland and their prohibition to establish themselves in this country will remain in force until the 1970s.

Year 1848

Rome's population revolts against the papal dictatorship. The pope is driven out of his home. But he is reinstalled in his power as of 1849 by the action of the French troops, dispatched on the spot by Louis-Napoleon Bonaparte, president of second French Republic. The opponents are then shot and the State of the Church becomes again an absolute monarchy whose sovereign is the pope. Thus, "Very Catholic kings" or "Presidents of the Republic"... very republican, one sees that for the French leaders, whatever the epoch, it is always the same combat: choosing Papacy is of primordial importance! Consequently, one understands better why the popes - including "Jean-Paul II" who currently drags himself in the Vatican (at the time of writing this book) - takes delight, as much as their suave visitors, in thinking and repeating that France is "the elder daughter of the Church!"

Year 1871

The pope decides to excommunicate any person who will take part in an unspecified election of the Italian state, because this one is defined as being "diabolic" since it had dared to deprive the popes of their secular state, certainly an "unforgivable sin" even if it were "confessed!"

This sentence of automatic excommunication will not prevent the pope from blessing the "Partito popolare a few years later," a party of Catholic inspiration, moreover lately set up by a priest.

1918 to 1945

Years of compromise. The Church actively supports the rise of totalitarianisms in Europe. In Austria, its support for Austro-Fascism is total.

In this environment, during the years preceding the arrival of Hitler to power, the members of the Catholic hierarchy did not remain inactive. Here are three examples:

From 1928-29 the Austrian priest Innitzer, publicly signs the request for joining Austria to Germany (the future « Anschluus») and delivers throughout the country a series of sermons in favour of this fascist Austria - Nazi Germany alliance.

He is quickly noticed by Monsignor Mgr. Pacelli, the future Pie XII, at that time Nuncio in Germany of the Pope Pie XI. Under the protection of Pacelli, Innitzer quickly advances through all the steps of the hierarchy. In 1932, he is named «Archbishop of Vienna» and then made «Cardinal» in 1933. Notably, in that year, all over the world, only seven personalities will be lifted to this supreme rank, although 18 offices were vacant.

The same year of 1932, another priest was noted, Monsignor GROËBER, appointed «Archbishop of Freiberg». He, barely appointed bishop, becomes «Member promoter of the S.S.» in 1933 and he pays his contributions to these Hitler «Special Sections.»

Supporting in his many writings the «Final Solution,» he will quickly be called «the brown bishop.» In 1935, one of his publications establishes him as «Champion of blood and race» and on January 30, 1939, he will speak in his "pastoral letter" on the topic, "Jews assassins of Jesus, always animated by an inexpiable murderous hatred".

Of this long list I will choose as third the one named HUDAL, a protégé of the first one cited, Innitzer. Hudal had been the Rector in Rome of the National Church of Austria and Germany since 1923. He will be recognized as of 1944, as «having ex-filtrated» several Nazis thanks to the Vatican networks, but in May of 1933 he distinguished himself already by declaring in his church before a floor of Nazi diplomats and dignitaries, «All German Catholics living abroad greet the advent of the New Reich whose philosophy is so much in tune with the national values as with the Christian values.»

That had at least the merit of being frank (!) but for us it is never but another confirmation of this «Holy alliance»...the horror of the Nazism with the hypocrisy of the Vatican!

In Italy, the Church signs a "Concordat" with the fascist regime that makes Catholicism the state religion: Italians can vote again without being excommunicated. Unfortunately, it is of little use in this period of dictatorship! The Church sacrifices in part its own associations, and all but the Catholic Action must integrate fascist organizations. The Vatican promises Mussolini to act in such a way that the Catholic Action is not tempted by antifascist actions.

In 1929, Mussolini, having signed with Pie XI the "Concordat" called «Patti Lateranensi,» is deemed by this pope as a man of providence («Uomo della provvidenza»). In 1932, the Catholic Action having been brought to its heels by the ecclesiastic hierarchy, in accordance with the dictator's wishes, Mussolini receives from the hands of the Pope the Order of «the golden spur» which is the highest distinction that the State of the Vatican grants.

In Germany, in January 1933, the «Zentrum» Catholic party, whose leader is a Catholic prelate (Prälat Kaas), votes full powers to Hitler. This last one can thus reach at the Reichstag the majority of 2/3 vote necessary to suspend the rights guaranteed by the constitution. With a very Christian charity, the good prelate also agrees to close an eye to the questionable litigious details of the Nazis, like the arrest of the communist deputies before the vote, etc.

Then the Church starts to negotiate a new "Concordat" with Germany: within this framework, it «sacrifices» Zentrum, then the only significant party that the Nazis had not outlawed. This was easily explained: this Catholic party had been instrumental in their attaining power. However, on July 5, 1933, Zentrum destroys itself: it auto-dissolves on request of the Catholic hierarchy, leaving the field free to the NSDAP (Hitler's party). From this point forward, NSDAP is the only and unique party in the country, an ideal tool to handle a population. This tool, of the kind required at all times by all manners of dictators, is offered here by the Catholic Church to the new chancellor of the Third Reich to enable him to transform himself into a Führer.

Hitler, in any case, already proclaimed himself Catholic in «Mein Kampf,» the work in which he announced his political program. In it, he also stated that he was convinced that he was an «instrument of God.» Nowadays still, many people would like others to admit that the Catholic Church did not have, at that time, the possibility of resisting the pressure imposed by Hitler. The proof that it most certainly did not want to oppose itself to this newborn monster, is that the Catholic Church put - and often for reasons more than futile - so many works on its list of prohibited books, never thought of putting «Mein Kampf» on the Index even before Hitler's rise to power.

It seems that the anti-Semite program of the future chancellor had nothing to displease the Church that, historically, had already acted so many times against the Jews. Hitler, in return, will not hesitate to express his recognition to it while making compulsory the prayer to Jesus in the German public school and by reintroducing the famous sentence «Gott mit uns» (God is with us) on the uniforms of the German army.

In Spain, a general attempts a military coup. He fails but this scuffle gives way to a civil war. No matter what it will cost the Spaniards, the Vatican and «His Holiness» decide to support him, the priests and the bishops will bless the guns of Franco, will pompously celebrate Te Deum for his victories against the forces of the republican government...although this one was legitimate!

This civil war will last 3 years, resulting in more than one million dead. Franco will not embarrass himself with the «laws of the war» and orders that the prisoners be shot. Then, setting himself up as a dictator - «enlightened,» without a doubt by his «spiritual adviser» - he will impose on Spain, under his boot and his yoke, 30 additional years of Catholic obscurantism and misfortune.

During the Second World War, the Vatican will know about the exterminations of Jews perpetrated by the Nazis. We will be told after the war that the pope hesitated, on several occasions, to make a public plea but that he finally refrained from making it, primarily fearful of Communism phobia, felt that a Russian victory would be «worse» than a German victory. On the other hand, in 1942, he will cry over the ruins of the good city of Rome on which bombs fall, and he will condemn with vehemence these bombardments of these allied troops to fight Fascism. But, oddly, he will forget to mention that his own political ally, Mussolini, had requested from Hitler «the honour of taking part in the bombardment on London.» But it is true that the pope does not live in London, he lives in Rome, and perhaps this does explain that, does it not?

Year 1948

The Pope declares that any person that would vote communist or that would help this party in some way would be automatically "excommunicated." The measure divides families, causes socially intolerable exclusions for many, and forces numerous Communists to retreat underground in rural zones. A striking illustration of these constraints exerted by the Italian society of the time is very precisely presented, amplified with the force of humour, in the dialogues of the film "Don Camillo" where Fernandel, who plays the part of the priest of a small village on the countryside, is confronted with the communist mayor who is, of course, anticlerical, the only other "notable" of this small village!

In facts (the true ones, those of life) the Italian priests indeed hurried to translate this decision with the weight of all their authority on their flocks so that everyone vote in favour of the great anticommunist party C. D. (Christian Democracy). That will not prevent this C. D. regime from lamentably breaking down in generalized corruption some time later in the middle of the 1990s.

Year 1961

Last edition of the Index (Index Additus Librorum Prohibitorum). Among the authors whose whole works are prohibited from reading by Catholics are: French writers, Jean-Paul Sartre, creator of «existentialist» philosophies then «materialist» and Andre Gide, champion of all freedoms, those of the body and the mind, as well as the Italian, technician of philosophy and psychology Alberto Pincherle Moravia, known as Alberto, proposing his solutions to the intellectual and social problems of his contemporaries. Fortunately for them the pyres of the «Holy Inquisition» were already extinguished, a few centuries earlier. Undoubtedly, they would have had to feel them too!

1980s

Certain observers had hoped, in 1978, that in John-Paul 1st, who had just been elected pope to everyone's surprise and who had, in his previous capacity as Bishop of Venice, been opposed to the dictatorial injunctions (financial among other) of the preceding Roman curia, that they would finally have a pope who would dedicate himself to an in-depth reform of the Catholic Church, so disappointing on many levels and for so long.

It is possible that their hope was not in vain, but in any case, it will have been short: 34 days in all, such was the duration of John-Paul 1st Pontificate. But during this short period, he had already found the occasion to specify with his close collaborators the diagram of the reforms of great importance that he intended to begin without delay. His program would include revision of the dogmas in the light of science, for example, as well as the various persons in charge of the government of the church. His intention was to remove the offices that "important eminences" occupied under poor pretence and that that its predecessors had hitherto never dared enjoin them to leave.

His sudden and brutal end remains still officially unexplained to date, and this due to the deliberate will of the principal persons in charge of the Vatican who were alive at the time of his death; the conditions of his death recognized by several people of his entourage as absolutely abnormal.

After his death these "dignitaries" of the church employed everything in their power to conceal the circumstances of his death. Among other ploys, the following example: his body was embalmed in the 14 hours after his death whereas the Italian law prohibited beginning an embalming less than 24 hours after death. By cross-referencing journalistic information, one can even note that the embalmers had been called in by "somebody of the Curia" 45 minutes before the "official" hour to which one found the pope dead in his bed!

This Vatican Curia, acting in this way, was hoping to oblige the Italian State to ignore the conditions of the tragic death of this 'flash' pope. Moreover, at the top of the government of the Vatican State, one always opposed the official requests of the Italian Justice by saying their requests are not available, the so-called Justice making a point of seeking the suspected causes of the pope's demise, whose death is quickly proven to be very favourable to the interests of some "eminences" positioned very high within the Catholic clergy.

Lo and behold, the State of the Vatican is "sovereign" - this since "the Latran agreements" concluded in 1929 between Pie XI and Mussolini, as you recall - it can thus afford to be unaccountable to anyone "down here", according to its language! But many human beings have the right to feel that one day it should be accountable, not to this virtual God that the first Christians invented themselves, but to the gods (plural) who are truly alive

185

"up there", from where they can see what occurs "down here!"

After this period of apparent liberalization and quickly disappointed illusions, Pope John-Paul II, enthusiastic admirer of works of Opus Dei, arrives at the head of the greatest religion in the world and joins again with the most terrible traditions of its frightening Church.

His condemnation of the condom as means of damming up the fight against AIDS causes an enormous number of deaths inevitably but difficult to estimate. He practices an active policy of sabotage of birth control measures in the Third World; but there too, the consequences of an action of this kind are hard to quantify as they are measured in terms of famine, misery, lack of medical care, and this, on the level of the poorest continents of the Earth (South America and Africa).

An example of his action in another field, always a lively "sport, as mentioned earlier, was the field of hunting for "heretics". He suspends "A Divinis" (for the time that will please God) two German theologians who had dared doubt, for one, the "papal infallibility," and another, "the Immaculate Conception" of Mary.

One can measure, only in this last example, the enormous difference between the action (or rather the "reaction") of John-Paul II and the broad-mindedness that the remarks of John-Paul 1¹ made from the top of the pulpit of a large church in Rome as he proclaimed in public: «Soon, my sisters, my brothers, we will have to re-examine the dogmas of our Church, in the light of today's Science.» It is true that few days separate these words from what one will call, prudently writing, «His premature death!»

Years 1990: Wars of religion in Yugoslavia

In the 1980s, Yugoslavia was one of the favourite vacation grounds for balneal holidays for Europeans. Yugoslav advertisements at the time praised the multi-religious character of the country as a tourist interest, for it is true that one can see in Mostar and in many of other charming villages the mosque and the church at one glance. Alas, the country broke down in a series of civil wars that one enjoys describing as "ethnic" whereas it is, in fact, real wars of religion.

The case of the war of Croatia is most flagrant. Serbs and Croats share the same ethnic origin and speak the same language, the Serbo-Croatian, that one calls Croato-Serb when it is written in Latin characters. The most ironic is that the "Serbo-Croatian" written in "Latin" characters, i.e., the "Croato-Serb", is today still the official language of the Yugoslav army which fights against NATO in Kosovo after having fought against the Croats at the beginning of the Nineties. Alas for these populations, the religion exists on their lands and it separates Croatians and Serbs: the "Croats" have been Christianized by Rome, they are thus "Catholic;" the Serbs, who write the Serbo-Croatian in Cyrillic characters, have been Christianized by the Byzantines, they are so "Orthodox." And the ones as much as the others cling to "their traditions."

When Milosevic began to stir the spectre of the "Great Serbia," Croatia declared its independence. At once, the Vatican and the German Federal Republic, whose chancellor of the time proclaimed himself "überzeugter Katholik» (convinced Catholic) recognized Catholic Croatia as an independent state. Consequently, the Vatican dispatched its nuncios in the entire West to obtain the recognition of the new Catholic state. The pope multiplied calls, prayers and masses for the independence of Croatia. During this time, the dictator of Croatia, former senior officer under the communist and Catholic regime, very observing, was laying off all the orthodox civil servants, i.e. «Serbs». He chooses as its national flag the old Oustachi banner that had committed genocide of approximately 600,000 Serbs between the years 40 and 44. That is how the civil war began!

One more proof that the Catholic Church took side: the war once finished, the Pope will beatify the cardinal Stepinac, he who had qualified Ante Palevitc, the Oustachi dictator of 1940-44, as «Gift of God» for Croatia and had supported him actively.

The war of Yugoslavia then continues in Bosnia where the members of the three religious groups (Catholic, Orthodox, Moslem) clash in a series of triangular combat whose civil populations are obviously the main victims.

The wars of Yugoslavia are an emblematic case of the catastrophes caused by the intolerance that is inherent with the «revealed» religions: religious communities clash, in the 20th century, in the name of religions that they received randomly during the expansion of various empires (Roman, Byzantine, and Ottoman) during the Middle-Age.

It is clear that «monotheist» Religions are a real danger to humanity, that they are vehicles of intolerance, of incentive to hatred, wars and conflicts. The fact is easily comprehensible: each monotheist religion will always assert that its god is «the good» god, the only «good God,» whereas for

187

each one, the others' god is «bad,» as he is not «the true» god and that consequently, all those who believe in this «false God» are «the infidels» and that they should be fought at all cost!

Whereas in fact, the truth is found in a universe where coexists a plurality of worlds, inhabited planets, and also some «human» gods (in the plural) who created us in their image.

19 – Christianity and the symbol of the Cross

Isn't it funny, isn't it indeed comical to see nowadays all Christians wearing as the Christian symbol, as symbol of their bond with Jesus...a cross!

This is so horrible! They are wearing an instrument of torture and death as a jewel around their neck or on their chest. They decorate their walls with this instrument, this symbol of suffering and death. Quite often they even display (put) it above their bed. As a matter of habit, they make the sign of the cross before praying, eating, starting a soccer game or taking a penalty shot in many sports events!

This Christian custom illustrates very well, once again, to what degree they are conditioned. They are fighting for principles, seeking to preserve them at all costs, with no knowledge of where these principles arose or what they represent. They are fighting to save acquired values without suspecting that they are not based on any fundamental truth.

The first Christians did not use the cross as their symbol. They used different signs of recognition such as fish; for example, one's head next to the other's tail represented the era of Pisces that began with the birth of Jesus, before our current era. The first Christians were also used other symbols: the shepherd, the swastika, the phoenix, the dove or two Greek letters, alpha and omega (the first and the last: the beginning and the end). All these signs were – and still are – clearly different from this horrible symbol of suffering and death that is the crucifixion cross!

The Catholic Church and behind it a flock of Christians following like sheep adopted the cross as their symbol four centuries after Jesus had been killed by crucifixion. Yes, four centuries, 400 years after his death! Actually, one of the first uses of the cross as a Christian emblem appeared on an announcement banner used by Constantine's army. Constantine, the murderous Roman emperor, converted to Christianity and then created the title of "Monarch of divine right" that he awarded to himself first. He used this banner with a cross during his war and conversion campaigns, campaigns carried out by force, during the 4th century A.D.

And now there they are! A vast number of ignorant Christians proud to be wearing this symbol! They are fools due to a lack of science, as the Bible said, a lack of knowledge. But we understand them: they are so conditioned...unconsciously conditioned! For that reason, the cross became for them a trivial symbol arising from the tradition. It is mechanically worn by Christians who venerate this known instrument of murder almost as much as the prophet who was crucified on it! Are they even aware of the fact that Jesus was a "Prophet", that is true...but not "the Messiah"...that is wrong? I'm sorry to tell them but it is important that they know this reality. Even after carefully reading Chapter 8 of this book, I'm not at all convinced of their awareness. I know that the conditioning they have endured for so many years, for so many generations, that it is now rooted in the individual and collective unconscious for most of them!

However, all Christian Africans should abandon this type of superstition for their own best interest. It would do them good to be aware that Jesus was a human prophet, that he wasn't the expected Messiah but that he taught love, compassion, and forgiveness. They could at the same time become aware also that by being who he was and who he is still, were he alive today, he would despise being portrayed as having died in this dreadful manner, the victim of human stupidity.

Because all Christians continue to sport, wear, or venerate the cross, they continue to perpetuate the human ignorance that cost Jesus his life. This is affirmed in the words Jesus spoke in his dying moments of the people who were executing him, "Father, forgive them for they know not what they are doing". If the Christians today know what they are doing, they will not venerate this instrument of torture by which Jesus was assassinated.

I ask of you, African Christians, especially to you, if Jesus had been guillotined, would you be sporting a guillotine around your necks? Would your churches be adorned with guillotines and severed heads? I would like, for once, Christian Africans, my friends, that you make the effort to think... once and for all...please! Think and, I assure you, you will feel better!

Jesus' teachings favored life and pleasure, not death and suffering! How man wars have been fought and how many millions of human beings killed in the name of this horrible symbol, the sight of which makes Jesus so sad when he sees it around your neck or displayed on military banners as he looks upon you "from the sky" where he now lives.

Knowing all this now, being fully aware of the charade played by the Church, can you still believe the lies? Reading these lines, the vast deception in which you've been shrouded, you and so many others like you, can you continue to play this bad game of fools?

One day Jesus will return with Elohim and with the forty or so other prophets that Elohim sent throughout the passing centuries from the day when these scientists and artists created our first ancestors here on Earth.

It has been written that he will be back and this has been reported by the traditions of all cultures: he will be back with his father Yahweh, with the other extraterrestrial creator gods, such as Lucifer and Satan and in company of other great prophets such as Osiris, Simon Kimbangu, Kimpa Vita, Simao Toko, Moses, Buddha, Muhammad, etc.

So when this day comes, will you welcome Jesus with images of his death and his suffering? Inside yourself, you must understand how deeply he loathes the cross! How could the remembrance of his suffering on the torture instrument be pleasant to him?

Know it – and truly admit it – as all "the scriptures" tell us, he is alive. Thanks to a sophisticated scientific process, one perfected by our creators in heaven over thousands of years, Jesus was recreated upon his death. Our researchers too, although still in technical early stages, will one day master this process as well.

This process, in simple terms, is called "cloning". In fact, it is cloning that holds the secret to eternal life from which Jesus benefited and still does. Some 2000 years later, Jesus resides on the planet of the eternals that the "sacred books" speak of; the Bible, the Koran, and others.

Christians simply need to reread certain Gospel passages and the Acts of the Apostles with consciousness and intelligence, without priory, with open eyes and heart. With this, they will understand that Jesus was not reincarnated as "a spirit" after his crucifixion, but in the flesh, happy to share a meal with his own incredulous disciples. You will find an example in the story of the Companions of Emmaus: Gospel Luc, CH XXIV, 13-16, 30-31, and especially 36-43. In fact, here I emphasize the last two verses: "They gave him a piece of grilled fish. He took it and did eat before them".

This is very eloquent isn't it! Simon Kimbangu appeared in the same way after his death and had been seen in many places and different locations at the same time. Each time our extraterrestrial creators played a part using a scientific technology far advanced in comparison to ours.

Any true admirer of Jesus, if he really loves him, should refuse to wear the cross that Jesus hates! Didn't he suffer enough? How can we admire him, be grateful for all the wisdom and teachings he gave to us, and still allow ourselves to make him suffer continually?

By the way, any true African should abandon the colonists' Christianity and return to his own polytheist religious traditions devoid of mystical hea-viness from the past and therefore placed under today's and tomorrow's science light. All Africans should look on Earth for who could be today the announced "Messiah". Once identified, we should be at his service because if Jesus were on earth today we would not be "a Christian" subservient to the laws of the Vatican, but at the service of this person: "The Messiah", "the Paraclete" whom the arrival has been announced many times (ex: Gospel John, Ch XVI, 7).

I strongly recommend to all black Christians who adore the symbol of the cross to read again Isaiah XLIV, 19-20, not only to read this passage, but also to understand it with intelligence:

> And none considereth in his heart, neither [is there] knowledge nor understanding to say, I have burned part of it in the fire; yea, also I have baked bread upon the coals thereof; I have roasted flesh, and eaten [it]: and shall I make the residue thereof an abomination? shall I fall down to the stock of a tree

> He feedeth on ashes: a deceived heart hath turned him aside, that he cannot deliver his soul, nor say, [Is there] not a lie in my right hand?

Once again, a Big "Christian" mistake: to make people adore a wood or metal piece transformed into a cross in Jesus' memory. A cross is not Jesus, a crossed wood or metal piece has no signification, absolutely nothing!

20. The polytheism of our African ancestors: source of truth

"A people without the knowledge of its past history, past religions, art and culture, is like a tree without roots".

MARCUS GARVEY

In most former African traditions, the word "Gods" is commonly used in their myths and legends. These "Gods" (in the plural form) are generally humanized, such that we could simply call them: beings with the same traits and characteristics of human beings. They may be of a smaller size, but the Gods are definitely physical beings.

We already know that in the **HEBREW** text of the Old Testament (the Torah), there are three main characters, they are called: **Yahweh, Lucifer** and **Satan**. These same humanized Gods are referred to in many myths and legends of the Bantu people though they often bear different names.

But before embarking on our big trip inside of Africa in order to prove this, let us imagine ourselves with the advantage of having wings so as to take flight, and begin a tour towards India and Asia.

In the **HINDU RELIGION**, there are, in fact, thousands of Gods, and Divinities. But in spite of their large quantity, we find coincidentally, that there are three main characters: **"Brahma"** (Yahweh), **"Shiva"** often presented as androgynous (Satan), and **"Vishnu"** (Lucifer).

Now let us go on our great African tour. We will start from the north of Africa and we shall cross the desert. With a little bit of luck, we shall find some of the last **TOUAREG NOMADS**. They will teach us that, for them the whole group of the sky divinities is called **"Emeli-hin"**. Phonetically this name seems rather close to Elohim...a good start!

Moving from the desert and heading toward the Atlantic Ocean, let us make a first stop with the purpose of getting acquainted with the **YORU-BAS**. It is in Nigeria and/or in Benin that we shall find them. The Yorubas are not only a tribe but also a religion. In their religion, there are several Gods, an assortment of Gods; the three main Gods are: **"OBATALA"**, the chief creator, who is androgynous (man/woman) and who would correspond to the "Yahweh" of the Torah. Another is **"YEMAYA"** who is the maternal strength of the creation and who would correspond to the "Lucifer" of the Torah. The third is **"ELEGUA"** who represents temptation and who would correspond to the "Satan" of the Torah. We can also notice that the Yoruba Religion was exported by the means of slavery and became the cradle of **"SANTERIA"**, a religion that is practiced in Brazil, in Cuba and in the United States. The descendants of slaves continued practicing the veneration of "Gods" though some aspects have regrettably changed, most notably the names of these Gods that have been changed into the names of Christian saints. The word "SANTERIA" for example means "the veneration of Saints".

While in Nigeria, we should also look closely at the **IBOS** for whom the leader of the Gods is called **"Ikenga"**, his direct assistant being called "Chiuke". And since we are still in Benin, knowing that there are a large number of voodoo "wizard" priests in this country, let us also take this opportunity to learn more about them. Just what is the religion of these people all about? Very simple: they have always venerated small beings that came from the sky. They recognize them as creators of Humankind, and call them the "Azizas". They also say that their leader is **"Yewe"** (almost Yahweh!). How interesting indeed!

Moving on from the Beninese to their neighbors, **Togo and Ghana**, let us look at what the **EWES** say. They call the Gods of the sky by the word «**Trowo**" (the "wo" ending indicates a plural), the leader of the Gods of the sky is **"Nana Bouclou"** (Yahweh), and the snake God **"Anyiewo"** (Lucifer).

Traveling along the Gulf of Guinea, we make another exciting discovery. According to the AKANS of Ghana, the leader of the Gods, their supreme God lived together with men on earth! He was outright physical, lived among men, and these men could approach him freely. The supreme God was man/woman (therefore androgynous) and was called **"Oboadee"** or sometimes **"Brekyirihunuade"**.

Traveling toward the southeast, we find the Rwandans (**TUTSIS**, **TWAS** and **HUTUS**) where the Monotheist Religion of colonizers committed so many obvious crimes, some more horrible than others.. Nevertheless, well-known ancient traditions remain and they demonstrate that all the geniuses that came from the sky are called **"Imandwa"** and the supreme God is called **"Imana"**. This god is a totally physique being who had conversations with men, and his interlocutors could see him, feel him, touch him, talk to him. In the presence of numerous witnesses it is said that he performed

196

wonders, revived dead people, or revitalized old and infirmed people with youthful bodies. For the Rwandans, it is this god Imana who created the first man. He created him in his image and in his likeness and He called him "Kazikamuntu" (Adam).

Before going down the West coast, let us go through the equatorial forest and the land of the PYGMIES. In their tradition, they show us that "**Arebati**" is the leader of the small beings who came from the sky. It is Him who created man from clay, ran blood through the man and breathed life into him.

Once we arrive at the Atlantic Ocean, we shall stop to meet the **FANGS** in Gabon where they will teach us that the three main Gods are "**Nzame**", "**Mebere**", and "**Nkwa**".

And to finish our tour we will head for THE CAPE.

In his rich country named "South Africa", the ZULUS will be the first ones to capture our attention because they imagine their ancestors as guardian angels coming from the sky. They pray to "**Amazulu**" which means in their language "the people of the sky". For Zulus, the leader of the Gods of the sky is "**Ukulunkulu**" (Yahweh), and his assistant who helped to work on the creation - the one who brought knowledge to men - is "**Unwaba**" (Lucifer). But in their cosmogony, there also exists a third important creator, "**Umvelinqangi**".

The Zulu people are known for being warlike and one of their famous kings of the past was "Shaka Zulu". But when we ask a white anthropologist the question, "What does the word "Zulu" mean, we generally get the answer, "Zulu" means "the sky". This is the reason why the Zulus are called "the people from the sky". Well, the usual answer! But the problem is that it is wrong and furthermore it is unfair to them.

In Zulu language, the word meaning the sky is "sibakabaka". There is another word that means *interplanetary space* and that word is "izulu". And still there is another word that means the infinite universe, "weduzulu". This word could also be used to mean "cosmic trips!» The understanding of these words is in no way the same as what the "expert anthropologist" claim for definitions, and the scope is not the same at all! This shows us clearly that the Zulus were aware that we can do interplanetary trips and have been aware for a very long time that these trips were possible. More importantly, they do not proclaim themselves as "the Zulus are people from the sky;" not at all. What they do claim is millennia ago, a people came from the sky to create life on earth. What's more, the Zulus, in their traditions, also speak about the fact that these people from the sky mated here on earth with some of the women whom they created and that the descendants coming from these "sexual" unions formed a race of kings and of tribal leaders.

References to our solar system, our galaxy, and to the knowledge about where the creators came from are all indicated by the Zulus in the term "Ingiyab". The name of the sun of the planet that is usually occupied by the creators is indicated by the name of "Isone Nkanyamba". The Zulus have always known and adopted the notion of infinity in time and space. For them, time and space are infinite and "one;" their word to indicate the infinity of space is "umkati" and to indicate the infinity of time is "isikati".

Do not allow yourself to be persuaded or deceived by a white anthropologist who would tell you that since the word "zulu" means "sky" that it makes the Zulus "the people from the sky". It is not true. It is the word "Amazulu" which indicates that they are a people from the sky, a people who came from "somewhere else", from another inhabited planet. In fact, «Amazulu» means the creator gods of the "Zulu" people and also of the whole humankind.

Then, before leaving this beautiful Africa, this continent that is so dear to us, we shall go into the heart of this last country we visited to find the **"BUSHMEN"** of Central South Africa and look at the roots of their words as well. The most important among the Gods who came from the sky are **"Cagn"**, (Yahweh), **"Dxui"**, **"Mantis"**, and **"Kwammanga"**.

As our trip ends, imagine leaving the South, South Africa, by boat in order that we may view the Cape of the same name, keeping in our heart the "good hope" that one day we will finally awaken the consciousness and wisdom of all the inhabitants of this superb country of Africa. It is poor today but so rich in human and material potential, rich in the potential of which its peace and happiness depend the most, religious potential. We hope this day will come as soon as possible.

We noticed during our pleasant trip throughtout Africa that the different ethnic groups, tribes, and clans are polytheists. There are numerous Gods, divinities, celestial beings who came from the sky, cosmic beings who came from far away.

198

Nevertheless, even in the midst of the majority of myths and legends of all these African people, there is a main God, like a President of all Gods, as the Chief-President of a people who came from the sky. We come to feel that there is an actual leader who is responsible for the work of creation of life on earth, just as there is a leader God in the original Bible in Hebrew, and it so happens that this leader is actually called Yahweh.

So, in summary, let us look at what names are used by all the African people that we know to indicate "Yahweh:"

"Ngai" for the **MASSAI** of Kenya and Tanzania; **"N'Kosi Yama'kosi"** for the **NDEMBELES** of Zimbabwe; **"Mahrem"** for the **AXUMITES** of Ethiopia; **"Nana Bulukus"** for the **FONS** in West Africa; **"Akuj"** for the **TURKANAS** of Kenya; **"Akongo"** for the **NGOMBES** of Kongo; **"Nzokomba"** for the **MONGOS** of Kongo; **"Kalumba"** for the **LUBAS** of Kongo; **"Katavi"** for the **NYAMWEZIS** of Tanzania; **"Amma"** for the **DOGONS** of Mali; **"Astar"** for a great number of people in Ethiopia and Somalia; **"Mbotumbo"** for the **BAULES** of Ivory Coast; **"Ndriannahary"** for the **MALGACHES**; **"Ajok"** for the **LOTUKOS** of Sudan; **"Quamta"** for the **XHOSAS** of South Africa; **"Ka Tyeleo"** for the **SENUFOS** of West Africa; **"Musisi-Kalunga"** for the **NDON-GAS** of Angola; **"Chiuta"** for the **TUMBUKAS** of Malawi; **"Rock-Sene"** for the **SERERS** of Gambia; **"Massim-Biambe"** for the **MUNDANGS** of Kongo; **"Huveane"** for the **BASUTOS** of Lesotho; **"Kyala"** for the **NYAKYUSUS** of Tanzania; **"Bumba"** for the **BOSHONGOS** of South Africa; **"Muluku"** for the **MOCOUAS** of Zambezi; **"Faro"** for the **BAMBARAS** of Burkina Faso and Niger; **"Wenna"** for the **MOSSIS** of Burkina Faso and Niger.

The leader God is also called **"Marcadit"** for the DINKAS of Sudan and, for them, the first man and the first woman he created, so forming the first couple (Adam and Eve) are called "Garang & Abuk".

We therefore have our own myths and legends that relate to the creation, and we have always had our own religions that relate to the genesis of Man. The Gods of our ancestors were humanized Gods who had human traits and characteristics. They were physical, made of flesh and blood, and they came down from the sky in their spacecrafts. They were many, they were a people, and they had at their head the supreme God who directed creation. In all the myths and legends of African people, the earth already existed. The Gods traveled to it and established life, animals, nature, and created men/women in their image and likeness.

The "cherubs" of the original Bible in Hebrew are also mentioned and we know them very well in our ancient traditions and cultures. They are the humanized gods of our ancestors, and most of the time, are described as celestial beings of small size and often of androgynous gender.

The elders in our villages have retained this knowledge and they still know stories about the small geniuses that came from the sky in silver-plated nuggets, in silver bowls, in the bright flying calabashes. They still know stories about genius-spirits who are in the forests and who help and guide men, who come in the caves to initiate and teach their knowledge to the leaders, or to those to whom they chose to pass it on.

In the Ivory Coast, these caves, these caverns of the old timers, have at the entrances images of these "spacecrafts of the Gods". These images have the shape of a flattened bell as if the rock had been cut with a knife in soft butter. The shapes are perfect and wholly represent those of a flattened bell!

In Ethiopia, there are stories well known by everybody, of King Solomon coming to visit the Queen of Sabah, arriving from Jerusalem in a flying chariot, and the length of time on board this spacecraft was that of lightning. And sometimes he even simply sent his flying chariot with gifts for the Queen of Sabah without making the journey himself.

In Old Egypt, the Ancients referred to areas around Mount Sinai as the "country of the blazing vessels"!

The flying silver-plated nuggets...the flying silver calabashes...the flying silver bowls...these are all terms from our traditions to describe the spacecrafts of the Gods, like the spacecraft of Yahweh. For our ancestors, Yahweh was the leader of the creation and President of the Gods. These descriptions are equivalent to those of the "Merkabah" in the original Bible in Hebrew (the flying chariot that is carrying the throne of Yahweh), to those of the Vimanas (the space ships of the gods described in the Hindu Mahabarata and Ramajna), or even of "the cloud" or "the glory of Yahweh", two expressions used many times in the Hebrew Bible. All these terms changed in the western languages - so long ago – to the term "Flying Saucers", replaced some years ago by that of UFO ("Unidentified Flying Objects").

But for us Africans, it is absolutely necessary that we rediscover our ancient traditions which are beautiful and which orbit the truth and in which we rediscover our "Gods" (in the plural), those of days gone by. Evidence

200

of our humanized Gods who are physical and who exist outright and who live and stay, of course, in the sky can be found in these traditions. When we understand this, we shall again be in the truth and total purity.

It is on this path that rests our "true" spirituality. It is here that we will travel the path of understanding, of consciousness, and of a harmonious opening of mind onto infinity, infinity in time and in space. Because today we are submerged in the invented notion of a "Unique God", immaterial, all-powerful, omnipresent, a way of conceiving the world imposed by our colonizers and their Religion, a distorted Christianity, we are often lead astray far enough as to act in the opposite way of the message of Peace and Love delivered by "Jesus Christ". And the "Prelates" of this religion have the audacity to claim themselves as official representatives.

And for us, working from this notion, all the so-called "values" that are instilled upon us (by force) only detract from the truth and put our minds to sleep. Moreover, masses of Africans pray to "Jesus the Saviour", but they will never find "their salvation" by following this path imposed by the West!

If Africa really wants to be saved, it must rid itself of these notions brought and imposed by the colonizer and "spiritually decolonise". It must rediscover the polytheist concepts that it had been taught for so long; it must rediscover its Human Gods who came from the sky; and lastly, it must analyze all of this in terms of both the science of today and the technologies of the future. For Africa, this is where the key to its own happy fulfilment lies and not in the Religion of the colonizer who came to alienate us, to destroy our identity, to take over our heritage. The colonizer, with a supreme malignity, made of each of us someone who could be tamed, molded, put down, domesticated, striving to maintain control over "the black" to make him a dependant, obedient, servile being, one who would never rebel against the "White Father" in cassock and his "holy" book, the New Testament.

I like this name "New" Testament; it is revealing! Naturally, this institution had to create something new, for the benefit of its cause, in order to accomplish its imperialist and mercantile mission. In order to stray the masses from the good way, "mislead" them, and to reach its aims, it had to move furtively as a shepherd (alas a "false shepherd") among the herd of so-called lost ewes. Bear in mind they had not been lost prior to this but became so only as a result of the shepherd's deception.

I prefer the Old Testament. I reject their "New" Testament as it wreaks of a contrived plot. My Old Testament is the "Humanized Gods" of my ancestors, it is the genesis, the history of creation told by my people, by our ancient people and I can compare it only to the Genesis of the true "Old Testament", the Torah.

There is a common truth in all the religious traditions of our ancestors in Africa whether it is in the South, in the West, in the East or in Central Africa. Through these traditions, the number of commonalities among all religions all over the world is enormous. Everywhere they speak about celestial beings that had a capacity for appearing and vanishing from human sight as they wished. Yahweh, according to the Hebrews, could appear suddenly to Moses, in a "burning bush", for example at a time when only birds could fly. For humans this will come too, but much later in their History!

In the majority of Bantu religious traditions, it is said that Yahweh and his other Gods, after having created men, left them and did not worry any more about them, departed at a given moment and left men alone on the Earth. And the traditions also say that before the departure of the Gods, there were free and easy exchanges between the creators and us, the humans they had created.

By way of example, in the religious traditions of Pygmies from Semang it is said: *"In the past a tree trunk was connecting the top of the cosmic mountain, the middle of the world, to the Sky; the communications with the Sky and the relations with the gods were thus easy and natural; because of a mistake, the communications were stopped and the gods withdrew even higher in the sky"*.

But let us also scan other traditions, other humans with a black skin, like the Arandas of central Australia: *"In the Sky, there is the Eternal young "altjira nditja", with the other Gods, they live there in a permanently green country, full of flowers and fruits, crossed by the milky way. They are all eternally young: the grand father distinguishing himself neither from his grandchildren nor from his great grandchildren; they are immortal like the stars, because death did not succeed in penetrating them"*. And for the Arandas too the communication with the Gods was easy, but was, for the same reason, suddenly stopped at a given time.

And in this case too, the link is easy to establish with the Hebrew Bible, the Torah, where Yahweh is translated as "the one who was, who is, and who will be", therefore "The Eternal" and obviously "Eternally young". How? Thanks to Science of course, science that gives access to eternal life. Through cloning, we earthlings begin to discover the secret of eternal life.

Now let us come back to the Great Envoy Prophet Simon Kimbangu to refer to his real teaching. But for that we have to call upon the Movement he created himself and called "Kintuadi" (which means Union) and not to the Church named " Kimbanguism". Kimbanguism was formed after Kimbangu's death by his junior son, collaborating with the colonial administration and ultimately betraying his father, the Prophet. Worse than this, the Kimbanguist Church later joined forces in the Kongo Kingdom with Mobotu Sese Seko, the horrible, bloodthirsty dictator that we all know.

What we have to keep constantly in mind is that the Prophet Simon Kimbangu was speaking of "Gods" in plural. This is undeniable. He spoke of a people living in the sky, and when he spoke of "our creators", (in the plural always!) "our fathers who are in the skies", he spoke with the precise following terms: "Bata Nzambi' A Mpungu". It is the colonizers who forced us to translate the word "Nzambi" to "God", compelling our subconscious in that way to refer to a unique God, immaterial and omnipresent (like this false "God" whom they invented and in whom they want us to believe at all costs!).

The word "Batata" is vitally important, because in all the Kongo languages this word "Batata" is inevitably in the plural without the possibility of any dispute; literally it means "The Fathers" or "Our Fathers" (in the plural once again). It is thus the equivalent of "Adonai" and of "Elohim" in Hebrew, these too incontrovertible and undeniable plurals.

When the Prophet Simon Kimbangu uses the following words: "Mpeve Ya Batata Nzambi' A Mpungu Tulendo" it can never be, in any case, a singular. This fact, all honest Kongos must admit that the French translation of this expression, such as we can read today in the scriptures of the Kimbanguist Church, is completely false, shamefully false. To write, "because the spirit of our all powerful God" is to completely distort the real meaning, because the true message of Simon Kimbangu is here talking about many people at the same time (still and always "in the plural") and not about a unique "God".

Furthermore, it is important to note the word "Nzambi" is also used by the people of Gabon where in some languages they also say "Nzame" or

"Nzambe". For example, for the Fangs of Gabon, the history of the origin of life on Earth is told in the Mvett: they speak about people coming from the sky and having a high technology, saying that their leader is "Nzame", that one of his brothers is "Zong" and that one of his sisters is "Nzigone". "Zong" is somewhat regarded as the "Satan"! The Mvett also tells that these gods (in plural, one more time) are "physical" beings that have a life like humans. They all are supreme creator gods and they are capable of feats beyond human understanding. Clearly, today we refer to these beings as highly advanced "Extraterrestrials".

In this chapter, I cannot forget to mention my friends, the **Dogons,** this gorgeous people living on the arid, dried up plateau of Bandiagara in Mali. Why especially not forget them? It is because their cosmogony is utterly fantastic. Indeed they have been, since their creation, holders of extraordinary cosmic knowledge that they pass on from generation to generation without ever having had telescopes or microscopes without any application in superior mathematics.

That being said, the Dogons have their own Genesis and, according to their Dogon ancestors, their creator gods might have come from the Sirius constellation. The Dogons claim they have had the knowledge for millennia of the fact that the star Sirius has two other satellite stars, in other words two "sister" stars with it. From the naked eye we can only see one star and it is only in 1862 that an American astronomer, Alvan Clarke, discovered that there was a second star revolving around Sirius, this thanks to a powerful telescope. The second star was named Sirius B. The Dogons had this knowledge for millennia...let us say, "since always"! How could they know that? Moreover, according to the information they have, they have also always claimed that there was a "Sirius C"! According to the Dogons, their ancestors, their creator gods, might have come from a planet that is in orbit around this third star, Sirius C, which we do not know yet.

But this goes even further. The Dogons have always been in possession of very precise data and of knowledge about Sirius. So, they assert that they always knew that Sirius had a satellite star, smaller than itself, Sirius B, but they specify that this second star, although smaller than Sirius (A), is heavier. This is why they have always called it "Po Tolo" or "Po-Digitaria" according to the name of an African cereal seed they use, also very small and very heavy. They also know that "Sirius B" completes its elliptical orbit around "Sirius A" every 50 years, thus the origin of the celebration of their big feast, the "Sigui feast", every 50 years.

Now these data about Sirius B have been confirmed by scientists of our day. But the Dogons possessed this information since the beginning of their history. They have preserved this throughout each generation on celestial maps of the sky and of Sirius, maps kept by their initiated Priests. In 1960, our astronomers were able to calculate exactly and with remarkable precision the period of revolution of Sirius B around Sirius A and determined that this revolution is made every 50.090 years! The Dogons always knew that!

And the Dogons go even further: they assert that there is one more star... let us say, "Sirius C". They call it "Emma Ya" or "Sorgo", and this star makes a revolution of 32 years around Sirius A, turning on a very eccentric elliptical orbit and which would be perpendicular to that of Sirius B! They have in their possession drawings and maps of these orbits, but above all, they say that this star Sirius C (Emma Ya) has several planets in orbit around it and that one of these planets is the home of their god creator, of their ancestors, who would have come to earth a long time ago aboard the Nomo which, according to their traditions, is an interstellar vessel whose shape is not unlike that of the "Apollo".

Nowadays, many astronomers begin to suspect that there could really be a "Sirius C" revolving around Sirius A. Using advanced equipment, they can determine changes of color of the system. From that, they believe that "Sirius C", as the Dogons say, could have a very flattened orbit, a little like a comet. By using a coronographer eclipsing the strong light of Sirius A, they can now see two travelling objects, but they cannot yet determine which of these objects presents a movement proper to the Sirius system (publication in the magazine "Astronomy and Astrophysics"). The astronomers Jean-Louis Duvent and Daniel Benest of the Observatory of Nice have used computer numeric simulations and their observations reinforce the likelihood of the existence of a third object of a weak mass in the surroundings of Sirius (Publication in the magazine "Ciel et Espace", 1995).

But our famous Dogons have yet more knowledge in astronomy that seems amazing for an African tribe having always lived isolated from any contact with other civilizations. For the Dogons, the chief, the leader of the creator gods is called "Amma", and for them the universe is infinite, but nevertheless measurable. They also say that there exist in the universe an infinite number of inhabited worlds and that they move away from the earth at very high speed in a coiled movement. They add that these coiled movements and elementary structures exist also at the infinitely small level that composes men; that is to say, the infinitely large (planets, solar systems, galaxies, milky ways) has the same configuration as the infinitely small (cells, molecules, atoms) which compose our bodies.

The Dogons have always known the different phases of Venus; they divide the Sky into 22 equal parts and into 266 constellations and assert that Venus has a "companion (which could be the asteroid Toro, recently discovered between Earth and Venus). They also know the four biggest satellites of Saturn, though invisible to the naked eye; but they do not know the planets that are beyond Saturn (Uranus, Neptune and Pluto)...

They maintain that they received their knowledge from a people who came from the sky and who created them, that these people from the sky came down to earth a very long time ago. They further claim that they brought with them vegetal fibres coming from plants of the "field of the Sky" and after they created life on earth, plants, animals, they created the first human couple who will then procreate the eight great ancestors of Humankind. Once their task was complete, Amma and the other gods returned to the Sky on aboard Nomo, their vessel.

This could not be clearer! Polytheism – belief in physical gods (in plural), of flesh and blood, space travellers – is the source of the truth. The Catholic Christian Church hides this truth and keeps us in ignorance in order to continue exercising its power upon men, a power which depends on the ignorance of the masses, on the blind belief of its followers, on an obscurantist supra-ocular belief of mysticism, on the mystery of god, an immaterial and omnipotent god who, in fact, does not exist.

Life in the universe is a trivial phenomenon. There exists in the infinite universe an infinity of worlds inhabited by "humanoids", fruits of a human creation. Thanks to science, there are men who create other men perpetually in the universe...ad infinitum! In black Africa, we have always know this. But because of slavery, religious assimilation, and colonization by the Christian west, with their unscrupulous use and abuse of power, our "genuine religions" that tell of people from the sky who created life on earth with science and art, have been stripped away.

I would like now to turn your attention to the "**AMERINDIANS**", these native people of the Americas, whom Christopher Colombus – believing he reached India – wrongly granted the name of "Indians", a name that remained theirs. I think especially of them because these people also had to undergo something rather similar to what so cruelly hit the African people: genocide perpetrated in the same way by the Christian colonizers coming from the West.

In the cultures of these native "Indians" they refer to what they call "the people coming from the sky". Indeed, according to their traditions today called "Indian", a "people coming from the sky" would have come in the past to teach them what they had to know about plants (biology) and how to live in harmony with Mother Earth and Father Sky. These beings coming from the sky would have also sent them Prophets to guide their people during the past eras. The beings contacted by this "people coming from the sky", the Prophets who so guided them were, among others: **Tenskwautawa, Smohalla** and **Wovoka**.

Many chiefs of these "Indian" American natives believe that the time has come to speak openly about some parts of their traditions, parts that they have been keeping secret until now, that is: their legends and stories concerning the creation and this people from the sky who came a long time ago on earth travelling in their "Thunderbirds", i.e., their spacecrafts.

These chiefs think that it is necessary now to inform that it is men and women of this "people of the sky" who created us, visiting us on the earth, walking among us during a certain time. Then at a given time, they returned to their own world, leaving alone on earth the man they had created so as to let him slowly progress till the day when he would be able to understand everything. At this very moment of complete understanding, the return of the "people from the sky" would be imminent and man would then understand his true origin, the true history of his planet and of his own genesis, in terms of living race.

These native traditions evoke their origin from the stars, the influence of the "people from the sky" in the development of their culture, their spiritual beliefs and their religious celebrations. But also, and above all, they speak of the imminent return of this "people from the sky"... a comeback expected for our time, the time when the colonizer's Church, liar and usurper, will come to collapse.

We Africans must absolutely keep our religious traditions - because they are right - and keep them the most perennial as possible. They are based on "polytheism", the belief in numerous Gods, while in the western world the belief in a multitude of celestial cosmic beings was erased little by little over time and replaced there by "monotheism", the belief in a unique God, created through a lie. That is not correct at all because the general rule that pre-existed before the birth of the Judaeo-Christian monotheism was the veneration of a multitude of Gods, this an ideology that has prevailed throughout time.

In this way, in venerating their Gods, polytheists never considered the leading God, Yahweh, as the only one. Here too we can establish the link with the Torah in Hebrew to show that our black ancestors knew the truth about this plurality of Gods. In fact, Yahweh is in no way alone in the Torah but surrounded by a great celestial court of which the whole, as in the Torah still, is called "Elohim". This word "Elohim" is a plural in Hebrew (the singular being "Eloha" or "Eloah") and "Elohim" means etymologically "those who came from the sky".

We also have to know that the use of "the plural of majesty", the "You" and "We" commonly used in French in place of a singular and only by conventions does not exist in Hebrew semantics. For example, what we hear in France such as "In this day of national holiday, We, the French Republic, conscious of the problems actually suffered by the French people, decided that…and so on and so on" (the usual political cant) is not translatable verbatim, at least, in the Hebrew language.

So, it is indeed a matter of a people, and most definitely this people that are indicated by the word "Elohim". For example, in the very first sentence of Genesis, biblical tale of the creation: *"In the beginning Elohim created the heaven and the earth"* (Genesis I, 1) or still, a little later, in (Genesis I, 27): *"So Elohim created man in his own image, in the image of Elohim created he him; male and female created he them"*. It is indeed that this plan of creation and its realization are the work of the Elohim people and that it is in their likeness, that the scientists of this people "Elohim" (males and females) created the human beings that we are.

Let us observe together, in the next chapter, to what extent our polytheist religious traditions were…and always are…in the truth.

208

21. Judeo-Christian Monotheism: entrapment, trickery, swindle?

«What revolts me in the Church is its dreadful lie, too constant lie, too methodical to find excuses. That there are in the Church, people of good faith, certainly. But then they are imbeciles. And even of those I am wary. Indeed they have moments of lucidity, they see emerging in front of them a howling objection, a leonine difficulty. Common sense, logic, should be to look at it, to realize what it is worth. Well, not at all. At that moment, they close their eyes; they do not want to go ahead, to see further, to control. No, it would be too terrible, to have erred so much, to have been deceived, fooled so much, is this possible! Then their only care is to think about something else. It would be too serious also, ashes and dust, ignorant, to rise up against so many witnesses, wise men, scientists, pure hearts»

-Excerpt from "Journal of a priest", chapter "the Church exposed",
published in 1956 (NRF Gallimard), written by Paul Jury,
Catholic priest having previously left the Church.

But wait, we will now move on to something that could shake you up, cause you to question your identity as Christian, Catholic, just like that. By education, by family tradition, purely out of habit, it is now religiously and politically correct to be Christian, Catholic!

The majority of Africans all read the same Bibles. There are for the French-speaking Africans and 14 main translations of the Bible in French. It should be known that the Bible, of which the original scriptures are in ancient Hebrew, was initially translated into Greek starting from the Aramaic text, then into Latin from the Greek text, to be translated finally into French, and into the other modern languages, beginning with English.

The 14 main translations in French are: those of Crampon, of Maredsous, of Osty, the one said "of Jerusalem", there are four of Catholic obedience; Ostervald, Segond, Darby, Scofield; the New World and "the Synodal one" are of Protestant or reform obedience; the one of OTB that is ecumenical; then there is also the one of Khan and the more recent one, of Chouraqui that are of Jewish obedience; only one was published under the direction of an Academic, it is that of Edouard Dhorme, Bibliothèque de la Pléiade, NRF, Gallimard.

Unfortunately, Africans do not read the version of Dhorme, or that of Chouraqui; they read those of Catholic or Protestant obedience. Well it is a pity for through the translations of Dhorme or Chouraqui, less altered and deformed, they could more easily provide viable links with the authentic religious traditions of their ancestors. The versions most read among Africans are only two in number; the one of Jerusalem in French, and the King James in English.

Thus, Christian Africans and all the other Christians of the world predominantly read Bibles that were recopied many times, retranslated, revised, corrected, and handled by copyists, interpreters, translators and editors of all kinds! This inevitably brings about divergences, inaccuracies, even some "errors" which the majority were introduced deliberately.

But then, is there a key to recover the truth, and if so where is it?

The key is to go to the source. But what is the source?

Well, they are the original Hebrew Scriptures with the names, the original substantives in Hebrew in the text. But beware; to find these original scriptures, they should be sought in "the Torah" (book written in ancient Hebrew and also named "Thorah" or "Tora"). That is where the original texts of the true "Pentateuch" are, together in the first 5 books of the Bible, "Genesis", "Exodus", etc. So what does one see in Hebrew in the Torah, the original Bible? Quite simply, we note there that the word "God" is nowhere to be found in the text! And if there is no word "God" in the original Hebrew Bible, it is that there was never a single God, immaterial, all-powerful!

In addition, as the "Bible" was originally written in Hebrew, it is thus in the Hebraic language that it must be taken into account with all the specificities and characteristics of this language with respect to vocabulary and grammar.

What is the word around which all is articulated in this first Hebrew Bible? This word is a name: the name "Elohim". And the first verse of the Bible, quoted in English at the end of the page in the preceding chapter, here it is now in Hebrew: "Bereshit bara Elohim et ha shamaim ve et ha eretz". This is simply translated into English by "In the beginning Elohim created the heavens and the Earth".

However, no one has the right to destroy a proper name when it is trans-

210

lated. Though different languages are used, a proper name must remain what it is; if not, the entire meaning of a text is altered. One cannot translate Elohim by "God" as to do so would oppose the most elementary deontology. And please do not suggest the idea that this translation is merely a "distraction", for, undoubtedly, this would repeat itself multiple times in each translation and would find itself used in all the translations!

It is truly an error here, yes, a deliberate error programmed in a grandiose way. It is necessary to recognize this because it is more than an error, a fraud, systematized misinformation. And it is exactly what was done! The most moderate of the terms that one can allot to such an action is expressed by the term "incorrect" and that is an understatement. More to the point, it is a total lack of intellectual honesty. To use the word "God" in the place of the word "Elohim", subject of an action verb as important as the verb "to create", is that the same thing? Absolutely not! The difference is enormous: this word and this one alone, voluntarily replaced by another, has lead to extremely serious consequences...reaching hundreds of millions of individuals!

Let us reconsider this word "Elohim" that we find in the first sentence of Genesis, important to say that its placement is "fundamental". Its contracted form is "El", its singular "Eloha" (or "Eloah") and "Elohim" itself is a plural. The Hebrew suffix "im" denotes plurality; it is undeniable and impossible to circumvent this. It should be recalled that the plural of majesty, of courtesy, does not exist in Hebrew, as explained above. It is so true that if one said in Hebrew "the Elohim" ("les Elohim" in French) a pleonasm would be made; it is necessary to use the word "Elohim" alone without the article "the" ("les" in French) preceding it to transform it into a plural. In Hebrew one cannot either say "the Elohas" ("les elohas" in French) for to express that one indicates more than one "Eloha". This twist does not exist. One quite simply says "Elohim;" it is, in this case, the only possible means to express the plural form of a word.

All that is needed to confirm this is to refer to the Larousse dictionary, edition 1965. It defines the word "Elohim" as the plural of the Hebrew word El or Eloha!

"Elohim" is thus a plural word that is often (but not always) used with a singular verb; Elohim said... Elohim made.... In French, words indicating a plurality are also used with a singular verb or plural following the determinant that precedes them. And so it is for words like humanity, family, troop, army, team, group, etc. These words are also not personalized plurals. Traditions common to all Semitic tribes told stories of the group of Elohim and this group of Elohim, was translated in semantic by the construction of the plural noun and the singular verb tense. There are many biblical references to the plural of majesty; this is a pure European fabrication and fraudulent! Once again, this kind of plural does not exist in the Hebraic language. Here are some biblical quotations that show us the bad faith of the bible translators and exegetes, these passages showing clearly that it is people coming from the sky:

> «...and ye shall be as Elohim» (Genesis 3, 5)
> «...the man is become as one of us...» (Genesis 3, 22)
> «That the sons of Elohim...» (Genesis 6, 1-2)
> «verily he is Elohim that judgeth in the earth» (Psalms 58, 11)
> «Yahweh... what is man? ... For thou hast made him a little lower than Elohim «(Psalm 8, 1, 4-5) etc

Thus, this plural word, central to the Bible, indicating the creative entity (one could say that this word "names" the creators), is indeed a perfectly well defined plural that indicates an entity of distinct individuals. In other words, this word "Elohim" designates people. But, why, in Christianity, did the Papacy put it aside, replaced by another one? Why did Judeo-Christian institutions accept it, they too setting aside the literal translation of the original term for one with a completely different meaning? Good question, which also leads us to ask the following: from where does this word "God" come from?

This word first appeared in French in the 9th century. Prior to this it did not exist in French. Compared to the millennia old history of the religions, this is very recent! Its origin is linked to an Indo-European source and its remote ancestor is the famous "Dei" that was used by the primitives in Europe to express the sunlight and other luminous phenomena observed in the sky. One can say that, etymologically, "Dei" meant and always means "light in the sky".

At a given time of their history the Romans adopted the name of Jupiter from the "Zeus" of the Greeks. This name - that of the supreme god in Greek mythology – "Zeus" was pronounced "Zeous" which gave way to "Deus" (Latin pronunciation: "De-ous"). And it is in this way that the French root "Di" emerged; the word "Dieu" god in French was born of the Latin "Deus" (in Latin declension, its genitive is "Dei". We give an example of it in this book by translating the two words "Opus Dei".)

With this word, "God", we are thus very far from an honest translation of the word "Elohim", this central word of the original Bible! On this subject it is interesting to note, because it is surely not without connection, that in the 4th century B.C., Aristotle made his contribution with a completely abstract concept that was popular at the time, the Latin expression that indicates it is even still used today. It is Aristotle who presented the theory of a universe governed by an "engine" (located... one does not know where) in this Great Whole that is the universe. It was the famous "Deus ex-machina", literally "God coming out of a machine", a kind of "Zeus-engine", to which nobody could understand anything but that was supposed to control this whole.

Stated another way, at his epoch Aristotle had come "to modernize" the old Zeus-Jupiter and that hit the jackpot! From there, Aristotle's theory was reshaped by Judaism and Christianity to strongly promote the concept of a "God", eternal, omniscient, immaterial, unique, evasive, invisible, pure spirit and not physical at all. And yet this divine being could be seen sitting on a small cloud smoothing his beautiful white beard, pointing the tip of his finger at his respectful creation...all this to amuse the gallery.

But what became less funny for humanity, was that the "representative on Earth" of this "God" so astutely invented - being then at the head of the most powerful world institution – could, a few centuries later by his own design, declare himself "infallible". Now, seriously! It is so much more comfortable from a seat of power to cast out with a single word those who would be inclined to dispute the prerogatives that one granted himself!

Bravo, African Catholics and Christians, for having given up the humanized Gods, the physical and human Gods of your ancestors, who populate in peace their planet somewhere in the universe in exchange for this product, this "white" concept that misinterprets the original Genesis completely.

By keeping your "polytheism", you would have undoubtedly avoided the great number of wars waged between "believers" of each "monotheistic" religion.

We must recognize that the councils of Latran, of the Vatican, and others still, including the Inquisition tribunals, did all that was needed for the Church to forcibly impose this clouded concept of "monotheism" to the European populations. It is useless to enumerate the details of all the monstrosities that were carried out so that this concept could triumph (to the exclusive profit of a few, unfortunately) Thus emerged the power of the Church and the world power of the Vatican; by camouflaging the truth and by crushing all rebellions, wherever they arose!

Thus how did one arrive at the generalization of a concept based on the idea that there is one "good" God while all others are inevitably bad? You know him well, this "good God". You know it is to him that our charming little ones do their "evening prayer" at the foot of their small bed, the one whose name the vulgar man uses to swear thus committing a serious "blasphemy" that our "good God" will necessarily punish, as "good" as he is. It is certainly true...since the priest said it again in the pulpit last Sunday!

And perhaps now as you read this book, you are thinking, "Nevertheless, all that the priest says it is certainly true". I feel what makes you shudder. Moreover, this "honest priest" in his sermon last Sunday again said to you from the top of the pulpit about this:

> *"Our "Good God", yes, he is good. But beware, the others are "bad" Gods. So I say to you, dear parishioners, believe in the Mother of us all, the Holy Blessed Virgin Mary that will help you and pray unto her Son, the true God, because those who believe in some other Gods than the "Good God" become inevitably bad. One sees each day all the misdeeds that they are able to do, but they will never go to heaven. They will not know the Paradise where the "Good God" reserves a place for you; he is waiting for you, you who suffer here below to unite yourself to his redemptive suffering, you who have been praying to him for so long and with so much enthusiasm"!*

It is interesting to study this works in the everyday life of each one because, most assuredly, it does work. It even works very well for a great number of Africans, this idea of a "good" God invented by the whites. The concept tranquillizes them. They are fed "good words" that reassure them and they find that "fabulous" for it is the right word to say it, here a question of fable, a pretty fairy tale, very well written and played, well fabricated, "virtual" ... to attract you and retain you in the family of their "Holy Church". I am, alas, sorry to tell you, this Church is far from being "holy" and of all that it tells you is not true. Deep within yourself, you know it. One needs only to reflect, listen and look to understand what is the truth. Stop behaving like ostriches; remove your heads from the sand of this "daily humdrum routine"!

Yes, it is really a fable, a story created in all aspects in order to dominate

214

people, even sometimes employing military force of allied countries, since the Vatican "does not have any divisions", as Stalin ironically observed. Yes, it is true, but the cardinals of its government, "the Curia", know perfectly how to use the armies of their many friends, queens, kings, dictators, and presidents of many countries, to their personal profit.

The Church thus succeeded in imposing the idea that its "God" was superior and that its concept of the world was the only valid concept. Its God being "the good" God, the only "good God;" all others without exception are "bad" gods. The idea has been insinuated in the heads of countless people, not only those who gather in "Saint Peter's Square" in Rome, that to believe in "gods" was a serious error and that belief in a God other than theirs was not only bad but was punishable. The ideas was suggested that it was the source of diseases, curses, and even of the presence of horrible "demons", as they say, quite as dangerous and mean as the "gods" themselves, excluding theirs, of course!

Throughout the centuries it was thus obligatory to favour the Catholic Church and its "good God" to avoid persecution! And that pressure worked very well with the support obviously of a great number of "powerful" of this world. One can recall, with an outline of "the material effectiveness" of its method, that in the "Holy City" of Rome half of the buildings, it is said, belong to the Vatican. This information is difficult to confirm, certainly, but as each of us knows, "One lends only to the rich"! Yes, for the Church, that worked very well, but much less for the millions of victims already left along the way, some of which I have outlined in several chapters of this book, and that will be even worse for the millions of victims soon to come.

So much horrid and iniquitous trickery!

In the original Hebrew Bible the two names that most frequently appear are Elohim (2,312 times) and Yahweh (6,499 times). But in addition to these, there are more, for example: Adonai, El-Shaddai, El-Elyon, El-King, El-Bethel, etc.

Once again, the word "God" in the name of which the colonizing Church claims to speak itself does not exist in "the true" Bible, the Torah, the original Bible, insofar as it is this word that basically explains the origin of our humanity!

But let us look at two other plurals of which we have just seen a short list.

First, "El-Shaddai" means "those from above" in Hebrew. And then the plural "Adonai" is also extremely interesting.

According to Judaic laws, it is forbidden for the Jews to pronounce the word "Elohim" as well as the word "Yahweh" because one of the commands dictated to Moses at the Sinai Mount says:

"Thou shalt not take the name of the YAHWEH thy Elohim in vain; for YAHWEH will not hold him guiltless that taketh his name in vain. (EXODUS 20, 7,)

Thus, in their prayers, many Jews read, say, and think the word "Adonai".

Where does this word "Adonai" come from? It is the plural of the Hebrew word "Adon" which means "Master". Thus "Adonai" means "the Masters". Consequently, "Adonai" is quite simply another Hebrew word to indicate "Elohim", this plural which means "the others" or "Those who came from the Sky".

The Catholics, the Church, all of Judeo-Christianity translated the whole of these names by "God", "the Almighty", "the Lord", which is entirely false and yet another grotesque intellectual swindle.

The verse of Genesis (I, 26) where, in the sixth day, Elohim says: «Let us make the man in our image, after our likeness!» this time takes all its meaning within the framework of the traditions of our ancestors. According to them, one can understand it easily; it is normal and even logical since their gods themselves "are humanized".

In certain passages of the Torah (Hebrew Bible), we also see mention of "Benei ha Elohim" which is literally translated as "the sons of Elohim". This also becomes comprehensible in the light of our authentic religious traditions that speak of people coming from the sky.

Especially important is the following passage from the Torah, worth pointing out because the Christian Catholic priests wish to hide it as much as possible for it disturbs them deeply. This passage becomes incredibly comprehensible in the light of our polytheist religions where the gods are humanized beings, physical, made of flesh and blood...thus, "human", as we are.

216

> [1] And it came to pass, when men began to multiply on the face of the earth, and daughters were born unto them, [2] That the sons of Elohim saw the daughters of men that they were fair; and they took them wives of all which they chose. [4] There were giants in the earth in those days; and also after that, when the sons of Elohim came in unto the daughters of men, and they bare children to them, the same became mighty men, which were of old, men of renown. «
>
> (Genesis 6, 1- 2 and 4)

I am particularly partial to this passage. It is a treat to place it under the nose of the African blacks in cassocks, at the service of the colonizer's Religion, at the service of the abominable Rome! How can they understand it if God is unique, immaterial and pure of spirit? Here the sons of Elohim are very clearly mentioned, of people who came from the sky, and of which some of the sons (men of the Elohim's planet) mated with the daughters of men (daughters of earthlings). This proves, coincidentally, that their seed, their sperm, is compatible with the ovules of our human partners...for "they had children with them"!

Nothing can be more logical, for they made us in their image, in their likeness. The Gods, these "sons of Elohim", are thus sexual, they are quite physical, have sexual organs like us, and certainly experience pleasure thanks to the use that they make of them. They saw that the girls of the men were beautiful. One could say that they were excited by the beauty and the charm of the earthlings. Educated by the religions of our African ancestors, this could be easy to understand. But on the other hand, the Church, Christianity, are quite embarrassed by these realities. How will it be able to escape this after all the opprobrium that it poured out in mass amounts of the topic of sex.

Sex is such an important element in the life of humans that to become master of it, to censure it to their liking, quickly became one of their preferred means of coercion to these "prude" Christians according to Paul, "the man of the lie", as he was called by Jesus' parents! Only, as the well-known saying goes, "chase the natural and it returns galloping". Doesn't it? However, sex is indeed "natural" and now that it returns in this biblical verse, what will they give for a twisted, quirky, ambiguous explanation? What will they find to try to escape from this bad step? What fairy tale will they invent to get out of it... while seeking to lull to sleep the little prepubescent children that they would like us to remain?

I can recall at least two times when I posed to committed Catholics the question of these multiple gods and the carnal unions of their "sons" with the "daughters of men". The bishop and the theologian in charge of great ecclesiastical responsibilities whom I had the occasion to question both attempted to reassure me in much the same way: "No, no, there is only one God! All that you read in the Bible is authentic and you must believe it...except this passage, because that one is an error that slipped there inopportunely". I don't have to tell you that I did find the argument a little light...and you?

Our ancestors spoke of "flying calabashes", of "flying silver nuggets", "flying silver bowls" when they described the machines of the "gods" that they saw moving in their African sky. Was this stupid? Not at all. In front of the same display, the Romans spoke of flying "shields;" perhaps the selected object reveals on their part a more quarrelsome temperament than ours...that's all! Once again, let us make a comparison with the original Jewish Bible, the Torah. It speaks of "the glory", the "chariot", "the cloud" transporting Elohim or Yahweh, and also about the "Merkabah" (the flying chariot transporting Yahweh on his throne). In the face of the unknown, each one applies words of the vernacular of his time...what else could he do?

Let us quote as example the three following verses:

> « [16] And the glory of the YAHWEH abode upon mount Sinai, and the cloud covered it six days: and the seventh day he called unto Moses out of the midst of the cloud. [17] And the sight of the glory of the YAHWEH was like devouring fire on the top of the mount in the eyes of the children of Israel. [18] And Moses went into the midst of the cloud, [...]
>
> «(Exodus 24, 16-18)

It is interesting that in the Bible, Elohim and Yahweh speak, act, move and are seen independently of the "Glory" which proves that they are not always inside the "Glory;" it is thus not part of their physical appearance! The word "Glory" in the French translations appears approximately two hundred times, and tries to translate its Hebrew correspondent "Kabod" of the original scriptures in ancient Hebrew. In fact, the very specific meaning of this old Hebrew word was "weight" or "heavy presence".

And the passage of Job 37, 15, 16 and 18 (Dhorme Edition), provides another proof of the activities on Earth of an «Eloah» when Elihou (Job 36, 1) questions Job in this way:

218

«[15] Dost thou know when Eloah disposed them, and caused the light of his cloud to shine?

[16] Dost thou know the balancings of the clouds, the wondrous works of him which is perfect in knowledge?

[18] Hast thou with him spread out the sky, which is strong, and as a molten looking glass?»

It is obviously a solid craft of metallic aspect equipped with an energy source that transports a passenger in the air, being maneuvered at the will of the passenger and it is, additionally, both light and very rapid:

"Here that Yahweh overlaps a fast cloud and goes to Egypt"(Isaiah 19, 1, Dhorme)
"Here, Elohim related to a fast cloud" (Darby version)
"[...] on a fast cloud" (Maredsous, TOB)
"[...] related to a light cloud" (Cramp)
"[...]overlapping on a fast cloud" (Kahn)
"[...]riding of the clouds"(Chouraqui)
"[...] Which overlaps in the celestial heights" (Khan)

We are now at the epoch of aeronautics and space exploration by man. It may be called a flying craft and that does not surprise anyone. Of course, at the time of these biblical accounts, that strongly astonished the primitives who witnessed it...and for a good reason, if they compared this spectacle with what they saw each day! In our times, crafts coming from elsewhere, capable of technological feats incomparably superior to those of the best terrestrial crafts, when they are observed by the eyes of our terrestrial contemporaries, are called "UFOs", "Unidentified Flying Objects". But they are always these same crafts of the gods of our ancestors, the same crafts as those named in the old religious scriptures: "fast cloud", "Glory of Yahweh", "ball of fire", "chariot of fire", "blazing cloud", or "Vimanas", (in the "Mahabarata" and Hindu "Ramajna") for example.

We also read in **Isaiah**, textually in 13, 5 (versions Khan, Jerusalem, Dhorme, Chouraqui):

«They come from a remote country, from the ends of heavens [...].»

And one sees, in Ezekiel, that their machines are capable of all the aerodynamic prowesses, in Ezekiel I, 14:

«the beings were and returned running, similar vision with the light-ning.»

On this same subject, other translations use the following expressions:

"[...] zigzagged"
"[...] thrusted in any direction" [OTB]
"making displacements like lightning"

One can read in the literature of the Kimbanguist Church that on seve-ral occasions during some ceremonies at Nkamba, Kongo-Kinshasa, in the lower Kongo, the Kimbanguists' stronghold where the Prophet Kimbangu began his works and where Kimbanguists have their great Temple, some brilliant celestial spheres appeared in the sky and were observed there by the followers present, that these scintillating spheres remained motion-less, hung in the sky for a long time during the night before disappearing suddenly. It was each time, quite simply, the flying crafts of our creator Gods!

Another interesting factor for the Christian and Catholic blacks: Jesus pre-sents himself in the Hebrew Bible (Chouraqui translation, John 10, 36) as follows: "I am Ben Elohim", i.e., I am child of Elohim. I am child of the Elohim people!

Our ancestors indeed knew the truth! But let us try to explore how Chris-tianity, the Church, could achieve such misinformation and especially by what means it could maintain this lie and camouflage such an enormous deception. To do so, it would be interesting that we study closely the famous councils that were used to build the power of the current Vatican and that of Christianity and how, together, they maintained their mystifi-cation.

By observing the semantics of the Semites people, one realizes quickly that all revolves around the word "El". One could say that "El" or "Elohim" (divinities coming from the sky) is presented as the central reference. In Semite languages "el" is omnipresent as prefix or suffix.

For example, notice the suffix in these names or first names: "Michael", "Gabriel", "Ezechiel", "Israel", "Raphael", "Azael", "Uriel", "Daniel", "Rael", "Gadrael", "Ismael", "Nathanael", etc.

As prefix it is often present in Arab-Semite names such as "El Aziz", "El Abdoul", "El Kadafhi", etc. Further, in Persia, one quite often hears people addressing themselves to the skies by saying "Elhim" or "Alhim" which is very close to "Allah", the most widely used among Arabs. In Babylon, "El" was pronounced "illuh" which later became "illuah", and from there the birth of the Arab word "Allah". In other words, the word "Eloah" of the Jews (singular of "Elohim") is the same one as the word "Allah" of Arabs. "Eloah" means "the one coming from the sky", as does Allah.

The common root of the two words being in the very old word "El" from which the plural "Elohim" is derived bears repeating as it is most important: "those who came from the sky". Moreover, "Bab" in Old Persian means "the Door" and the etymology of "Babel" "the door where the El's came" or, stated more precisely, "Door by where the Elohim came;" better still, "the door by where arrived those who descended from the sky"!

All the qualifiers given by the Bible to Elohim, to Yahweh, demonstrate the accuracy with which our ancestors referred to the visitors who descended from the sky as humanized, human, physical "gods". Indeed, these qualifiers agree very objectively with the human nature, and I quote the following examples: "hai" (alive), "ganna" (jealous), "king" (who sees), and then the correspondents of "demanding", "selective", etc.

Now let us look closely to the name "El-Elyon" that we find in the original Bible in ancient Hebrew. It is quite the precise name of a "divine" being, of a character among Elohim, among the sons of Elohim, therefore among the Gods. His sanctuary was located among the Cananeans in Salem (Jerusalem). The priest Melchizedek was assigned to guard this sanctuary. The true etymology of this name with its generic "El" associated to the adjective "Yon" means loosely but simultaneously as "deep" and "remote" in space and time. One could perhaps speak of him as a "being of the Elohim people who came from afar, from the depths of the cosmos".

And for those eventual sceptics, understand that there is no ambiguity on the distinct natures of "Yahweh" and "Elohim", the two names being often differentiated in the passages from the Hebrew scriptures. Here again, with pleasure, some examples:

«*I will praise thee [Yahweh] with my whole heart: before the Elohim will I sing praise unto thee*». *(Psalms138, 1)*

«*Yahweh*
[...] What is man, that thou art mindful of him [...]?
[...] For thou hast made him a little lower than the Elohim (Psalms 8, 1, 4-5)

"Again there was a day when the sons of ELOHIM came to present themselves before Yahweh, and Satan came also among them to present himself before YAHWEH". (JOB 2, 1)

[...] And Elohim said, Behold, the man is become as one of us, to know good and evil: [...]» (Genesis 3, 22)

It is quite clear, Yahweh is the leader of these people, he has the highest position in their hierarchy, and Satan is an "Eloha" of these same people, as is Lucifer. We can clearly say once more that this is a matter of physical beings coming from space in their flying machines. It is they who our ancestors venerated in our traditional religions, and rightly so, and not an "immaterial unique God" as the colonizer tried to lead us to believe with his diversions and plots.

Let us think for one moment. The Christian Church is completely divided. There are among its core some Catholics, some renovators, other traditionalists; there are Protestants, Anglicans, Orthodox, etc. If there were so many dissensions during 2000 years of Christianity, it is because of one fundamental question, the question of truth. A clear and faultless truth would not bring dispute or divergence within a group. If there were so many divisions among the members of the Christian religion it is because the truth that this religion preaches is deformed. For a very long time, this religion has not espoused the truth; it does not proclaim the "true truth", as our children say. The essential truth that this religion should have brought to humanity from the beginning has been voluntarily occulted by those who had the responsibility of spreading it in the world and, unfortunately today, it is still partially occulted by their successors.

What is important to understand is that the universe is infinite, that there is infinity in time and space, that the universe can have no "center" neither a "beginning" nor an "end" since it is precisely "infinite". However, among our fellow men that could not understand during past epochs, two types of very different reasoning developed:

-    *There are those for whom in their mind "God" is a concept that, in fact, does not mean anything other than "infinity", something eter-*

222

nal, omnipresent and impalpable, but not having any power on the individuals that we are.

-And there are those who hide behind the word "God", a white bearded being sitting on his cloud and that would have created man in his image, that would be the only existing being of all eternity and that would absolutely have all power on the poor and weak creatures that we would be!

But what happened exactly? How could we have misled ourselves in such an absurd concept? Answer: since the beginning, there was an extraordinary amalgam between two concepts, two realities totally different but that were mingled under the same appellation that we have to call by its real name... an "uncontrolled appellation". The Elohim, our creators, had explained to our ancestors, the first men, that there was on one side "infinity", present everywhere, an "eternal" reality (we are part of it, and it is part of us) and on the other hand are the Elohim, "humanoids" having 50,000 years of scientific and philosophical advancements on us and who created us in their image.

Little by little, we attributed to the Elohim the attributes of infinity, which is partly true for they succeeded in becoming "eternals" thanks to their science. And then we attributed to infinity the power to manifest by sending us messengers, our creators. This is also partly true since the Elohim are kind of the instruments of infinity in their creation of intelligent beings similar to them. Unfortunately, we neglected the enormous difference existing between the Elohim and infinity: infinity does not watch us, either directly or permanently and it has no awareness of our individual acts. For the infinity in time and space, whether humanity enters a golden age or self-destructs has no importance whatsoever, no more than our finger molecule that we leave on a scarf while caressing it. Infinity is a concept without identity that cannot have any conscience of our own existence, nor of its own, nor of anything else, for that matter.

We should not transform our creators, the Elohim, as beings that we should venerate on our knees or prostrate ourselves in adoration. No, we should consider them as our great brothers from the infinity that we should love, for we one day would like to be loved by those whom we will be able to create in turn.

The time of blind faith is over; the time of understanding is now...and this

223

always with Love as the constant factor both in the decisions we make and in our actions.

Our creators had seven bases on Earth, seven laboratories, that is why certain scriptures talk about the seven eyes of Yahweh on Earth. In each of these laboratories they created life, including human beings in their image and likeness, and the first man in the laboratory located in the Garden of Eden. Why seven bases, seven laboratories in all? Because in the beginning there were seven different races and in creating life on Earth they recreated on Earth their seven original races. Therefore, there are among our creators in the sky among the Elohim some beings that are black, white, yellow, red, etc. Kimpa Vita and Simon Kimbangu were truthful when they said, "The black man was created by black creators...and there are some Kongos in the Heavens"!

There are those books that the Church has always attempted to hide for there are many truths in those manuscripts, stated or called "apocrypha" (rejected, not recognized, forbidden by the Church). The Church is not at ease in this; the angels are not at all asexual beings, clearly being what we call today extraterrestrials! The creator god: Men? Answer: Yes! And the Church ventured at all costs to eliminate everywhere this fact that the gods are humans. One of these books or Apocrypha manuscripts that bother the Church is pre-diluvial (prior to the deluge). It is the book of Enoch. Let us look closely at Chapter 7,1-2, 10-11, which closely follows the one from Genesis 6, 1-4; the one from Enoch being much more explicit:

> *Enoch 7:1 It happened after the sons of men had multiplied in those days, that daughters were born to them, elegant and beautiful. Enoch 7: 2 And when the angels, the sons of heaven, beheld them, they became enamoured of them, saying to each other, Come, let us select for ourselves wives from the progeny of men, and let us beget children. Enoch 7: 10 Then they took wives, each choosing for himself; whom they began to approach (they copulated with them)... Enoch 7: 11 And the women conceiving brought forth giants.*

If you want to find illustrations proving to what extent flying crafts, spacecrafts, flying saucers, UFOs were present in biblical scenes, throughout time from Moses to Jesus, and even prior to that, go to the following website: **www.nlongi.be** . Their presence can also be seen in Buddha's time and during the ancient Hinduism in the far Orient, as in the stories and miracles surrounding the prophet Simon Kimbangu. Our creators, these beings who "came from the sky", have always been here, were always present, they have always observed the great events happening on Earth and

224

assisted in particular all the prophets they had sent or contacted throughout the different epochs. They are the ones at the origin of the great religions that we know on Earth. Judge for yourself what you see in these illustrations on **www.nlongi.be**!

To conclude this chapter, let us stay in the field of interplanetary spacecrafts and enjoy it with radiant display of testimonies and declarations coming from scientists, cosmonauts, astronauts and political men, all men of renown.

This list of persons and their contributions on this subject, declared or written, is far from being exhaustive. The heaven is not vast enough to receive a vessel large enough to contain all that exists and is known. But I offer to you my selection of a few of these rockets, each one brighter than the next:

Declarations of great and renowned scientists:

The famous physician Stephen Hawking, who was invited to the White House, declared on American TV, on March 6, 1998:
"Of course it is possible that UFOs really contain extraterrestrials as a lot of people think, and that the government hides it".

Doctor Herman Oberth, one of the fathers of rockets, now retired, declared in 1960 to a group of journalists:
"UFOs are conceived and controlled by beings of the highest intelligence (...) There is no doubt in my mind that these objects are some kind of interplanetary spacecrafts (...) I think that some extraterrestrial intelligences observe the Earth and have been visiting us for thousands of years".

Mr. Maurice Chatelain, one of the designers of the Apollo program, responsible for NASA's communications, declared in 1979 that the length of the transmission of the dialogue between the control tower on the ground and Apollo 11 technically allowed NASA to censure some information coming from the astronauts and he even declared this:
"All APOLLO and GEMINI flights were followed from a distance and sometimes very close, by spacecrafts of extraterrestrial origin. Each time, the astronauts would inform "Mission Control" on the ground who enjoined them to keep the most complete silence".

He also declared in other circumstances, that everyone at NASA knew that astronauts were observing UFOs, but that a strict order was given to all, i.e.:
"Never talk about it".

Doctor Dino Dini, NASA space engineer, made a quite stunning revelation during a TV show in Switzerland in 1997 about UFOs witnessed during the Apollo 11 flight:
"Everywhere confusion reigns, during the last war, during the Gulf war, everywhere chaos is triggered, these flying disks appear. They come from stations posted near the Earth (...) Neil Armstrong (the first astronaut to set foot on the Moon) saw objects that were following him, spacecrafts following Apollo, and also some living beings. Some spacecrafts also followed the other Apollo missions. This is an attested reality. We are the ones who hampered global speech, for we were given orders in this regard. We were greatly frightened when we understood the enormous difference between our technology, our science and the one of the UFOs. Thus it is obvious that it leads us to globally give negative opinions. Undeniably, the disappointing fact is that we have no explanation because our science is still practically primitive in comparison to the one of those planets where the spacecrafts come from".

Dr Lee Katchen, physicist, atmospheric expert at NASA, declared on June 7, 1968, that he was convinced that UFOs were of extraterrestrial origins and pronounced the following words:
"UFO observations are so common that the militaries don't have time to take care of it. So they erase them from their screens. The main defense systems (SAGE network) have UFO filters integrated and when one appears, they simply ignore it".

In a memorandum declassified by the Canadian government and dated November 21, 1950, Wilbert Smith writes:
"The subject is of high confidentiality for the US government, more secret even than the bomb H. Flying saucers exist and their operation mode is unknown".

Declarations of astronauts, cosmonauts and pilots:

Scott Carpenter who participated to the Mercury program, declared:
"At no moment while they were in space, were the astronauts alone: they were under permanent surveillance by UFOs".

The Senator Colonel John Glenn, the first American astronaut declared:
"Certain reports on UFOs are well-founded".

Some years later, on Tuesday, March 6, 2001, he also declared on NBC:
"In these glorious days, I was very uncomfortable when we were asked to say things we did not want to say and of denying others. Certain people were asking us, you know, were you alone up there? We never answered the truth, nevertheless we saw things up there, strange things, but we know what we saw up there. And we couldn't really say anything. Our superiors were really afraid of that, they were afraid of a kind of "War of the worlds" and of the general panic in the streets. Thus we had to stay silent. And now we see these things only in our nightmares or perhaps in films and some are really close to the truth".

Major Gordon Cooper declared having seen some UFOs in the fifties as a fighter pilot:
"During many consecutive days we observed metallic crafts shaped like flying saucers, at very high altitude above the airbase, and we tried to close in on them, but they were able to change direction more rapidly than our fighters. I truly believe that UFOs exist and that the true unexplained cases come from another technologically advanced civilization".

In 1985, about 30 years later, Gordon Cooper made a solemn declaration at the UN:
"I think that these extraterrestrial crafts and their crew who visit the Earth from other planets are evidently more technologically advanced than us. I think we need a high level coordinated program to collect and analyze scientifically the data from the whole planet on the different kinds of encounters in order to determine how to best interact with our visitors in a friendly way. We should first show them that we learned to solve our problems in a peaceful way rather than by war, before being accepted as a full fledge member of the universal team. This admission would offer our world some fantastic possibilities of progress in all domains. It seems then certain that the UN has an acquired right to deal with this subject in an appropriate and quick

manner. For years, I lived with a secret, the secret imposed to all NASA specialists and astronauts. I can now reveal that every day, in the USA, our radars spot some objects of which the form and nature are unknown. There are thousands of reports of witnesses and numerous documents to prove it, but nobody wants to make them public. Why? Because the authorities are afraid that people will imagine a species of horrible invaders. Thus the word remains: We must avoid panic at all cost".

The astronaut Edgar D Mitchell, who piloted the Apollo 14 lunar module, declared in 1971:
"We all know that UFOs are real, the question is: where do they come from?

He also declared during a public lecture:
"I am convinced that other forms of life exist in the universe. The question is to know what their degree of advancement is, how many more thousands of years over us. From what I know today, from what I saw and experienced, I think that the proof is positive and much of it is classified 'Top-Secret' by the government".

The Russian cosmonaut, Georgiy M. Grechko, who participated in many Soyuz and Salyut missions declared:
"If I was free to say what I saw in space, people would be stunned".

The commander pilot J. Howard, declared having seen an immense flying cigar accompanied by ten flying saucers and said:
"They must be some kind of aerial crafts from another world".

The commander pilot W"B" Nash declared having seen and observed 6 large flying disks and said:
"I think that these crafts were operated by extraterrestrial intelligence".

Declarations of politicians:

Jimmy Carter, President of the United States from 1977 to 1981, declared during his presidential campaign before being elected as President:
«If I am elected president, I will see to it that all information held by this country on the observations of UFOS is available for the public and the scientists. I am convinced that UFOs exist because I saw one.»

228

Once elected, he did not do anything, but perhaps he could not (?)

Mr. Mikhail Gorbachev, President of the USSR, declared on May 4, 1990, to the newspaper "Soviet Youth":
«*The UFO phenomenon really exists and it must be treated seriously*».

The Admiral Roscoe H. Hillenkoetter, who was the first director of the C.I.A. declared on February 27, 1960:
«*It is high time for Congress to let the truth burst out thanks to public auditions [...] but by the official secrecy and the ridicule, one led the citizens to believe that UFOs are nonsense. To hide the facts, the Air Force reduced to silence its personnel*».

Mr. Albert M. Chop, deputy manager of NASA public relations who was also a spokesman of the US Air Force within the Project Blue Book declared:
«*I have been convinced for a long time that flying saucers are real and of extraterrestrial origin. Moreover, we are being observed by beings coming from space.*»

Mr. Dick D'Amato, specialist in national and international security for Senator Robert Byrd and member of the US National Security Council declared in 1991:
«*... An occult faction of the government, of an incredible power, held secret information on the UFOs and they illegally spent enormous sums of money in this operation.*»

Mr. Nick Pope, civil servant with the Defense ministry of Great Britain, who was at the heart of secret research on UFOs for the government during 4 years, from 1991 to 1994, had created sensation while declaring later:
«*I believe in extraterrestrials.*»

...and he published a book: "Open Skies, Closed Minds". He had access to "top secret" information. His seniors in rank became furious about it, but Mr. Nick Pope did not retract.

22. The true origin of the Gospels of the Christian Churches

« The Virginity of Mary? An aberration.
The Bible? A fabric of lies.
Theologians? Pedants who frown in order to give themselves airs.
No, women are not less intelligent than men.
No, church people should not enjoy such considerable goods but,
content themselves with some broth;
no, Spanish did not do well when discovering America, because they
raped other people's lives. »

- GIORDANO BRUNO (1548 - 1600) -

The word "Gospel" comes from the Old English "good spell" which means "good news" (as in French "Evangile", and from the Greek "Euaggelion"). However, there is one first thing to say about these Gospels: they are all "according to" someone, according to Matthew, according to Mark, according to Luke, according to John. We have no certainty regarding the identity of their authors.

And a second thing: the Christian clergy likes having us believe that when we speak about the gospels it is a matter of a unique writing from initial texts. It is a pity for them but this is completely false! The texts have been reshaped and again reshaped, manipulated and again manipulated. The fact is easily demonstrated by the exegetics who looked into these texts, but the Christian clergy is still skillfully concealing this information. We understand it: if the truth were to be known on this subject... it would not be "good news" at all but, on the contrary, the most appalling news!

Let us quote on this subject the interesting work of Father Kannengiesser: "Faith in resurrection and resurrection of faith" (1974) in which he writes, "We must not take literally the facts about Jesus as reported by the Gospels that are only occasional or fighting works [whose writers...] recorded in writing the traditions of their communities about Jesus".

This is most interesting when one takes into account that none of the authors of the Gospels was an eyewitness of what he has written, none! Kannengiesser refers to fights, but why? Because the Gospels are a selection of texts, a collection of texts, made in a particular context and especially in the context of a struggle between Christian communities, between Judeo-Christians and Paulinians (the disciples of Paul).

231

The evangelical texts we have today are based on the result of an update done 100 years after the death of Jesus, and this following previous revisions which in turn followed earlier revisions, the whole thing, the entire texts being compilations from different sources (in the plural, please!)

These Gospels are not the first Christian documents! For example, the "Epistle of Paul to the Thessalonians" precedes them by at least 50 years. And it must be noted, Paul was judged by his contemporaries as someone who betrayed the thinking of Jesus. All Apostles regarded him as a traitor, yet Paul will become known as the great builder and founder of Christianity as we still know it today! If not for Paul, and later the Emperor Constantine, Christianity would bear no semblance to what it is today, nor the gospels.

It must be said, even if we must say it with deep regret, that this Religion, these four Gospels, most of the texts comprising the "New Testament" constitutes an overwhelming betrayal of the philosophy and teachings of Jesus.

There is no known record prior to the year 140 that relates the existence of any evangelical texts. Around 170, according to the evaluation of O.T.B. Œcumenical Translation of the Bible), appeared a canonical status for these four Gospels. OTB is clearly states that evangelical texts were adapted "to diverse milieus", were answering "the needs of the churches", were expressing "a thought on the Scriptures", and replying "even on occasion to adversary arguments, and" [they were] "collected and put down in writing according to their own viewpoint, what was given to them by oral traditions"!

In other words, quite often these texts were sorted, collected, selected and modified according the "needs" and personal "viewpoints" of those who prepared them.

Nevertheless, at the "Vatican II" council (Rome, 1962-1965), a council initiated by John 23rd, affectionately referred to by Christians as the "Good Pope John", together with the cardinals who composed this learned assembly, all expert liars, Pope John concluded and customarily declared to the world without shame:

« *The Church [...] asserts without hesitation, the historicity of the 4 Gospels that transmits faithfully what Jesus, the son of God, during his life among men, really did and taught for their eternal salvation*

232

until the day he was removed to heaven [...] ».

This is false but, once again, here the lie is particularly blatant and grotesque!

Let us see the reality more closely:

Concerning Matthew, it is now more often admitted that he was not a companion of Jesus, after all, that the author was Jewish, that he used a Palestinian vocabulary and that the text was written in Greek. It has also been discovered that the author belonged to a Judeo-Christian community and that he was at odds with Judaism.

Concerning Mark, it is not the book of an apostle, but the story of someone who was probably a disciple of an apostle (that makes a difference!). There are many Latin references in his text therefore it could have been written in Rome, according to this theory. This text is directed to Christians who do not live in Palestine.

Then, concerning Luke, Kannengiesser gives the following example:

> *"Luke is the most sensitive and the most literary, he has all the qualities of a real novelist"*, his gospel is written in classic Greek without barbarism. OTB says: "The first concern of Luke is not to describe the facts in their material exactitude".

Lastly, concerning John, the most diverse opinions are put forward. OTB says that: "All leads us to believe that the presently divulged text had several authors". Others believe that subsequent additions were made. Total confusion prevails as to who is actually responsible for this gospel. In any case, here, as with the other three authors, we are left with the unknown as to their identities. With this, it is easy to understand why these four gospels are described as "according to" and not assigned the name directly.

It is interesting to remember that, at least at the present state of our knowledge, there is no document written by an eyewitness of Jesus' life, that the gospels are in fact only a compilation of information concerning the public life of Jesus and that this information emanated from oral traditions and documents that have disappeared! Those "documents that disappeared" had been intermediaries between the oral tradition and the final documents.

233

But why did they disappear? And who made them disappear? Could it be those already named above and in particular the Great Roman Emperor Constantine the 1st? The very people that expect us, at all cost, to believe that these gospels are a faithful transmission of the life and words of Jesus, and obviously, the Vatican? Everybody has the right, at least, to ask the question, even those who have no particular ability to investigate for themselves!

The so-called original texts, to which the sophist-theologians often refer, never existed. These are copies dated from the fourth to tenth centuries of our era. The number of copies of previous versions is about 1500, but they are inconsistent. It was possible to identify 80,000 variants and there is not a single page of these so-called original texts that is not a current topic of contradiction. From copy to copy these texts were transformed, modified, manipulated and adapted to correspond to "the needs", quoting the words of OTB. They are full of mistakes and deceptions - several hundreds of thousands are counted - that are easy to identify and that are well known.

The most important collection of these "mistakes" is the "Codex Sinaiticus" that, like the "Codex Vaticanus", dates from the fourth century. It was discovered in 1844 in a library of the Monastery of Saint Catherine in the Sinai. It contains no less than 16,000 manual corrections in all attributed to seven different translators-copyists. Some passages saw three revisions with the passing of time; its final text completely different than the first. Mr. Friedrich Delitzsch, author of a dictionary of ancient Hebrew and distinguished specialist of the Bible has detected more than 3,000 serious mistakes in this text that however belongs to the canon of the Catholic Church.

Normally when we speak about an "initial text", this supposes the existence of, obviously, an initial document. But still we need for it to be really "initial", that it is a matter of a first version and that it can be guaranteed "authentic", that its origin is clear and unquestionable. In the case of the four gospels, virtually none of the text answers to such a definition, not even partially.

We can understand fully the words of Jean Schorer, rector of the Cathedral Saint-Pierre in Geneva, though his words are most blunt: "The thesis that the New Testament is fully inspired from "God" is very simply unjustifiable"

234

All true atheists - the ones seeing "God" as an invention of man - will quite obviously share his opinion, it goes without saying.

But let us go back to the falsifications. On this subject Robert Kehl of the University of Zurich makes this observation: "It often appears that one passage is corrected by someone and then once again by another copyist, translator, in order to receive a complete different meaning, and this according to dogmatic concepts of such or such theological school that must be taken into account. All this made the texts a terrible shambles and deformed them".

The majority of Christians are ignorant. People who form that majority believe that the Bible always existed like it is today and that, from the beginning of its existence, it was always under the form they know now. They think "their" Bible, comprising the Old and the New Testament, always had the texts that comprise it today.

They are ignorant, first of all, of the simple fact that for two centuries the first Christians had no documents at all, except the Old Testament that was written before the birth of Jesus-Christ. Furthermore, at that time, the present canonic version of the Old Testament was not yet chosen nor fixed by the strategists of the Vatican, or at least their predecessors, to avoid an anachronism.

They also ignore the fighting, quarreling, wars, and confrontations that took place for centuries between the diverse schools and varied trends of Christian thinking. In more recent history, we recall the attempted murder of Pope John Paul 1st in 1978 only 34 days into a pontificate that was proving a trend toward reform (we can still dream!) It appeared that he may work toward replacing past deplorable habits ranging from the "Mafioso way" of the past to the condemnation of contraception, all habits admittedly very beneficial to the interests of some prelates but appalling for the general masses.

All these conflicts were caused by serious disagreements on the doctrines to be implemented and the dogmas that the papacy intended to impose on the "Christian people" and on the world, because such has always been the size of its ambition.

The majority of Christians I am speaking about evidently ignores the necessity to introduce a common basis of doctrine promulgated by these violent internal fights. And they also ignore, I have grounds to support,

235

that in order to lever these hazards, this basis was built and set up - only 200 years after Jesus' death - on the plinth of several compromises, in particular: It must be said and made it known everywhere that these "holy" texts are inspired from "God", that these texts we enter in the canon of our church are "the word of God"! Of course, in the eyes of the "high" hierarchy of this church, it went without saying that all the other texts (or all the texts of others, as you wish) should compulsorily be regarded by the whole world as "null and void".

In all fairness and as a simple logic, the ones who distorted the Scriptures to this extent should not claim the right to make theology a science, which has been done for a long time, nor to proclaim that with them, with their Catholic Church, the Vatican is the only one holder of the authentic "word of God". Rather they should be ashamed to facilitate such a false organization.

With regard to their cassocked African valets, the cassock being black or red, those who put themselves in the service of this Mafioso church should be even more ashamed, thinking that they abjured the religion of their ancestors, an honest religion, and abandoned in adversity all their African brothers and sisters, locked up in the claws of this Roman Religion often against their own consciousness!

As we just have seen there is enough to question the seriousness of the information transmitted by "the four gospels". Not only are there numerous differences between the four, it can be noted more easily by consulting "the Synoptics" where all four texts are shown in adjacent columns (one per evangelist) to allow an immediate comparison. Numerous divergences are, of course, about grammar and vocabulary details, others about words, but there are also more serious discrepancies in which meanings of whole passages are modified. Most importantly, in this form, it is impossible to tally with each other the different tables of the genealogy of Jesus.

Moreover, there are facts in these four gospels that contradict each other from one text to another demonstrating well that these texts were abundantly altered with the intention of facilitating the integration of some fragments each time kept to become canonic. And in doing this work, the Church did not want - or did not know how - to take into account the existence of multiple mistakes; it left them in place. We saw above what the concerned specialists where thinking about it! At any rate, how could the Church overcome all these problems with documents whose texts have been altered so many times?

236

WHITE POISON

23 - Paul, builder of Christianity:
Man of lies and of anti-Semitism

"The Catholic Church always acts for its own good, says nothing when it should be talking, I say, when it is getting too dangerous, it hides behind Jesus Christ, exploited for thousands of years"
Thomas Bernhard Austrian writer (1931-1989)

Without any doubt it can be easily said that Paul is, by his apostolic and theological work, the true founder of Christianity. It is Paul who made Christianity a universal religion.

Very particular attention has to be paid to this character because it is he who laid the foundations of Christianity. Likewise, when alive this man was a paradox, and today he remains the most disconcerting paradox of the entire history of religions. He remains the character that began Christianity and the same character that ferociously took an active part in the Jerusalem's Sanhedrin battle against the zealots and other "messianics". He is a double-sided character, who on one side established Christianity on a worldwide plan and on the other persecuted Jesus' disciples! Yes, the founder of Christianity persecuted Jesus disciples as well as members of Jesus' own family!

This is also the only "saint" known as the person responsible for another "saint's" murder, of Etienne, the proto-martyr, stoned in Jerusalem around the year 37. It is reported that Paul, on his way to Damascus in the year 36, had a recurring vision of Jesus, a vision he recounted repeatedly and that threatened to upend his entire life.

Another one of Paul's personal specificities is that he speaks outrageous words with respect to Jews that brings us to ask ourselves this question: was he really himself a Jew? Because he is responsible not only for a break up in the Jewish people but for one within the Christian community. In fact, quickly he presents himself as Simon Peter's rival to whom Jesus told, before leaving Earth "[...] you are Peter and on this rock I will build my church[...]" (MTT.,XVI,18). In this, according to the Gospels recognized by the Church, Peter therefore took advantage of a legitimacy granted by Jesus during his life on Earth.

But Paul himself, perhaps driven by a desire for worthiness, took pride in a legitimacy given by Jesus during a conversation between themselves in private on their way to Damascus in the year 36, therefore after Jesus' "resurrection" and "ascension" into the Heaven. In that Jesus was now "resurrected" and "gone to heaven", Peter and Paul decided to share their respective functions in this way: as the first Christians were from Jewish and Pagan communities, they agreed that the task of converting Jews would be left to Peter, the Pagans' conversion to Paul. From then, the former will continue to respect the Mosaic Law, while the latter will deride the Law of Moses, a law that they estimated archaic and absolutely out of date!

To all his detractors, Paul would oppose systematically the faith in the Christ resurrected and in this way will blur everything. He will further impose systematically his own interpretation of events by taking advantage of this famous singular adventure...still the one he pretends having lived on the way to Damascus.

From this conflict, a true phobia against the Law would give rise unto him and the consequences would be disastrous: the Jews' fidelity to Moses Law will increase their "stubbornness". So, because of Paul, the pagans would begin to consider Jews as vindictive beings, people who transformed "the Law" in occasion of power and not capable of escaping this bad penchant, at the risk of suffocating "the good news" brought by Jesus. This would likewise lead the same pagans to affirm that Jews separate themselves deliberately from the human gender with their own cult and their own eating habits, and to further themselves as misers to "the Law". Ultimately, with a religious climate not unlike that of today, pagans would perceive the Jews as "god-killers" (the ones who killed "God").

In other words, it is with Paul, with the founder of the actual Christianity, in the early years of its foundation that anti-Semitism was born and immediately took its sinister flight.

Let us not forget that the " Nazarene Christians" had been persecuted by non-converted Jews and later by Romans. We have to know also that Paul's predication takes place when the second temple was trembling on its bases, and that at that time the Temple's police were persecuting the original apostles. The latter will start to disappear one after the other, only a small handful will stay, but they will also disappear after the destruction of the Temple of Jerusalem by the Romans in the year 70.

We can easily say that without Paul, Christianity would have probably never existed. But we must add that Paul, by taking advantage of Jesus' teachings and by interpreting it just as he wished - against the Apostolic Council of Jerusalem's wishes, among others - changed the destiny of the world by betraying this Jesus that he had known himself and that he presented after his death as his Master! Jesus, we can say, never had the intention of developing a religion based on such dogmas as the ones imposed by the Christian religion presumably in his name. He, from where he is now, must be displeased, at the very least, to see that Christianity has developed on erroneous interpretations of his teachings. What else can we say!

All of the above the Roman Catholic Church knows very well to be true but it continues to maintain deliberately its monstrous hypocrisy. In this view, we understand much better the diverse efforts by the Catholic Church to delay the publication of the "Dead Sea Scrolls Manuscripts" (Qumran's Manuscripts) and also the degree of its intervention into the research on the Qumran.

There is cause to be seriously suspicious about its actions under the circumstances, considering the rigidity of framework of this research and the consensus of cover concerning the content and dating of those manuscripts, especially when we know how these could destroy the traditional Christian theology, indeed, could even call Christianity's fundamental dogma into question. Do these scrolls contain compromising information that would contradict the Tradition? We absolutely have the right to ask questions, considering that there are no impartial studies concerning them.

Are these scrolls "pre-Christian" or "post-Christian"or both at the same time, as "Larousse Dictionaries" asserts? (The scrolls have been dated both 2nd century B.C. and 1st century A.D.) It would be important to know because if they are from before the Christian era, they jeopardize the original Christ by demonstrating that his words and teachings were from a way of thinking that was already "in the air". And, if they are from the time during which Jesus lived, that would be even more troubling for the Church because the title "master of justice", as mentioned in these texts could have been assigned to Jesus himself, proving that his contemporaries did not consider him as someone "divine". This would be quite embarrassing for the Church because it fervently wishes to compel the whole world to believe that he is "Son of God" and "God the Son", second person of its murky invention: "The Holy Trinity"!

The also very important fact is that these texts would highlight an existing split within the Jesus' disciple's community, with the condemnation by the apostles of the one who was the founder of Christianity: Paul. Further-more, it is interesting to note, he is also referred to as "man of lies" in the Qumran Manuscripts!

From numerous published studies, we are led to believe that the dating of the "Dead sea Scrolls Manuscripts" has been over estimated, that the Church swayed their interpretation to precede Christ in order to not call Paul's teaching into question, a teaching disputed by Jesus' disciples. The foundation of the Church was built on this "Man of lies" and not on Peter, as Jesus had decided when he was still on Earth, this according to the Gospels officially approved by the Church!

Beginning with Paul, "Man of lies", as he aptly named in these precious manuscripts, the first red page (the "blood-red" of the martyrs) of Chris-tianity will be written. But, how could we as black Africans incorporate ourselves into such a page and in subsequent ones that were at least as black as red?

We need the courage to look for and to find the answer to this question, as unpleasant as it could be to know it! Because being a supporter of this religion is like being an integral part of these numerous pages of cruelty (these "red pages" are detailed in Chapter 18). Because the atrocities that we discover in those pages are not only part of the past, they also trouble our present life. They continue to be written with every passing day, every passing moment (the horrible and progressive ravages of AIDS are only one example!). Then how is it that we who suffered so much and continue to suffer also contribute to the writing of these pages that are so appalling for us as well as for so many beings, humans like us?

This Christian Religion, responsible for a multitude of monstrous atrocities over hundreds of years, is not our religion; this is not part of our African heritage! It is a religion coming from the outside that we have been forced into it with blood and with a multitude of deep humiliations.

Fortunately, "the beginning of the end" is at hand for this religious im-posture that has endured more than two thousand years. Thanks to the discovery of the Nag Hammadi manuscripts in Egypt in 1945 and the Qu-mram discovered in Palestine in 1947, the truth now appears. It is due to these manuscripts that we learn that the first steps of Christianity were completely different from what was set forth that we would believe, even today. Markedly different trends existed within this new Religion; the first Christian groups were killing each other in Rome or in Jerusalem like two

242

mafia rival bands in New York at the time of Al Capone.

These manuscripts bring us the proof that Jesus was not "God" in person, that he was married and had descendants, that he did not suffer on the cross, that he was not "the announced Messiah", but that he was a "human Prophet", these notions alone a great deal to consider. The truth is that Jesus was one in a succession of Prophets, several preceded him and others will come after him. Evidence of this can further be found in the "writings" and/or "traditions" of many civilizations...including ours, our black civilization that we can be proud of. What are we waiting for to understand that this is where the truth lays? As soon as we understand it our life will finally blossom into happiness...because we have been created for the happiness of being!

The manuscripts discovered in Nag Hammadi include fifty two different texts of which the nine principal scriptures are the Apocryphon of John, the Apocalypse of Peter, the Apocalypse of Paul, the Gospel of Thomas, the Gospel of Philip, the Gospel of the truth, the Egyptian Gospel, the Secret Book of Jack, and the letter of Peter to Philip.

All these texts were known by the first Christians but were declared as apocryphal and heretic by the Christian Church of Rome built by Paul, the man of lies and later also by the roman Emperor Constantine. The Gospel of Thomas, as it appears in the Nag Hammadi manuscripts, is a text written in the year 140 in Coptic, but it is a translation of a Greek text written in the year 50, therefore long before the four orthodox gospels according to Mark, Luke, Mathew and John, two of which even date back to the year 110. At the time of the Roman Emperor Constantine and the Pope Sylvester possession of the Nag Hammadi heretic texts were punishable by death! Why?

24. Jesus: the lie surrounding his sexual life, his succession and his "divinity"

«The disarray of the Christians comes in great part from the lack of information on the part of the theologians and historians of the Church which, in order to deny the facts susceptible of provoking a scandal, operate in two ways: either they distort the facts and make them say the opposite, or they camouflage the truth.»

Joachim Kahl, Doctor of theology, University Philippe Marbour, Germany-

The two key persons who were in great part responsible for the image of Christianity as we know it today are, without any doubt, Paul, previously Saul the Pharisee, who will bring Christianity to the level of a universal religion (chapter 23 of this work is devoted to him entirely), and also the ambiguous personality who was Constantine, the Roman Emperor, "Constantine 1st the Great", who reigned during the 4th century from 306 to 337.

We must first understand that Constantine was the Great Master of the official religion, the pagan cult of the invincible sun (in Latin, "Sol Invictus") in Rome prior to the arrival of Christianity. During his reign, Constantine suddenly faced a serious problem: the sudden boom and the rapid expansion of Christianity in the middle of his Empire, where Christians and pagans confronted each other; the occasioned risks of instability and divisions in the midst of his Empire.

Constantine was a pragmatic businessman. He understood that Christianity was expanding more and more and that he was best suited to join sides with that new religion that was taking off like a shot. From that moment his only question was: "how do you convert the pagans to Christianity?"

Perhaps this discerning emperor was only interested in power; perhaps he was also inspired by the illustrious example of Paul, "the liar". At any rate, the most formidable solution he could arrive at to resolve the problem was to pretend to be himself inspired by "God" and converted to Christianity, which was simply the use of a political trickery on his part since serious historical clues prove that in reality he was only baptized to Christianity much later, on his death bed!

In order to reach his desired goal, Constantine resorted to skilful ruses, establishing compromises and realizing the fusion of important dates as a way to introduce rituals and pagan symbols in developing Christian tradition. In other terms, he comes up with a crossbred religion, a hybrid religion, understandable and acceptable by all his subjects. By looking at it closely we can see that a great number of pagan traces still exist today within Christian symbolism, and most of them are signed by the hand of Constantine, for example:

The solar disc used by the Egyptian gods for displacement has become the halo of the Christian saints
The mitre
The altar

The Eucharist (by eating the body of Christ-god)
At first, Christians were honouring the Jewish Sabbath (logical since Jesus was a Jewish rabbi!); their day of rest was then on Saturday. It is Constantine who moved it in order to make it coincide with the celebration of the pagan god "Mithra" (solar god of ancient Iran). So the great multitude of "ignorant" Christians, indeed "uncultivated", celebrate each Sunday, the day of the sun, by going to the dominical service without knowing why, even today. (note "sun" in the word "Sunday" in English, "Sonntag" in German, "zondag" in Dutch to designate "Sunday" which means, literally translated to French: "Day of the Sun"). In addition, these same Christians meanwhile practice lots of pagan rituals like receiving the Eucharist without ever being conscious of what they are doing, or why.

Such behaviour is so ridiculous as to be comical. It only deserves great shouts of laughter!

The Roman Emperor Constantine simply used the figure of "Jesus" as he did with Christianity for political ends, but by doing so he has shaped the face of Christianity deeply and for a very long time...since it still exists today!
In order to achieve his political goals, Constantine would convene a council. It will be the first ecumenical council of Nice (in 325), the "credo" being already, more or less, the one espoused by Catholics today! It should be mentioned that Pope Sylvester, the "pontiff" at the time, was not present but sent two delegates to attend the council. But in short, even if Constantine was only the President of honour of that Council and Ozius of Cordue was the presiding President, it is Constantine who, in fact, was the true

246

director, the primary decision maker, in short the presiding President...he was the one.

It appears that during this assembly, that Constantine ordered and financed the compilation of a New Testament. This commissioned work would exclude from all the Gospels all information referring to the human aspect of Jesus. It was imperative for him that Jesus appears to be "divine" even if it meant to adapt the text to achieve that goal: Jesus must especially not appear to be a mortal or a man amongst men, having lived a manly life as any other man. To this end, the gospels showing the human aspect of Jesus were gathered, put aside, destroyed, and burned! We can say with certainty from that point on the original life of Jesus was totally banished. And Pope Sylvester remained quiet; he agreed, in fact, that it suited well the Church of Rome.

When a Christian talks to me about the New Testament, I laugh and answer: "Oh yes, you mean Constantine's Bible"! (Indeed we dedicate in this work the entire Chapter 22 to the true origin of the Christian gospels. It is truly enlightening, as you can judge for yourself!).

So, the New Testament would have been in great part written and compiled according to the specifically well defined political program of the Roman Emperor Constantine the 1st for whom the "divinity" of Jesus was to be promoted, that influence would consolidate the imperial power of Constantine, a power nonetheless already well established thanks to his numerous military victories.

It is that Roman Emperor, a bloodthirsty murderer, (he assassinated his wife and his own son) who inaugurated around 327 the first Vatican basilica, the Saint-Peter Basilica, erected on his command and of course, he will be later on canonized by the Church!

It is obvious that a part of the original story of Jesus was banned in this manner as Jesus does not appear in text as a man amongst men.

Let us consider famous painter Leonardo da Vinci (1452-1519), a great mischievous joker who was, according to several sources, a flamboyant homosexual, everything but a good "follower" of the Church. One of his most famous paintings is "the Last Supper" (the last meal of Jesus with his 12 apostles). We should examine this painting very carefully as several "initiated" persons have discreetly concealed in their works of art (paintings, writings, etc.) certain symbolic gestures which only they were aware.

That famous painting was intended to portray 13 men, Jesus and his twelve apostles, during the last meal. But at closer inspection of the painting we see, at the right hand of Jesus, a woman, not a man! It is a young and pretty woman, sensuous; she has a magnificent head of red hair and her hands are delicately poised on the table! Who is this woman? And what motive would a man like Leonardo da Vinci have for drawing her in that painting? What message did he want to transmit by doing so? What is there so important surrounding this woman and consequently also surrounding the figure of Jesus?

We could surmise that this young woman may very well be Mary Magdalene, who was not a prostitute as they would like us to believe but likely the outright companion of Jesus, in other words his "wife", the woman he was married to!

Mary Magdalene represents one of the most nagging nightmares of the Vatican, of the prude Catholic Christian Church. A large scale campaign of slander must have been organized in order to portray her as a prostitute in order to mask, perhaps, a secret that would bring the Church, Christianity and the Vatican to collapse!

Look closely at The Last Supper by Leonardo da Vinci, to the right of Jesus where he has painted a companion of Jesus, probably Mary Magdalene. During the time of this famed painter, the symbol for femininity was the "V" from Venus. And to illustrate in a subliminal way that it is a woman in his painting, Leonardo da Vinci shows us a perfect "V" between Jesus and the person sitting on his right. Jesus had a wife, a companion, several women, and several companions! Jesus was a Jewish rabbi, he was a Jew; and in those days Jewish society proscribed celibacy. This is a fact!

Many Gnostic gospels in the Coptic papyrus of Nag Hammadi and the Aramaic manuscripts from the Dead Sea, such as the Gospel from Philip, relate amorous physical relationships between Jesus and Mary Magdalene. Jesus and Mary Magdalene more than likely had sexual relations together! And it is also likely that Jesus had other companions or mistresses. It seems that there is amongst those apocryphal gospels, the gospel of "Mary Magdalene". Oh, yes! In that gospel, Peter's jealousy toward Mary Magdalene is noted. It is Peter who cannot accept the fact that Jesus loves Mary Magdalene so much, that Jesus loves her more than everybody else, and that he has accepted her...but for what and in what capacity? Quite simply, knowing his end was near, might have given the succession of his movement, of his Ministry to Mary Magdalene, to a woman! Quite possibly!

Jesus had completely revolutionized the Jewish customs of his times. We must note that the said customs were based on the Mosaic law that discri-

248

minated against women, subjected them to the contempt of men, these men were to beware of the woman "temptress", "source of evil". It was even imposed on them to display disgust for the "impure" woman. And ultimately, the Mosaic law decreed that only boys were to be schooled, the sons (besides some still continue to apply that precept to the letter!) On the other side, Jesus enjoyed being surrounded by women who tended to him; and the women surrounding him were numerous: Mary Magdalene, Jane, Suzan, Mary Salome, Mary the sister of Martha, etc.

But amongst all those women he clearly had one "chosen", a regular companion, Mary Magdalene, whom he loved deeply...to such a degree that he brings her more teaching than to his apostles...and they are jealous of her, particularly the apostle Peter who does not hide it and cannot tolerate it.

We should be clear about this: the first community of apostles following the death of Jesus probably should have been directed by a woman. Would Jesus have entrusted his succession to a woman and that woman would have been called Mary Magdalene!? In that case Jesus would have in this way reinstated all women discriminated against for such a long time by the sexist Jewish Mosaic law.

And in his painting " the Last Supper", (refer to the illustrations on page X of the central note book) Leonardo da Vinci apparently illustrates the feelings of Peter towards Mary Magdalene. To the right of Mary Magdalene Peter appears leaning toward her while holding his hand in a menacing gesture as though to slice her throat with a knife! Furthermore, between the two apostles to the left of Jesus there is a hand surging out holding a dagger. When counting everyone's arms, we see that this hand does not belong to anyone; this hand is anonymous; it is without a visible body in the painting but it seems to be directed towards Mary Magdalene! Explanation: is Mary Magdalene going to be a person to be eliminated after the death of Jesus; will she be killed? Will the Apostles bring about her demise following the death of Jesus?

Neither the Church of Paul or the Church of Peter were the legitimate succession of the Ministry of Jesus. The only legitimate Church was probably the one of Mary Magdalene, the one chosen by Jesus!

We should also remember that Mary Magdalene was very poor, but, nevertheless, a princess from the tribe of Benjamin (one of the twelve tribes of Israel), therefore from royal ancestry. And Jesus was from the house of David, descendant of Salomon, king of the Jews. So we had here two lineage of royal blood united through marriage, united as a couple!

Is it a simple fact that Jesus certainly had a rich and full sexual life, that Mary Magdalene was his wife, his regular companion and that Jesus maybe had named her to succeed him, in order to direct his Spiritual Movement in case he was to disappear. Is this one of the facts the Church, the Vatican especially, was in earnest to conceal, to keep secret, as with certain Secret Societies or secret Orders? Most likely! Was not Leonardo da Vinci the Great Master of a Secret Order, priory of Scion!

All the Great Masters of the Priory of Scion were libertine on the sexual level. Two of the Great Masters, Leonardo da Vinci and Jean Cocteau, were homosexuals of great appetite. Leonardo da Vinci renders, I believe, both secretly and symbolically, a great honour to the original teachings of Jesus, to libertine sexuality, to guilt-free sexuality, in another one of his famous paintings, "the Jocund" or, more precisely, "the Mona Lisa".

We should look more closely at this painting as well and ask, why is it famous? The mysterious face and the famed smile of the Mona Lisa (the Jocund)...what lies behind that smile? Well, the male god of sex and pleasure of the ancient Egyptians was "Amon" (interesting that a popular brand of prophylactics is called Amon) and its female counterpart, the goddess of fertility, of pleasure and of sexuality was Isis. So on one side we have Isis of which the ancient pictogram was L'ISA and on the other side AMON... AMON LISA... and so it evolved, the "MONA LISA".

I personally believe here that Leonardo da Vinci was winking secretly to the sexual divinity, to orgasm, to pleasure, to the union between feminine and masculine by painting a figure somewhat androgynous, half man, half woman, the Mona Lisa. We might even say that he has painted a self-portrait (there is a striking resemblance between himself and that of Mona Lisa), the young homosexual Leonardo da Vinci often disguised himself as a "drag queen" of the time!

But we understand why the Church and the Roman Emperor Constantine tried to slander the person of Mary Magdalene; she presented a formidable obstacle to their false affirmation that Jesus was "divine"!

The Christian Catholic Church continues to lie, continues to manipulate the masses by ensnaring them in lies. The Pope John-Paul II was a learned person but he stubbornly lied along with the rest of the higher officials of the Vatican. They are all lying, from A to Z. Their foundation – based on a "divine" Jesus who would never have associated with any woman on earth – is just as stupid as it is false: it is a wilful lie!

We should also take notice that many esteemed people, including Professor Geza Vermes of the renowned University of Oxford stipulate that "The gospels maintain a complete silence about the marital status of Jesus. We have here an unusual situation in the antic Jewish world that would deserve a detailed inquest"! Nowhere is there an allusion to the ultimate celibacy of Jesus...nowhere!

An amusing account in the fourth gospel is the story of the wedding in Canaan where Jesus is undoubtedly present but where the groom and the bride remain completely anonymous, so insignificant that their names are not mentioned...very amusing! Moreover, Jesus is present on this occasion at a time when he has not yet entered the "public" life described in the Bible. More to the point and quite interesting, it is his mother at his side, at closer inspection of the account, who rather seems to be the hostess, tending to guests' needs, ordering wine and other instructions of the servants! We have always been brought to believe that Jesus and his mother were only guests at that wedding, but with another look, it could very well be that it was the wedding of Jesus himself! It is at that wedding that Jesus made his first "miracle", the changing of water into wine. The head-waiter having tasted the new wine, declares, "Call the groom" and tells him "any man serves first the good wine and, when everyone is drunk, the bad one. You, you have kept the good wine for now"! It is clear here that the major-domo is speaking to the "groom"...so to Jesus?!

We can be grateful to that Egyptian peasant who found in December 1945 near the village of Nag Hammadi in Upper Egypt a clay jar containing thirteen parchments wrapped in leather. Some of those parchments of Nag Hammadi shaped the very first Christian literature and in no way reflect negatively on prior standing of the gospels. Quite to the contrary, because they have not been subject to reshuffling or to alterations they are much more faithful to the historical truth than the falsified gospels.

What can be discovered in these manuscripts? In Mary Magdalene's gospel we can clearly read that Peter is jealous of Mary Magdalene and he even questions the other disciples by asking them: "Are we really going to have to listen to her? Did he really prefer her over us?" The gospel of Philip in the manuscripts of Nag Hammadi says the following: "the companion of Jesus was Mary Magdalene. Jesus loved her more than the disciples and often kissed her on the mouth. The other disciples, he points out, were offended without trying to hide their disagreement, and asked Jesus: Why do you love her more than each one of us? And Jesus answered: Why should I not love her more than you?" Let it be clear, Jesus had a companion. He was probably married, with a sexual life certainly well endowed, as all prophets had.

The main thing to remember from all of this is that part of the history of Jesus is one of the biggest campaigns of world disinformation. Shame on the Vatican, shame on the Christian Church in its entirety for deliberately abusing the human credibility!

It is also interesting to note that the ancient Judaic traditions contained sexual rituals inside the Temple of Solomon where followers sought the "cosmic Orgasm" which allowed them to be "one" with the universe, with the cosmos, by mating with priestesses, hierodules. Let us note here that the black African Prophetess Kimpa Vita, around 1700, engaged in sexual rituals during the religious ceremonies of her spiritual Movement (for this she was, obviously, declared a heretic, a witch, and was burned at the stake with her baby in her arms with the care of the "holy Catholic Inquisition"!)

Jesus perpetuated a teaching based on the notion of the awakening of the spirit through the awakening of the body and the importance of pleasure and enjoyment, facilitating one's ability to open up the spirit to the cosmos, to infinity.

Another thing we can note is that Jesus could very well have bequeathed the direction, the pedagogy of his ministry to a woman, Mary Magdalene, because he was a "feminist". He certainly must have insisted on the importance of the feminine values and femininity for the blossoming of human society. In other words, he must have predicated that femininity be sacred and vital.

Consequently the monotheist religions that discriminate and lower the women today (Christianity, Islam and Judaism) wander from the truth and are "sexist", "machos" and "discriminating". They violate an original teaching that they have betrayed, mutilated, eradicated, changed or refused in order to soil the humans with a feeling of guilt and encumber their life with heavy taboos regarding sex, pleasure, sensuality and nudity of the body. The deformed teaching given us is certainly grotesque, but mostly false!

24. Jesus: the lie surrounding his sexual life, his succession and his "divinity"

WHITE POISON

25. The Grand Secret

I will now reveal to you what is, according to my convictions, the ultimate "secret", the one that lies at the highest level of the Catholic Church and at the highest level of some Freemasonic currents and Secret Orders. Of course, this secret does not involve the people at the bottom of the ladder, but those at the highest level in the hierarchy, those who know and possess the secret knowledge and whose mission it is to keep them secret. They are a few people, strictly selected, "high-ranking" in civil society, most of them very wealthy, and often at the head of a country or in a "high-ranking" position in the Vatican.

Besides, among the loges that haunt the halls of the Vatican, we can recall the famous P2 loge that created a scandal in the 70s and 80s with, among other things, the laundering of dirty money and the enormous financial misappropriations that not only led to serious tremors at the Milan stock market but also to the death of Milanese magistrate Emilio Alessandrini, assassinated on January 29th, 1979, shortly after he opened an investigation on the Banco Ambrosiano. Giorgio Ambrosoli, manager of this very "Vatican" bank was also murdered shortly after and his boss, Roberto Calvi, (a very "good friend" of Cardinal Giovani B. Montini, before he became Pope Paul VI) "had committed suicide" under a bridge of the Thames in London on June 17/18, 1982.

In fact, David Yallop, who reported the information above in his book written in 1985, specified that the investigation on the "Vatican bank" leading to the death of Magistrate E. Alessandrini had still not been reopened. Of course, we know that the legal system needs "some time" to get started, but still more than six years to find a successor to a murdered judge... even if we admit that candidates to such a succession are not numerous, it is still taking a rather long time for justice to move along, wouldn't you agree?

This secret so important that only "great leaders of this world" would be allowed to know it, well, here it is:

Long ago, an extraterrestrial civilization much more advanced than our own came to Earth and created all life forms, including human beings, whom they created in their own image and likeness, thanks to a perfect mastery of DNA and genetic engineering. They were mistaken for gods by our primitive ancestors, and now, in all ancient civilizations, we can find traces of their presence on Earth. They were at the root of all the old religions on Earth.

Indeed, at one point, after cohabiting with the men and women that they created on Earth and after procreating with them, both human species being sexually compatible with one another, they decided to leave the Earth.

They then sent, or contacted several men and women on Earth, who became their messengers, their Prophets. It is they, the known male and female Prophets, who were at the origin of the religious movements, some of which became the major religions of today, with millions of followers.

All of these Prophets came at different times, each according to the specific circumstances of their time. Today's era has just begun. It follows "the Age of Pisces" and is called "the Age of Apocalypse" (from the Greek word "Apokalupsis" which means "revelation"). But why "revelation?" Because it is this era, our era, in which we will see the birth and the arrival of the last of the Messengers on Earth, the "Messiah" as foretold in all traditions and religions, the one who will completely lift the veil on the mystery of god.

That is the fabulous secret: a new revelation awaits us!

It will be the last revelation brought to our humanity by our creators. Therefore, it is extremely important for each of us to know about it. Considering all the consequences of such information, it would be criminal to keep it secret.

This last messenger, the "announced messenger", the one who brings the revelation, is already here, but people in the Vatican and some in the Freemasons refuse to acknowledge him. Even worse, knowing who he is, they may try to eliminate him, because all these "high-ranking leaders", whether in the Freemasonry or the Vatican, are afraid of what he is going to reveal, fearing that the worldwide knowledge of this message will put their interests in jeopardy and cause them to lose their heinous powers, powers built over time on the "mystery of God", and constantly reinforced with all their secrets.

Here are the truths they dedicate themselves to concealing from you in order to maintain their power:

256

a. There is no single, immaterial and almighty God;

b. We have been created by physical beings from space;

c. The one we call Yahweh or Allah, is the president of the "Council of the Eternals", i.e., the "government" of the planet of our creators;

d. The one named Satan is the leader of the opposition party on this planet, and is sometimes called upon for consultation by Yahweh himself.

But Satan has always fought against this experimentation by their scientists, venturing on Earth to create human beings like themselves, "in their image and likeness" as written in the Torah and the Bible (and also in other "sacred books").

The one known as Lucifer is the one who led on Earth a group of creators and who many times disobeyed the directives of their mother planet, especially after they were forbidden to create humans in their own image. His group, nevertheless, achieved this creation, giving birth to our very first ancestors.

This group also dismissed the ban of revealing to the first created humans how they had been created.

Because of their multiple violations, the members of this group were exiled from their mother planet for awhile and, as punishment, were condemned to live on Earth with the humans. This is why this group is often symbolized as the "Serpent" crawling on the terrestrial ground.

However, these incorrigible extra-terrestrials who were forced to stay on Earth, these disgraced angels called "Nephilim" in the original ancient Hebrew Bible, disobeyed another order one more time, that of having sexual intercourse with their creation. The result of these unions left a progeny on Earth called "Gibborim" in the original ancient Hebrew Bible.

The "great initiated" were determined to hide all these truths from us. Also know that a few prophets were hybrid human beings, i.e., half human and half extra-terrestrial. This is a logical result of inbreeding by inseminating a woman of the Earth with the sperm of one of the extraterrestrial creators. Or the opposite is also possible, i.e., by sexual intercourse of a woman from their planet with a man from the Earth. As mentioned, these unions can result in the birth of a child; for instance, the beginning of Shintoism in Japan where their first Emperor was born from the union of an extraterrestrial woman and a man of the Earth.

These so called "initiated" also know the explanation of many things that remain "mysterious" to the public. For example, they know:

a. That behind all the miracles accomplished by the Prophets of Old, there is the intervention of these beings from another planet who, thanks to their thousands of years of scientific advancement on us, can easily accomplish what we can only blissfully call "wonders" because of our embryonic scientific knowledge!

b. That in books, tales and/or artistic works, everything that portrays or talks about "cherubs" or "angels", refers to this People, these physical beings of flesh and blood with a physique similar to that of our children's, and whose planet is not in our solar system, but in our galaxy.

c. That the inhabitants of this planet, for a long time already, have been traveling to observe us; their spacecrafts have been noticed in the sky since Antiquity. Over the centuries, they have successively been called "flying chariots", "fireballs", "cloud of fire", "glory of Yahweh", "fast cloud", "vimanas" (in Hindu scriptures), "Merkabah" (in Judaic language), "El Boraq" (in the Koran), "solar discs" or "flying suns" (in ancient Egypt and among the Mayas, Incas and other Aztecs).

These are the same spacecrafts that today we commonly call "UFOs" or simply "flying saucers", referring to ordinary objects, just as Roman soldiers called them "flying shields". All these vehicles – because that is what we are talking about – are the spaceships of these particular extraterrestrial peoples who created us. They could also be those of other extraterrestrial peoples authorized by our creators to come and observe us.

Another important thing that these "great prelates of the Roman Curia" or these "Great Masters of the Masonic Loges" know is that the last of the Prophets must be born in the West. They are perfectly aware of his country of origin, France. The Vatican even helped the antichrist, Hitler, to try to find him and kill him, this "last of the Prophets".

Once more, in all its cruelty, history repeated itself: the king Herod tried to find and kill Jesus, but since he didn't succeed...

> " Then Herod,[...] was exceeding wroth, and sent forth, and slew all the children that were in Bethlehem, and in all the coasts thereof, from two years old and under..." ,(Matthew II, 16)

Before him, the Pharaoh also tried to find and kill Moses, but the Pharaoh's daughter managed to "save him from the waters". There was also a similar story around Krishna, "avatar" of Vishnu in the Hindu Pantheon.

And in the middle of the last century our humanity has seen a redoubtable new wound open up (this time, perpetrated on an industrial scale!): the holocaust of the Jews. One of the main reasons of this absolute horror was precisely to look for the "Messiah". The obvious goal of the promoters of this vast action was to kill this "future nuisance", in order to change the course of human history.

The "initiated" Jews know full well what the motivation of this new massacre of their own people was and they also know that the Vatican was the Nazis' accomplice in this annihilation attempt...or perhaps the Nazis were the Vatican's accomplices. Who knows? In any case, Hitler had a passion for prophecies regarding the "last of the Prophets". He knew where and when he was supposed to be born. It was at a time when he, the Fuhrer, would set out to conquer the world (Herod was also possessed with the Prophecies regarding Jesus!). In addition - and this is one of the best hidden aspects of Hitler's life - the German dictator, known as a good Christian and keen on esoteric philosophies, was secretly fascinated by UFOs and everything related to extraterrestrials. The Nazis searched all over France in vain, hoping to find the one their Fuhrer was looking for. Unfortunately, they now know, beyond a doubt, that their search failed, despite the deaths of countless innocent people.

In fact, this last messenger, also announced by Simon Kimbangu, will reveal to the world in simple language, who these angels, "Cherubs" and "Seraphs" (in Hebrew: "Keroubim" and "Seraphim") mentioned by our African Prophets were, who these small beings that thousands of people saw in the streets of Kinshasa were, who fought the colonial army to help the Congolese People free itself, and lastly, who our humanized gods (in plural!) precisely were.

He will bring us, terrestrials, "the Truth" that most of us are waiting for.

He will not talk in the name of a unique and immaterial God, but in the name of an entire People, in the name of Gods (always in plural). And, for Africa, he will engage in a discourse that will encourage Africans to find their roots, to decolonize themselves, and to leave and abjure the Christian and/or catholic religion which is nothing but a scurvy masquerade.

Yet, these "initiated" we mentioned previously, are perfectly aware of everything I have just explained to you! They know that the coming of this "last of the Prophets", the arrival of this ultimate "messenger from the sky" will mean the end of Christianity. They know it and this makes them tremble and afraid. In fact, seeing the Pope's current conditions, I do not think I am too far from the truth when I say he is shaking. Actually, that is what he does all day long to such a point that I wonder how he can hold onto his instrument when he has to satisfy an urgent need. He shakes so much that he must spray all over the bathroom. He must find it difficult to hit the spot!

All these "high dignitaries", or at least the people declaring themselves as such, know that the collapse of the Church is predicted, and that in the near future we can expect a contact between our extraterrestrial creators and us, because they will officially come back when their current Ambassador on Earth, the true "Messiah", will have achieved his mission.

But why do these initiated people try to hide the truth? Why do they try to change the course of history since stopping this course is an impossible mission, and they know it? What pushes them to act in this way? What is their profound motivation?

Furthermore, they are fully aware of the grotesque lie around what happened on October 13, 1917, in Fatima. They are aware that the dance of the sun as described by a crowd of more than 50,000 people – therefore a huge number of witnesses – was neither a miracle nor a divine apparition, but instead, the apparition of a shiny aircraft, a spacecraft. Many people gathered at the place where three herdsman claim to have seen the Virgin Mary appear before them. And indeed, something out of the ordinary happened in the sky on that day. Would you like the description of a witness? This person wrote his testimony a few days after the event. His name is Mr. Jose Proenca de Almaeida Garrett. At the time, he was professor of medicine at the Coimbra University. Here is his testimony:

> *"It was still raining around 1PM, when three children arrived where the apparitions took place. Around 1:30PM where the children were, a column of thin, fine and bluish smoke, which extended up to perhaps two meters above their heads, then faded at that height. The smoke dissipated abruptly, and after some time, it came back to occur a second time, then a third time..".*

> *There was no fire, and then around 2PM, the crowd looked at the sky, towards this "Sun" which dissipated the dense layer of clouds. ... I turned around toward this "magnet" which attracted all the stares, and I could see it, like a very clear disc, with its sharp edge, bright and shiny which gleamed without hurting the eyes.*

> *It appeared as a flat and shiny disc, carved out of a pearl shell. It did not look like a contemplated sun through the fog, there was none at that time, for the disc was not obscured, nor diffused or hazy, it stood out clearly in the sky, with a sharp edge, like a large game board. The pearl-like disc was doing flip flop maneuvers. This was not the twinkling of a star in all its brilliance. It turned on itself with impetuous speed. Again, we could hear a clamor in the crowd, like a cry of anguish. This blood-red 'Sun', in fact, kept its rapid movement of rotation, seemed to free itself from the firmament, and suddenly plunged towards the Earth, threatening to crush us with its fiery mass. These were terrifying seconds.*

> *Busy staring at this 'sun,' I noticed that everything darkened around me. I looked around me, and then far away to the horizon, and everything was in the amethyst color. The objects, the sky and the atmosphere all had the same color. A big purple-blue oak was rising up in front of me, and creating a thick shadow on the ground. May others try to explain this".*

Other official documents of testimony allow us to claim that this huge flying disc was seen by people standing 4 to 5 kilometers away, and who did not share at all the emotion and expectations of the crowd in Cova de Iria:

> *"I was staring at this star, it looked pale and without its blinding brightness; it looked like a snowball turning on itself. Suddenly it seemed to do zigzag manoeuvres, threatening to fall on the Earth".*

When we analyze these descriptions, we can only agree, in all intellectual honesty and sheltered from any religious conditioning, that we are talking about an engine in the shape of a disc, a saucer, a sphere, even slightly ovoid, moving randomly above the crowd and showing all the characteristics of what we call today a UFO or a flying saucer! There are many details in the descriptions: the sudden changes in color, the fireball aspect, the bright light effects, a non-blinding light, a high speed rotation, the silence of the aircraft (silent engines), sudden apparitions and disappearances. All this is characteristic of all the contemporary eye-witness accounts of UFO sightings. Whether you accept it or not, it is a fact. And the Church as well as people in high positions in the secret Masonic societies know it.

The Fatima "revelations" became a chief preoccupation in the Vatican because the conclusions of the discourses about the "Virgin" unequivocally described the end of the Catholic Church. Of course, the Popes were careful to never allude to this fact. And for the past 88 years, Fatima has been marked with the stamp of the Catholic fear, and rightfully so.

If we consider the 20 centuries of religious wars, crusades, colonialism, discrimination toward the Jews, Protestants, Cathars, People of color, the Inquisition, witch hunts, and nowadays wide scale pedophilia, anti-science sentiments, implicit accomplice to the Aids pandemic, it is obvious that "Mary" and her "step father", the eternal Yahweh, anticipated that the end of this Roman institution would one day come, for it has betrayed the simple and basic teachings of its prophet Jesus. Thus, this is what the de-mystified Fatima should be!

Moreover, Fatima did announce the one who would come after Jesus to accomplish the prophecies of the Apocalypse of John (Apocalypse meaning "revelation" in Greek), the end of the myth of "God", and the prophecies of Papa Simon Kimbangu for the African continent and the black Man. With the coming of this Messiah that is announced as well as the Messages that he brings we can agree that Fatima is coming to pass.

The mystery of "God", this entity, and through its armament, is responsible for the death of hundreds of millions of people for the past 2000 years. We can now understand that they are the Elohim of the Bible, extraterrestrials and human beings coming from another planet who, thanks to science, created all life on Earth around 13,000 years ago. It is they, the Elohim (plural Hebrew word unjustly translated as "God"), who have sent all the Prophets including Jesus. The Parousia is being prepared by the second Son, brother of Jesus, who is the one announced to bring the reve-

262

lation. He is here on Earth now to end deism and to bring the good news; to build an Embassy on a neutral land to welcome the Creators, beings like ourselves but more technologically advanced than we are.

They will come back within the next 30 years with Moses, Elijah, Ezekiel, Kimpa Vita, Simon Kimbangu, the Buddha, Mohammed, Jesus, and all the other Prophets of Old as written in many scriptures and as revealed by the "secrets" of Fatima. You can agree or not. May those who have eyes see and understand. The prophecies are coming to pass and it is time to recognize this. Often times the truth is as simple as it is unbelievable. May those interested in this truth seriously do their own research and understand that the one who was announced for all peoples of the Earth is here. The one announced by African Prophet Papa Simon Kimbangu as the "Nkua Tulendo", whose role is to accomplish the "Dipanda Dianzole" (total freeing of the black man), is alive and among us.

Pope John Paul II turned the mystery of Fatima into a veritable Fatima circus especially after the assassination attempt made against him in 1981 at Saint-Peter's Place. He claimed that it was the Virgin Mary in person who saved him from this attempt and that it was part of the revelations of Fatima, i.e., that a miracle saved him through the Virgin Mary. How pathetic and untrue and well orchestrated by the Vatican! Today, this bullet surrounded by precious stones is the jewel before which many faithful Catholics come to pray after the sanctifying ordeal of crossing the Basilica Esplanade on their knees. The Vatican is lying! On May 13th, 2000, at the end of the beatification of the shepherds from Fatima, Cardinal Angelo Sodano announced the so-called revelation of the third part of Fatima's secret message. This revelation was about John Paul II and the Vatican published the entire message on June 26th, 2000. That message is a lie. The truth is that the message reveals the end of the Church, the coming of Jesus of Nazareth's brother who would come to destroy the myth of "god", and finally the imminent arrival of our celestial human creators. There is the truth!

So why insist on hiding it all and not reveal what they know? Why? Why their unrestrained quest for power? Why their unrelenting quest for money in order for some Masonic currents to dominate the world? What animates these particular secret societies where everything revolves around money and power? Why? What, in their view, became more important than the truth itself? And what could have motivated them to the point of disregarding the Truth? Since the foundation of the Vatican was built on a lie and has evolved in a lie, the answer is easy to understand. It cannot lose its power, this supreme power for which it has always strived and for which the real mission it gave itself lays. This is their ultimate goal and nothing is going to change this. But regarding the particular Masonic loges, it is more difficult to understand their resoluteness?

Personally, I can formulate two hypotheses to answer this. I take full responsibility for these hypotheses as I am aware that I could be wrong. But of the different paths I took in my search for an understanding, the path that led me to these hypotheses is the one that appeared to me as the most logical, while admitting the possibility that I could be wrong. That is why I am only talking about speculations; they emanate from the pondering of my brain and even personally, just for my own sake, I consider them as pure speculations, until more clues will come along to confirm what I am about to write.

Meanwhile, expressing these theories will give me the opportunity to feel the immense joy of destroying another vile Christian myth and the one of fighting against another despicable Christian aberration, i.e., the "Christian" belief in a devil called "Satan". Could it be intentional?

So, let us take a closer look in the next chapter at this well-known Satan, to support my first hypothesis, and then at the history of the twelve Tribes of Israel for the second hypothesis.

WHITE POISON

26. The mystery of Satan and the history behind the Twelve Tribes of Israel.

a. The Mystery of Satan

Just as there is no good, unique, immaterial, and almighty "god", there is no so-called "devil", as we were told to believe either. This character that incarnates evil, destruction, and the end of the world does not exist, at least not under the notion that was imposed upon us. Not at all!

Satan is simply a human being embodied in flesh and blood. He is part of the sons of the Elohim, of those people who came from the sky, the extraterrestrials, and who created all life on Earth, including human beings "in their image". His name is Satan and it is just a name like any other name.

If he plays a role among the three great characters of this extraterrestrial people, the other two being Yahweh and Lucifer, it is for a very specific reason.

This reason, which can easily be deduced from the scriptures, is that Satan was against "man;" from the beginning of this "experimentation", he was against the creation of man. So once "man" was created, Satan received on many occasions the authority to challenge man to see if he was "good" or to see how far he would travel if he chose a path of evil. Satan was also given permission to test man's faithfulness when given a mission or a teaching.

 The different tests applied by Satan are known. Those imposed on Job, for example, as outlined in the Book of Job, are just a few. On this subject in the "scriptures" we read that the majority of the Prophets and other "subjects" were challenged by "Satan" with the sanction of the entire Elohim population and the authorization of Yahweh. They were tested often to determine whether they were worthy of their mission, if they would be faithful, and if they could be relied upon by the Elohim.

Whether Satan's tests involved Zoroaster, Moses, Job, Jesus, or other "Prophets" and subjects, they were quickly noticed and identified in different religions. That is how, and here again is only one example, in numerous Bantu religious traditions there is mention of a "god of temptation" who tests man in a very clever way.

Let us try to use our mind a bit by removing ourselves from the blind and nonsensical beliefs commonly generated by the fright of this Christian "devil" and by simply asking the following question: Why was Satan against the creation of humans?

We can easily understand that on the Elohim's planet part of the population was against the experiments that some of their scientists were carrying out and therefore called for the creation of a bioethics committee whose purpose would be to control, or at least, supervise these genetic experiments. The real concern from this part of the population was the fear for their own civilization.

We can easily understand why a majority tried to forbid certain genetic engineering experiments since the same situation is happening here on Earth right now and this, from the moment scientists started talking about cloning. But an opposition movement of such proportion must obviously have a face or, to put it more succinctly, a "leader", a "president".

So, if at this moment in their history, these people already have the science and the energy needed to travel in space, can leave their solar system and travel within their own galaxy, we can anticipate how things would work on their planet. There would be parliamentary debates, the important question of genetic engineering would be debated at large and everyone would bring their own arguments to the table. And, knowing from experience that it is impossible to stop scientific progress, a solution or a suitable compromise would have to be reached, if not for all, for at least a reasonable majority.

And this is how the leaders of this planet would finally give the team of scientists and artists, who are interested in these experiments, an authorization to continue these new combined artistic and genetic engineering ventures. The only condition is that they be done on a planet in their galaxy but far away from the one their fellow humans live on.

Well, this is indeed what took place several thousand years ago: the scientists and artists, sons and daughters of the Elohim, chose the planet Earth to continue their experiments. Simultaneously, this revolutionary trend, of which Satan is the leader, received various guarantees with a certain freedom to control what these creation teams would carry out. One of these vouches could have been, for instance, that the creators be forbidden to create beings that are in "their image". But, as referenced in the scriptures, we clearly read that there was, at one point, a will by some to bypass

268

this restriction. This is the case of Lucifer who, along with his teammates, was responsible for our creation and who deliberately chose to disregard such an injunction.

This is what led Satan and his supporters to think that nothing good could come out of this endeavour and that it would turn bad or turn toward evil, which is not any better! Seeing this, his group reacted as any opposition party would have. Eventually, Satan expressed his views and was able to have his voice heard by the government on his planet. In the end, he made proposals and asked for certain measures to be taken.

But what would infuriate Satan even more were the two other facts that the scriptures also tell us about very explicitly. Initially, Lucifer's group would not only create beings "in their image", but they would also explain to these beings why they, their creators, are not gods, but humans made of flesh and blood and that they came from the sky in physical flying machines. Hence, this explains the name "Lucifer" given to the character who heads this group of creators and which means "light bearer" or the one who brings "the fruit" of knowledge to the first man.

When studying the scriptures we can then understand that the mother planet would punish this group of creators, i.e., sanction those who disobeyed. This is symbolically well represented by "the Serpent who is condemned to crawl on Earth in the dust". This "Serpent" refers to the team of creators who were prohibited from returning to their planet and condemned to remain on the Earth with our ancestors, as explained in the Bible. Of course, Satan was not pleased with this sanction which he considered to be too mild and requested the destruction of this group's creations. And to defend his point of view he accumulated enough evidence to support his claim and thus succeeded in making them admit that only evil could come out of man.

Then comes a third disobedience from this banned group of extraterrestrials. Some of the members of Lucifer's group would have sexual intercourse with those they had created. Children would be born from these sexual unions, and the earthlings would then obtain weapons from their creators. Of course, at first it would be for the sole purpose of hunting for their survival but very quickly it would degenerate and men would begin to kill one another with these weapons. Unfortunately, with what we are seeing today in the 20th and 21st century one must wonder about the purpose of all this "progress" throughout the ages when considering that violence has not diminished at all.

269

Yet, these observations would bring additional support to Satan when pre-senting his case before the members of the Parliament of the planet of the Elohim. At this point, his arguments would win the hearts of the members and a decision is made: this experiment is a failure. All life on Earth must be destroyed and Lucifer's group (the "fallen angels" called "Nephilim" in the Hebrew scriptures) must be repatriated to the Elohim's planet.

But once more, Lucifer's group would disobey and before being repatria-ted to the Elohim's planet, they decide to save those whom they conside-red to be the most successful among the descendants of the beings that they created. Among them, there is Noah to whom the group provides a spaceship that would protect him and all the species inside from the destruction. It is in this vessel orbiting high above the Earth that several humans and the genetic codes of several animal species were preserved and protected against the flood.

It is noteworthy that traces of the existence of this "flood" can be found in the traditions of almost all civilizations. Indeed, the simple truth is that Noah's ark was, in fact, a spaceship that orbited above the Earth, and not a boat floating on the surface of the turbulent oceans. One needs only ponder the possibility that these events actually occurred in this way.

Thus, a destruction of incredible magnitude and caused by these extrater-restrial beings took place destroying all life on Earth. And according to the scriptures a certain amount of time goes by before the Elohim decide, for one reason or another, to create life on Earth again by using the genetic codes preserved in Noah's vessel. All of this takes place despite Satan's objections as well as that of his supporters who continue to believe that nothing good can come from man and that this decision can only have serious consequences. Yet, he was forced to abide by the decision of the majority of the people in his government.

It is at that particular time however that the gods decide to let man pro-gress on his own and without assistance. The Bantu traditions speak about this period as the period when the gods are absent, when Yahweh gave up on man and left him alone. That is why the Bantus understand very easily what I have just exposed.

As time passes, we witness that the Elohim chose to have beings born of men who would then be ultimately charged with giving birth to religions for the purpose of preserving traces of their work at a time when men would have reached a level of scientific knowledge so that he can understand. It is here that the era of Prophets begins. And it is here, as described in the scriptures, that Satan will challenge each Prophet's faithfulness to our creators.

How does Satan proceed to test these people chosen by the Elohim? One can read in the scriptures that Satan never tests a Prophet before he is contacted and starts a certain mission. Only then does Satan intervene. With the promise of wealth, power, and material abundance, he would attempt blasphemy toward the Elohim and Yahweh, encourage denunciation, and urge his subject from his appointed mission, rallying constantly to win favour with Satan. This is how the notorious Christian Theological "devil" operates!

Coincidentally, this word "devil", only used to frighten us, where does it come from? Excellent question! From the Greek word «diabolos» which means "slanderer", quite simply. This explains it, doesn't it!

Moreover, on several occasions Jesus calls this slanderer by his name in the scriptures, he names him quite naturally "Satan"! The Book of Job is extremely interesting and quite eloquent on this subject, because it demonstrates perfectly that Yahweh and Satan know each other extremely well and that they maintain a more than friendly relation, very fraternal, full of mutual respect! (JOB 1, 6-12). One also sees very clearly in Job that within the Elohim's political structure, Yahweh has a higher position than that of Satan.

Here we have the "devil Satan" demystified, stripped of his forked tail, of his menacing horns and his pointed ears. Here he is finally rid of his masquerade and found in his "human" costume, and rightly so, having been part of the humanized gods in the authentic Bantu religions, those that existed prior to the period of religious colonization imposed on the African continent by the lying and usurping Christian churches!

Let us return to my earlier hypothesis, simple but bears repeating. It is certain that Satan and his supporters must always be very concerned with the high degree of aggression demonstrated by the human species, their rejection of good and the choice of evil men so often makes, and their flagrant displays of unconsciousness. We could also say with certainty that Satan continues to observe and test humanity, and that he and many others on the planet of the Elohim will be convinced that the creation of our humanity did not fail only when men will unite to suppress and overcome greed, power, and war.

On the basis of the fact that the universe is infinite, a fact that our contemporary scientists increasingly recognize, with infinite forms of life in the universe, there is also an infinity of people who create life on an infinite number of planets, therefore an infinite number of people creators, and an infinite number of people created. One can admit that all these people are in full evolution between a "primitive" stage and a scientific era of advanced technologies that will enable them one day to become creators themselves.

One can predict that the people who controlled their external energies as much as their internal impulses of aggression, having developed a deep wisdom at the same time, are thus peaceful and conscious people. From this fact one can consider that these beings evolved from self-destruction permanently.

From this state of consciousness and existence, they can, if they wish, create life in the universe since they master intergalactic travels outside of their solar system, and can communicate with people of this level of wisdom and science, to exchange and promulgate cosmic laws for the safeguard of the universal balance.

In other words, these wise people whose populations are not "morons", thanks to their use of science, and based on their common wisdom, could establish laws that ensure that people demonstrating aggressive or violent behaviour would not have access to certain energies that would jeopardize the balance of the universe, a balance these sages would have created and of which everyone benefits.

It is appropriate, perhaps even compulsory, that before giving a certain scientific, technological heritage to beings recently created, that we be fully convinced that they would not make ill use of it. We must ensure that this humanity is well under way toward a planetary conscience, toward total disarmament and universal peace.

With this in mind, this humanity would have to be able to unlock certain bolts, to break down certain barriers; for example, to respect the differences in religions, races and cultures, even to experience joy in enriching themselves of their discovery. It will always be necessary to undergo Satan's tests and challenges, testing men's capacity for good and evil, corruption and magnanimity, to resist temptation, selfishness, greed, and power. Only continual testing will determine how far men can go in his unconsciousness and choice of altruistic evildoing for personal gains.

272

So that it can access the great family of intergalactic civilizations, it would be necessary, and understandably so, that humanity proves, in one way or another, that it is worthy of receiving the particular scientific heritage that would allow it this access to the cosmic level.

Most certainly, the time will come when humanity must prove its worthiness. Logically, this will occur when the course of its evolution leads it to discover energies which could bring forth its self-destruction. At this moment of its history, humanity will be preserved, provided it has reached a level of wisdom and planetary consciousness that is equal or higher to its level of technological progress.

I believe our terrestrial humanity arrived at this crucial moment: We discovered the atom and atomic energy, subsequently accumulating enormous stocks of nuclear weapons capable of obliterating the planet several hundreds of times!

Knowing that this time would come for us, I believe the Elohim granted Satan one final test for mankind allowing us to then choose our fate, and observing to see if we would finally choose the right path. Since then, the Elohim have not intervened again and men has been left alone to pass this final test.

It is true that there are reasons for us to be shaken when we see the frightening number of things far away from the "right path" that currently occur on Earth. There is so much evil that is done on our small blue planet at the detriment of a large part of its population. All it takes is to see how wars are senselessly repeated, how conflicts are born that cannot be ceased, how alliances are made and destroyed unless the objectives are wealth and power, all with total disregard and respect for the human being.

Look at how the armament industry benefits those who decree wars themselves and who shamefully gain exorbitant sums by selling weapons on both sides of the front, without taking into account neither the life nor the pain of the sons and daughters of the Earth.

Look at certain "humanitarian" institutions which, by definition, claim to guide humanity toward peace, happiness, and prosperity. These same institutions, I say, are instrumental to the profit of the rich and mislead us with their claims for equity for the poor countries of the Earth.

We can really ask some questions about the true goal of organizations such as the UN, NATO, the World Bank, the International Monetary Fund, WTO (the World Trade Organization), et cetera. When we know how these world organizations function, generally contrary to what they are supposed to do, one can wonder whether they are not infiltrated up to the neck by agents. Which agents? Those of secret societies whose only goal, once again, is the accumulation of wealth and power for the profit of a handful of unscrupulous individuals.

Why wouldn't Satan have, at a given moment, contacted certain members of an important secret society, or a small group of very powerful people on the financial and economic level, or certain people of very powerful families on the financial level, people who, perhaps, would already have a certain secret basic knowledge? Why wouldn't certain Freemason lodges have been created starting from a contact with Satan in the past? It is unclear, but I must really ask the question.

Within the framework of my assumption, which is only one assumption and not more than that, it could be that Satan put these people to the test by proposing to them a pact that could have been formulated, for example, in the following way:

"I, Satan, and those numerous who support me think that men is bad and do not share the opinion of Yahweh and Lucifer. Men are negative and would self destroy sooner or later. We do not wish to see this humanity continuing to exist. We propose to you to help us accelerate this self-destruction. In any case, men are the fruits of a failed creation. If you refuse to help us, you would know poverty, suffering, imprisonment, and death at the hands of your brothers, the men".

"If you accept, by creating racial tensions on Earth, ethnic conflicts, inequality, the oppression of the people, by installing dictatorships, by creating wars of religion, while sustaining your own religion, Judeo-Christianity, and by raising the white race to domination over the entire world, then you and all who help you would be saved from the final cataclysm. You will be taken aboard our vessels and we would allow you to come back to Earth when everything would have been destroyed. Then you may implant a new humanity, a new world order that you would govern to your liking, with our help.

If you accept the mission, you will be supported financially. You would become wealthy and powerful. But foremost, if you accept this mis-

sion, you and those you choose would have eternal life.

We offer you to help us accelerate the final disaster on Earth that would only purify the universe of beings who do not deserve to exist. To achieve this, you might activate various racisms to exist in men, you could establish spiritual and political movements that would secretly facilitate this goal, fostering fears everywhere which, in turn, would increase the arms' stockpile, aggression, intolerance, and racial and religious hatred.

In any event, the cause of humanity is lost. Sooner or later it will self-destroy. It is up to you to gradually accelerate that by acting in a subversive manner so that Yahweh and all who share his philosophy will not recognize your efforts.

Don't you think that a very restricted group of people could possibly have accepted such a proposal in the past? If this pact were not an assumption but a reality this could explain why things on Earth turn out so badly, why so many wars follow one after the other, be they "racial", "ethnic", "religious", or of "economic interest". Our humanity does not identify a difference. That could also explain why one speaks in the Bible about good and evil, that one speaks also of Armageddon, presented like a combat between the sons and daughters of light against the sons and daughters of darkness, combat that should take place within our time.

In this case, on one side, the sons and daughters of darkness would be **those of the group having accepted the "evil"** and keeping the secrecy on what they know. But on the other side there would be the first cited, the sons and daughters of light. They would be **those who really work for Love**, peace, good and fraternity.

And among these beings of light, there would be, now in our current epoch, those who would follow and help "the last of the Prophets" as announced, "the Messiah", knowing that he would be challenged by the others, those of darkness who would organize an international plot to slow down the impulse of the revolutionary Movement that the Messiah would have founded. These sons and daughters of darkness would organize campaigns to discredit the image of this "last of the Prophets" and would use slander towards him, would defame him, and mock him, thus influencing the masses to ask for his "crucifixion".

This will be accomplished with the support of the press, media-liars totally influenced by the sons and daughters of darkness. Media will employ every tactic of "those of darkness" to force indifference among the sons and daughters of light, to persuade them to accept war and conflict, to blind them with stupid national patriotisms, and forcing racial, cultural and religious division. Thus these media would then be used to standardize the thought of people, to turn them like a herd of bleating sheep guided unwittingly to hurl themselves into the sea.

Simultaneously, we will see the Vatican and its networks make a final-hour attempt to "save face", to change the course of history, in order to continue its existence and spread of power. This Vatican that secretly continues to create wars of civilization, that is still on a crusade such as the Crusades in past centuries, but under the guise and protection of secret societies with its agents working in anonymity.

It's interesting to note the words of our modern age "Roman emperor" or the leader of the 21st century Crusades, President George W. Bush, "We are on a new crusade"!

In any case, there are certainly many questions that can be raised with regard to the current state of our planet. And remember that all that you have prior in this chapter are my assumptions, but one observation remains clear: the Vatican has perpetuated an infinite degree of evil on Earth by its actions and subversive behaviour. Tidily concealed behind its opulent exterior, the Vatican continues to withhold the Truth while wealth accumulates and its power spreads. After twenty centuries of greed and lust, the Vatican continues to lead humanity to loss and demise.

If he held with sincerity to the logic of Love that he repeats daily, the Pope should start by excommunicating President Bush who claims to be a "good Christian", who prays before authorizing the deployment of bombs that would kill innocent populations, who claims that "God is with him", (as Hitler displayed on the belts of his soldiers) who prays daily so that "God blesses the United States". He prays so that God and Jesus bless his bombs that would kill innocent civilians, non-combatants, adults and children. It is a complete aberration; it is so contrary to Jesus' teaching that in principle the pope should excommunicate him immediately.

But, of course, Pope John-Paul II would not excommunicate President Bush. He would do nothing about it for there are so many truths hidden behind the mask of kindness of the Vatican prelates. The entire hierarchy of the Vatican, "the Curia", support civil and religious wars.

26. The mystery of Satan and the history behind the Twelve Tribes of Israel.

Throughout their history, more than two thousand years, the Vatican has waged war and violent actions of all nature against those who did not accept their religious authority, whose views differed from theirs. Whether atheists, polytheists, no philosophical view mattered than their own. This is as true today as at any other point in history, and it is time that we become aware of this reality. The Vatican requires submission and has stopped at nothing to achieve it.

But there is perhaps still something else that could greatly obstruct the Christian West, a quandary to me. Why do Christians refuse to recognize the true place of "the black men" in the history of humanity and, in particular, his place in the history of the religions? Dating back to ancient Greece, then to Rome, even to current time in Europe and around the world, but none so much as in the Christian Western world. Why then is it so difficult to recognize the black men and give him his place in the history of Humanity, the Sciences, and the history of the religions?

For the moment, I do not have a formal answer to this question. But I persist in asking because it is important to do so. More importantly, it is our imperative that blacks should be the first to find a just and suitable answer to the question that has disturbed our lives for hundreds of years.

Could this objective of smothering "the black men" be also one of the goals of this plot of silence, one of the reasons of this secrecy that should be maintained at all costs, a mission of secrecy that has prevailed for over two thousand years?

What does the Vatican stand to gain by maintaining this secret, relying on a tacit agreement made between persons from other secret orders (Opus Dei, Jesuit Order, the Order of Malta, etc.) What stigma surrounds the black men that obligate these orders to unite against them?

Until these questions are answered... Bravo to Catholicism and to Christianity! You have misled us so well!

In any case, it is further reason for us to look at this subject more seriously together in the following chapter. But in order to understand the "supporters and tenants" of these lies, let us first study the history of the twelve Tribes of Israel. In this we will discover and perhaps understand the opposition to the Truth, a deliberate denunciation of the Elohim, the people of our Creator-gods .

b. The History of the Twelve Tribes of Israel

After the death of King Solomon, builder of the first Temple, a great political and moral decline occurred. A religious schism occurred within the
Hebrew kingdom, dividing it into two. The ten Tribes of the North seceded
and formed the kingdom of Israel while the two Tribes of the South (Benjamin and Judas) formed with Jerusalem the kingdom of Judea.

Succeeding King Solomon were two enemy brothers, forming two rival states and thus destroying the harmonious unity created by their predecessor.
The history of the kingdom of Israel and the ten Tribes of the North was
short and without glory. In 721 B.C., Nebuchadnezzar, King of Babylon,
(Assyrians) destroyed and dispersed the ten Tribes that comprised the dis-
sident kingdom of Israel, having broken the alliance with their creators in
the heaven.

In 587 B.C., the kingdom of Judea succumbed the blows of the Babylonians. Between 586 B.C. and 581 B.C., Judea saw a large-scale exodus and
deportation toward Babylonia. In Jerusalem the Babylonians dismantled
the Temple.

We can thus say that long ago there were two Hebrew kingdoms, namely
that of Israel with the ten Tribes of the North and that of Judea with the
two Tribes of the South (the Tribe of Judas and that of Benjamin) and that
the ten Tribes of the North, having broken the alliance, never submitted
again to their creators, the Elohim.

From then on, the Kingdom of the North, Israel and its ten Tribes, would
disappear from the map much earlier than the kingdom of Judea. With the
crumbling of the Kingdom of the North by the Assyrian kings in 721 B.C.,
the ten Tribes of the North were deported and their populations dispersed.
But to where?

Following this deportation, certain members of the ten Israeli Tribes of
the North joined their brothers of the Kingdom of Judea, ending the strife
that had existed between them and that of the two Tribes of the South,
ultimately and symbolically restoring the union of the twelve Tribes and
resuming their alliance with the Elohim.

However, a significant number of members of the ten lost Tribes, disappeared, remaining obstinate toward the Elohim. They continued to be "irre-
ducible", thus maintaining the fracture in the alliance and their rebellion

278

against the Elohim. The misfortunes experienced by their forefathers and the tests undergone in exile had instilled in them this rebellion towards their creators, the Elohim. They, by way of consequence, had then repudiated the Alliance (the famous original "Alliance" between Yahweh Elohim and "the chosen people"). Let's recall this: in return for their obedience to the Elohim and their respect for this grand plan had been this portion of the "Promised Land", land which would later be taken back when the ten Tribes broke the Alliance.

In fact, a large portion of the ten Tribes of the North would not return to Jerusalem after their deportation by Assyrian kings. Its members would recover their freedom, abandon the worship of YHWH and Elohim, even go so far as to repudiate their name, "Israel". And although their leaders knew the secrets of the great celestial plan, of the great intent of the Elohim, they would make every effort to thwart this great plan in the centuries to come. And it is thus then that one would see them denounce the Elohim, systematically develop a spirit of opposition to Yahweh and organize themselves to automatically thwart any development favoring the great plan of Yahweh and the Elohim. Among others, they would be at the origin of many organizations that would be opposed to the "sons and daughters of light" working for the completion of the grand plan of the Elohim. They would become savage enemies of those who remained faithful to the Alliance formed by the Elohim. This was the case of the children of Judas; the Jews and the Bantu Tribes of Africa, related to the Tribes of Judas and Benjamin. But to where could these rebels of the ten Tribes of Israel have immigrated? Are they still "lost?"

This we know from our historians who have traced their journey. Some arrived near the valley of the large river of Central Europe, the Danube, and where some historians have found derivatives of "Dan" (the Tribe of "Dan" is one of the ten lost Tribes). This migration ultimately led them to Denmark, whose name, "Den-Mark", is partly composed of the Tribe of "Dan". Moreover, in these countries or regions hundreds of tombs were found carrying the Hebraic inscriptions and dating from the time of the exile of the children of Israel.

After their deportation from Israel and driven out of Jerusalem by Assyrian kings, the ten Tribes of Israel, the ten Tribes of the North, would, in fact, disappear from history for many centuries. Where did they go? They traveled to the north, toward the valley of the Danube, toward Denmark, as is the case with the Tribe of "Dan", but also toward other regions deep into Europe for the other nine Tribes. It is sure and certain that the ten lost

Tribes were not all destroyed and even that some knew an extraordinary odyssey!

One can note that in 113 B.C., the Romans were astonished and surprised by a sudden attack by those called "Kimbri" who invaded Wales. Who were these "Kimbris"? Well, probably none other than members of the lost Tribes of Israel (in Hebrew: "beit-Khumri" means the "house", the "family"). According to certain serious historians, the Angles, the Saxons, the Jutes, the Danes, the Goths, the Normans... would only be descendants of these ten Tribes... those will in their turn, later, invade the United Kingdom, and will become its kings. It is not by accident that we can find among former kings of Ireland three kings named "David" and three kings named "Solomon", this well before the birth of Christianity!

Many respectable figures such as Queen Victoria, King Edward VII, statesmen, generals, admirals, and countless other people consider that the United Kingdom was formerly populated by the members of the ten Tribes of Israel. There exists in England and in the United States a "British World Federation" whose hundreds of thousands of members share this thought!

It is told that between the four feet of the opulent throne on which Her Majesty the Queen of England majestically sits lies the stone on which David, King of Israel, had once enthroned himself in Jerusalem!

Having not yet been invited by Her Majesty into her palace to validate this theory, I would like to share this unsubstantiated claim: Members of the British World Federation are certain that the Anglo-Saxon populations, English as well as American, comprise Israel (the ten Tribes of Israel) to whom so much was promised in the Bible. According to the Federation, it is the "British people" that the Kingdom of Peter is intended, as mentioned in the Book of Daniel, a Kingdom that must encompass all the Earth! Some subscribers to this theory go even as far as to identify Great Britain with Ephraim (another one of the ten lost Tribes), and the United States to Manasseh (yet another)! Is it by chance that Englishmen would assign themselves the name of "British?" Not at all! In Hebrew, this word would translate as "the child of Israel", "the child of the Alliance;" "brit" meaning "alliance" and "ish" meaning "man"! In these circles, it is said that the Queen of England's ancestry links her as far back as Solomon.

It is clear that the Germans, the Austrians, the English, assert their Saxon origin, but at the same time it is also necessary to remember and recognize that the French clergy, the nobility, and the French royalty has the same origin. It belongs to the Saxon family, as does the Belgian dynasty (of Saxon Coburg, in Walloon language). Hugues Capet, founder of the Capetian dynasty that reigned in France until the French Revolution, belonged to the family of Saxony. He was, in 987, elected king of France by the Assembly of Senlis made up of the majority of nobles and Saxon monks. Among them was Gerbert the Saxon who will later become Pope in 999 under the name of Sylvester II. Interesting, isn't it!

Most interesting! And why? Because the Saxons would evidently be the direct descendants of the ten Tribes of Israel and one would think that the Saxons, the Angles, the Danes, the Goths, the Normans are none other than the ten lost Tribes of Israel who became "anti-Elohim", having denounced the Elohim and broken allegiance with Yahweh. Which could bring us, in all logic, to the following conclusion: in all of the Saxon circles, whether they belong to the royalty, the nobility or the clergy, there remains this aversion towards those of Judas who remained faithful to the Elohim. Throughout time, there has been in these circles, the European Dynasties, i.e., the British, Danish, Belgian, Norwegian, Spanish crowns, etc., an "anti-Elohim" attitude, a will and determination to thwart the grand plan of the Elohim. And this mentality also exists in the Vatican!

When we see that these Saxons, or descendants of the ten lost Tribes, came as far as occupy the throne of the Pope in Rome in the Vatican, i.e., Sylvester II, this undoubtedly perpetuates the "anti-Elohim" position of the Vatican and its refusal to recognize the Elohim, thus denying the Truth! We can understand a little better why the Vatican persists in hiding the Truth, couldn't we! We also better understand the current political scene where we see the British and the USA form a unified front as to their political orientation (the two Wars in Iraq, the support for Israel against Palestinians, etc.). You see that we understand better now!

The Bible reports to us that, speaking to him about his wife:

« [15] And Elohim said unto Abraham, as for Sarai thy wife, thou shalt not call her name Sarai, but Sarah shall her name be.
[16] [...] I will bless her, and she shall be a mother of nations; kings of people shall be of her.» (GENESIS 17, 15-16)

What nations are those? The Angles, the Saxons, Goths, Danes, etc., all descendants of the ten lost Tribes of Israel that once formed one of the two Hebrew Kingdoms, and mainly that of the North, the Kingdom of Israel, opposed to the Kingdom of the South, that of Judas. These old Tribes considered after their dispersion in Europe that the Bible spoke about their Nations to them, that only they could really be regarded as the "Nation of Israel". And apparently, we see that there is a constant search for the application of this Biblical word that applies very well to the British Empire with its Commonwealth, gathering many countries, linked by a common allegiance to the English Crown! In Psalms 89, verse 21, 24, 26 and 28 it is said: «[21] I have found David my servant; [24] And I will beat down his foes before his face, [26] I will set his hand also in the sea, and his right hand in the rivers. [28] Also I will make him my firstborn, higher than the kings of the earth". These are indeed those that the British Crown, the Saxons and the Angles, applied from the very start of the 18th century and until the middle of the 20th century, hence the famous expression of ages ago "Britain rules the seas".

And why these descendants of the ten Tribes of Israel, who probably became the kings, the dynasties in Europe, could not have met explicitly to this end, that to conquer nations, believing that it was their destiny, and thinking that if they did just this, if they succeeded in achieving this goal, it would be a new challenge to the Elohim. It would again be a true rebellion towards the Elohim. Moreover, by acting in such a way they would do nothing but perpetuate their opposition to what the Elohim ultimately expect from them. Didn't they meet for that, for example, during the Great Conference of Berlin in 1884, where they decided among themselves of the "colonization", of the conquest of many nations, to share Africa between descendant crowns of the ten lost Tribes of Israel? It is highly possible, it is only an assumption, certainly, but highly credible nonetheless!

The German Kaiser, Guillaume II, the one who set in motion the First World War in 1914, was related to the royal family of England and he recognized himself as the great grandson of King David the Hebrew!

The Goths, instead of calling themselves "sons of Israel", considering their hostile attitude towards the Elohim, having disavowed the Elohim, would be satisfied to call themselves "Aryans".

One can say that the Hebrew people, at one time in their history, were divided into two antagonistic branches, the one that remained faithful to the Elohim (Judas) and the other becoming anti-Elohim (Israel and its ten Tribes). Thus descendants of the ten lost Tribes (the Saxon, Angles, Goths, the Aryan, the Danes, etc.) would start to develop a thesis according to which, as described in the Bible, all prophecies intended for "Israel" relate to them, them directly, and that those specifying the name of Judas would pertain to the second faction (Judas, or more particularly the "Jews", including the "black Jews of Africa").

Hitler was very aware of this system of thought! He did not choose the word "Aryan" randomly to designate as being "superior to any other", in his opinion, the "Aryan race"! Hitler would come to develop contempt and hatred for the other race, the one of Judas which remained faithful to the Elohim. He would then basically align himself with the anti-Elohim thesis and, like that of the ten lost Tribes, dedicate himself to destroying the grand plan of the Elohim. He would seize every opportunity to undermine the plan, to capture and kill the Messiah proclaimed for these times, as he was keenly aware that the Messiah would be born during his lifetime.

We are forced to note that this trend of non-recognition, non-consideration, non-obedience, non-acceptance of the Elohim, in short, this denial of the Elohim is indeed still present today. And we find the root of this denouncement in the history of the ten Tribes of Israel of the Hebrew Kingdom of the North.

Hitler, anti-Elohim, by declaring war on Elohim, those who sent the Christ 19 centuries earlier, by preventing certain prophecies to pass, by attacking the faithful followers of the Elohim, i.e., Jews and Blacks of Judas, he would fulfill the role of the Antichrist as was foretold for the end of time. He would rid the world of the announced Messiah and of the Elohim's allies, the Jews and Blacks of the two Tribes of Judas.

It is known that Hitler was a member of a secret society called "Thule Gesellschaft" of which one of the Great Masters was Rudolf Hess, Hitler's mentor. For this secret society, the inequality of the human races was an absolute dogma: the superiority went to the Nordic race, the "Aryan" race. This secret society recognizes and admits the existence of "external or extraterrestrial" powers that intervene in the life and the history of humanity. These powers are called "supermen" but not "Gods". For this secret society, these extraterrestrials did not deserve the superlative of "Gods" but only that of "supermen" because the civilization on their planet is only more advanced than ours, because it was born a few millennia earlier than that of Earth. Obviously these "supermen", these "external powers", are the Elohim of the Bible and Hitler would fight them in order to destroy their grand plan, the one destined to save humanity! Hitler and his followers worked from the following premise: it is the duty of the people of the North, the "Aryan", the Saxon, etc., to create on Earth a race of "supermen" who will fight against the Elohim. He would perpetuate the battle against the Elohim with the assistance of the Vatican and many other powerful allies, Franco, Mussolini, Pétain, for example.

Thus, the essential role of the «Great Masters» of the secret society "Thule Gesellschaft", such as Rudolf Hess, was to tend to the preservation of the "absolute secret" concerning the grand plan of the Elohim and also to the application and orchestration of human plans to thwart the celestial plan conceived by our creators, that they still conceive and offer with generosity for the benefit of our humanity. Fortunately, as history demonstrates, the Nazi regime was unsuccessful in rallying the Anglo-Saxons to aid in their fight against the Elohim! Quite the contrary! The question we can ask, in light of the current state of our world, is: "What about today? Where are these 'sons of darkness' today?"

One can certainly say that there was in the 20th century a kind of resurgence of this spirit of rebellion against the "Gods", against the Elohim, a spirit which was the same one initiated against the Creator Gods some 2500 years earlier by the ten "lost" Tribes of Israel.

And for Hitler, Rudolf Hess and other Nazi "initiates", this rebellion was to find its apotheosis in the capture and the assassination of the Messiah, of the Elohim's Messenger, he whose birth was foreseen for their time, somewhere in France. They would implement a plan that would have changed the course of the history of humanity, to supplant the grand plan of the Elohim with one that would mean the complete annihilation of all humans faithful to the Elohim, those of Judas, the Jews and the Blacks, so that they, the Aryans, could employ the unscrupulous use of science to the profit of their treachery, the race of "Aryan supermen"!

Further, the "race of the Lords", masterminded by Hitler, Rudolf Hess and other initiates, once Masters of the world, would confront the Elohim and thus avenge the centuries of humiliations and affronts of all kinds that the Elohim would have inflicted to the ten "lost" Tribes of Israel and to their descendants! In the hope of conquering "the sky" with interplanetary flying machines and to wage war with the Elohim, Hitler and Hess issued unlimited appropriations in men and hardware to Werner Von Braun, the father of rockets, as well as total support for research and development of the atomic bomb. Pure madness when one takes into account the immeasurable technological advance the Elohim have over us.

Ultimately, millions of "Jews" (of the two Tribes of Judas) would go to their death in the gas chambers, still praying YHWH (Yahweh), praying to their allies, the Elohim, many knowing what awaited them. The anti-Elohim despicable madness of Hitler and his regime, and even others in the Vatican, would cost the lives of forty million human beings! Ironic that in this mass planetary slaughter, where nearly six million "Jews" were put to death, massacred, and assassinated, many of the very assassins bore false pretence as the descendants of their brothers of the ten lost Tribes of Israel!

Throughout time on Earth humans have constantly thwarted the celestial plan of our creators, the "Elohim"! Nevertheless, the Elohim have intervened and guided humanity fully into the Messianic era. In 1948, the United Nations proclaimed the creation in Palestine of an independent Hebrew state, such as was announced in Prophecies, and as described previously, Ephraim being the Hebrew Kingdom of the North, Israel, that of the ten "lost" Tribes of Israel, and Judas being the Kingdom of the South, the one whose population had remained faithful to the Elohim:

> «[11] And it shall come to pass in that day, that Yahweh shall set his hand again the second time to recover the remnant of his people. [12] And he shall set up an ensign for the nations, and shall assemble the outcasts of Israel, and gather together the dispersed of Judah from the four corners of the earth.[13] ...and the adversaries of Judah shall be cut off: Ephraim shall not envy Judah, and Judah shall not vex Ephraim". (Isaiah XI, 11, 12 and 13)

But it may be that the State of Israel of today and the descendants of the ten lost Tribes, e.g., the European royal families, the great European nobility, even the Vatican, persist in not wanting to recognize the last of the messengers sent by the Elohim; the Messiah, Maitreya, Nkua Tulendo, or New Paraclete. Humans always being free (and responsible) for their acts, it is most probable that there is again nowadays a trend of opposition towards the Elohim, and that again some choose to keep "a stiff neck" towards them and their vast and generous celestial plan. And even if I regretted deeply that it was so, sincerely, I believe that we could still be confronted with this kind of harmful and most deplorable attitude.

With the modern day thirst for power so prevalent, and for several reasons, it is possible that there could be a plot to suppress the entire truth by some powerful individuals for whom maintaining power has become more important than respecting the Truth. Indeed, with enormous interests in maintaining power at stake, it becomes easy to disregard this fundamental Truth. Personally, once again, I think that the power mongers among us today could very likely organize themselves as in centuries past, disguising their efforts in political and religious rhetoric, as we most often see on a daily basis, to thwart the grand plan of the Elohim and to continue to conceal the Truth.

To achieve their ends they will continue to plan secretly so that the belief in a unique immaterial and omnipotent God is preserved. As history shows, this initiative is led by the Vatican, closely followed by the Zionist Jews of Israel, and other high level Freemasons who persist in conveying the belief in "God". And although today many know his existence, precisely who and where he is, they refuse to officially recognize the actual presence on Earth of the "Messiah".

Although we do not agree with them, we can, however, understand their motivation. They are sufficiently informed of the scriptures to know that one of the main missions on Earth of the Messiah will be to abolish the belief in this "God" who does not exist. They know that he is the one who will lift the veil on "the mystery of God", but all of their influence, all of their power, is built precisely on this same mystery. They also know that this Messiah will come to speak in the name of the Elohim, of our creator Gods in the plural, in the name of this celestial people coming from the sky. And they fear, and with good reason, that his words are as unpleasant to hear as those of his predecessor, Jesus, had been to the ears of their Pharisee ancestors.

What solution remains then? The solution rests with those who remained faithful to the Elohim, to those having found new or renewed allegiance with the Elohim. The solution lies with those who openly recognize their last "Envoy", the Messiah, the Nkua Tulendo.

Is there still somewhere on Earth a branch of the two Tribes of the Kingdom of the South, of Judas, that could seize this role, the role of reuniting with the Elohim? Yes, and these people are in Black Africa. They are all the Bantus and black people of Africa. Believe it, the last will be first, the New Jerusalem has already set foot in Africa. If the State of Israel and the West continue to fix their gaze in a direction opposite to that indicated by the Elohim, then Black Africa can look again in the proper direction and completely reunite with the Elohim. Joining again with our fathers who are in the Skies will be the greatest happiness of all of Africa and ultimately for the entire world.

It is up to you, my brothers and sisters of Africa, to decide. The decision is yours. Look carefully at your old traditions, look at your history, look at your authentic religions, and look at the authentic legends and genesis about creation, and of man, and of all that lives on Earth. Acting accordingly, you will realize unequivocally that the "Elohim" are everywhere, in all that I have just enumerated, that they are only Love and that they love you like their own children.

Restore the bond with them, recognize them, and give up the Churches and Religions of those who betrayed them. Give up the Religions of those who parted with them, of those who are in rebellion towards them. Recover your religious purity by mending the broken link with them. Be their "allies". Be sons and daughters of the light of the Elohim by rejecting the Religious Institutions developed by those who broke the link, who not only refuse to accept them but flatly reject the possibility of their existence. Abandon their camp, this fortress in which they have forced you to reject your ancestry, to abandon your history, and in which they strive to eradicate your authentic religions that speak of the celestial beings who came from the sky, the Elohim of the original Hebrew bible.

You, African men and women, a multitude of realities that belonged to you were concealed from you, stolen from you. And the chapter that you will now read will perhaps reveal all that you have been denied. The gaze of our creators, the Elohim, is turned towards you right now, you African men and women, who are reading these lines. The Elohim observe you, feel you and hope that your people will be able to recognize them without delay. Your time has come!

The true "Israel" is not an unspecified State nor a federation of States or Nations. "Israel" is everywhere on Earth. It is where a person who recognizes the Elohim as our creators and who recognizes their last envoy as the awaited Messiah. These are the true "Jewish" people of today, the true "House of Israel".

Today, "Israel" is comprised of those people who avow with sincerity and solemnity that the Elohim are our creators by attesting their faith to the Elohim through their son. For once again a son of Yahweh walks the same ground as us. But this one is and will remain their last "Envoy Prophet", as proclaimed by his predecessor in Black Africa, Simon Kimbangu, as "Nkua Tulendo", the one who will come with a specific message for Africa, a message enabling it to decolonise itself completely. From that point forward, fulfilling the mission that is hers: become the "future" of humanity, an open door on her golden age, the age of this full and beneficial realization of herself. If she decides to do so and devotes herself entirely to the mission, it is an attainable goal!

This "History of the twelve Tribes of Israel" as I have described to you, is my second hypothesis to try to explain this "plot", or "boycott", or mission created to conceal the truth, to maintain distance between men and their extraterrestrial creators, the Elohim, these "people coming from the sky". I am hopeful that my efforts will further explain this predisposition of anti-Elohim on Earth, the historic trend toward destroying the grand plan as foretold and enacted by Yahweh Elohim, signs of which can easily be verified by the reading of the true Bible.

To further explain, we have, on the one hand, an anti-Elohim trend beginning with the ten "lost" Tribes of Israel and perpetuated secretly at the highest level by certain Masonic lodges from generation to generation. And then, on the other hand, there would be "Satan", authorized one last time to challenge humanity before its possible entry into the intergalactic era by utilizing the enormous capabilities placed at his disposal and by placing one last hurdle for humanity to overcome.

This hurdle, or temptation, may be presented to only one carefully chosen important person or to many who compose a worldly power family. But Satan will attempt to seduce them, promising them many things such as money, power, and the realization of all their desires, and including eternal life. He would ensure that they would become Masters of the world if they follow his plan, a plan that is in direct opposition to that of Yahweh.

Satan, as you recall, is the leader of the political opposition on the Elohim's planet. He would thus be authorized by those aligned with the thinking of Yahweh, to place an obstacle and challenge man's fortitude, his strength to overcome temptation, or if, in his weakness, he may align himself with evil. To overcome this hurdle would be a supreme test of man's goodness, that to disparage war and conflict of any kind will enable him to know the joy of applauding our fathers return to Earth, to profit from their scientific heritage and infinite knowledge. He will have to achieve a level of planetary conscience based on supreme universal values of Love and Non-violence. As you know, we have many hurdles yet to overcome.

In addition, for 2000 years, man has been forced to deal with another obstacle, that of the despicable Vatican. Contrary to the words of its senile and mumbling "leader", to the effect that "the Catholic Religion is a religion of Love and Compassion", history has shown, and detailed repeatedly in this work, that the Vatican probably is the most dangerous criminal institution on Earth.

Within the framework of my first hypothesis, I alluded to the fact that Satan may have contacted key characters originating in the ten "lost" Tribes of Israel, characters whose descendants still remain the "anti-Elohim". If this were the case, is it possible that the Vatican is nothing more than a shelter in service to Satan? Certainly a theory that demands consideration!

In my view, the Vatican is certainly already spearheaded by those who work against the Elohim, those who have the means of executing their plan on Earth. And in this, since they agreed to oppose Yahweh, they are "the satanic ones"! As a matter of fact, it is Napoleon speaking on the Jesuit Order (a powerful religious order to which the Pope would bow in secrecy), who made the following remarks:

> «*The Jesuits are a military organization, not a religious Order. Their chief is the leader of an army; he is not the abbot of a monastery. And their goal is power, absolute, universal, the power in its most despotic exercise.*»!

It is obvious, in my opinion, that for a long time things have not been going well on Earth and that the future or fate of humanity is not good. There exist "dark" alliances that continue to create conflicts, wars of race and religion, that create classes of rich and poor, that pit people against each other, man against man, these alliances having governed at the highest level and been encamped in each side of these perpetual conflicts.

I firmly believe that the simple and good Catholic Christian, as some describe as "Mister everyone", is merely a person who has been betrayed unknowingly. His unlimited trust and naïve belief that each successive Pope was the one true "representative of God on Earth", when in fact they were just people like himself gave rise to a level of veneration that has continued until today. In truth, the Vatican, this "holy place", was never anything more than an anti-Elohim temple built in the service of evil by males, might I add.

Concerning Freemasons, the same holds true. Yet, I am absolutely convinced that those who did not advance to the highest levels within their order are unaware that they were snared in the same immense net of power and are unwittingly directed by the institutions of the Vatican, the Jesuits, and other such orders. These institutions venerate an Antichrist religious tradition and have never observed the worship of Yahweh, the submission that must represent absolute love and respect for our fathers, the Elohim. On the contrary, they denounce the Elohim, they who possess an absolute Love. Yahweh, Lucifer, Satan... although their visions may vary, they love one another and delight whenever man chooses good over evil.

Just like the large majority of Christians all over the world, the various small Freemasons are unaware that Rome and its acolytes, of which their "Great Masters" are part, actually refuse to accept the plan of Yahweh, the "Grand Architect" of our humanity. Quite to the contrary, they fight as much as possible to prevent the realization of this fantastic project!

The righteous on Earth will do the utmost to have non-violence and the truth triumph. They will fight for Love, fraternity and intelligence and will not be saddened if they see that the majority of men continue to be violent, aggressive and stupid. They must imperceptibly lead men to develop a planetary conscience.

The heritage of our creators, the Elohim, is ready. All that is needed is for the child, our humanity, to not die while being born. May peace reign on Earth for men of goodwill. And the Vatican, at its highest level, the Pope, the Cardinals, are not among these men, they are the disguises of "evil".

Amen

26. The mystery of Satan and the history behind the Twelve Tribes of Israel.

WHITE POISON

27. The "all men are born equal" of the Christian Democracies

"When you go back into the past and find out where you once were, then you will know that you weren't always at this level, that you once attained a higher level, had made great achievements, contributions to societies, civilization, science and so forth. And you know that if you once did it, you can do it again; you automatically get the incentive, the inspiration and the energy necessary to duplicate what our forefathers formerly did".

– EL HADJ EL SHABAZZ (Malcolm X) –

This title sentence is the famous sentence immortalized by the 3rd President of the United States, Thomas Jefferson. It is written in the Declaration of Independence of the United States. Its sentiment is nice, but it means absolutely nothing. In it lies the implication that "all white men are born equal", in the mind of our founding fathers whose faith rested in the Church and Christendom, a church that has always espoused affinity with the extreme right, fascism, and neo-fascism.

This is not surprising. The Church has always walked hand in hand with "racist" movements. God is "white" and Jesus is also "white" and this walk is absolutely necessary in order to maintain the Power of the "Christian Church", to continue to keep its followers in blindness and ignorance, a following that remains fearful to question why.

And who does the Church claim as its biggest "dummies" of all? The Blacks as they were conquered by the Religion of the colonizer which has been the tool of control, domination, conditioning, and total degradation.

With as bad a hand as this one, of course it must be concealed. And perhaps the best way this is done is by accepting blacks within the clergy. Like black puppets, they are maneuvered into revered positions as bishops and cardinals, thus misleading the black populace into believing their presence is valued and important. Those blacks accepted into leadership at the Vatican are our greatest traitors. Being "uncultivated", and although having the best intentions, they have been misled with the "truth" and ultimately betray their people although unwitting to them.

The United States is so proud of Thomas Jefferson's sentence "all men are born equal" that they tirelessly proclaim it loud and clear in their speeches. Sadly, the truth is a different matter! In his only book, titled "Notes on the State of Virginia", Thomas Jefferson makes his own thinking clear. He formulates and presents his theory that white men are intellectually superior to black men. He explains, word for word and among other things, that it would be impossible for a black person to understand the mathematical formula included in the famous book of Euclid, called "the Elements"!

That is the truth about the thinking of this Christian believer born Thomas Jefferson and 3rd President of the United States. He proclaimed in "his" book (he wrote only one) that Africans are inferior to whites and that they cannot grasp the basis of mathematics! This is a stereotype that has prevailed until today among a large number of white mathematicians.

In regards to blacks, however, it is very important to note that only half of this story has been told. Why has the other half been concealed? How can we explain the fact that there is, apparently, a consensus to continue to suppress this fact for as long as possible?

In searching for the truth, we cannot overlook "The Elements", quoted by Jefferson and described as the second-most printed book in the history of humanity, second only to the Bible. "The Elements" was written by Euclid some 2300 years ago during the splendid era of Alexandria. Euclid is considered by many to be the greatest mathematician of all time.

And yet, writings, documents, history, demonstrate that Euclid was of African origin. And most interesting, Euclid never traveled beyond the African continent, never took his teachings into Europe. And yet some Western history books teach that Euclid was Greek. How can this be so when he was born in Africa, raised in Africa, educated in Africa, and never left? I am anxious for an explanation to this contradiction from our historians.

The only rational explanation that comes to mind is how embarrassed the leaders of the Christian Democracies, where Jesus is depicted as white, where the saints are white, where the angels are white, where God is white with a white beard, might feel to admit and acknowledge that the father of mathematics is, in fact, black, an authentic Negro.

But how were they able to capitulate such an enormous lie into the minds of so many people?

294

In my opinion, it is very simple. There exist very old books on the history of mathematics in which we can read that ancient Egypt was not part of Africa, but actually part of Greece. History shows that Alexander the Great did conquer Egypt, establishing the famous city of Alexandria in his conquest. But as we come to understand the continental divisions that have occurred over hundreds of years, we can understand more easily the confusion and logistics of where these ancient cities and civilizations had originally rest. Perpetuating disinformation such as "Egypt is not in Africa" has lent to centuries of confusion.

And how is Euclid presented in picture in the West? As a white male, old, and with white hair. This picture, this image of Euclid that is being diffused, was created 2000 years after his death estimated circa 300 B.C. (And I gladly remind you that Euclid passed away in Africa). Bearing in mind that no "authentic" pictures of Jesus and his followers exist when they were living, how too could a picture of Euclid have been taken (three centuries earlier) that depicts him as white? Who, over time, had the audacity to portray this famous African as white?

The "true" reality is completely different from the distorted story that has been told. An important number of Greek scientists and philosophers of the antiquity were born, raised, and educated on the continent of Africa. Among them were many people of African origin, most black, without question. There is no shred of evidence that Euclid traveled outside of Africa. Therefore, we can assume that he was a full-blooded native African, quite simply.

As for the written history of the black race, it is important to remember that many history books only tell what their authors are permitted to tell or to publish i.e., they only tell half of the truths, and these books are full of misguided and misleading information. For example, consider the unsubstantiated entry by our colonizers concerning our ancestors, the Gauls, a generalized misinformation that has been passed forward from generation to generation causing irreversible damage to so many of our black children.

Clearly, the Western Christian Democracies and the Church of Rome certainly would have no interest in reconsidering the historic truths. It may disturb black Christians to hear the truth but quite frankly, this is the least of my worries because what is of utmost importance is the reality and for the truth to be finally revealed. It is time for Africa to ask herself the right questions and to begin teaching the truth to its children for their own sake. The truth lies outside of Christendom and the model of Christian Democracies.

Euclid was African! And this part of science was a present, a generous gift, offered by Ancient Africa to the modern western world.

Today, the result of this campaign of disinformation is plain. Whites, and even a majority of blacks, have laid claim to the idea that the white man holds superiority in mathematics and think that the African contribution in this field is nonexistent. An African today who is brilliant in science is, most often, not considered for what he is but rather considered as an ano-maly, a rare case, different from other Africans, unique, special, a bizarre accident, or even a mistake of nature. When will this narrow-minded point of view be abandoned?

Another striking example in mathematics is the one of a Nigerian from the Ibos tribe, Dr. Emeagwali, now living in the US. In 1989, Dr. Emeagwali developed a mathematical formulation whereby the simultaneous use of 65,000 processors from separate computers would allow the realization of 3.1 billion calculations per second. Brilliant! And thanks to his work, he is now regarded as one of the fathers of the Internet. The result of his research enabled computer scientists to understand the capabilities of "super computers" and to implement a system allowing a multitude of computers to communicate with each other simultaneously.

Dr. Emeagwali is black. But when the time came to introduce him to the public and it became necessary to publish a picture of him, an interesting thing happened. His first photo, showing him as black, was rejected and replaced with a drawing of a white man which was then widely released through the scientific community.

Why? An illustrator tried to justify his submission by suggesting that Dr. Emeagwali might have traces of white blood, as seen in his facial features. Ridiculous! Dr. Emeagwali is a handsome black Bantu with distinguishing features very much characteristic of Negroes. One need only view his ori-ginal photo to decide for himself.

When will the so-called Christian Democracies and the Church decide to tell the Truth about such matters? When? In my opinion, we must not wait for a decision. The time is now. It is best for us to take charge of the actions necessary to reveal the truth. Fundamentally, we must first re-nounce our association with these white religious organizations.

For hundreds of years, the Virgin Mary (who was not a virgin, coincidentally) has been depicted in paintings and other artistic renderings as beautiful and pure white! And for hundreds of years, man has accepted these renderings without question and without thinking. In reality, paintings done prior to the Renaissance period depicted the Madonna with features similar to that of a black woman. Further, the Christ child is represented with brown and black features.

Consider also the Egyptians, Jordanians, Yemenites, to name a few. Do you see white people among them? I see brown people and black people.

The artistic illustrations of the Madonna and the Christ Child done by Michelangelo Buanarroti and Leonardo da Vinci, Freemason and Grand Master of the Sion Order lodge, as all white are certainly personal artistic offerings. But they cannot mislead me. Their creations are the fruit of purely speculative, hypothetical, and erroneous, imagination. Or perhaps their vision was guided by a specific political and strategic will prominent during their time. This too fits well into a policy or scheme designed to mislead the masses and further subdue the popularity of the black race.

The Scriptures vouch very clearly the fact that Moses had a Kushite (Ethiopian) wife. What color are people in Ethiopia? And if Moses had children with this woman, what color would they be, according to you?

But according to popular opinion, everyone is white; Jesus' mother, Jesus, Joseph, etc. Everybody is white! Why is this so? Because the euro-centrist Christian thought is fundamentally a colonial thought, and consequently racist. Strategically, by negative reinforcement, man is led to uphold the intellectual supremacy of the white man while creating an inferiority complex among blacks. By doing so, an entire subconscious of a race of people is affected and the entire African continent as well.

According to my research, I can contend and insist that Jesus, his mother, Mary, Moses, and others all had dark complexions, a fact that many western Christian democracies are unwilling to accept. This is not surprising given the intense level of conditioning, misconception, and reinforcement they receive, thanks to the unavoidable "media-liars".

When we read history books, we can see that chemistry already existed at the time of Ancient Egypt in Black Africa. But what is the meaning of the word "chemistry?" It means "science of the black man"! In our western universities, will you see the origin of chemistry being taught? Will you see a professor refer to his "science of the black man" book when teaching chemistry? You know the answer...NO!

The word "chemistry" finds its root in the word "Kemet". "Kemet" is the ancient word for what we today call Egypt. And in ancient Egyptian "Kemet" is translated as "The land of Blacks"! In which chemistry manual will you find this important detail in the introduction?

Fortunately, there are a few exceptions and as they are so rare, it is all the more enjoyable to point them out. Isaac Asimov is the author of more than 500 books, including The Biographical Encyclopedia of Sciences in which he acknowledges that:

a.Mathematics, science and technology are gifts from ancient Africans.
b.an African called Imhotep is one of the fathers of medicine;
c.an African is the father of Architecture;
d.an African is the first scientist in written History;
e.all the first Greek Scientists have been taught in Africa by Africans
He also acknowledges that:
f.all these "Greek scientists" lived and worked in Africa.
g.Some were even born in Africa.

Well, well, good morning again Euclid!

The oldest mathematics manuals on Earth are called the "Rhind Papyrus" and the "Moscow Papyrus". They are kept in Moscow and in Berlin and are made from antique papyrus which comes from the Valley of the Nile. As far as I know the Nile flows in Africa and is described as this continent's principle waterway. Or could I be wrong?

The Berlin Papyrus was given the name of Alexander Rhind, a simple Scot traveler who purchased them. But why were they not given the name of the person who wrote them, an African named "Ahmes?" Why have the Christian Democracies overlooked this fact as well? Further still, the Moscow Papyrus was found in Africa, not in Moscow, and therefore we must ask the same question.
 Books are typically named based on their authors as well as for scientific discoveries. Why does this fundamental rule change with regard to Africa and to blacks? Why do the Western Christian democracies insist on "Euro-

298

peanizing" African books and discoveries? Would they allow us to "Africanize" their European books and discoveries?

In the immortal words of Napolean, "History is only a suitable lie"!

To elaborate on this previous point, let us look closer at the subject of writing. In our chapter, "The systematic denigration perpetuated by those with a high leadership inside the church", we looked at the mission of the church to force blacks to abandon their history and heritage and to foster a mentality of inferiority among black people. To this end, senior prelates and other missionaries claimed that the black man had no true writing history and no place in history, no civilization.

Let us attempt to verify the truth.

According to specialists, the four original sources of writing in the history of humanity would be listed chronologically as the following; the writing system of Ancient Egypt (circa 3400 B.C.) (therefore a system of a "negro" writing), then the Sumerian writing, the Chinese writing (circa 1766 B.C), and the Mayan writing (circa 500 B.C). In his "Plato's Phaedras" (274 B.C), Socrates recalls to the collective Greek memory that "ta grammata", i.e., the letters, the grammar, the writing systems, were invented in Kemet (in Ancient Black Egypt).

By examining Greek history, many interesting facts are revealed that have long been concealed or overlooked. For example, it is a black man named Cadmus who instructed inhabitants of Greece in his time, the "Hellenes", of the art of writing, which was later handed down by them to Romans. And from this was derived Latin. And from this, French, Spanish, Portuguese, and numerous other languages evolved, we have Cadmus, a negro, to thank.

On this matter a particularly substantial source of information can be found from "Diodorus of Sicily". This historian from Ancient Greece but from a Sicilian background traveled in Egypt around 59 B.C. Diodorus chronicled his journeys and ultimately composed what is known as "The Historic Library", a universal history of mankind. This work is comprised of forty books and deals with the origin of humanity through the expedition in Gaul of Julius Caesar in 54 B.C. (see DIODORUS OF SICILY, BOOK I, 4,7). Diodorus enjoyed wide popularity with the Hellenes' elite of his time.

In "The Historic Library", Diodorus recounts the story of a Negro man with

Egyptian heritage named Cadmus, the same who instructed letters to the Hellenes. (See DIODORUS OF SICILY, BOOK III, LXVII.1, HISTORIC LIBRARY, ed. "Les Belles Lettres").

Indeed Cadmus was the first person to adapt letters to this language later referred to as "the Greek language". He would assign a name to each letter and establish a connection to each. Therefore, as history shows us, we can say that this fundamental contribution to the intellectual life of Men was not the fruit of a Hellenic intelligence (not even Greek), but the fruit of a Negroid intelligence! And yet with unscrupulous bias, the "tremendous history of Greek civilization" has continued to be taught in Europe with total disregard for the truth, that blacks have played a vital role in the advancement of civilization. "Me? I said 'strange'?... how strange"! to quote the famous French actor, Louis Jouvet, might be a typical response to such a claim.

Another important and fundamental aspect to be aware of and to further support Diodorus' contribution concerning Cadmus would be that of another famous Greek writer, Herodotus. Herodutus also presents Cadmus as the architect of the written language and its evolution throughout Europe. (see Herodotus, Book V, 58) Herodotus confirms that Cadmus and his entourage traveled to Greece to bring and share his knowledge, traveling from the coastal region of Phoenicia, now known as Israel. It is here that Cadmus lived among the Canaanites.

Let us look carefully at what these ancient texts tell us about these regions and their inhabitants. Canaan would have belonged to Ham (black son of Noah) and to his descendants. This might explain the number of exchanges and connections between Canaan and Egypt during this time (where "KaM" means "black", "burnt", hence the name "Ham" given to the black son of Noah). Further, it could be said that Canaan was conquered by Negro pharaohs, perhaps even Osiris, the Great Prophet and black half-God (see Chapter 7) who, during this time, traveled extensively throughout what we now call "Europe". It could further explain the great similarities between the rites and customs of Canaanites, Phoenicians, and Egyptians.

I offer this as proof for your consideration. In the year 2000, a team of archeologists led by Pierre de Miroschedji made an important discovery in the heretofore obscured history of black Africa, much to our pleasure! The French publication, "Le Figaro", in its September 25, 2000, edition offers this excerpt entitled, "Gaza, Conquerors' Path:"

"[...] just unearthed incredible foundations and walls of a city 97% Egyptian, stretching over ten hectares". In the discovery of this fortress that guarded the border between Egypt and the country of Canaan, what's most important, is the date: the medium Bronze Age. Between the end of 4000 and the beginning of 3000 B.C, Egyptians had already established a colony here. And Pierre Miroschedji adds: "it means a thousand years before what we estimated being the time of the Colonial Egyptian Empire".*

And so you see, well before Thoutmosis III, one of the pharaohs of the 18th dynasty, (1505/1484-1450 B.C.), perhaps two or three centuries before the time of the pharaoh, Narmer ("Negro" founder of the Egyptian empire, 3rd to 6th dynasty, from 2778 B.C. to 2260 B.C.), the Kamits or KaM took possession of Canaan and so of Phoenicia.

You will recall that the name "KaM" means "black" and is the real name of the inhabitants of Egypt. Yes, contrary to the words of our esteemed historians, these conquerors lived nearly fifty centuries ago. And it is these black conquerors from Phoenicia who brought the craft of writing to Greece. And according to the texts of Ras-Shamra of Ugarit in northern Phoenicia, their real ancestors, the Canaanites, hailed from the south, from Egypt. (See "Conteneau, Oriental Manual of Archeology, 1791)

They indeed came from Africa despite what some western uncultivated, perhaps misguided or dishonest, authors may say. And with amusement, they have confused African Egypt with European Greece, altering Euclid's race from black to white, as though a black man was not capable of such an achievement.

Having reviewed these historic accounts, the truth concerning Cadmus, the negro, the man who brought writing to Greece and, via a chain reaction, to the rest of Europe and beyond, becomes crystal clear. But for further edification, consider the following passages as well.

> 1- *The Bible of Sanchoniathon, a Phoenician book, acknowledges clearly that writing was invented by Egyptians (Blacks!) and then passed on to Phoenicians (see Theophilus Obenga, the scientific renaissance of Africa, African Diaspora, Paris, 1994).*

> 2- *Professor John Chadwick's words:*

"The alphabet writing is generally considered a Semitic (i.e. Phoenician) invention, but the Egyptian writing opened the door to this system". (See John Chadwick, At the origins of the Greek language, Paris, Gallimard, 1972, p 70 and 71).

And if there is still doubt in your mind, here is the icing on the cake:

3- In his writings, "The Pleading", Greek poet, Eschylus (claimed by some to be the creator of the antic tragedy) reveals to us the genealogy of Cadmus, and he is not the only one to do so. As revealed in his book, Cadmus is the grandson of Lo, the daughter of the King of Argos. The City of Argos was located in the Peloponnesian Peninsula, that is to say, Pelasgos. Quoting the poet Asios of Samos and Greek Pausanias, "and the black soil created Pelasgos in the likeness of Gods". From this, some ancient authors (and the Greek Pausanias) contend that King Pelasgos was a Negro, therefore was his descendent, Cadmus, as well. (Source: Black Athena, Martin Bernal, Tome 1, PUF Edition).

a)   The "father of the church", Eusèbe of Cesare, "Inachos", that is to say, Lo's progenitor, was indeed a Black from Egypt. This may be explained by Eschylus' passage in "Prometheus", a passage confirming the negritude of Lo's son, "Epaphos" who is Cadmus' grand-father: "and to recall how Zeus brought the child into the world, the one you will give birth to [speaking to Lo] will be the black Epaphus, who will cultivate the entire country watered by the large flow of the Nile" (Source: Eschylus, Prometheus, v. 846-852)

b)   The logographer, Pherecyde (first half of the 5th century) confirms that Cadmus was the son of the Egyptian, "Agenor" (himself son of the Negro "Epaphus") and of a black girl from the Nile. (Therefore Cadmus had a black father and mother).

c)Agenor, Egyptian subject and Cadmus' father, must have later been nominated by the Egyptian power as leader of the city of Tyr in Phoenicia because it is precisely there that we find him again. So, for Hecatee of Abdera and Diodorus of Sicily, Cadmus was originally

302

from Egypt and from the city of Thebes in particular, as outlined by Alexander Tourraix (Ref. Alexander Tourraix, The Orient, Greek Mirage, PUFC, The 'Belles Lettres' Edition).

All these facts and many others ultimately confirm Cadmus' negritude (see the most ancient Greek paintings of Cadmus).

Having outlined Cadmus' lineage by Eschylus and confirmed this by Pherecyde, authenticating his pure black heritage, it is equally exciting to tell you that he is also the brother of "Europe", a black girl to whom the European continent owes its name. Funny, isn't it? And yet, I fear that few white Europeans will appreciate this touch of humor.

Nevertheless, the teaching of writing to Hellenes, the Greeks' ancestors, is historically based on this anecdote: an African black named Cadmus came to search out his sister Europe on a Continent to which posterity will grant the name of this black woman.

On the admission of Herodotus, it is the only valid explanation for the origin of the European continent's name. Abducted by Hellenes or Cretans (Herodotus does not come to a decision), EUROPE will be taken to this continent, which will become "European" and it is when he went to look for her that Cadmus set his foot on this continent. The teaching of writing to Greeks, Latins and others is based on this theory. Some ancient relics found in Greece still exist that give credence to this thought.

As you can well understand, all of this is very embarrassing for the Christian West, to be sure. And throughout time, the Vatican has taken great pains to remove any trace of these historic facts. It is fully aware of this true lineage but all of it is concealed at the highest level of this institution's hierarchy and its 'secret service' agencies, such as the "Opus Dei". Indeed, the Vatican has, time and again, exercised its own form of propaganda and has succeeded in concealing the real position of the black man in the history of humanity, in the history of religions and of the Bible. All this is suppressed by the white Catholic Christian Church whose power is based on a monstrous accumulation of lies and crimes.

Many saints in the Bible and in history were blacks (St. Francis of Assisi and many others). So why wouldn't Jesus have been of mixed-race? Numerous sources, frescos, paintings and cults show a Madonna, the Virgin Mary, as a black. Why would this be contrary to the truth?

It is clear to me that the Vatican and numerous Masonic orders have concealed countless other details about the history of humanity. Even if they view themselves historically as rivals, each must continue their campaign of deception or lose their power, thus the likely tacit agreement between them. Indeed, to reveal that the origin of the word, "Europe", comes from the name of a black woman, which is, in reality, nothing more than a detail in the history of humanity, would be seriously detrimental to both their causes.

Let us not lose sight of the fact that Osiris and Isis played a predominant role in the rites and beliefs of the first Christians and that a lot of symbolism around Osiris and Isis is coming back today through the heretics in Europe (Cathars, Templars, Zion Prior, etc.)

Ladies and Gentlemen, Christian blacks, by being "faithful" to Christian Churches, you perpetuate these lies and grotesque misconceptions. Every day that you engage in this belief, you continue to denounce your true place in history. Because of this, this universal orchestration of lies, Africa remains in misery, poverty, and overwhelming misfortune.

Africa must accept being dominated by others, exploited by the western world. In the eyes of Westerners, Africa serves two purposes; as a depository for their waste (for a small fee, of course), and as a place of predilection for the deployment of military activities (highly lucrative to some but promoting death and violence for the rest of the world, including innocent civilians of their own countries). And when these world leaders supply the various world armies with weapons from their factories, there is no doubt that they are fully aware of the consequences of their actions. Ladies and Gentlemen, Black Christians, the Christian Churches of the whites keep you in the dark, in servitude, in slavery and in a form of permanent colonization that you may never have fully realized. Until now!

For you and for all your descendants and for the benefit of the entire planet, it is URGENT that you become aware of the realities in which we are living today.

The baron Dominique Vivant DENON (1747-1825) was a famous French draftsman (see the illustration on page XI of the central booklet). He was a member of Bonaparte's expedition to Egypt before becoming the director general of French Museums under Napoleon the 1st. Talented draftsman and engraver, Napoleon Bonaparte enlisted him for his expedition to Egypt (1798-1799). His mission was to gather, through drawings, historical traces of Ancient Egypt. As we know, photography was not available to him at that time.

During his expedition, he made a drawing of the famed Sphinx' face. But it was his own comments, written at the foot of the monument, which were much more beautiful:

> "I just had the time to observe the Sphinx, which deserves to be drawn with the most scrupulous care, as it has never been done in this way. Though its proportions are huge, the well-preserved outlines are as smooth as pure: the expression of the head is soft, graceful and calm; the character is African: but the mouth of which the lips are thick has softness in the movement and a truly admirable delicacy of execution; it is flesh and life".

Further in his comment of the Egyptian art, he wrote: "as for the Character of their human face, borrowing nothing from other nations, they copied their own nature that was more graceful than beautiful [...] in all, the African character, of which the Negro is the charge and perhaps the principle" (op.cit. p.168). (Page 203, Source: Vivant DENON, "Voyage to Lower and Upper Egypt during General Bonaparte's campaigns, Paris, 1st Issue Didot l'Aîné, 1802; reissue, Pygmalion/Gerard Watelet, 1990,p.109.)

How did we so suddenly, so sharply, fall into a regression with such serious consequences? Consider these two thoughts : the Gods who were living with our ancestors returned to their home, and we were left to the victimization of slavery. We will see very soon what "conclusion" we could draw from all of that. But first let us look at the future of Africa should it choose to embrace science instead of Christiany.

There are still people who doubt that ANCIENT EGYPT was populated and controlled by blacks, that pharaohs and queens were handsome and beautiful Negroes, that it is indeed blacks who had reached a level of civilization and a degree of science decidedly superior to those in other regions of the world at that time. In others words, that there was a time when blacks brought knowledge and light to white people, a time in history when whites were "savages" in comparison to blacks, and that sciences such as architecture, perfumes, chemistry, mathematics, astronomy, letters, et cetera, and other major contributions typically ascribed to white people could have been done by blacks. (See in the central booklet a few nice pictures illustrating this reality, page I and XI to XVI)

When we have been able to control the thought of a man, by having imposed one's religion upon this man, there is no reason to be worried about either his reactions or his actions. Because he is like a domestic dog or a circus lion, well trained. Is this really the way the majority of Africans want to live? I hope not!

There was a time when Africans were bearers of light for whites. But looking at the Black Christians today, the sentiment I feel is that Africa's light is fading, and worse, that it draws its light from Christianity. I must emphatically exclaim: "Beware!! It is an illusion of light; it is false, nicely put together, but false and deceptive nonetheless. Africa, you have allowed yourself to be hypnotized by this mystification. You have lost the light you once had"!

But today, Africa can rediscover its light. And to do so, it must abandon the illusion cast by the Christian light. Remember that there was a time when you were not in darkness until a light came from elsewhere.

28. Africa and Science

"When you are ready to leave for work, be aware that half of all the things and all the appliances that you have used before leaving were invented by Blacks".

- Martin Luther King Jr -

We have seen in this work to what extent and with what tenacity the Church has always rivalled the progress of science. From this point forward, it is plain to see what is good and right for Africa; simply put, all that the Church opposes, and science especially. So it is very much in the best interest of Africa to support science whenever possible and without trepidation, provided the scientific advancement is non-violent in its goal.

One thing is certain; virtually nothing will be able to stop the advancement of science, no church, nor any millennial Christianity. So it is imperative that an intelligent Africa fix its sights on the future and not with the past.

And what is the future? Science and progress. And what is the past? The Church and Christianity.

In order for Africa to restore its health and its drive, it must divorce itself from the Church and join into a loving relationship with Science; this for its consummate happiness.

In the very near future, as science and technologies evolve, Africa will find itself equally evolved to that of western countries. It is conceivable that it may even surpass these nations in its capabilities as the painstaking progression of scientific knowledge experienced in Europe will have passed. Indeed, science will progress at lightning speed. And this progression will follow an exponential curve in which the horizontal axis (x-axis) representing 'time' will become shorter and shorter as the vertical axis (y-axis) representing 'scientific discoveries' will grow. This means that the progression of technology will occur in shorter and shorter periods of time.

Let us examine this not only in mathematical reasoning, but in reality. During the last twenty years, man has seen more discoveries in the millennia of human history than in those preceding twenty years. And the exponential curve of this scientific progress is only at its starting point, thanks to the remarkably increased power of computers each year.

As we continue on this trend, over the next ten years we will make even more discoveries to surpass those made during this prior twenty-year period. Continuing to rise and turn ever closer to the vertical axis of the exponential curve, the progression of science will again be reduced in half to five years, where more discoveries will be made in that time period than in all the preceding years combined, and so on. Imagine when a scientific discovery will occur in a single moment!

At that precise point in time, man will have reached a phase known as 'singularity' and which is in its infancy today. This ultimate moment will be the one when he will have discovered all that there is to discover, or at least he will know all the general aspects of science, and every universal biological principle, in every field. Man will continue to make discoveries and to do research. But it may be for cultural purposes or for his pleasure, or for artistic reasons, but one thing is for certain is that he will have come to know all that is essential for him to know.

It is precisely at that crucial moment, at the beginning of the rise of this exponential curve of Science, that Africa will see its chance within its intellectual grasp. And it must seize this moment! For Africa has one of the greatest advantages over the West ever known in terms of the science and technologies of tomorrow: purity. Africa has preserved an extraordinary purity and prevailed over a culture and mentality weighed down by a heavy past that Westerners are constantly entangled in.

It is Africa that has the purity that Westerners have lost. Diametrically, the West is crushed by its Judeo-Christianity. It is heavy, dusty, obscurantist, "conservative". This is how the Catholic Church is seen, carrying the flame of that stupid "Judeo-Christian ethic", howling at every opportunity, "Halt the progress of Science"! It is an obsession, even if nowadays it no longer has the power to send scientists at the stake for their revolutionary work, it often tries everything it can to stop science in areas where it is about to create the most controversy.

This retrograde attitude is motivated by the persisting fear of the ecclesiastic hierarchy that a great number of its dogmas will be shattered, ridiculous dogmas that are outdated but that nonetheless the Church still insists on imposing on the whole world!

Africa must quell its fear concerning this matter. It must consider all the benefits that those new technologies can bring to its continent to deliver it from misery and to continuously improve the quality of life of its inhabitants. The western powers are intent on subjecting Africa to the phases of industrialisation that they have undergone themselves; thus ensuring their advancement over Africa and to maintain its under-developed state, a "developing continent", as they delight in saying. They are being polite, but this in no way commits them to helping this "poor" continent in order to make it "rich". No point in dreaming!

Through their courteous guise, the Westerners are attempting to hide a well-orchestrated plan of neo-colonization. Well, no! This time it won't be so simple. Africa can now oppose itself to the realization of one of their new "machiavellian plans". Thanks to its talents, its genius, its freshness and purity, Africa will rise quickly and directly to a level identical to all developed countries, perhaps even overtake them. It is possible for her provided it seizes Science and places it at the service of man, that it grabs the new technologies that the West dismisses in the name of its restricted "moral code". Now is the time for Africa to find the awareness that will save her.

The only poison that will prevent the success of Africa in this endeavour is non other than this "white poison", for which this book was titled. She manufactures this poison in her head and is often tempted to intoxication by it. But she must vomit it completely, abandon it, once and for all, this poison that she has come to know so well as: her "inferiority complex" to the whites! Africans must eliminate this poison forever. They don't need to feel inferior to anyone, certainly not towards whites whose fundamental qualities are seldom superior to those of the blacks!

There is a vast number geniuses in Africa, a large reservoir, but it is necessary that the young geniuses and inventors be able to grow and flourish in an environment that allows their genius to germinate and bloom. For this, they must have access to knowledge, science, education, and information. And all of this is now possible, thanks to the Internet.

Mozart could never have expressed his talent, his immense musical prowess and genius if he had grown in an environment without access to instruments or facilities to use them. The backing, the instruments, the tools, access to knowledge, is what has always been unavailable to these numerous African geniuses. Throughout their history, the foremost concern of their parents was to bring food to their table. Even today, many young African geniuses wonder daily if and when their next meal will come. This situation will change very soon if we organize ourselves correctly and if we demonstrate that good will and solidarity can exist between us.

What are those sciences and new technologies that can allow Africa to eliminate the barriers that stall their advancement? They are:

a. *The Internet;*
b. *GMOs (Genetically Modified Organisms),solution to the problems of hunger and malnutrition;*
c. *Nanotechnology;*
d. *Therapeutic cloning;*
e. *Robotics (biological robots)*

By accessing the Internet, millions of young Africans will have instant access to the best education, to all information, to all knowledge, and to all scientific publications. They will also benefit from the wisdom of the best professors in the world, even "attend" American universities via the Internet. Even now, many US universities offer online classes, testing, and degree programs, all without attending in person.

That's the future! To get an "on-line" education from the professors most competent in their academic discipline without the burden of travel or campus living expenses.

Thanks to the beneficial effects of those electronic techniques, hundreds of millions of young Africans will be linked to each other, even to the whole world, from behind their small screen. A conditioning of the masses will never be possible again because the Internet allows the immediate exchange of information and ideas between two individuals once they become connected.

In this way, the Internet will be for Africa like an electric pulse that links neurons in the brain as it stimulates global consciousness. The young have to be trained extensively in Internet usage and in computer science in Africa by making available to them the necessary computers, energy, and Internet links. This must be done today, not tomorrow.

GMOs are the solution for eradicating hunger in Africa and in the whole world. Thanks to genetics, we will finally be able to produce greater quantities of food in Africa where there is such a cruel lack of it at the present time.

310

The Genetically Modified Organisms are the future. They bring with them countless advantages. Firstly, they will significantly reduce the amount of pesticides and weed-killers used in cultivation, already some of the most serious sources of pollutants for our people. And, as recently demonstrated with genetically modified yellow rice, the GMOs will bring us important sources of vitamins that our African populations so desperately need.

It is far too easy for the plump Westerners to proclaim from atop their ivory towers that genetically modified organisms are dangerous. First of all, it is again a lie. But above all, it is better to have this food than to have no food at all, a fact well known in Africa but that Westerners do not understand, this to their satisfaction. In Africa, having experienced the pain of starvation and malnutrition, what is more hazardous for the health of the poor is not to have any food at all. Next to this absolute evil, the rest pales into insignificance.

Even if the production of genetically modified organisms has not been perfected, we must continue with their experiments in order to improve them and be able to present them in their perfected form. All the fears intentionally conveyed by some with regard to those new species are without basis; they are only based on ignorance.

Until now, the desired genetic modifications were obtained through centuries of slow selections done by gardeners or breeders. The genetically modified foods are the result of manipulation of the same order but done over a much shorter period of time.

Nobody fears the wheat that was selected over centuries in order to increase production or the steps taken to prevent it from mixing with wild wheat, or worried that dairy cows that produce 20 times more milk than the wild species would "contaminate" the latter.

Not only will the genetically modified species bring food in abundance to Africa and reduce pollution but they will also allow us to discover or rediscover fruits and vegetables with extraordinary flavours. The tastes of food are, in fact, contained in their genes. Through this method, we will have sweeter fruits and with a more pronounced taste without having to add refined sugar to increase our enjoyment.

Imagine that all the fruits and vegetables indigenous to the African continent are grown naturally and without chemical additives, their flavours enhanced one hundred times over. Bananas, pineapples, et cetera. All this

311

is possible and within the reach of tomorrow's Africa.

The same will apply to animals. A salmon capable of growth ten times faster than the wild species was recently created through genetic modification. Western opponents who claim to be "ecological" are trying to block its commercialisation under the pretext of the result of accidental cross-breeding with the wild species. So what is the danger in this? We would have salmon ten times bigger than before. Where would the problem be? I doubt that fishermen would complain about this phenomenon anymore than those who know famine would, those who are literally dying from hunger!

Better...or worse! This depends on your point of view. Now geneticists are proposing to sterilize these genetically modified salmon simply to stifle complaints from stubborn westerners who oppose this progress in science.

And the taste of those genetically modified salmons can even be enhanced. We will even be able to modify the genes that control the taste of the flesh and thus give it more flavour. We will achieve the same with meat. Beef with fresh meat having the same taste and tenderness as aged meat, even more tasty and tender than what we commonly consider "normal;" this will also be possible. The modification method will apply to all forms of food now at our disposal.

Africa must distance herself from the "conservative" and narrow-minded European Christian thinking and welcome the genetic progress at our threshold. We have the ability to improve the quality of life of men; we must first begin with Africans themselves.

Why are these "conservatives" shocked by genetically modifying an animal to become food for people? Are they shocked by the head of one of those horrible looking dogs such as the bull-terrier, the bulldog, the Yorkshire or the Chihuahua? No! Yet those species come from the wolf or the wild dog and are the result of genetic selections. The only difference between the transformation of a GMO and the domestication of the ancient wolf to one of man's beloved "pets" is the time it took to achieve the result, centuries. It's that simple.

And simply because that operation took centuries, nobody protests. Everybody accepts with admiration a nude cat without a single hair and with skin that creases simply because the genetic modification took centuries. How stupid!

312

We Africans, to the greatest benefit of our present and future children, must not fall into the trap set by western conservative thinking. In fact, we must turn our back on it and seize science and new technologies with open arms in order to improve our quality of life, our well-being. And you will soon see the rest of humanity follow us. Remember the Bible passage: "Every man is brutish in his lack of knowledge"!

Computers will quickly surpass the capabilities of the human brain. In fact, we can ascertain that it is already the case, especially in the areas of memory capacity and the ability to calculate. Yet with the development of artificial intelligence and neuronal computers, the computers' performance, including its capacity to create and/or adapt to new surroundings, will become more powerful than what the most brilliant human brain can perform. And this capability will surpass not only our most brilliant chess champions, for instance, but our computer designers as well. Amusing, no? The ability to create machines that are more intelligent than those who created them is quite fascinating indeed.

This advancement will drastically change all the socio-economic structures of the world and perpetuate an unprecedented development in the History of Humanity. How unfortunate for those who will not seize the opportunity to take advantage of it!

Then will come nanotechnology, a phase in scientific history that Africa must not miss. Most definitely, Africa must be certain to be a pioneer in this field. Nanotechnology promises to replace labour in all industries producing raw material, industrial as well as agricultural.

The use of microscopic robots able to work at the molecular level will allow mines to extract minerals without miners, factories without workers to transform them into usable materials, farms without farmers to transform chemical substances into vegetable matter or meat products without the use of plants or animals. The nanobots (nano-robots) will be able to produce everything we need since they work directly at the nano (one billionth -10-9) scale. Their role is to reassemble atoms and molecules and so create the basic constituents of all matter.

If we need iron, for example, all that will be required is to insert billions of nanobots into the ground. They will then extract iron ore, transport it by automated means towards the factories where it will then be inserted into machines, computers really, where other nanobots are programmed to transform it into pure iron. All those operations will be done automatically, without producing any waste. The same method will be employed for cotton, for example, and all other materials. Machines will produce cotton directly from atoms composing its matter without having to use the plant.

Nourishing the populations will finally become a thing of the past!

If we want a piece of chicken, for example, it will be as simple as inserting the chemical components of chicken flesh into a device much like our modern day microwaves, full of the flavour we would expect of the best grain-fed chicken but without the hormones or other chemical producs. Fish, other meats, fruits...in fact, every food possible and imaginable will be at our disposal.

Each type of food has a specific chemical composition and can be re-created chemically by simple manipulation of atoms and molecules by nanobots. These instruments will be programmed for purifying the rivers and, ultimately the oceans, the same ones that are currently being used as huge waste receptacles.

With this advancement, there will no longer be a need for a work force, employees, labourers, etc. At this time we will need to establish a minimum revenue for each human being, a guaranteed income from his birth to his death, an allowance that will give him the pleasure of living a decent life. This "existence revenue", call it what you will, will afford each person the basic necessities of life; shelter, food, clothing, and fun, something we can really call "living"!

Nanotechnology will bring about the freedom of the human being. It will resolve a great number of problems, beginning with lodging and food. "Living apartments" will be designed using a subtle mixture of biology, electronics and nanotechnology. And the ultimate pleasure... nanobots will build them without any construction workers. Each apartment or other types of lodging will be connected to running water, to food production apparatus, all chosen by the occupant. No longer will food be a commodity for only the rich. No one will ever have to "eat caviar with a ladle to be noticed; anyway, it is stupid...it is not better with a ladle", to quote the Italian-Frenchman Colucci (or Coluche). And as for amusement and pleasure, computer science will introduce to every human being the access to virtual reality.

This equality will engender an incomparable world of love and fraternity.

314

Each and every one of us will have the pleasure of creating original works of art that we can offer to our loved ones without expectation of compensation since money will have become a thing of the past. For those endeavouring in fields of scientific research, of course, they can do so also without the motivation and necessity of earning a living. No, now it will be just "for the fun of it", or still with the inclination to progress, pure and simple.

It would be normal, even desirable, for these artists and researchers, whose works bring additional happiness to their fellow citizens, to gain some advantages such as the right to choose to live in large individual homes or other dwellings, for instance, as their work benefits the entire human community.

Soon in such a society, hospitals will become almost obsolete; the benefits of nanotechnology and cloning will allow the repair of human beings up to the limit of longevity programmed in their cells.

All of this is not science fiction for the next century; it will come to pass sooner than we can imagine.

It is quite probable that, at first, the western world will try to hinder the progress of nanotechnology because those in positions of power and wealth will customarily oppose sharing these benefits with others. They will not want to give up on this powerful monetary system and be reluctant to share these technologies with the poor, those "at the bottom". More precisely, using an expression by French politicians and voiced by Jacques Brel, "Those people, Sir, have always gotten richer by impoverishing and exploiting even more 'those at the bottom.'" As seen in Africa, they exploit and crush them unscrupulously.

We can safely bet that they won't be willing to allow Africa the benefits of the progress of science. Despite their nice speeches promising "help for development", these people who control the reins of world power are far from admitting that what they intend to do is to control Africa and further from providing relief. This reality weighs us down every day of our lives.

This is where the role of the blacks in the Diaspora will become very important, essential, especially those African-Americans in the United States who identify more and more with their African roots, their African origins. There are an increasing number of distinguished scholars and millionaires in the black Diaspora in the United States. In fact, there is a magazine in the US dedicated to black millionaires. It will be their role to bring these technologies to Africa as soon as possible, to deliver Africa from its endemic misery and to ensure that it realizes equal footing with the West, or to advance since it is within their capability.

I have just stated that this is not a thing of fiction. To be clear, this will occur in the next twenty years. Africans, are you going to find your proper place in this new contest? Africa, are you finally going to find the part that you will be able to play in the great concert of the Nations?

It is quite possible. Africa has all the genius, all the brilliance it needs. It must only give itself the proper means, especially to its youth, to all the budding geniuses that it has, so that they can express it and make their genius shine forth.

However, we must constantly be wary of the pernicious idea instilled and reinforced through "mental manipulation", a wholesale manipulation of people of all race, but particularly of blacks. This idea is "the inferiority of blacks to whites". And we have to acknowledge that this very long campaign of lies, astutely orchestrated and always by the same exploiters, has produced fearsome results. This "inferiority complex", this "White Poison" is most regrettable because it is false. Nevertheless, our "black spirits" have been imbued with it, a harmful burden that we must cast off... quickly, now!!

Because it is nothing more than a fraudulent falsification of reality, a fancifully orchestrated attempt to promote black inferiority. And to prove the existence of that odious manipulation, I will reveal to you, my African brothers and sisters, information that architects of this campaign wish to conceal from the black population of the world, perhaps to the white population as well.

Here are the facts. They are numerous; countless black inventors and scholars, descended from slaves, thus African blacks or Negroes, but living in the United States. Several are responsible for inventions that we, people of all color, use every day; proof that environment, access to information, the availability to adequate tools are all that we need to foster the artistry and creativity of our various "geniuses".

Here are a few examples of some inventions and ideas discovered by blacks, African-Americans living in the USA, between 1800 and the present time:

316

a. The first machine for planting corn and cotton

b. The wagon coupler for railroads

c. The extraction of shampoo, vinegar, soap, ink, synthetic rubber

d. The process of using cotton in the manufacturing of isolation boards, paper, ropes, and paving blocks

e. The creation, from Soya, of a plastic material that Henry Ford used in certain automobile parts

f. The flash drying process that allows the conservation of food without altering neither the taste nor the appearance

g. The manufacturing of hard plastics

h. The telegraph

i. The pacemaker

j. The procedures for the use of chemotherapy

k. The second kidney transplant in the world

l. The evaporator that allowed the production of sugar of great quality, and that same system was used for the production of condensed milk, soap, gelatine, strong glue, etc.,

m. The device capable of lubricating steam machines while in operation

n. The gas mask

o. The first refrigerating apparatus transportable on long distances

p. The anemometer that allows measuring fluid turbulence

q. The paint gun

r. The image converter able to detect electromagnetic radiation

s. The spectrograph camera used by Apollo 16 on the moon (the first telescope used from another celestial body)

t. Traffic lights

u. The harpoon (fishing tool)

v. and so on... the list is far from being exhaustive!

And since we just evoked their various successes, it would be good to pay tribute to all those black scholars and inventors by listing some of their names: George Washington Carver, Ernest Everett Just, Lloyd A Hall, Percy L. Julian, Lloyd Albert Quarterman, Ralph Gardner, Lewis Latimer, Granville T. Woods, Otis Boykin, William A. Hinton, Louis Wright, Charles Drew, Jane Cook Wright, Samuel Kountz, Arnold Maloney, Shirley a. Jackson, Patricia S. Cowings, David Blackwell, Norbert Rillieux, Elijah McCoy, Garret A Morgan, Georges Carruthers, etc. The list is endless.

Yves Antoine has written, among many works, a specific essay on just this topic, "Black Inventors and Scholars", publisher: L'Harmattan, Paris. And we are happy to offer him this mention.

I wanted to share with you this information as it contradicts the "image of the black" as has been told for so long and still persists today. It is an image so integrated in the human mind that nearly everyone harbours this misconception. While many people disagree, the generally accepted view of blacks is that we are good in music, sports, and dancing. And without knowing us better, assume that everything else is beyond our capability.

The problem is that this is completely false. We have proven our ability to excel in many fields, even fields of science. It would appear as though there is a large-scale attempt by the human community as a whole to dismiss our talents, to ignore our competence in varied disciplines. As if this "human community" would prefer that our essential skills remain unknown and unused. Further, there is a contention that blacks are completely incompetent in the field of finance. Is that so! Who received the Nobel Prize in Economics in 1979? A black man, William Arthur Lewis! And, in fact, in Medical Science, who performed the first open heart operation in 1893 in Chicago? A black man: Doctor Daniel Hale Williams!

The black universe, the universe of negritude, the universe of Africa and the Africans is just as infinite as are the universes of other populations. We have already brought a lot to modern science but it has remained well hidden. But now beware! Let it be known, Mr. and Mrs. Westerner, we are beginning to see clearly!

And we Africans, let us be well aware – it is vital to our future – if all this truth has been concealed, it is because a certain white Christianity has always leaned on its so called "scientific" racism to justify its invention of inequality between the races. It is in order to reinforce that woolly theory that it would like for our competences to remain occult and that the blacks themselves remain ignorant about what they are capable of doing.

Its reasoning is very simple: the more we would be informed, the more we would become confident and the more we would copy the models of success that we would see around us, always to better ourselves. And this "way of doing" would put in peril the supremacy of power, presented as "spiritual", of the directors of the said Christianity. But moreover and

318

most importantly, this would greatly harm their businesses, threaten their exorbitant lifestyles, the "worldly" goods they acquire from enormous power, the wealth and power they insist on keeping above all else, and have for 2000 years!

But you might be saying: "Would a spiritual decolonisation also have implications at the political, economic and social levels?" Of course! It is only logical. If we get rid of that fearsome instrument that has allowed political, economic and social colonisation, namely the Christian/Catholic Religion, we face a new political, economic and social vision that will again change Africa, but in the right direction this time! This "re-conversion" will, at the same time, "re-draw" Africa at all levels. Not only will there be a return to the roots, to traditions and to authentic religions, but also an enormous adjustment at the political, economic and social levels will follow because all the clocks will be set at the right time! We will briefly approach these essential questions in the next two chapters.

WHITE POISON

29. A return towards the old natural borders that preceded Christian colonization

"If I were chief of one of the people of Nigritia (an African country), I hereby declare that I would build gallows at the country's borders and unremittingly hang the first European who would dare cross" -
Jean Jacques Rousseau

The spiritual decolonization of Africa will generate a total liberation of the whole continent. There will be automatically a global change, a continental awakening, a new wind, a new momentum, a revolution reaching all the levels of life. It is completely logical. There will be a general return to authenticity. That cannot fail to happen. Inevitably, the spiritual revolution will generate many other revolutions in its path. One of them, and not the least, will be the abandonment of all conflicts of a geopolitical nature. This will be done as soon as our old borders are returned to us, our "true" borders that existed prior to the era of "Christian" colonisation. This transformation will be done for the greatest happiness of Africa, and everyone will realize its beneficial effects.

When these "Christian" colonizers arrived on our immense continent, they decided among themselves to create states that had not existed prior to their arrival. Like a children's game, the inhabitants were merely pawns whose very existence was considered meaningless. With maps of Africa before them, they randomly traced discretionary lines on paper denoting their playing fields, or borders, this according to a well-known principle, "the strongest always wins". These arbitrary borders were created for "the needs of the cause", plain and simple, to better aid the Westerners distribute the plunder of the local resources. (See, The famous Geographical Conference of Brussels in 1876 and the International Conference of Berlin of 1884 to 1885).

And how do you suspect that the general Act of the African Conference of Berlin begins?

With the sentence "In the name of Almighty God..." followed by "His Majesty the Emperor of Germany, King of Prussia, His Majesty the Emperor of Austria, King of Bohemia, etc.., and Apostolic King of Hungary, His Majesty the King of Belgians, His Majesty the King of Denmark, His Majesty the King of Spain, President of the French Republic,

321

> *Her Majesty the Queen of the United Kingdom of Great Britain and Ireland, Imperatrice of India, His Majesty the King of Italy, His Majesty the King of the Netherlands, Great Duke of Luxemburg, etc.., His Majesty the King of Portugal and the Algarve, etc.., His Majesty the Emperor of all Russia, His Majesty the King of Sweden and Norwegian, etc.., and His Majesty the Emperor of Ottomans, all wanting to solve, in a spirit of mutual agreement, the most favourable conditions to the development of commerce and the civilization of certain regions in Africa [...]"!!*

Please! "In the name of Almighty God"! As if it were Yahweh the eternal who gave them the order, the mission, or the permission to savagely go colonize Africa! Whose "God" is it? It must be theirs because I don't know of any immaterial, omnipotent, and unique "God" that they came to impose upon us for he does not exist. Quite the contrary! From high up in the skies, our creator gods, the Elohim of the original Hebrew Bible, have seen it all. They have seen this grotesque and inhumane plan being orchestrated among Christian European dynasties and consequently decided send a black Prophet whose mission it would be to combat and fight against this monstrous plan. His name: Prophet Papa Simon Kimbangu. The "God" that they imposed upon us does not exist!

From the very beginning, the harmful consequences of their exploits were immediately and widely felt. Within one African state, it was not uncommon to find more than one hundred distinct groups of people having virtually nothing in common with their neighbours. In most cases, their traditions, their customs, and sometimes their language were so diverse that they were only able to communicate using the language of their colonizer. With this, it became of primary importance to learn and assimilate their language in order to survive.

The organization of these territories was also fraught with problems. When the colonizers arrived, most inexperienced in centralization, they decreed that all peoples of the land would live together within common borders and that a capital city would be designated from which the affairs of all the land would be orchestrated. The only "fault" of the people was to not have the technological advancement otherwise they might have rejected the usurping invaders.

The colonial power forcibly imposed its authority on Africans who endured the tyranny by remaining united. But despite their efforts to remain unified, some ethnic groups hostile to their own, feeling the injustice, pro-

322

gressively gave rise to the first rebellious movements militating in favour of a decolonization.

Years passed and decolonisation was finally complete. Its results were inescapable in a world that claimed this exploitation was wrong and did not rely on the brute force of armies. Thus the colonial powers returned to their homes, leaving in place a central power and administration modeled after European governments but which held nothing in account for ethnic realities, local cultures, social traditions or organizations. Such is the case of the Bantus, for example.

And it is then, as political independence was gained, that difficulties of a new nature began! Ethnic problems began to arise throughout the country as indigenous groups installed to power began to exercise the rules left to them by the white colonists.

It is at the time of decolonization that independence should have been given back to all the people gathered arbitrarily by the colonizing forces. A myriad of small independent states would thus have been created. This process would have made it possible to avoid the onslaught of ethnic wars that we know today. It would have favoured the creation of a Federation similar to that of the United States of America (the USA). This federation could have been named "USAF" (the United States of Africa) and, as Europe has just now realized, it would have been in its best interest to establish a single African currency, which could have been called the "Afro". And why not!

It is not too late to return to the source of the problem by destroying the states and the borders created by the colonial powers. In this, a spiritual revolution would arise, this renewed transformation would fuel the revolution.

But in order to achieve a transformation of this scope, it is necessary that all independent parties, secessionists, confederations, and federations join in concert to assist each other, to forge ahead in the same direction and with the same vigorous collective momentum.

It is this spirit of fraternity that will facilitate the effective and functional decolonization of all Africa. It is in this that resides the "sine qua non" condition required for our continent to survive and flourish.

It is necessary to dispense, once and for all, with these arbitrary borders that have no basis in reality, whether cultural, ethnic, religious or geopolitical. Simple lines traced on maps by completely unconscious colonial civil servants, these are our African borders. Horror in its purest form, it is like a rotted fruit fallen from the tree of human silliness, collected and exploited by a small group of people who represent the rot of the human spirit. If we Africans wish to escape the problems which colonization has inflicted on us for so long, we must embark on the true decolonisation of our continent at once. And it is important to recognize that decolonisation must begin with the dissolution of the artificial states created by the colonist exploiters, including the centralized governments that were also established for their own interest and gain.

Moreover, and of the utmost necessity, it is vital that this decolonisation be orchestrated only by Africans, that no outside source be involved in the restructuring of Africa. It will become vitally important that we organize our strongest people into positions that will unify all of us in our mission, rally us peacefully in the same direction, to the complete success of this project.

Any African today who refuses to find appeal in this grand collective effort, who wants no part of this process of decolonization, I say to him directly: he is a traitor to his ancestors, those who were conquered, humiliated, persecuted; he is a coward of the highest degree; he does not deserve to be called "African;" because he no longer is at that point, he is without a "soul", he is a "living dead". In fact, he is dead but does not yet know it. It is necessary that we face reality: the old colonial powers, in reality, do not do anything to really help the Africans, content that they are to continue to plunder the diverse natural resources of this immense and rich continent. The only thing that the neo-colonizers do is to renew the methods, taking advantage of the current local conflicts in order to better mask their politico-economic chicaneries. Obviously, in a state that saw one or more ethnic conflicts and various rebellions, it is so much easier to maintain corruption to profit from the natural resources of that country while continuing to pretend it is officially "decolonized" when in fact, it is purely for "the gallery", the watchful eyes of the world.

If each ethnic group, or each people, could have within their territory and their natural resources a true power supported by real means, i.e., police force, justice, administration, whether their own and/or those of the USAF, it would be much more difficult for the Western plunderers to manipulate prices and production via the powerful multinationals as they currently do. What's more, each conflict even officially "condemned" or "deplored" makes it possible for the Western manufacturers of weapons to realize substantial profits. To elaborate more clearly, these "merchants of death" do not want to lose their "juicy markets".

In the current geopolitical context, the larger the country is, artificial, the more this country is easily controlled by the former colonizers who, in reality, never really granted true independence and who wittingly continue to monitor their progress from afar. Actually, they monitor much more closely than they admit, especially when their armed forces are concerned.

Quite often, you might notice, that whenever an African head of state wishes to establish a privileged relationship with another head of state other than the former colonizing state i.e., the "controlling state", words change but the reality remains the same and armed forces are sent back to the country to put it back on the "proper" course. They are even often accompanied by "friendly" troops such as those of other western states, now also turned into controlling states. What frequently occurs, as the former colonial powers deem necessary, guarding their own interest, of course, is for certain local leaders to be replaced or even "eliminated" with ones more sympathetic to their overall mission. It is the armed forces in place that discretely takes care of this matter.

Unfortunately, at the time some governors were replaced, it was discovered that certain African chiefs did not remain indifferent to the huge deposits made in their names in Swiss bank accounts. Denouncing this activity and fixing our sights on the future, it is important for us to "forgive and forget", "the past is the past", but remain vigilant to remove all the malingering remainders of colonization.

It is necessary that the Africans awake from the deep sleep which leads to forgetfulness. It is over! And the pretty fairy tale with which Westerners rocked us for such a long time is also over. What comes to replace them is concrete: it is necessary for us to break down the borders imposed by our colonizers and to dismantle all the states that we ourselves did not choose.

Those among you who follow the walk of the world with acuity may ask, "What will happen with the UN?" It is true that this organization was sometimes a cruel foe of Africa, acting as the servant of certain western powers. But again, keeping our sights firmly fixed on the future, if we could ensure both forgiveness from this organization and a commitment to act with honesty to supervise the creation of new states, states represented by the natural and ancestral boundaries as had existed before the colonization, then we would consider how best to work with this organization but not without serious guarantees.

The natural riches of Africa could finally be returned to the local populations, those people who have been dispossessed of it for a great number of
years. With the help of these resources, each ethnic group and each nation
could thus find its roots, its traditions and its language.

A second African language, a national language, could be adopted so
that all the inhabitants of the large African continent can communicate
between one another in one common tongue. We might, for example,
choose Ki-Swahili, already spoken in many countries. It is best, I feel, that
the chosen language not be that of a former colonizer. It could, however,
be English. Yes, English is the language of a former colonizer, but we must
consider the lesser of all evils. And we must be mindful that English is fast
becoming the international language and therefore should be adopted by
the old French and Belgian colonies.

Lastly, it is time for us, as Africans, to become wary of the guise of "coo-
peration" that the old colonizing countries claim to offer to the service of
Africa. It is false. They are nothing but agents commissioned to maintain
control so that the so-called "Independence" remains merely a word, a
meaningless word, with no bearing on reality. It is now time that we declare true independence and end this pretence.

Let us take in hand our destiny by rejecting overall all the structures that
were imposed to us by force.

For a better understanding of the execrable consequences that resulted
when Christian colonizers arbitrarily assigned borders within Africa, both
at the political level as well as the economic and social levels, consider
the example of the Belgian ex-Gongo, ex-Zaire, the current Democratic
Republic of Congo.

It is clear that this State owes its existence solely to the results of a
one-man enterprise, that of Leopold II (1835-1909), King of Belgium, who
claimed this immense territory as his "private, personal property". During his reign, King Leopold II and his men successfully subjugated entire
kingdoms, empires, sultanates, ethnic groups, clans, and total familial
tribes to his service. (Refer to the famous "Geographical Conference" of
Brussels in 1876 and to the "International Conference of Berlin" of 1884-
1885).

In all cases, these classes of people which I described above, prior to Leopold's intervention, had been organized in social groups, each one being

326

homogeneous and autonomous. But as a consequence of the arbitrary and despicable parcelling of their respective territories, many being parcelled into several plots, some can be found today belonging to several different state-controlled units.

Cases like this are not random. I offer you a short overview of some of the autonomous social groups confined to this new state, Kongo-Kinshasa, the "monster state" created by King Leopold II. This state, with branches stretching over a distance equal to the road from Paris to Moscow, is eighty times the size of Belgium and nearly five times that of France. Here is the list of these groups:

a. *The Kongo Kingdom on the two banks of the large river*
b. *The Kuba Kingdom, located between Kasaï to the west, Sankuru to the north and Lulua to the south*
c. *The Luba Kingdom, between Lubilash, Mbujimai, Lomami, Maniema, Luvua and Luapula*
d. *The Lunda Empire, from the high plateaus of Katanga to Angola, Kwango-Kwilu and Zimbabwe*
e. *The Kingdom of Msiri around Lake Tanganyika*
f. *The Zande Sultanates in the north*
g. *The Mangbetu Sultanates in the north*

Briefly enumerated, these are only some of the most important social and state-controlled units, integral parts of the vast territory that is known today as DRC, the Democratic Republic of Congo. This artificial and un-manageable "monster", DRC, in reality, still remains under the control of western powers since its rise to independence.

More serious still is the case of certain populations which were found divided and distributed among several distinct governances, even after treaties were signed. For example, Kongo remains a Belgian (Kongo-Kinshasa) and a French (Kongo-Brazzaville) possession. The Lundas populations are another example of being the possession of three countries: Belgium, Portuguese, and Great Britain. Still another example, the Tshokwe people belong partly to the Belgian Kongo as well as to Angola and Rhodesia (now Zimbabwe). All this lends to such complexity, really the antipodes of "biblical simplicity". Wouldn't you agree?

At the time, late nineteenth century, the situation was crystal clear; fuelled by their desire for prestige and stimulated by the colonial competition that was fully engaged, the powers gathered at the Berlin meeting had no special interest in the creation of homogeneous sets, neither in the social field, the economic field, and much less, the political field.

This was most especially the case for the countries that succumbed to Léopold II, King of the Belgians, by far the greatest landowner with his private African domain. The DRC of today by far exceeds the stretch of the ranches of American Presidents!

King Leopold was satisfied purely and simply to seize the indigenous lands and to distribute their concessions to companies known as "colonization companies", true subsidiary companies of his own private company named, "the State of Kongo" of which he was the only "Lord and...Master after God".

But as anyone can see, we have never seen this so-called "God almighty" come to make the least remonstrance with any "Lord and Master" whomsoever. It is true that this commandment to have utter respect for the "God in the skies" above the "Lord and Master" on earth is an earthly concern and originates with "those from below" and not "those from above". It is men of earth who declared themselves Lord and Master, making themselves accountable to no one. This sentiment has prevailed throughout time. Ultimately, in all of these campaigns to partition Africa with simple lines on a map, the historic and sociological realities of Africa were never a consideration. All of the Christian colonial powers, particularly France and Belgium, acting as Lords and Masters, agreed to leave free course to the wretched and disparaging design of Africa.

For them, Africa was one immense vacant land, having never known any other Master but them, whereas, quite to the contrary, Black Africa was precisely, and it remains so, a continent where the leaders of the land (the emperors, the kings, sultans, chiefs) had, and still have a determining importance in the social and religious structures in place on their lands.

These are deep wounds that colonizing Christendom has caused in Africa! Throughout each border, from the Ivory Coast to Nigeria, for example, ethnic groups are divided in two, in three...

Let us reconsider the fate reserved for Kongo. King Leopold's highest concern was to conquer a maximum number of territories without regard for the serious scarring his exploits would cause Africa, without thought

328

for how he might heal her wounds. Thus he parcelled the old Lunda Empire between the Belgian Kongo (Katanga), Angola, northern Zambia and northern Zimbabwe. This single empire was divided into four plots, each one forming a different and new state. Another example of the consequences of this surgical division of the territories is the tribes of the Zande Sultanate whose border now overlaps the equatorial province of the DRC, that of the Central African Republic and that of Sudan. A single sultanate distributed between three distinct states!

Kinshasa, Brazzaville, Kwango, the north of Angola and Point-Black had formerly formed the old "Bakongo kingdom", a kingdom which had actually known several centuries of existence prior to 1885 when "small civil servants" drew pencil lines that would divide it among France, Belgium, and Portugal.

However, any African, because it is engrained in him, must acknowledge that the tribal conscience bears something essential that is not shared by the national conscience, the latter attached to the artificial countries that colonizing western Christendom imposed on us by force.

Moreover, at the time in which we live now, the beginning of this third millennium of the Christian civilization (but only of this acknowledged millennium, since it is true that we evoked the role of Egypt and Phoenicia more than 5000 years ago) we, as Africans, can see that the tribal conscience still remains stronger than the national conscience, as seen in the majority of African countries

Another apparent observation: the realization of a national conscience in countries with so many ethnic diversities could only be fulfilled by the yoke of a centralizing dictatorship. And yet, what do we see today? Colonizing dictatorships or regimes paid by "Christian" Western powers. Africa does not want that anymore. It does not want to hear about it anymore either. Too much is too much. It is time to turn the page! Inevitably though, the political units established in these countries created artificially become fragile and their controllers clearly start becoming aware of it.
That can seem to be paradoxical, but in fact, today this fragility of the governments is a good thing for us because the African political, social and economic structures are young. They are the fruits inherited from the structures that the "Christian" colonial powers left us and, because we are young, these can easily be reversed. Thanks to our youth, we have the flexibility necessary to replace with unprecedented speed the existing structures with ones that will be more appropriate for our use.

The after-effects of colonization no longer need demonstration. It is a plain fact, established and well documented. In this perspective, the Katangese secession of the Sixties, for example, which was founded on a regional idiosyncrasy with mainly economic motivation, was a marvellous phenomenon, conceived and produced by a talented and generous man, Mr. Moise Kapend Tshombe. At the risk of losing his life, this political leader, descended from a former reigning family, had a very clear and spontaneous vision bout the events of his time and about the long-term future of Africa. I am particularly proud to pay tribute to him here.

I insist vehemently that it is essential that every African understand the importance of "spiritual decolonisation". Our entire future depends on it. The emancipation of Africa comes from this. The African unity will start from this. All of the real development of the continent will be based on this change of mentality. The real liberation of Africa will be the twin sister of the spiritual liberation among each one of us. It is on this rock that the creation of the United States of Africa will find its point of anchoring. The introduction of a single African currency will be one of the consequences. The autonomy of the regions will be another. Thirdly, will be the creation of an African army having as its unique function to keep peace throughout the continent. This will be the ultimate result!

What more can we expect? Let us use our mind. Let us put all of our neurons into action and move to gain the happiness of an African identity devoid of the chains of this degrading colonization and from which Africa can free itself once and for all.
With all that we know, we can no longer claim to be Christians! We are Africans. We have our unique and specific African identity. We are whole human beings and we don't need the recognition, though well overdue, of Christendom to know that it is the species of Man of which we are part.

We, Africans, have never considered ourselves to be "wild beasts". We are conscious and are filled with humanity. Since the day of our birth, we are human beings like every human being on the planet, regardless of what color our skin is!

And what a beautiful selection there will be among the African leaders because a spiritual decolonization in Africa, as we saw earlier, will generate changes at the political, economic and social levels. Yes, it will be a true "revolution" which will lead Africa to insist that their welfare be placed in the hands of competent and honest African heads of state, people who are truly dedicated in service to the interests of Africa as a whole and to the

330

interests of their family and clans in particular.

Indeed, as we have seen in the past, during the Negro slave trade, there were "traitor" chiefs who collaborated with pro-slavers. Wretched as it is, we know it to be true. At the time, it was black slaves who were exported like cattle, by tens of thousands of tons. But today, it's important that we know who the current "traitor" African chiefs are and what "goods" they are exporting by the tens of thousands of tons.

Africa sells and exports today on a massive scale its biotope, its environment, i.e., its soul. And it also sells its wood, its coffee, its rubber, its cotton, its cocoa, its oils, its ores, etc. Its soil "Saharanises", and is becoming a desert. Africa empties itself of its substance: this invaluable substance, it sells it to the Western economies and industries. And in exchange for what? For some apples and other crumbs!

The traitor chiefs of today are African politicians placed at levels of responsibility in our countries but whom, in reality, are at the service of neo-colonialism by the bonds of the free masons. It is they, these chiefs of modern times, who sell Africa to the Masters of the Occident.

On the day when the decolonization of Africa will be started by means of a de-Christianization of the African populations, the African people will ask them to return accounts of their management that is as disastrous for the countries which were entrusted to them as it is profitable for certain Western interests.

This moment will come when Africa is spiritually liberated from the yoke of the Religion of the colonizer. But it will not be able to come before. This phase of spiritual liberation is necessary because it will unify Africa. It is this that will truly bring her the strength to carry out this major transformation, which will be a saviour for the continent and all its inhabitants because it will be beneficial and it will endure.

A just return of things... Yes! But a return of just things too!

WHITE POISON

30. For a restoration of the sacred royalties linked to the people from the sky

A spiritual decolonization of our continent will certainly bring about in a natural manner a beautiful return to customary authorities in Africa. It will be necessary that the future African governments have at their center a kind of "Great Council" made up of the Customary Authorities, Chiefs and Priests of the African Authentic Religions, such as Kimbanguism, cited here only as an example. In any case, the religions of the colonizers of along ago will absolutely have to be excluded from this "Great Council". As far as the future governments, they will also have to be deprived of any trace of colonization!

The entire components of these "Great Councils" will constitute the cradle of the history of our continent and those who will compose them will remain the guards of the heart and the spirit of the whole of Africa because these beings are our collective inheritance, that which neither colonization, nor the great dictatorships of the "black puppets" of the Occident managed to uproot. The role of each of the "Great Councils" within the government where it will sit will be to give to the politics of this government a full legitimacy. It will also tend to the safeguarding of the local part of the total inheritance of Africa in the country where it is situated.

Since the first nominal independences that began in the Sixties, the first African dictators were all put into place by and for the Occident and, whether it be Mobutu Sese Seko, Omar Bongo, Eyadema or others, each one tried to obtain a complete legitimacy but for all of them their efforts were in vain.

Why was it impossible for them? Even if it is little known to Westerners, the answer is rather simple: in Black Africa, legitimacy is something that is "sacred". It is a gift that the Gods Creators offered to the ancestor and that he, in turn, transmits to the most deserving in the community. Nobody will manage to diminish the strength of this traditional custom among Africans of Black Africa and it is "mission impossible" for those who try!

Moreover, after the total failure of the European model imposed at the political and spiritual levels since the independences of the Sixties, the popularity of the chiefs re-emerges stronger than before. And rightly so, as is the case of those whom we call Mwant Yaav for the Lundas, the M'Siri for the Bayekes, and the Oba, the Ooni, or the Kabyesi elsewhere in Africa.

All of these chiefs see their popularity reborn to the immense pleasure of Africa that rediscovers its roots prior to colonization.

It should be known that nowadays there remains approximately fifty monarchs and/or emperors, distinguished people in Africa. The fact is, as we consult them more, so does their prestige increase. Long ago, these leaders concerned the colonizers, as they still worry current African regimes formed after nominal independences. This is completely normal because they possess sacred legitimacy and thus they will have to be included in the politics of the future African governments. Their legitimacy dates back to the year 1000, and for some, even further!

At the center of the vast majority of black African populations, there is a cosmogonical profile of the royalty that is sacred. Indeed, very often there exist at the root of the dynastic lineages one or several clans of celestial origins. Traditions even sometimes explain that these lineages arose from little beings or "geniuses" whose origin was celestial!

Let us take a look at what is being said regarding the dynasties of Rwanda:

> "Shyerezo had a sterile wife named Gasani. In the absence of her husband Gasani will give birth to a child whose magical conception took place in the sky; Shyerezo will later learn from a conversation with a messenger that his sterile wife gave birth. Shyerezo orders that the baby be put to death but the torturers will hide him. The child will grow with his older brother "Mututsi", and will be named "Kigwa". He will spend his life in exile with his brother and sister".

> But "Kigwa" means "the one who fell" [from the sky..?]; he unites with his sister "Nyampundu" and engendered a royal lineage called "Ibimanuka", which means "those who have come down" [from the sky..?]. Moreover, the first descendants of "Kigwa" will all bear names that clearly make reference to their celestial origin. After "Kigwa" we find "Kimanuka", in the genealogy, which means "the one who came down", and then we find "Kijuru", which means "the one from the sky".

> In other words, the Tutsi-Rwanda dynasty suggests an impregnation "by the sky" of the ancestor of this dynasty, from which a mediating function between the sky and the Earth takes place. From this, the "Ega" clan, "Nyampundu" progeny, will exclusively provide all

334

the wives to the first series of ancestors of "Ibimanuka" [those who came from the sky]. In Rwanda it is also said that... ""Kigwa" pierced through the celestial sky with an iron hammer to find its way to the Earth".

It is not all! Let us continue our voyage back in history:

A "religious" dynasty has also developed in the past in Rwanda but this one has no link to the one described above. Instead, it will be the founder of an initiation cult to which chief "Ryangombe" is given the title of king by his disciples. At the center of this "religious" dynastic cult called "kubandwa", little spirits (or geniuses) called "Imandwa" were revered and the chief's (or president's) name was "Imana" [Yahweh]. And in the 18th century the "kubandwa" religion was officially recognized at the court of the king of Rwanda of the dynasty aforementioned.

This religion met with great success with the Hutu and Twa peasant people and, as a result, will give many officiating priests. Thus, Ryangombe governed Rwanda with the king of the dynastic lineage of "Kigwa". It is said that Ryangombe established his kingdom at the top of the Karisimbi volcano where the blessed initiated people spent their time in joy, playfulness, and blossoming while in the company of "Imandwa", the little geniuses that came from the sky. This way of life was a huge contrast to the life of those who were not initiated into this cult. In addition it was said of Ryangombe that he could transport himself high, between the sky and the Earth and that he owned the tree of life of the initiated. It was also said that he was the king of the "Imandwa".

In the society of this king of the "Imandwa" was the sharing of goods and wealth divided equally between all the individuals, no matter what their social status. It was, in fact, a true revolution that brought about profound structural reforms. It was said that Ryangombe inaugurated a new kingdom mid-way between the sky and the Earth and that his disciples could, through him, communicate with the immortal or eternal spirits, i.e., the little geniuses called "Imandwa". Ryangombe was a hero, a purely "religious" king, essentially "spiritual" and certainly not a "warrior" king. He was, at the time, the founder of a religion that we can call "salvation religion", and this is why he was also called, rightfully so, the "liberating king".

In Uganda and in the north east of Tanzania, Ryangombe also appears in the pantheon of the spirits. It is often said that Ryangombe and his religion was simply the resurrection of a very ancient cult that existed before and that was called the cult of the "Cwezi spirits", from which derived the Rwandan cult of the "Imandwa" people (these geniuses who came from the sky). In Tanzania and in Bunyamwezi, as well as in certain parts of Burundi, the cult of the "Cwezi spirits" was also known and observed. And ironically, the Lunda (or Ruund) people of the Lunda Empire – the one I come from – also have a sacred royalty which involves princess "Lueji", also called "Ruweji", who was visited by a hero, son of the sky, and impregnated by him even though she was believed to be sterile. In the ruund or Lunda language, the supreme god, Yahweh, is called "Tshinaweji" or "Tshinawezi", while the son of Ruweji, who was the founder of the Ruund or Lunda Empire was called "Yaav Naweji" (often written as Nawej) or "Yaav Nawezi", with the same ending "wezi".

And this is not all! Our Zulu brothers, from South Africa, call the very bright star of the gods of the sky "Khwezi"! Interesting, no? As for the Venda and the Thonga people, they call the bright star of the planet of the gods "Khwekheti" and this star is nothing more than "Sirius", place of origin of the creator gods, according to the Dogon tribe of Mali!

Let's now take a look at the history of the origins of the Luba Kingdom or the Luba dynasty:

"The Luba hero, at the origin of the Luba Kingdom, is "Mbidi Kiluwe", who, according to the Luba tradition, was a Prince who came from the sky. After bringing fecundity to the Earth through a son called "Kalala Ilunga", he returned to the sky and his son created the new dynasty".

Let us now look at the Venda, the Kuba, and the Karanga people of Zimbabwe:

"The Venda royalty is also linked to a celestial genius called "Raluvhumba", who appeared in a "ball of fire" and his place of predilection was a "sacred" cavern. He was appearing on top of the rock overlooking the cavern and the king, who was a descendant of "Raluvhumba and who was praying to him with all his people, had to go to him".

336

"As for the Kuba people, their first king was a descendant of "Mboom", or "Nyeem apong", the master of the sky. Among the Kuba of central Africa, in the Democratic Republic of Congo, the king is a sacred person because he is the living representative of "God" on Earth. In fact, a Kuba adage says: "If I sleep, it is the king; if I eat, it is the king; if I drink, it is the king. Not because he creates me but because without him it would be anarchy". Moreover, the Kuba people warn the sovereign leader during his enthronization by reminding him, "tyranny leads to death".

"The Karanga people of the Great Zimbabwe, the place where the pyramids of Zimbabwe were erected, say that at the beginning "Mwari" [Yahweh] created the first man that they call "Mwetsi" [Adam]. But "Mwetsi" lamented that he was lonely so "Mwari" granted him (with) a spouse [Eve] and subsequently another spouse... it is also said that later the "serpent" [the fallen angels led by Lucifer] mated with the women of "Mwetsi", and that much later, a celestial genius called "Madzivoa", joined their people and mated with the Karanga princesses i.e., the daughters of the king. The ancient Karanga people worshipped this stranger, or genius from the sky".

Among the Pende people of Central Africa, the sovereignty, "magical" source of power, comes from elsewhere, from the sky. The same applies to the Ashanti people of Western Africa. The throne, or Ashanti Sovereign power, is of celestial origin. And the list of all the religions and African royalties, coming from the sky, goes on and on!

It is clear and obvious that there is, in Africa, an indisputable link between a large number of royalties and these cosmic beings, hence "celestial" since they "came from the sky". These "angels" of the Bible, also known as our "creator-gods", are the Elohim of the original Hebrew Bible. And the precise reason why the kings and queens were considered "sacred", or "of divine origin", is because they had "blood from the creator-gods" running through their veins!

It is of primary and utmost importance that all the people of black Africa recover from their old traditions traces of these beings that came from the sky. They are our humanized celestial creator-gods of flesh and blood like us. And it was for our utmost good that they physically and sexually mated with a large number of our ancestors!

These small beings, or geniuses, that came from the sky, have a special and primordial place in numerous traditions and religions. Whether Judaism or Christianity, it is also clearly stated in Genesis VI, 1, 2, and 4, that these sons of Elohim sexually mated with their creation. Likewise, Islam mentions the "Djinns" who are the "small spirits coming from the sky" and who are sometimes falsely associated to demons by those who refuse or cannot face the facts. It is clearly stated that they are "humans", neither rebellious to "Allah", (Eloah-Yahweh), nor enemy to man.

The legend of the "Djinns" in Islam is perfectly comparable to that of the Cherubim of the Bible, or that of the "Imandwa", or "Cwezi" in black Africa. Moreover, it is said of these "Djinns" that they had the reputation of maintaining sexual relations with humans. It is for this reason that Sufism was not very well perceived by authorities as certain aspects of the doctrine taught the possibility of having intimate relations with "God". But despite the fact that Sufism was severely persecuted, it did not stop it from developing in many countries from Egypt to Iran!

For this century where all "racists" prevail Africa would have no writings, and thus no history. This is completely false. It is imperative that all Africans and also all the Blacks of the Diaspora restore to memory a crucial date for our entire continent: November 15, 1884. On this date, Bismarck, having overcome France thirteen years prior and having proclaimed himself "Emperor of Germany", and then "Chancellor of the 2nd Reich", initiated the "International Conference of Berlin" in his city. His work was completed in 1885 with a treaty that would distribute ignominiously and arbitrarily all African territories among the various colonial powers which had "officially" seized the land, its natural riches, and once again, its inhabitants.

The indoctrination of this treaty meant the smothering of several centuries of history, of a millennium of a history squelched by a horde of scurvy colonialists accompanied by their soldiers killing "the rebellious blacks" and by their missionaries converting "the pagan savages"!

Kingdoms, empires, sultanates, were beaten down in one blow. Virtually vanished. It is only now that we slowly begin to rediscover them gradually. Thanks to the marvellous advancement of the Internet, this once lost history is now available, carefully documented, both minute details and wholesale facts.

We should be aware though that this "victorious colonization", often executed cavalierly, was far from having been carried out honourably. We saw, for example, in their unbridled race for the best conquest, colonizers forcibly convinced illiterate African kings to ascribe a check mark to the bottom of a treaty of protectorate, "signing away", by the same token, all of their goods and powers, and much more, in some cases!

Summarizing precisely, the process of colonizing countries in the "Christian" tradition began in the most inhumane manner and ended with the most scandalous.

First, let us address the English. They practiced the "indirect rule" by leaving certain autonomy to the sovereigns in place in exchange for respect for their trusteeship.

The Christian French simply replaced uncooperative kings with obedient leaders. Power was transferred to their own men who remained directly under their control. This manner of operation indeed reveals a widely accepted view of the "state of mind" of the "average Frenchmen", one belying that they are superior to everyone else before even taking the time of becoming acquainted.

And let us also look at the country of Belgium, they tiny nation that caused so much damage, Christian Belgium. More than other countries, it still practices racism toward blacks. And worse, if outwardly encourages racism among blacks. In Rwanda-Urundi, for example, the Belgians orchestrated conflicts between the Hutus, Tutsis and Twas, one against another. (See Chapter 14 of this book for more information on the Rwandan genocide.)

Without exception, the Belgians deceived all dynasties within Kongo. Illiterate black kings naively believed that they were signing into commercial free trade agreements for economic partnership and they inadvertently signed over complete power to Belgian supervision. One can say, "totalitarian"!

For those kings who recognized the subversive intentions of the colonizer and began to rebel, their retribution was simple and barbaric: they were executed. Here are three examples: the M'Siri of the Bayekes in Katanga, and two Mwant Yaav of the Lundas. For others, deportation was their sentence, exiled to remote regions of central Africa, separated from their family and totally isolated from their people. Most of them lived under these conditions until their death. Such was the case of the big chief Muluba "Kasongo-Nyembo" in Belgian Kongo. Before the arrival of the colonizer, chief Kasongo-Nyembo reigned over the Muluba Kingdom. When the colonizer arrived, he refused to submit to their power. Seven tribes under his reign received their freedom from the occupier. The remainder of the Kingdom was divided. They left him the South, and the North was given to his brother Kabongo. Despite this forced division, Kasongo-Nyembo did not acknowledge defeat and did not cease fighting against foreign presence on his territory. For his antagonism toward the colonizer, he was exiled in 1905 and remained in isolation until his death in October, 1917, having never seen his country again.

Fortunately, in Africa, history is not so easily erased. Perhaps this is because it is recorded in the heads, and not on paper! Admittedly, within two generations, colonization suppressed the powers of our monarchs. But a return to the Customary Authorities and to Nobility as well as their new participation in political life of the regions can occur again. And it will, I am convinced, very soon!

Do you want to have an idea of some of the great important kings who still hold office in Black Africa? Here is a list:

The King of the Kubas, Nyimi Kok Mabiintsh III ;

The Lunda (Ruund) Emperor, Mwant Yav Mushid III

The Ashanti Emperor, Osei Tutu II

The Zulu King, Goodwill Zwelethini, descendent of the legendary Shaka Zulu

King Hapi IV from Bana

The XIVth Fo of Bandjoun

The Sultan of Foumban, El Hadj Seidou Njimoluh Njoya

The Sultan of Sokoto, Abubakar Sidiq

The Ekegbian of Benin, J.I. Inneh

The Emir of Katsina, El Hadj Mamadou Kabir Usaman

30. For a restoration of the sacred royalties linked to the people from the sky

The Lozi King, Litunga Yela Ilute

Langevin, The King of Abomey

Kigeri V, the "Mwami" of Rwanda

The sovereign King of Swaziland, Mswati III ;

The Morro Naaba, Emperor of the Mossi

The Bayeke King, Mwami Mwenda Munongo M'Siri

Oseadeeyo Addo Dankwa III, King of Akopong-Akuaper

Salomon Igbino Ghodua, King Oba Erediauwa of Benin

Agboli Agbo Dedjlani, King of Abomey

The King of Goulmou-Fada

The King of Bousouma

The sovereign King Letsie III of Lesotho

The King Solomon I, Omukama, King of the Bunyoro

How can one conceive of directing an African country, created artificially and under false pretence by a treaty such as that of the Berlin Conference, knowing the existence of similar entities included inside (and outside) the borders of this state were organized as the result of scandalously drawn lines in 1885 on the map of Africa, lines which never retraced the borders of the historical kingdoms? It is a total and absolute aberration!

The leaders of the current governments who still deal with the Western powers, ex-colonizers, remain skewered on their privilege of power, continuing to grant longevity to the execrable treaty of Berlin. By doing so, they continue to betray their people of today and their ancestors of yes-

341

WHITE POISON

31. Appeal to the Kimbanguist and Kush people

It is to Kimbanguists, to all Kimbanguists, whom I formulate this appeal. Wherever they may be on this Earth, they all have the duty to act for the Prophecies of the Great Envoy, the Prophet Simon Kimbangu, to be achieved. You may have noticed that our creator-godsare indeed physical beings and that they move in machines that are of material construction. On a regular basis, these machines can be detected by our terrestrial radars. Our F16 fighter planes are also sometimes able to identify them on their radarscopes. Note that on radar one can perceive only material objects. Collective hallucinations or holograms and the like do not give rise to the images displayed on the screens of our civil or military radar.

On several occasions during Kimbanguist ceremonies, celestial spheres, flying saucers, were seen in Nkamba, the fief of Kimbanguism, the native village of the Prophet Simon Kimbangu, which houses the large temple of Kimbanguism and which is called the "New Jerusalem".

These luminous celestial spheres, fixed on the firmament in the sky of Nkamba and not making any noise are none other than the machines in which move our creator-gods , the Elohim of the original Hebrew Bible. The ancient Egyptians called these machines "solar discs". It is said that the god of the gods, "RA", traveled in a "solar disc". Those celestial spheres that appeared in Nkamba are those solar discs which the former Egyptians talked about, as did the god of the god of the ancient Egyptians. It is the "Nzambi", the "Mpungu", the "Mungu", such as he is called in the local languages of your people.

If these celestial spheres appeared, it is proof that "Nzambi", or "Yahweh", the eternal mentioned in the Hebrew Bible came to observe you in Nkamba. He looks at you as the physical being that he is. He comes to sensitize you in order to prepare you for the revelation.

Because we have now entered the age of the revelation, the age of the Apocalypse, the veil of the mystery of god will finally be raised. In Greek, apokalupsis is translated as "revelation. This era is also referred to as the era of Aquarius, as the era when knowledge is poured upon humanity, the era when all mysteries will be revealed and demystified. During this time, thanks to science, man will finally be able to understand and abandon his old supra ocular beliefs. The era is here. It is written in the "sacred books" that when this era arrives, there would be signs in the sky. These signs are the appearance of UFO's (Unidentified Flying Objects) and it is no coincidence that these appearances occurred in Nkamba, none whatsoever.

The Roman Catholic Church, Rome, the Vatican, with the support of its powerful political allies, have undertaken a global campaign to silence the questions concerning UFO's, flying saucers. Knowing full well that they do exist and, in fact, have millennia of scientific advancement over us, they fiercely deny the existence of other civilizations in the universe. They also know that these vehicles commonly referred to as UFO's have been coming to observe us for a very long time. The Roman curia and its allies also know that they are our creators who visit us but engage in every tactic to conceal this truth from us.

The Great Kimbangu Envoy has always fought the Roman Church, acknowledging it as a lying, usurping, hypocrite of the truth. You Kimbanguists continue this historic battle that your Prophet initiated. Do not give it up and look at the stars, look at the skies. Somewhere in our galaxy lies the planet of our creators. They depend enormously on Africa to find its place in the era of the second independence, an independence that will ultimately be "true" independence, and that will announce the total liberation of the black race, the total and final decolonization of the black man.

The work at hand, that which you have just read, will be fought vehemently by the Roman Catholic Church together with its base of allies. Depending in large part on its partners in Africa, France and Belgium, they will again employ every tactic to safeguard its power and its web of deceit. But this time their efforts will be in vain. Kimbanguists, give up the name "Christian"! Leave the claws of spiritual colonization completely! Leave the ecumenical fortress of the Churches in Rome or Geneva! Be revolutionaries and continue on the way indicated by the Prophet Kimbangu and not another!

Give up the assembly of those whom Rome and its curia have entrenched in their mission, those whom this Christian Church has "standardized", conditioned, and aligned. Do not compromise with the clan of those who were the torturers of the Prophet Kimbangu!

One of the preferred tactics of the Church and the Vatican has been to estrange the princes and chiefs of Africa from their families, their children, taking them to the metropolises of Europe to indoctrinate them in their centers of formation. Once trained in the studies that would shape them, train them, they would return to their native Africa. Now "tamed", these leaders were both useful and pleasing to the curia. Do not be mislead; their plan was well calculated!

But nothing is lost. The current kimbanguist leaders such as Papa Dialungani Kimbangu Kiangani can rejoin the battle of their grand-father Papa Simon Kimbangu at any time. Today they face a battle of conscience. But the time to please Rome and the different African leaders currently sold to the neo-colonialism is over. Now the time has come to fully reveal the truth and all the truth! And I have confidence in the Kimbanguist leaders; they will follow the good path.

Many are those among you who know that there were "odd" apparitions in Nkamba. Your testimonies are numerous but no one really wants to shed light on what happened because it is too troubling and embarrassing for many. Indeed, revealing the truth could be cause for some serious changes. Nevertheless, complete light can be shed on this subject inside this very work.

Note, for example, the apparitions in Nkamba one Wednesday in 1924 at precisely 8:40 a.m. It is there that nine UFO's, nine luminous spheres appeared. According to eyewitness accounts, the vessels formed a perfect circular configuration, their diameter approximately twelve meters each. Among these nine vehicles, witnesses recount, one was larger than the others. It is this larger one, seeming to bear more "import" than the rest, that descended slowly and silently before landing on the ground. It is on this site where the highest building in Nkamba, the "New Jerasulem", was erected, the building that we call "nzo ya mitinu", "the house of the kings". Once this grand machine had landed, the Prophet Kimbangu emerged, proclaiming to those who were witnessing this astounding vision, that he had returned to see his family, a people sorely mistreated throughout history. The Prophet then took one of his sons aboard the flying saucer and rose again into the sky.

There are manuscripts in the Lingala language that report these events and these apparitions of UFOs in Nkamba, including filmed testimonies of the inhabitants of the village of Nkamba. The young Kongolese cinematographer, Roch William Ondongo is currently directing a documentary on this very subject. With so much resistance to the truth, this is a bold and beautiful undertaking for Ondongo.

Even for Ondongo, the young son of a kimbanguist pastor, obtaining information on the subject has not been an easy task. The fact is information of this type is widely concealed from all people, kimbanguists included.

The flying objects seen in the sky over Nkamba are no longer "unidentified". Their identity is indeed well known! To this end, simply reflect by yourself using your intelligence. The word intelligence, you recall, comes from the Latin word, "interlegere" meaning to "establish links". So let us make good and logical links. Who could be the pilot of those "material" machines that brought Kimbangu to Nkamba on that historic day?

The answer is obvious: they are our creators. It can be no one else. And they have continued to come from their remote planet somewhere in the stars. It is they who delivered to us earthlings the prophets Moses, Ezekiel, Buddha, Jesus, Muhammad, Zoroaster, The Bab, Krishna, Kimpa Vita, Simao Toko, and many more, including the one whom you undoubtedly know best, Simon Kimbangu. It is them, our extraterrestrial creators, who have assisted these Prophets and Prophetesses throughout time. It is with the guidance of our creators that these outstanding individuals could carry out their missions, from "miracle cures" to delivering a message to their contemporaries, a rich and timely message.

All these Prophets are one and indivisible, each being a link of the same chain. They share a principle orientation, one often coming to complete the mission of the prophet before him. Most often, the coming of another prophet is announced by his predecessor. All of these prophets had, each one in his time, to accomplish a mission adapted to the various temporary needs of the people among which they lived and operated.

Today we entered the Messianic era, announced by the various Prophets, the arrival of Nkua Tulendo predicted by Simon Kimbangu. Open your eyes and your ears. He is here. But also understand that he too has been fought and ridiculed by the same people our Prophet Kimbangu warned us of, i.e., the Vatican, Christianity, and colonial powers, France, Belgium, and other European dynasties. (Remember that France is the First Daughter of the Catholic Church.) They all will unify their strengths to reject "the Messiah" for they are aware that this "last prophet" will not come to plead in their favour. He will not come to please them. Quite to the contrary and, in fact, they are astutely conscious and dreadfully oppose his arrival.

Nkua Tulendo, this Great King Prophet, whom Kimbangu announced his arrival, not only has the role of revealing the secrets of our origins by joining again the bond with our creator-gods(in the plural) that was broken, not only does he promise a splendid future for us thanks to science, but he also implicates himself in current politics so as to enrich the future lives of all man. And to a greater end, he dedicates himself to the plight of those countries most deeply affected by the selfishness and brutality of colonization, the foremost being Black Africa. And so his role of Messiah, the last Prophet, bringing the final message of our creators, is not only spiritual, religious, it is also political. It is with courage and tenacity by his word and in his writings, he makes known all that he has to say.

The Western Powers are also well aware of what I tell you and will make every effort to divert the attention and focus of the people of the Messiah, Nkua Tulendo. To this end, they will defame him, ridicule him, calumniate him. They will present him as a liar, an illuminated swindler, a baseless guru, the leader of a dangerous sect. This is their current tactic, facilitated by the "lying media" which they own in large number. Do not fall prey to those who victimized you for so many years. Do not allow yourself to be influenced by the media. Read and reflect, disseminate information for yourself and allow your conscience to determine the truth. Be wary of what the whites will deliver to you concerning this "last Prophet". Return to your old traditions; they speak generously of those who came from the sky. You will easily be able to establish a link to these objects that appeared in the sky over Nkamba.

Those Western Powers, particularly Belgium, and the Roman Church are trustees of the "Colonial Archives of Belgium". And it is in these archives that we will find a great deal written about the Great Envoy Prophet Simon Kimbangu. These "higher authorities" know that the true and imminent liberation of the blacks throughout the world is upon us. They know that the end of the domination of Africa by whites is also now. And further, they know that it is on the borders of the ancient Kongo kingdom that this conflagration will occur.

With a wealth of information at their disposal, these parties are completely aware that the basin of Kongo-Nile is a location vital to this resurrection of Africa. It is from there that all of Africa will ultimately rid itself of white domination and finally know its "second independence". A true independence as foretold by the Great Special Envoy of our Father creators: Prophet Simon Kimbangu.

The Nkua Tulendo announced by Prophet Kimbangu, is "the Messiah" for all the people of the Earth for all time. And moreover, he has a very important message for Africa, the continent our creators hold most dear. He is not black. He is white. Yet he is "black African" in his heart and his spirit.

347

He speaks in the name of his Father who is in the Heaven, i.e., Nzambi, Mpungu or Yahweh the eternal (in Hebrew), this "supreme being" who is "President of the Council of the Eternals" on the remote planet of our creators. And so it was predicted by our Creators in their grand celestial plan. If he had sent a "black" to come to lead Dipanda Dianzole (the true independence and liberation of the black man), this man would not have been taken seriously. He would have been regarded as a revolutionary, somebody who shouts loudly, a rebel and no more than that. Thus it is a white man that comes to speak for Africa as it is up to a "white" to repair the affects of white colonization in Africa. This white man will be seen by certain people from his own race as a traitor and they will seek to deter his mission, to kill him. And believe me, they seek to kill him, but as long as he is still necessary on Earth, that he still has things to say and do, he will benefit from the protection of our creators, the Elohim, and nothing will happen to him! He is not here to perform "miracles" through the intervention of our creators nor is he here to tell us to believe, as past Prophets have, but rather to use our intelligence!

All Kimbanguists all over the whole world must become active militant for a pure and simple abolition of the arbitrary African borders, unilaterally fixed by the Colonial Powers at the time of the Conference of Berlin in 1884-1885. These vacuous borders are the source of all the geopolitical conflicts that Africa knows. It is these borders that have confined Africa in neo-colonialism. All Kimbanguists must take part in this combat so that the natural borders preceding colonization are restored. In these arbitrarily organized countries, the fruits of these colonial borders imposed by force, the African leaders currently in power have no legitimacy. The legitimacy belongs, in fact and in rights, to the old kingdoms, the old empires, and the old sultanates of before the era of colonization, this within the framework of very precise natural and historical borders. The second "true" independence preached by Prophet Kimbangu passes by this salutary rebuilding. Do not be misled; it is an obligatory passage. But, more importantly, this rebuilding must be done in absolute non-violence, peacefully and democratically, and according to the wishes of the majority of the people. Without any blood and without any violence!

Fight for the access to independences, federalism or confederations of states. Fight in favour of federative or confederative tendencies. Let nothing stop you in your quest to claim your rights, for your freedom to choose your destiny within the borders of your ancestors in the kingdoms of long ago, where the throne was occupied by those who came from the sky, a truly legitimate authority. The old Kingdoms and Empires of days gone by will live again and ultimately they alone will decide if they want to constitute or consist of federations or confederations of several States. But, once again, this must be done in absolute non-violence, peacefully and democratically!

None of the current African presidents who maintain and support these artificial borders deserve your support. They do nothing but facilitate and support the neo-colonialism objective because they are, in reality, concerned only with personal stakes, power and pleasing the former master colonizers.

Refer to chapter 29 of this work "A return towards the old natural borders that preceded Christian colonization". You will find there a more detailed analysis of these problems. Restore the old Kingdom Kongo, if you are Mukongo and Téké, for example. It is your duty and is precisely what the Prophet Kimbangu has asked of you. The Nkua Tulendo also shares this vision.

You must be asking yourself the question, "Must we now abandon Kimbangu to follow the Movement of "Nkua Tulendo?" Not necessarily. In fact, do as you see fit. You may remain kimbanguists. But if you do so, then be "true" kimbanguists; in this, denounce your Christianity! When all is achieved, the Prophet Simon Kimbangu will return aboard one of the same machines as he appeared in Nkamba. He will come in the company of some of the great prophets; Moses, Buddha, Jesus, Muhammad, and Kimpa Vita, among others, and in the company of Yahweh and others creators. It is the Nkua Tulendo who will welcome them all together in a residence built to accommodate their return, if possible, in Africa.

That will be a reality if the African people succeed in bringing the "Dipanda Dianzole" to fruition, the second independence announced by Simon Kimbangu. This is the sine qua non condition for a glorious return of the Prophet Simon Kimbangu to his place in the heart of Africa and welcomed by Nkua Tulendo with the blessing of Yahweh the eternal and his people, the Elohim of the original Hebrew Bible.

It is not by chance that Jerusalem is situated in Africa. The "New Jerusalem, the one "coming down from the sky", has already known its foundation in Africa. As it is written, "The last will be first".
One of the missions of the Nkua Tulendo is to prepare the welcoming of our Fathers who are in the heaven in the company of the former Prophets sent by them. But first, it is necessary to succeed in the "Dipanda Dianzole",

the second independence or total decolonisation. And this will begin with the destruction of the artificial borders, the physical or virtual restoration of the old kingdoms, empires and other political structures of society, and the abandonment by the African masses of Catholicism and Western Christendom. We have no choice but to go through these phases.

The majority among you are Bakongos and Tekes. In this, originating from the various ethnic groups of the old Kongo Kingdom, and recognizing that there are also kimbanguists in many other African ethnic groups dispersed throughout Africa and also in the Diaspora, know that you are not alone in this mission.

Many other people will undertake the exact same mission as you. They will support you in the acquisition of this second "true" independence, the Dipanda Dianzole that will be achieved by the simultaneous action of many people, because many other people now understand that spiritual decolonization is where their only source of salvation lies.

Indeed a diversity of people other than those who constitute the Kongo Kingdom of long ago of which the Prophet Kimbangu and the Prophetess Kimpa Vita were children, others I say, will lead with you an action comparable to yours. These will not base themselves directly on the Prophet Kimbangu and his prophecies. They will base themselves on their own history that also goes back to biblical days and more particularly to the history of the Empire of Kush, history connected to that of the descent of Cham, the black son of Noah and to biblical prophecies concerning the people of Kush for this era, "the Messianic era".

Your brothers Tutsi, Tushi, Tuku, Kushi, BanyaMulenge, Hima, Hema, Luba, Lunda-Ruund, Bororo, Turkana, Somali, Gallas, Fula, Masai, etc., who are all people constituting the old biblical Empire of Kush, will initiate the same mission and they will pursue it by your side.

Concerning the history of «Kush», the Catholic Church and Rome also concealed many things from you. In the hebrew language, blacks are traditionnaly referred to with the word «Kush». If you travel to Israël today, you will hear hebrews refer to blacks with the word «Kush» in the singular and «Kushim» in plural. Where does this word originate? What is this famous history of "Kush" and of their people? What is the link with the prophecies of Kimbangu, the Dipanda Dianzole, and the total liberation of the black people and the coming of the Nkua Tulendo? We should examine this more closely, remembering that the black people do not need a "white" interpretation of the Bible nor to espouse white catholic Religions to understand their place in the history of the Bible.

Refer to the Old Testament, precisely, Chapter 2 of The Book of Genesis. There, in Verses 8 through 14, is the following passage:

> *"And Yahweh planted a garden in Eden, in the east; and there he put the man whom he had formed. And out of the ground Yahweh made to grow every tree that is pleasant to the sight, and good for food; the tree of life also in the midst of the garden, and the tree of knowledge of good and evil. And a river flowed out of Eden to water the garden; and from thence it was parted, and became into four heads. The name of the first is Pishôn: that is it which compasseth the whole land of Havilah, where there is gold; And the gold of that land is good: there is bdellium and the onyx stone. And the name of the second river is Gihon: the same is it that compasseth the whole land of Ethiopia (Kush). And the name of the third river is Hiddekel: that is it which goeth toward the east of Assyria. And the fourth river is Euphrates.*

The rivers Hiddekel and Euphrates are of less interest here, but let us look at what we can say concerning the rivers Pishôn and Gihon and especially the country of Havilah and the country of Kush. It is quite interesting.

Expressed differently, the Garden of Eden was not a small garden, but a very vast territory (or laboratory). It extended from the East until it reached the source of a river, therefore to the source of a large fresh water tank that will nourish all this vast Garden of Eden, and this river will give rise to four arms. This large tank of fresh water is located in the area of the Great Lakes (Lake Tanganyika, etc), and the first river, Pishôn, is the White Nile of which the source is in Rwanda at the border with Kongo (D.R.C.). This river surrounds the country of Havilah. And the second river, the Gihon, which surrounds all the country of Kush is the Blue Nile.

Therefore, the biblical Garden of Eden was very vast, extending from the East to the area of the Great Lakes in the heart of Africa, where one precisely finds gold, bdellium and stone of onyx. This is a well-known fact! Perhaps now you will begin to understand why there is endless crisis and war in the area of the Great Lakes. The stake is surely very different there, more than what you might have imagined! It also should be remembered that at that time there was still only one continent. We had not yet identified "continents" and, much less, the "the continental drift". Therefore the eastern side where man had first been situated was quite different from that of our current East. The East was defined in relation to a precise point, clearly. But which point? It is at the source of the Pishôn River, the White Nile, on the Rwanda-Uganda-Kongo border. Over time, many rabbis have confirmed that location of the Garden of Eden!

Do not be misled; the oldest history of humanity, to our knowledge, is that of "Kush". Moreover, it is "Kush" that will give rise to Egypt and not the reverse. The moment of the meeting between "Kush" and the Pharaoh of Egypt is well documented in history. But the precise origin of "Kush", because it is so ancient, we cannot be sure.

When one spoke in biblical language of "the land of Israel", this was not limited at all to the territory of the State known today as the "Hebrew State of Israel". These are two entirely separate regions. The southernmost border of Israel was, at the time, the Zambezi, and the heart of the Garden of Eden was at the source of the White Nile, the Pishôn, on the Rwanda-Uganda-Kongo border, where the first man was created.

The Hebrew Jews populating the State of Israel today have no historic recollection of the Garden of Eden. When asked, notice that they do not know or can no longer recall. Whereas we, in the Royal Courses of the people of Kush, we have restored this fact. We still know! Further, The Hebrew Jews of the current State of Israel cannot describe the true borders of biblical Israel. Therefore, since the creation of the State of Israel in 1948 until today, there has never been a true definition of the borders of Israel. The State of Israel, in its constitution, does not clearly define its borders. In fact, it has no borders. During talks to outline a constitution, Israel's rabbis prohibited defining borders, claiming, "You do not know where the exact borders of Israel are"!

The first Jewish Zionist Congress, under the direction of Theodor Herzl, had as its objective the creation of a Jewish national hearth, i.e., "a Jewish State". This Congress took place in 1897, in Basel, a Swiss city on the eastern border of France. Several future Congresses also met in Basel (Basle). In April 1903, Uganda was presented to Herzl and the Zionist Jews as a proposed country in which the Jewish State could be created. It would not be the Palestine of long ago that would be proposed but rather a country in the heart of Black Africa: Uganda. And in July of the same year Herzl would also study the possibilities of Jewish immigration to Kongo! And where do you imagine this immigration would take place? In the area of the Great Lakes! Then, at the time of the Sixth Congress (August 22-28, 1903), a conflict arises over the selection of Uganda, Zionists of Russo-Polish origin insisting to overturn the decision in favour of Uganda. Discussions continued in February 1904 to name Uganda as the new Jewish state. Herzl enthusiastically maintained his support for this choice but became ill in June of that year, passing away on July 3. Talks were resumed that included Chaim Weitzman (who later became the first Israeli president) and David Ben Gourion (Prime Minister under Weitzman) and together they encouraged discussion in favour of Palestine as the place where the State of Israel would be founded.

Why was Uganda the first selection as the country of preference? Why was the consideration of this country a priority to Theodor Herzl, the father of "Zionism", a movement to which he will devote his entire life? Why would he have also examined the possibility of Kongo? Do you really think this was a coincidence? With such a delicate question in the balance, where to found the State of Israel, fulfilling the prophecies written in the Bible, could choosing a country in full Black Africa, "the Negroes" place, have been left to chance? Not on your life! The possibility was underscored by a strong motivation! But what? Because it is there at the Uganda-Rwanda-Burundi-Kongo border that the Pishôn, this river that nurtures "the garden of Eden" finds its source! It is there where the land of Havilah is located. (It is from this that **towns and cities** such as Huvira in Kongo received their names, **and note that in a lot of local languages like kyniruanda there is no letter «R» to be pronounced, the letter «R» is there often pronounced or replaced by an «L», so Huvira = Huvila or Havila**).

And, beside the fact that the first man and woman, Adam and Eve, created by our creators from space, were created there,

in the area of the source of the Pishôn (White Nile), there where the tree of science was located, or in other words the laboratory where

the first man came out, Adam and Eve were blacks! Yes, this is also one of the things Rome and very well initiated rabbis know damn well, and that they have kept secret and hidden untill today!!!

It should be known that at the time of these Zionist Congresses the southernmost source of the White Nile was mistakenly situated at Lake Victoria in Uganda. It was later discovered that the true source lied further south near the Rwanda-Burundi-Kongo border. Those who took part in the Zionist congresses rejected the choice of Uganda and chose Palestine, quite simply because, to their memory, the history of Eden was too dis-

353

tant, even unknown to them. Thus their choice was made on Jerusalem, to Palestine, the place of the Temple, because the history of the Temple was closer to them, less obscured in the darkness of their collective memory. In fact, it was only King David who made Jerasulam his capital. To your re-collection, where had the capital of Israel, in the territory of Kush, been? In any case, one thing is sure: Meroe (Sudan) was, at a very distant point in time, considered the capital of Kush, therefore of Israel.

We, royalties of Africa, having safeguarded the memory of "Kush", of "Havilah", can say to the Jews of Israel, the current Hebrew State, that the borders of origin of "Israel" were the borders of "Kush" and that its Southern border was the Zambezi or, more precisely still, the southern-most border of the South-Kushite Nation of Shaba (Saba, Sheba), i.e., the Lunda Empire, which extends until part of the Zambezi.

Let us look at the biblical writings again. Who were the characters of the name of "Kush" and "Havilah". The answer is simple. After the flood, the descendants of Noah would again repopulate the Earth. But Noah had three sons; Shem, Japheth and Cham. We know that Shem is the ancestor of the Semites. Within this branch, Ishmael (son of Abraham) will be the ancestor of the Arab branch, and Isaac (other son of Abraham) will be the ancestor of the Jewish branch. Let us leave Japheth br iefly and discuss Cham who was the black son of Noah. Cham was the father of four sons, all "black;" Kush, Mizraim, Put and Canaan. This is the first historical mention of the name of "Kush". In turn, Kush would have three sons, also black; Seba, Havilah, and Sabtah. This is the first mention of "Havilah", but also of "Seba".

Before completing this analysis. Let us revel for a moment in a small but pleasant bit of history, showing to what degree this beautiful part of his-tory was concealed over time, this to the benefit of the white race and to the disadvantage of the black, as chance would have it. At a given time in history, there would be a crossing, a mixture, between the descendants of Shem (son of Noah, ancestor of the Semites) and the descendants of Cham (the black son of Noah); that would occur when a nephew of Abraham, Lot, married a "black" daughter of Canaan Of this union between the nephew of Abraham (descendant of Shem) and this daughter of Canaan (descen-dant of Cham) would be born two girls who will give rise to the branch of Moabites (mixture between "Shem" and "Cham;" one can say, to some extent, a mixture between blacks and Semites).

It is in this branch of Moabites that will be born Ruth and the "Jewish" filiations starting with the mother. It is from "Ruth, the Canaanite", such as she was called, or "Ruth, the black one", or "Ruth, the brown one, that all of the great kings of Israel were descended; Solomon, David, and Jesus! Did Solomon, David, and Jesus have black blood coursing through them, their heritage dating back to Cham, through Ruth? Yes, it is undeniable! What was then their skin colour? Well, certainly not, "snow white"!

What else do the writings tell us? Following certain events that included the displacement of people after the tragedy of Babel, the people of Kush would travel toward the south, Canaanites to the east toward Asia. This would explain why so many in people in India have dark complexions (this is only an assumption). And the descendants of Kush; Havilah, Seba, Sabtah, where would they settle? They became situated in the aforementioned "country of Havilah" and "the country of Kush", where the rivers Pishôn and Gihon begin.

The Bible (Genesis) even tells us very clearly that Abraham, with his wife and son, Lot, and all his possessions, leaves Egypt and travels to the south to settle in the land of Hawilah (Havilah-Huvira) which is one of the geographical areas now known where Abraham and his descendants lived.

Geographical maps dating back to between 1600 and 1700 A.D. illustrate an important part of current Africa with the name of "Ethiopia" and a particular area by the name of "Empire of Kush and of Sheba". All this is connected to the lineage of "Kush", the small black son of Noah, but also to the lineage of Seba (son of Kush). Later, the Queen of Seba (Sheba) will be united with King Solomon and she will bear him children, furthering the line of descent.

At these times, the name "Africa" did not exist yet. To refer to this territory, one spoke about the land of "Cham", (Kem, Kam, Chemet), land of "Kush", land of "Sheba", and land of Ethiopia (not named Ethiopia at the time, but a very vast territory). The lands of the Kushite empire received the name "Ifriqiya" (Africa) after the invasion of one of the Arab kings of the Yemen which bore the name "Ifriqos bin Qais bin Saifi". This king would seize the lands of the North (the Maghreb, etc) and consequently those lands would bear a name referring to him, i.e., "Ifriqiya" (Africa). Today, the entire continent is known by everyone as Africa, a name that is just a derivative of an Arab king who conquered the land.

But the history of "Kush" and "Havilah" still remain in the area of the Great Lakes of Africa. It is still alive, more now than ever before. Why did

355

we call the area of Katanga by the name of "Shaba (Sabtah, Sheba)?"

This return to our history preceding the era of slavery and colonization, embarrasses (one might say "annoys") many people, in particular, the Vatican and its allies (France, Belgium, etc.). Why? Because a return to our origins, consideration of this history which is ours will force us to become aware of our "great biblical past" and allow us to understand that our own history is truly glorious. Consequently, we can abandon the Vatican and its lies.

They fear us rediscovering our biblical "Jewish" origins and that we may be inclined to seek even more our old traditions and our authentic roots. But what they fear the most through this process is that we will once again discover "the Truth", that which they worked odiously at concealing from us for twenty centuries.

And there are very particular people who raise the highest concern for Rome and the Vatican; the Hima, or Tutsi people. And why? Historically, Tutsis have always refused to be converted to Catholicism, to Christianity. But in addition to that, they are the living embodiment of Havilah, of Kush. From the beginning of recorded time, the Tutsis were the spearhead, the elite troops of the black Pharaohs and of the crown of Sheba. In ancient times they were the guardians of the source of the River Pishôn (the White Nile). They are the descendants of the elite troops of King Solomon. They were the Great Archers of the Court of King Solomon. Upon their death, Tutsis kings were embalmed in the same manner as the great pharaohs.

The Tutsi Kingdoms were marvellous living shrines to the sovereignty of King Solomon on the African land, on the land of "Kush". Everything in the organization of the Tutsi kingdoms before the arrival of the slave system and of colonialism was centered on the rites of the temple of Solomon of long ago, such as, for example, the social organization around the "russet-red cow". The russet-red cow bears a mystical connection to the Temple of Solomon where the immense herds of "Russet-red Cows" were devoted to sacrifices in the Temple and the permanent purification of the House of Israel (See the Old Testament). The Constitution for their kingdoms was the "Torah" in its most literal pre-Talmudic form. Their constitution was aptly called "the Constitution of the Bull". Their instrument of Government was the "Stick of Moses" which represented their belonging to the people of Israel.

The biblical festivals for the Tutsis were of enormous proportion prior to

356

the arrival of the Catholic Christian colonizer, as they had been at the time of the Temple in the time of Solomon. The Halakhah Tutsis, for example, carefully safeguarded encoded references to their festivals. Among many rituals preserved was their annual festival called "Umuganuro", which means "Festival of Return". During this celebration that lasted eight days, sacred oxen were sacrificed to symbolize the "rise toward Jerasulem". There is a clear and obvious parallel that can be made between the Pharaonic practices and those of the Tutsis when referring to the culture of the 18th Egyptian dynasty. This explains the mosaic faith of Tutsis. One needs to know that the legal system of the Tutsis, prior to colonization, plainly mirrored that of the Deutoronomic Code, this without any advance knowledge of this code!

In history, there are many accounts of travellers who witnessed the Jewish-Hebraic occupation by Tutsis. Let us quote, for example, the famous exploring traveller, Eldad Hadani, a Spanish Jew of the 9th century A.D. who attests in his writings to the authenticity and anteriority of the mosaic civilizations of the tribes of Israel living around the Pishôn on the sacred lands of Havilah. In 883, he writes to the Jews of Spain to inform them of his finding. He even specifies that the faith of these people is exemplary and that their Talmud is Hebraic. But, on one hand, these people have not known of rabbis as the rabbinical system only came with the second Temple, the Temple of David, and the Tutsis only knew the first Temple, that of Solomon!

After the death of King Solomon and with the Assyrian invasion of the Temple and of Jerasulem, it would be the troops of "Kush" led by the "Tutsi" elite that will run to the aid of Jerusalem. Legend also has it that they helped to save the Ark of the Covenant of the Temple and carried it with them to the land of "Kush" in Ethiopia. The famous drums of Burundi are nothing other than the drums of Solomon, the drums that were played in the Court of Solomon. The guardians of these drums were the Shebatic sovereigns of Havilah where the biblical Pishôn runs, the White Nile.

Concerning the possession of the land, the Tutsi Kingdoms strictly applied the contract of emphyteutic lease, such as is mentioned in the Old Testament. This "contract of term lease" was called "Ubugererwa" and could, to some extent, be translated as "contract concluded with a foreigner" because, according to the "Constitution of the Bull", the land could not belong to an individual and the individual could only borrow it for certain lengths of time. The "Russet-red Cows" could be the only sole owner of the land. This is in line with indications in the Old Testament concerning property.

From ancient time, the ancestors of Tutsis, Hebrews from Kush, took a particular care and assiduity in celebrating the family rite of the consumption of "Matsah – Umutsimah;" ritual bread manufactured from a cereal, "Uburo", known for not fermenting when making contact with water. At Passover, this bread was eaten in small portions called "uruhalah-hallah". The original "Matsah" of the Kushite Hebrews was accompanied by a particularly bitter vegetable species called "Isogi". For Tutsis, the celebration of Passover occurred long before the arrival of the Christian evangelization in Africa, a regulation for all their people. During this celebration, they commemorated, as a family, the deprivations endured in the desert during the forty years of Exodus, which led them from the Holy Land to the Promised Land. Moshe (Moses) was their spiritual Chief and their Chief of War. The "stick of Return" ("Intahe" in Tutsi language) supported their strength in combat and in the administration of justice, this according to the recommendations of the Kushite Patriarch "Jethro" to his son-in-law Moshe. And it is during this extremely testing Exodus that the Hebrews received the "Law Written" from Yahweh the Eternal. The Kush Tutsis always called this celebration "Kurya Umwaka" (literally "to consume the year") in accordance with the Law promulgated by Moshe, in Exodus chap.12, verse 1-2: "And Yahweh spoke unto Moses and Aaron in the land of Egypt, saying, this month shall be unto you the beginning of months: it shall be the first month of the year to you". And so the celebration of "Kurya umwaka" always commemorated New Year's Day of their "Kushite" calendar!

In order to disparage the historic truth about the Tutsis and to depict them as a wandering tribe who only recently settled in the area of the Great Lakes, erroneous information has been set forth designating them as descendants of Cham and originating in Abyssinia (current Ethiopia). But in fact, the Tutsis have populated this area since the dawn of time, since biblical times. Do not be fooled by this literature that comes from a catholic anti-Semite machination that has tried to eradicate Tutsis from the surface of the Earth, because, in their view, Tutsis' knowledge is vast, they refuse to convert, and they obstruct a greater plan.

Why, in your opinion, has Catholicism, in the second half of the last century, perpetrated three actions of genocide on the Tutsi people? For what reason, in your estimation, did Catholicism, by fanaticizing Hutus whom were already converted to this Roman religion thus undertake to exterminate more than 1 million Tutsis under the horrible conditions that we know? Why? Solely to remove these people from the face of the Earth, people who, in the eyes of the Vatican, are guilty of knowing too much about the history of the black man and the fact that his history repeatedly connects him to times of the Old Testament.

It is not for nothing that the newspaper "Jerusalem Post" in its edition of November 23, 1998, declared the following: "

> *We launch an appeal to Israel and the International Community to condemn and undertake actions against any anti-Jew violence, perpetrated by the non-Israelis throughout Africa, on more than 500,000 Tutsi-Hebrew Israelis in Rwanda"!*

For Rome, Tutsis represent the living memory of the Hebraic people of Havilah and Kush. And in addition, they have the audacity to persist in their refusal to convert to Catholicism or eventually to another branch of Christianity. Consequently, in the opinion of the "high prelates" of the sinister Roman curia, this qualifies that they be eliminated. For them, no other solution is possible! Fortunately, the Roman curia could not bring their plan to fruition and, for our greater happiness, the Tutsi nation still thrives today!

It should be remembered that when the Bible speaks to us about the isolated tribes of Israel *"on the other banks of Ethiopia"* it is indeed of the people of Kush and Havilah that it speaks of, of these people dwelling in the area of the Great Lakes, the people of the basin of the White Nile. The very prestigious Talmudist RASHI (Rabbi Shlomo Ben Yitzhak) affirms it clearly: this geographical territory is in the area of the Great Lakes (Uganda, Rwanda, Burundi, Kivu, Shaba-Katanga, Luba), he says.

The Roman Catholic Church, with its allies, developed an entire strategy to safeguard its power in Africa. Be wary, as with the plague, of all Christian NGOs and other "good catholic charities" installed on our premises. They are often nothing but screens, concealing intelligence agents in the service of Rome. An entire enterprise of hatred has developed in Central Africa toward the Tutsis, toward the Rwandans. This campaign was knowingly orchestrated by the agents of Rome. Pointing their fingers at Tutsis and transforming them into "scapegoats", they made them responsible for all the evils, for all the problems, for all the existing plagues, unceasingly presenting Tutsis as being the evil in person, "the devil" himself, and all Tutsis as invaders, people full with arrogance, etc... And, unfortunately, this unhealthy propaganda succeeded noticeably well once again. To be convinced, one only has to see the number of Kongolese who became, in the last few decades, bearers of intense hatred toward Tutsis, often to the point of murder.

We point out the lesson offered by the history of a recent past, the 1930's, when the same machination took place in Nazi Germany. The "Jews" were designated as authors of the economic crisis, transformed into "scape-goats", responsible for all the evils and misfortunes of society at the time. And we all know what resulted from this. Let us not allow this to happen to Tutsis on our premises in Africa! Never! Do not let yourself fall into this pernicious spiral by offering an inattentive or resigned ear to the unhealthy remarks that we hear in passing. For example, recall the words of a certain Kongolese politician who sometimes in the past referred to Tutsis as "Inyenzi", which means cockroach, microbe, or insect. At the beginning of the Nazi era, Jews were also spoken about in this manner in Germany and bordering countries. The result was the holocaust!

We should never allow that between us in Black Africa. Never... I mean never!
UNESCO spent millions of dollars between 1984 and 1987 to carry out excavations in the Area of the Great Lakes, to do archaeological research there. But never was a report published on this subject... not one. Why? Because everything demonstrates the presence of Tutsis in this area since millennia before the time of Jesus and that, actually, Hutus came there well after them. In other words, compared to the Tutsis, the Hutus settled there only recently. The catholic clergy did nothing but propagate lies on this subject. In fact, the Hutus, once transformed into fanatics of Catholicism, their Church encouraged them to assert these lands as their own since, it said, these lands being "Bantu", it was supposedly legitimate that they return to the Hutus. The Catholic Church wasted no time in making these incontestably false allegations not only to the Hutus, but also to the other Africans. The one and only aim set by this Church was the extermination, another holocaust, a new Shoah, against Tutsis this time, so that these guardians of the oldest history, that which goes back to King Solomon and the great patriarchs of the Bible, disappear!

Tutsis are not our enemies; they are our brothers. Our enemy is Rome; it is the Vatican; and it is Catholicism! It is said that there is a "Bantu theory" for some and a "hamitic theory" for others, so-called "strangers coming from somewhere else" that does not correspond to anything. This is only an invention of circumstance, nothing else! To say that the "Kushite civilization" does not exist and that there is, for the black race, only one civilization, the "Bantu civilization" is just as false. Do not let yourself be fooled nor cradled by murky theories like these. They belong to those generated by the agents of Rome in order to divide us and to make us forget the real history of "Kush" with the exact and precise position of its borders that date back to the biblical Genesis.

This false "Bantu theory" dates back to the 1950s already, and in 1959 it led to the extermination of hundreds of thousands of Tutsis in Rwanda. The argument they used to justify the unjustifiable: "these people do not belong here...they should go back home to Ethiopia". Some ten years later, between 1960 and 1970, they would use linguistic formulas to perpetuate further this so-called "Bantu theory". It would resemble a pure frame-up, again so artfully orchestrated that one could even call this "missionary raciology"! But where do you believe that such wild flights of fancy are elaborated? In many places, to be sure, but one most prominent would be that of "the Franco-Burundian School of History", established in Paris. Yes, France again, the "first daughter of the Church", and whose school would play a key role in their mission.

Although this manipulation came primarily from white capitals, Rome, Paris, etc, there were also, unfortunately, black allies among them. Omar Bongo, President of Gabon, Great Master in Freemasonry and a man cherished by France, conversely was always ready to serve the great interests of the West whenever necessary. In 1982, it was Bongo who inaugurated the "Center of Bantu Civilization", immediately receiving the recognition of the European States. Are you surprised? And so it is! And who would be installed as the head of the aforementioned "Center of Bantu Civilization?" The Kongolese Theophilus Obenga. And do not think that this was entirely by chance for this man is a pure product of the Sorbonne, Parisian school reputed as being the premier institution of the Universities of France. In fact, France aimed only to show by means of this famous "Center of Bantu Civilization", with money obviously, that the Kushite and Semitic civilizations do not exist in Africa, that only the Bantu civilization prevails, regardless of the facts which prove that this is pure aberration.

According to the result of the alleged "scientific" studies, the following principle was presented: if Tutsis are not Bantu, while they live in a Bantu place, then they are "foreigners". It is in this very subtle "Bantu theory" that division was spawned among the children of Black Africa. In this context, ecclesiastics such as the Abbot Alexis Kagame who, around 1967, traveled to Rome to study (encamped with the enemy) returning later to Africa with a completely conditioned spirit. They return with ideas that are more eccentric than the ones before them such as the Roman "Bantu-Rwandan" thesis!

Let us, once and for all, deal with this question: the Tutsis were established in the area of the Great Lakes at least 2500 years before the dawn of the Christian era. They are not newly-arrived foreigners. Who can claim to justify the clouded theory of Tutsi immigration, for there exists no real foundation allowing him, neither in historical testimonies of the area or in the local traditions. Certain parts of the Kivu lands were taken away from the Hima - Tutsis by colonization and placed within the artificial borders of Belgian ex-Kongo. It is clear that a "Bantu" theory that would concern every African cannot exist!

We must return to our authenticity, to our old traditions...to our Truth!

The enemy is Rome. I repeat this; it is the Roman Catholic Church and its "Holy See" of the Vatican. It is the Vatican always that we find behind these well orchestrated divisions, behind the falsification of history, behind this imposing "enginery" especially designed to make us forget our "true" history. Understand this well! But why does this Church preoccupy herself so deeply with all of this with its fanaticized, conditioned, corrupted catholic African black allies?

To better understand the reason for the Church's vehement opposition to black Africa, we should initially realize that the persons in charge of the Vatican, and their allies, are completely aware that prophecies of the Prophet Kimbangu announce the imminent end of the domination of the Christian Churches in Africa and that this will simultaneously involve the disappearance of the secular domination on this continent by people of white race, their domination being only one extension of that of Rome.

However, the plentiful information available to these "high world authorities" tells them:

> a. *of the role that the area of the Great Lakes will have to play in the deep upheavals that will intervene in the next few years... and also*
> b. *of the very particular participation which will be assigned to the Tutsi people in the course of these events.*

As they have a great stake in the area surrounding the Great Lakes, and more precisely still, from the land of Kush, the land of Havilah (ref. Genesis 2), so in lies their vehemence toward the Tutsis,

Here, extracted from the Bible, writings of a poetic style, Isaiah 18, 1-3 and 7:

"Woe to the land [...]
which is beyond the rivers of Ethiopia,
That sendeth ambassadors by the sea,
even in vessels of bulrushes upon the waters, saying,
Go, ye swift messengers,
to a nation scattered and peeled,
[...]
to a people terrible from their beginning hitherto;
a nation meted out and trodden down,
whose land the rivers have spoiled!
All ye inhabitants of the world,
and dwellers on the earth,
see ye, when he lifteth up an ensign on the mountains;
and when he bloweth a trumpet, hear ye.
[...]
In that time shall the present be brought unto Yahweh
of hosts of a people scattered and peeled,
and from a people terrible from their beginning hitherto;
a nation meted out and trodden under foot,
whose land the rivers have spoiled,
to the place of the name of Yahweh of hosts, the mount Zion".

This passage speaks of the area of the Great Lakes, Uganda, Kivu, Rwanda, Shaba-Katanga, Burundi, and Kasai where the mountains and rivers meet. Long ago, all the territory of Kush went from Nubia to Somalia, Djibouti, Ethiopia, Eritrea, Uganda, Rwanda, Burundi, Kivu, Shaba-Katanga, Kasai, and Kenya. The scattered and peeled nation about which the Prophet Isaiah speaks is this nation of Kush, the nation of the men of high size (ref. Isaiah 45, 14) and others. The Tutsis on their mountains of Rwanda-Urundi, the people of "Kush" would present a gift to Yahweh of the armies. This gift is the fruition of what the Prophet Kimbangu calls "the second independence", or in other words, a return to the old natural borders that existed before the era of colonization.

It will mean a return to the borders of Kush. This state will once again formally unite as a confederation of numerous states based on the sovereignties of long ago which, in this region and at that time, swore allegiance to the crown of Sheba, to the line of descent of King Solomon. When this happens, we will again be free, truly independent, released from the white domination, fruit of the domination of Rome. With this freedom, we would finally realize the constitution of the new states that will be born everywhere in Africa, a great Federation: the "United States of Africa". "Dipanda Dianzole" will flourish in all the corners of Black Africa. Of course, the enemy will do everything in its power to keep maintain the current artificial borders because they are the cornerstones on which its power was built. Its control and its complete domination of Africa depend on these borders for foundation.

Kongolese, it is true that the President of Rwanda, Mr. Kagame, who is also Tutsi, leads a disastrous policy towards Kongo. He has nothing to seek in Kinshasa; he should be satisfied to do politics in his own country. Do not draw up against all Tutsis of Rwanda-Urundi-Uganda. Doing so would be a grave mistake, as not all Tutsis present your problem. Do not fall into this trap tended by Rome, well tended again by the Vatican and its Kongolese and its assorted allies. It is very important, paramount, to understand that to organize such a mission would be to fall into this additional trap tended again by Rome. Rather look at the intrigues of this Catholic and Roman Church. Observe the Vatican. It is where our only true enemy lies. It uses its powerful "concoctions" to lull us to sleep, potent "powders" to hypnotize us. They will again create scapegoats to exterminate without scruple. In fact, this time it is the Tutsis that Rome tries to muzzle with the complicity of its "First Daughter", France. Proven by their actions in 1994, France supports and aids the genocidal Catholics carry out their atrocities, the extermination of Tutsis in the Area of the Great Lakes. You cannot allow this abomination to happen again. You must immediately oppose it with the greatest conviction.

May the "Dipanda Dianzole" start with you, faithful of the Prophet Simon Kibamgu! Do not be afraid. The Heaven looks at you. And from the top of the Heaven, the Prophet Kimbangu, Yahweh the Eternal, and the other Prophets and creators will approve your action because they approve this way of thinking. And here on Earth the Nkua Tulendo also approves. Claim your legitimate sovereignty. It is high time to dispense with this "colonization". And may the Prophecies of Simon Kimbangu as well as those of Isaiah be accomplished according to the will of Yahweh the Eternal. And who knows, once we commence this action, perhaps it is possible that the sky will intervene to support and accelerate the result of this second independence. But in any event, it is imperative that we begin, that it be initiated by us. The sky will not start it for us. By initiating the mission ourselves, we will demonstrate consciousness and will, and we will deserve all that will then follow.

364

On this subject, in the Old Testament, Yahweh the Eternal says, "Concerning the people of the lands of Kush and all the people of the Old Kingdoms, such as the Kongo Kingdom, for example, when time comes, he, Yahweh, the President of the Planet of the Eternals, he will return each clan onto their own, because the land of Kush belongs to them. In other words, in these times, the old kingdoms and empires will be restored and "colonization" will be nothing more but an empty word.

To further elaborate, I will quote you the example of people whom I love very much: the Masai people of Kenya. The mission described above has begun; the plan to restore their lands has been activated. The territories of these people, their ancestral lands, belong to the lands of the old empire of Kush. In 2004, the Masai began to exert unprecedented pressure on the Kenyan government in order that their ancestral lands be returned to them, having had them confiscated from them in 1904 by the British colonizer.

However, in 1904, the United Kingdom and the Masai signed an agreement stipulating that the British could freely dispose of their lands until August 15, 2004! But the 2004 term of the agreement has passed!! At this point, the Masai immediately began to claim their ancestral lands and to demand of the authorities of Kenya more than 600 million dollars in financial compensation because their ancestral lands are now occupied by other ethnic groups, even, but to a lesser degree, by whites! We are referring to a million hectares of lands! Generously, the Masai did not lay claim to those lands that were distributed by the government to farmers of other ethnic groups after the departure of the British colonists immediately following their access to independence. It is important to note, in order to understand fully, that the Masai had been excluded from this distribution of lands.

In Nairobi, capital of Kenya, the police force violently repressed a demonstration by the Masai that was held though it was prohibited. A Masai was even killed in the center of Kenya because he had allowed his herd to feed on lands that he asserted belonged to him but, in fact, belonged to a great white landowner! In the two weeks following August 15, 2004, expiration date of the treaty, 104 Masai were arrested for actions of land claim. How did the Government of Kenya react? It was satisfied to say the following thing: "the 1904 treaty in question was exceeded by the events and all the problems involved in the land were solved by the independence of Kenya in 1963".

But, in reality, there is absolutely nothing solved. The borders of Kenya of 1963 are those that were traced by the colonizer in 1885 at the time of the Conference of Berlin. Kenya is an artificial country, a pure product of colonization. The Masai have the legitimate right to assert their ancestral lands in order to have one day their sovereign and constitutional "Massailand" within an important confederation of States adhering in its turn to an even greater Federation, that of the "United States of Africa" where all people will be represented equally, including the Masai.

And to the north of Kenya, there are the Samburu people who claim their autonomy, people who have secessionist tendencies, who have the firm intention of reclaiming their lands, and whose inhabitants want to be once again attached to their "Somali" brothers living on other side of the border in Somalia. All this completely forms part of the process of decolonization. Let us stop with the colonial borders and return to our old borders, the truly legitimate ones! And let us do this in a totally non-violent way by creating political parties that claim this right!

And you, Kimbanguists, you are a force, a power, by your number, by the religion which binds you, the religion of the "Kintuadi "of the Prophet Simon Kimbangu, who exhorts you to lead to good term the "Dipanda Dianzole", the second independence.

Up to you to play. Amen! Or, in other words, so be it!

32. "Prayers" and "Miracles"

"From 1858 to 1972, miraculous cures noted in Lourdes, France by the religious authorities: 72.
Fatal traffic accidents on the road of the pilgrimage: 4,272".

- MICHEL AUDIARD, scenario writer and French dialogist (1920-1985) -

Before we arrive at the conclusion of this work, here are two subjects that I feel we should look at in more detail because they adversely affect Africans today.

Africans have always been a spiritual people as evidenced by the tribute we have paid to our creator-gods through our various social activities for many years. This is wonderful, and it needs to remain so. We must continue to pray, sing and dance for our creators, our humanized gods...but it should be done with consciousness. This is so different from an imposed "liturgy" "from above" and whose rituals are often so incomprehensible to the majority of "believers" that they are, invariably, meaningless!

To love our "human" gods, to thank them with consciousness, i.e., with the knowledge of what they really are: not "supernatural" beings, or ethereal. No, they are really "human beings" like ourselves, but we are ever mindful however that they precede us in the fields of science and wisdom by tens of thousands of years. This also makes quite a difference!

That is what our creator-gods wish. They want that our Love for them rest on consciousness and comprehension and not on this blind "faith", the "coalman's faith", that Christianity brought to us and continues to impose on us. They prefer those who love them with their consciousness rather than with their faith for it is consciousness that makes us similar to them.

Those who know and recognize that the creator-gods, this Elohim people, are not "supernatural" beings, those who understand that the enormous difference existing between them and us takes its source in a tremendous scientific gap and continue to love our celestial creators in all consciousness, then the love that they send to them touches them at the deepest of their vast and very subtle sensitivity.

It is thus important to understand that "the supernatural" does not exist.

367

All that exists is "natural". What we are tempted to call "supernatural" is what has not yet been explained scientifically, but this will one day change.

To illustrate this point, among the multitude of possible examples, we will take only one. What is more "natural" today than to get on a plane and fly over an ocean? Well, if we had the same state of mind as our descendants had living only 150 or 200 years ago, we would undoubtedly qualify this mode of transportation as "supernatural" or "miraculous" and we would say that it is reserved only for "cherubs" and other "angels" coming from the sky.

Christianity taught us to pray to a "God" whom it deems as "unique", "immaterial", "supernatural". But such an entity does not exist! Our ancestors did not speak in this way to our humanized gods of long ago. Our ancestors addressed the gods directly in their songs and prayers. They knew them by their names, as a human being calling another by name.

Let us reflect a little. Christianity came to Africa and it taught us that God is a "supernatural" being, "immaterial", "invisible", that He is omnipotent, very powerful and that He created man "in his image and his likeness". Good! But if I use my intelligence, I note that there is a huge inconsistency. How, if He is "supernatural". could this "God" have created "in his image and his likeness" a being that is completely "natural?" Because I am "natural", and it is what we all are, "natural", "visible", and "palpable", not "supernatural", "invisible", and "immaterial".

The proof of such evidence doesn't need to be shown; any rational, intelligent, healthy and functioning mind should be able to deduce: "I am natural", I am "human", and I was made "in the image and the likeness of those who made me; therefore, they are inevitably human, "natural", "visible", and "palpable".

And now, we can easily understand why our creators said to our primitive ancestors, as related in the Old Testament: "Son of man stand upright on your legs" which means, in other words: "do not bow down by kneeling like that in front of us, but instead love us with your consciousness". And, what did the Christian Religion do to answer this wish? It perpetuated a reverence and love for their immaterial God so that Christians of all races would drag themselves forever on their knees in total unconsciousness!

The meaning of the original prayer was also completely disfigured by Christendom. In fact, there are only two true prayers in the original meaning of this action and only these two, no others! The first one is the attempt of telepathic communication with the creators. Man's brain is like a large transmitter-receiver able to send and receive a multitude of clear waves and thoughts. This is telepathy. Certain Prophets of ancient times, certain wise men, had the capability of being in telepathic contact with the creator-gods when those were on Earth or near the Earth. But when the creator-gods were on their remote planet, elsewhere in our galaxy, this communication with them was not possible, neither for the Prophets nor for the Wise men.

It is for this reason that the creator-gods installed on Earth the famous "Ark of the Covenant", a "transmitter-receiver" station, as we would call it now. This apparatus had its own source of energy - an atomic battery, quite certainly - and it allowed man to come into contact with the creators due to certain manipulations of its levers (named in the bible, "Horns of the Altar", e.g., in. "I Kings, I, 50" and "I Kings, 2, 28").

The use and displacements of this "Ark" are often mentioned in the Bible (e.g. in "II Samuel, 6, 6-7", "II Samuel, 6, 9-12" and "I Kings, 2 - 26").

The use of this Ark was certainly not without risk. This apparatus was to be handled with technical precautions. Our ancestors, ignorant due to lack of science, could have had no knowledge. According to the Bible, among many accounts, the Philistines stole the Ark and took it to their chief Dagon. Having no knowledge of the dangers of the apparatus, they were most likely electrocuted through mishandling. Many among the Philistines met their death from burns ("bubons", in the Bible) due surely to the dangerous radiation emitted by the radioactive products integrated in this communication device (I Samuel 5, 1-9).

Moreover, with the situation of this telepathy "station", the words of Yahweh could be heard by certain "initiated" ones such as Elijah and Samuel, his young companion at the time. In the Bible, in I Samuel, the entire chapter 3 recounts for us the following scene. Samuel is laying next to the device and Yahweh calls him. But twice Samuel, perhaps still not initiated enough, thinks that it is Elijah who is in the next room that is calling him. He goes to see him but Elijah explains to him that it is Yahweh who is calling him. He sends him back by saying: "Go to bed and, if you are called, you will say: Speak Yahweh, for your servant is listening to you". Then the dialogue is established, from the first sentences that today two radio operators would use: "Samuel, Samuel! "Speak, for your servant is listening". At this epoch, the expression "I hear you loud and clear" was not used yet!

That was the true original meaning of the prayer: an attempt at communication with the creator-gods. And there, one fully understands the ongoing teaching by the Bantu traditions that demonstrate to us that there was a time when the communication between men and gods was easy. There was, at one time, an easy connection between the Earth and the heavens. Then came a time when this link was broken and, in this form at least, it is still not restored to date. In light of this, one understands better all the truth that is in our traditions... and the importance for us to rediscover them.

Another passage in the Bible (Psalms, 139, 4-6) attests beautifully as to what was then this original prayer, based on a telepathic connection between the Creators and those they had chosen to guide the people, the Prophets and the wise men, telepathic men and women. These latter established the link between the creators and us earthlings, their creations, in acting as sort of a bridge.

In these three verses of Psalm, it is King David who speaks to Yahweh, and here is exactly what he says to him:

> *"For there is not a word in my tongue, but, lo, O YAHWEH, thou knowest it altogether. Thou hast beset me behind and before, and laid thine hand upon me. Such knowledge is too wonderful for me; it is high, I cannot attain unto it".*

The word "knowledge" is here really appropriate in the sense of scientific knowledge. It is in this, a matter of science, which could not be understood by our ancestors. "Primitives, such as they were, like David, King of Israel, were in no way able to "attain unto it".

Let us not forget that our ancestors were primitives! The Apostles who followed Jesus, all without exception, were completely "ignorant" for lack of science. They had no knowledge whatsoever, not even of any basic notion; they had no understanding of chromosomes, DNA molecules, or any related subject. Compared to today's students learning genetics, elementary molecular biology and other sciences, they were ignorant. We should be well aware of this fact!

The Hebrews, by the means of this instrument named the "Ark of the Co-venant", communicated with the Elohim:

> *"And YAHWEH spoke unto Moses, saying, Speak unto the children of Israel, that they bring me an offering [...]*
> *And let them make me a sanctuary; that I may dwell among them [the Hebrews].[...]*
> *And they shall make an ark of shittim wood [...].*
> *And thou shalt overlay it with pure gold [...]*
> *And there I will meet with thee, and I will commune with thee, [...] [to communicate to you] all things which I will give thee in commandment unto the children of Israel.*
>
> (Exodus 25, 1-2, 8, 10-11 and 22)

From Moses (1230 B.C.) to Solomon (930 B.C.) the communications (prayers) were constant between the Elohim and the Hebrews by the means of this Ark, this "telecommunication" station amplifying the telepathic abilities of Hebrew earthlings.

By referring to this first meaning of the original prayer, any human being nowadays can try to attempt a telepathic contact with our creator-gods and pray onto them in this way. Humans who so wish can even gather in assembly and decide, for example, that they will gather on a precise hour and day to send our creators waves and thoughts of Love. But above all, we should speak to them only of beautiful things for the sake of pleasing them; that is all!

And in this is another example of Christianity's enormous stupidity. Pardon my bluntness but there is no other suitable way to express this. The Chris-tian Churches have traditionally led their parishioners in prayer to the heavens without awareness for the intention or purpose of their prayers. And one more time, once again, Christians played along, leading African Christians as champions in this foolishness. They pray to lament themsel-ves so they can cry, to be forgiven, to ask for wealth and prosperity, to keep or recover health, to succeed in their university exams or even to score on a penalty during a soccer match; to implore that their wives give birth to a son, to complain about this or that. In short what they dare call "a prayer" is, in fact, complete and utter total nonsense!

They pray to their creators and to the heavens each time things go wrong! But the bottom line is, it's a logical attitude. It is the by-product of this Christian foolishness that teaches that "God the son" was sent to erase the sin of man and that man is now on Earth to suffer. This Christian precept is absolute folly. It is another grotesque invention by this "Paul", who later would be sanctified but, as necessity would have it, is still the "man of lie", the one who betrayed the original teaching of Jesus the Prophet to whom he pretended to serve.

Coincidentally, there have been numerous people sanctified by the Church but none was less worthy than "Saint" Paul, also known as Saul, the founding father of the Christian movement.

Paul is responsible for numerous erroneous personal creations and interpretations. He decreed, among other things, that Jesus died suffering to atone a certain sin of men. And this aberration was completely formalized by Rome when the Council of Carthage, in 418 A.D., established into doctrine the "original sin" that says that all men are born sullied with this sin which they would somehow all inherit from their first parents Adam and Eve. That is also pure nonsense!

The result of this ridiculous mentality is that the "Christian" is educated in an atmosphere in which he feels constant guilt. He feels as though he must constantly ask for forgiveness; Protestants ask directly for forgiveness while Catholics add another layer and must confess their "sins" to a priest.

And as if all that was not enough to make people feel guilty, there is a "good God" that perpetually watches over the Christian, even when he masturbates. (I can only imagine the quality of the masturbation of the good black Christian, "solemn believer", who thinks that the "good God" at this precise moment is looking down on him with an annoyed look. How relaxed he must feel indeed!)

This great overkill with "venial" or "deadly" sins is so inane and could easily demonstrate that this Christian guilt complex is based on a gross error! Let's first note that the Bible speaks of a "forbidden" fruit and not of an "apple" and that this fruit has nothing to do with sexuality (which many false shepherds have been trying for ages to have their flocks believe).

This subtly used error goes back to the distortion of scriptures, completely disfigured by translations and copies done and redone by Rome and its scribes perhaps already under the order of the emperor Constantine. For in reality, the "Vulgate"(official Latin translation of the Catholic Bible) when it speaks of disobedience towards "God" committed by Eve first and then by Adam, it uses the word "fructus", that is indeed translated by "fruit". But in its figurative sense, the word also means "beneficial", such as the fruit of an action, a salvation, ones work.

When a Roman, in popular Latin, wanted to designate the fruit-object that one picks off the tree and that is sold at the market, he used the literal meaning, the word "pomum". And it is this term that in the minds unduly took the place of "fructus" and gave birth to our famous Christian "apple", the one our first parents should not have eaten. And so it goes, again and always "nonsense"!

The tree of knowledge of good and evil of which Adam and Eve had assimilated the "benefit" (the fruit, in the figurative sense) is in no way the ridiculous apple tree of the Christian imagery, an image indeed naive, but voluntarily chosen by certain twisted and perverse Roman minds. And from then on, the "Adam's apple" was well stuck in the throat of Christians, be they whites or blacks just as the so-called "apple picked by Eve" remains stupidly stuck in the sexual guilt of countless Christian women and their mates by contagious effect!

Indeed, Christianity never ceases to tie all this shame to sexual practice, to sensuality and pleasure, whereas it has nothing to do with that whatsoever. John Paul II, just as your predecessors, you were a "false shepherd". You manipulated the scriptures to better enslave hordes of Christians around the world. No "mea culpa" is to be made as to libido and sexual pleasure, and no institution, religious or other, should impose the slightest subordination as to sexual practices and sensuality between consenting adults.

The real Elohim Bible does not advocate any of that! Nowhere does it mention about an original sin committed by humanity on this point or on any other! John Paul II, I repeat, was a "false shepherd" and a liar!

So you had no reason to reproach those who have innocent but minor sexual practices. On the contrary, many among them, even all of them, would have had the right to reproach you, to you who said you were the "sovereign pontiff", "the infallible one". The lies you uttered while addressing these issues were fraught with disastrous consequences, and you should have been reproached with vehemence, given that your message had such tremendous influence "urbi and orbi" (to the city and the world), to a public so long conditioned by the incredible misinformation propagated by your Church!

The so-called original sin does not play any part in the Old Testament and Jesus never spoke of it, and never remotely alluded to it! The biblical texts of the Old Testament teach in many instances, that each one is responsible for his own actions. It is our pitiful "Saint" Paul who introduced confusion into his epistles by referring to a shortcoming of Adam's and therefore penalizing the following generations. So many misguided perceptions came from this detestable Paul for whom any hope could only come from the sacrifice of Jesus.

Thus, to explain the death of Jesus, according to Paul and others in the Jesus Movement, we were given only one explanation: the sacrifice. And as if this were not enough, Paul, unfortunately as much a «sweet talker» as a «great liar,» would additionally insist that Jesus died for our sins through his crucifixion. In itself, this is another blatant example of stupidity, as heavy as the tipcart of guilt it involves! Paul interprets the death of Jesus as a willed and necessary sacrifice! Result of all that? Suffering was glorified as a favour coming from heaven!

Not too long ago, our oppressed, humiliated, "those at the bottom" were counselled not to revolt but to "carry their cross", to take part in the sacrifice of Jesus! What would be the purpose? One answer only: to help the Powerful "to maintain order", whether just or unjust. And today, this precept still remains: for Africans as well as others, for those whom the enforced "order" has been unjust for centuries, and for those to whom one continues to say, in answer to their sufferings: "Pray and carry your cross in the name of the Lord Jesus-Christ. He, the God of Love, upon your death will reward you in heaven. These beautiful words have never had their desired effect of lessening the suffering, but it calms them, and so the "maintenance of law and order" so much desired is greatly facilitated to the benefit of "those at the top"!

Now, to all those African Christians who by the millions complain, lament, and direct their supplications towards the heavens: "Oh, Nzambi, come to deliver us from our sufferings", "Oh, forgive us for our sins", "Oh, Nzambi, please this, please that". I say emphatically, that is completely useless. These words are insults in the eyes of our creators! You show grotesque unconsciousness toward them! To act in such a way is to prove that one is "stupid for lack of science"! So, please, cease your jeremiads; they are useless and harmful!

It is when all is going well that you should address our creators. It is then necessary to send them only love, consciously. We have nothing to ask the heavens, and it is useless to request something from the heavens when things are bad. The gods instilled in each man "individual responsibility". Man is responsible for everything that happens to him, this as much on the individual level as on the collective level. This is so and endless prayers cannot change it! It is high time for Africans to understand that, those who have specialized in prayer groups of lamenting, complaining, crying and spending their time asking our creators for worldly things!

So few of us have understood that. Yet the teachings of the Biblical Prophets are clear on this subject: "Help yourself and the heavens will help you"! What does that mean? You want to pray for yourself, then you should address prayers to yourself and you will receive. This is the second meaning of the original prayer, the first being the telepathic attempt at contact with the gods, only to send them thoughts of Love and of recognition and nothing more. This, I repeat.

For anything else there is the second original prayer: individual prayer to oneself. "Pray and it will be given to you in abundance". But pray to whom? The prayer is for us; we pray for ourselves; and further, we pray to the gods who are in the heavens to please them. This will be good for ourselves in all respects, as all the prayer will be reciprocal.

The second benefit of original prayer is the magic of "creative visualization" or the art of "positive thinking". It is one of the great secret mechanisms instilled deeply in man by these creators. Whether one speaks about it as "technique" or "prayer" is insignificant. In any case, it is a marvellous tool that allows man to achieve his goals, his objectives, and his dreams.

It should be known however that this "individual prayer", in order to achieve its desired goal and to effect positive change, requires stimulation: "positive imagination".

None of the objects surrounding us, none of the inventions we enjoy, was created without it first occurring in the form of ideas, of thoughts inside someone's brain. The creative abilities of an intelligent human brain are numerous and those of an intelligent humanity are infinite. Each phase, each step, each detail of this work that is the creation, took its origin in an idea, a thought that was visualized, sometimes individually, sometimes collectively by one or more of our creators.

Man can use his imagination to invent or create but also to achieve the personal goals he wishes and decides to fulfill. And this can be on all levels be they professional or emotional, philosophical or psychological.

The great secret of this prayer lies in the following fact: The neurons of our brain are nourished by the channel of our five senses; touch, hearing, sight, taste and smell. We are in constant interaction with our environment through our senses. We should therefore try to permanently improve the quality of our sensory perceptions in order to increase the quality of our inter-neuronal connections.

But in addition to our senses, there is another channel that nourishes our neurons. It is our imagination. With our eyes closed, it functions the instant we begin to imagine or create images on the giant screen of our mind. And there, it is without intermediary; connected in closed circuit, the images inside our brain travel from one neuron to another. It is no longer information perceived on the outside through our senses. And imagination offers the tremendous advantage of not forcing this information to pass through our perception grid; the imaginary is using memory to realize direct connections inside the brain.

In a state of relaxation, eyes closed, man can imagine what will make him grow, what he might like to develop; certain human qualities, for example. But be wary; it is important to recognize that the imagination can sometimes destabilize as well.

It is also interesting to know that our neurons are physically unable to differentiate between what is really lived through the senses and what is imagined! But better still, what we imagine is stronger for our brain than what we actually live through the channel of our senses. The brain feels information that it receives through imagination much more strongly, with more precision.

Moreover, "visualize" is composed of 2 Latin words; visus" (past participle of the verb "videor" which means "what is seen") and "alius" (of which the genitive "alis" means "in another way"). Thus one can truly say that "to visualize" is to see in image, in imagination. And this ability "to visualize" can be used to affirm oneself. "Affirm" comes from the Latin "affirmare" (or "adfirmare") and means "to make firm, strengthen, prove, establish".

In short, practicing this form of original prayer, using this secret mechanism that the creators instilled in man, the ability to visualize, corresponds to this thought: to pray is to represent through one's capacity of imagination, to put into image the goal that one has set and to live it as if it was already reached by affirming it with words, thoughts, and adequate emotions.

Our thoughts are energy and they sculpt us, just as they shape our environment. Through visualization we use the electromagnetic potential of our brain. We give ourselves the energy necessary to achieve the visualized goal. Visualization and affirmations (autosuggestion) program and reprogram our brain, change our convictions, destroy our prejudices, make the individuals that we are more aware of our responsibility toward the choices we have to make in our lives. Here are some examples of affirmations:

a.   *I am always energetic when I rise in the morning (accompanied by the fact of visualizing yourself as such in the morning);*

b.   *I love myself with all my flaws. (and visualize yourself full of self-Love);*

c.   *My body is my temple; I love it; I stop poisoning it; I stop smoking. (and visualize yourself vomiting when nicotine is breathed in, therefore making a neuro-associative connection during visualization, connecting smoke to a great displeasure).*

Obviously, one must always choose feasible objectives, and primarily, what we want to embark upon must please us. From there, the objective must be profitable, and of course, one must be versed in achieving it and truly wish to obtain it. It is really necessary to have conviction in "embarking" on the path of the selected objective and to know very precisely what result one hopes to achieve. It is important to conceive a visualization that is not static, that we can see ourselves already having what we wish for; the scene must be realistic, credible and one must see oneself there. It is important to have an inward attitude that is just, that will accompany all the process of visualization, i.e., a positive state of mind. In short, we should be well prepared and have planned well the whole of what we will visualize.

Once this is clear for you, sit down, relax, close your eyes, breathe several times deeply, then concentrate deep within yourself, relax while remaining awake and conscious. And there imagine in this setting a scene in which you are a participant, you are an actor. This scene is presently happening; the emotion that you add to the scene will vitalize it. The more intense your positive feelings, the better your experience will be. In the scene you are creating in your mind, use your sensual abilities to their maximum, with as many details as possible. Also introduce obstacles on your personal path into your visualization, obstacles that you can surmount with ease. Visualize all of this with conviction; you will feel the situations as if this scene is real.

Decide on a devotion of individual prayers for the chosen objective for, say, 3 times per day for 21 days. Then is the moment of fruition; the religious scriptures say on this subject. «You reap what you sow.» The scene you have imagined in your mind, visualization together with the affirmation, all that will germinate and bear its fruits. You will see.

Creative visualization is neither a refuge, neither an evasion, nor a call to invoke miracles. This true prayer that creative visualization is requires that we carefully consider what we have had the tendency to ask of our creators in the heaven in the past, this due to "Christian" ignorance.

This form of prayer, visualization, does not consist of abstract thoughts. A human being can only succeed in this exercise if he is fully aware and responsible for what he thinks, thus aware that he is himself responsible for what happens to him, and that humanity itself is, also, responsible for what happens to it.

The ideal moments for this form of individual prayer are the periods immediately following the wakening or those that just precede sleep. This is due to the type of cerebral waves that we naturally produce at these times.

It is interesting to realize that our brain is like a muscle, and that the billions of neurons that constitute it are like muscle fibres. These famous neurons that fill up our skull and through which our thoughts form and circulate are obviously the essential elements of our nervous system. However, they are not any less physical than the fibres in our muscles, the biceps of the arm or femoral of the thigh.

This tiny course of anatomy is merely to help us understand that one must maintain and train the mental as much as the physical, perhaps even more so, for mental condition is more important than physical condition, the second one dependent to a great extent on the first. We can say that the development of these neuronal fibres through positive thinking, positive imagination, and creative visualization (the individual prayer) is the key to the proper functioning of our whole being. And so remember these important words: «For our brain, what we imagine is stronger than reality.» This is of paramount importance for in this lies one of the greatest secrets of man.

Man has looked everywhere to find this key; on the highest mountains, in the deepest oceans, in the heart of the most impenetrable forests, further in the most remote deserts, everywhere... and he never found it! Moreover, he had no better chances of finding it than a drunkard losing his keys in a dark corner, and looking for them under a street lamp, saying, "Here I will find them because I can see clearly"!

Indeed, it is not where man looked that the gods had hidden this secret key. It was not outside of him. It was, and always is, deep down inside of him at the core of his own consciousness! But one thing is certain; for man to touch with his finger the "naked" body of his consciousness and finally find this key so sought after, he must first decide to abandon the "Christian" unconsciousness that still inhabits his own consciousness and continues to damage it.

Finally, it is important for Africans to demystify what "Christian miracles" are!

Whether they were the healings performed by Jesus, Simon Kimbangu, Simao Toko, Buddha, or yet other Prophets; or whether it was Jesus who walked on water; or of the Red Sea parting to let Moses and his people pass, closing up on the Egyptians; whether it was the multiplication of loaves, the trumpets breaking down the walls of Jericho, and so on, these do not represent "miracles", as such. They were only "scientific achievements" to some extent, orchestrated by our humanized gods who are in heaven, and who have, as we have already stated, tens of thousands of years of scientific advancement over us.

All that we can imagine on Earth, they can accomplish, and have already for millennia past. We men of the 21st century are aware of the enormous scientific gap between our contemporaries and our ancestors inhabiting prehistoric caves. Well, the gap between us and our creators is all of this, if not of greater significance. But we should consider this in reverse direction this time. It is much more difficult to have our imagination go in this direction, in the direction of the future progress of science. It's true! For example, how can we manage to imagine all that earthlings will have discovered in 10 to 20 thousand years from now?

Taking again the example mentioned above, but relating however to a period of time definitely shorter (let us say, 150 to 200 years), one realizes already that for our great-grandfathers who considered the horse as "the most beautiful conquest of man" and who only had in mind the history of Jonas in his whale as mode of transportation of an "odd" kind, it would have been quite difficult to imagine that in 1 or 2 centuries, would fly each day across the sky, not some little angels, but some metal birds transporting in their belly hundreds of women, men and children that it would deposit hours later healthy and safe on the other side of Earth.

Thus, the scientific gap between our creators and us is so tremendous that they could easily now, despite the importance of our recent progress in this field, show us "achievements" that would be called "miracles" by all our contemporaries. There would be among us just a very small number, the most intelligent, the most evolved who would realize that they are only applications of sciences not yet discovered nor understood by men of the Earth. It is necessary for our minds to realize that our creators' level of knowledge is such that even our most eminent scientists cannot begin to imagine what they are capable of.

Moreover, if they desired, they could perform "scientific miracles" before our eyes that would panic the majority of humanity, with the rare exception, as we just said, of some particularly evolved minds! It would be very easy for them. To assimilate the level of fear this would invoke, we need only to imagine the fear of nearly 50,000 spectators who witnessed the "miracle of Fatima", further perpetuated by the lies and secrets which the Vatican maintains on this subject, even if it means not abiding by its own word.

Our creators did carry out some scientific operations from afar to the attention of Jesus, Simon Kimbangu and other Prophets in order to help them and support them in their missions to lend credibility for their contemporaries and to ensure that traces of their work would endure throughout time until the present generation, that of the Revelation, the era of Aquarius, this generation that will be able one day to understand thanks to Science.

Concerning "miracles" in places of pilgrimage or elsewhere, they are:

a. *Either actions operated remotely by our creators themselves, in order to test the reaction of humans and their degree of credulity related to the level of science that they managed to develop on Earth;*

b. *Or achievements related to autosuggestion created by the individuals themselves setting out a mental dynamic; in this case it is the power of the brain that operates the healing, but in that all is of a mental nature, it is here a question of "mental conditioning".*

There are no "miracles", as such. There is no "supernatural". Natural and tangible things can surprise us, but it is only something "natural" but not yet explained and beyond our scientific understanding that allows ourselves go and qualify it as "supernatural".

We have to be aware that the potential of the human brain has not yet been fully understood by our current scientists. All that we know here on Earth today without understanding it and without our scientists being able to give us an explanation for it yet is due to our creators. Science is the most important thing for man and especially for the Africa of today. It is science that will be able to solve all the problems of Africa and Africans, whereas all that the "Christian" prayer has ever done to this day is crippled us, and nothing more. Let us say this once again because it is true:

"Every man is brutish without knowledge". [For lack of science]

(Jeremiah 10, 14)

Africa has always known true religiosity throughout the continent but, thanks to the stranglehold of Christianity, it is waning, and this is indeed sad. The true Mass, the true Eucharist, what is it? It is to be in communion with the infinite. It is to be in communion with everything that surrounds us; nature, plants, animals, stars, the sun, the moon. And the water of the river, the water that symbolizes so well the cycle of infinity in time and space, and that constitutes the greatest part of the molecules of our body, always had a sacred place in African spirituality. Water is the very symbol of the communion with Life.

To be religious it is to be connected to the universe through one's senses. It is to feel infinity constantly. It is to stand at the edge of an ocean and to be conscious that this ocean is, in fact, just one tiny droplet of water on the huge gardens of infinity where our terrestrial sphere is itself merely one tiny grain of sand that glides in the universe. It is becoming the tree we caress or the flower we contemplate; it is blossoming in the tree, it is floating in the white cloud, it is becoming the song of the songbird. It is "to be", connected to oneself, connected to others, connected to our Creators, connected to life in the universe, connected to infinity. It is becoming infinity that becomes aware of itself. And there, one is happy, one is in blissfulness without reason. Inexplicably, we laugh without reason and become "cosmic", and it is comical. Quite simply one "is"!

Being religious is all of this simultaneously. It is to feel how our neurons flirt with the stars of the Milky Way. It is to feel how the stars tickle our neurons and other cells. At this point, one becomes the star and life becomes a succession of moments of eternity. The infinitely small sparkles inside us and we also feel connected to the infinitely large.

Being religious in front of a beautiful sunset is to enjoy it fully. It is to eat and drink this "sunset" and to digest it very slowly, savouring it for a long time to follow, quietly as we go about our lives. It is to contemplate the sunset while completely becoming this sunset for a short moment, by feeling all of our cells that become a sunset. We become its color and its heat. We become aware that at the same time in the infinitely small inside us, there is an infinity of sunsets, just as there is an infinity of sunsets in the infinitely large that compose us. There, the seized and lived moment is "eternal", and unquestionably religious.

It is what our ancestors knew all too well and were keen on teaching our children: all human beings must respect nature, plants, animals and all other life forms because all is "one", all is indivisible, all is without any separation, all is "unity", bound by the links of "true" religiosity, felt in the meditative or contemplative state, the source of interior meditation, the source of happiness, key of the greatest of Sciences, the Science of "being".

Our wise ancestors taught all of that to children. They taught them how to transform the past into the future through the fully seized and lived present moment. For example, they were taught to pick a fruit on the tree with respect and religiosity for the tree carrying this fruit, always being mindful that the plants and the trees, just like animals and men, suffer when one cuts or tears a branch or limb. They were further taught to become aware of the cycle that this fruit in the infinite will go through, that energy and matter are eternally one, that matter becomes energy

382

and that energy becomes again matter, that nothing is lost in the universe, and that everything has always existed either in the form of matter or in the form of energy. Everything is in perpetual transformation, that our body will claim the juice and the flesh of this fruit so that they become a part of our being.

Indeed, certain particles of this fruit will be used to form, for example, some new skin cells on our body and other particles of this same fruit will be forwarded to our brain to transform into energy and to become our future thoughts.

That is religiosity. A religiosity also taught by Jesus who, before dining with his disciples, would show the food and say, "This is my flesh, this is my blood", demonstrating his communion with the infinite cycle of time and space and all those who were with him became aware that mind and matter are eternally "one".

Similarly, the words, "You are dust and you will return to dust" also become meaningful, completely comprehensible. All is infinity in time and in space; we are composed of eternal matter. Ultimately, "to be" is "being the infinite that becomes aware of itself". That is true religiosity, letting our consciousness exude, and finding happiness in the opening of ones mind to infinity. There the greatest human quality manifests itself: humility, word derived from "humus", which means soil or dust.

This awareness gives way to the notions that one feels living inside: the universe is infinite, life in the universe is a trivial phenomenon, there is an infinite number of planets in the universe and they are inhabited by an infinite number of consciousnesses having an infinite number of different physical forms. Life in the universe is the fruit of an intelligent act; humans create humans in their image and their likeness, and this ad infinitum and on an infinite number of planets.

At this point, one is happy, quite simply, and one naturally has a thought of Love and gratitude for the people who are most important to us in the universe. One addresses those who compose it, those who created us, a bond of Love, human to human, without any lamentation towards the Heaven. One transmits only beauty to them, only love, in the songs and dances through which one pays tribute to them.

Christianity came to separate us from all that, to our greater misfortune. We should now, immediately, recover the roots and traditions that relate to our human, palpable, physical gods, those who are called in the original Bible in ancient Hebrew "Elohim".

By leading his people in prayer during the year 2003 to encourage rains in Europe to offset high temperatures and the threat of fire, Pope John Paul II, it can be said, was guilty of obscurantism. He addressed himself to hundreds of pilgrims and tourists who came to visit him in his summer residence south of Rome. He first expressed to them his condolences for the many victims who died following the period of great heat, and told them after, «I ask you to join me in my prayer for the victims of this heat wave and ask you all to ask with enthusiasm the Lord to give to the Earth that is thirsty the refreshment of rain!» These are his words as cited in Castel Gandolfo in the summer of 2003. (Source: HTTP://news.bbc.co.uk/2/hi/europe/3139549.stm).

What a silly notion! What an insult to all the meteorologists of the world and an insult to Science! A God supposedly so immaterial, unique, invisible, and omnipotent as to humble himself to create rain on request!! It is, once again, a famous encouragement by the False Shepherd so that people sink always further into superstition and mysticism.

In any event, though John-Paul II prayed together with all of his pilgrims, the rain did not fall when their prayer ended, neither in the following days or even the weeks after, proving that even Papal prayers are useless and ineffective. They are strictly powerless, just like this unique and immaterial God is inevitably powerless… since he does not exist! It is obvious that it will begin to rain eventually in a place where rain is sorely needed and, surely, before this moment, somebody, somewhere in the world will have prayed. Then would Jean-Paul II, this usurper, have credited his religion for that? Most likely since this was, and still is, within the framework of the application of the Pope's usual policy of dragging along the masses as far away from the truth as possible.

Do not grant any importance to the prayers of the Pope of Rome. He must surely not be appreciated in Heaven by our creators who are "human" and "physical" beings, who are scientists and artists, but above all "scientists".

This is why, each time we utilize a scientific approach, we please them, for in this we act like them and show them that we are conscious of being made in their image and anxious to exploit all the possibilities that they designed in us. Science is most important for man and not the obscurantist and mind numbing prayers of any Pope.

Once again, let us recall how this sentence is important:

"Every man is brutish without knowledge".[For lack of science]
(Jeremiah 10, 14)

Logically thinking, according to this verse written in the "Old Testament", the "sacred" book of the Catholic Church, one might also say, "For lack of Science, the Pope of Rome is a moron"! To speak in such a way is not to insult him directly; it is merely making a simple observation...of biblical exegesis!

It is undeniable that spirituality is necessary to the well being of individuals and the survival of the human species, but is the belief in an almighty, immaterial god necessary to satisfy our need for spirituality? The answer given today by neurobiologists is NO! This response from Science is categorical: "The human brain was genetically designed to encourage religious experiences, the religious feeling".

Our brain is thus biologically programmed to experience states of transcendence or states of meditation. And so, the "mystical" experience is an inward adventure of which we had not yet completely understood the mechanisms. But what we do know already, thanks to Science, is that this very powerful immaterial god is in the head of each one of us and not at all outside. In fact, we are talking about an inward mirage.

To elaborate on this subject, let us look at the work of neurobiologist Michael Persinger, as he was the first to give a scientific explanation to these "mystical" phenomena. In particular, Persinger studied the case of people who said they had an experience of communication with god in a near death situation. Many of these people happened to be resuscitated whereas they had been declared in a state of clinical death prior to that.

Thousands of people having experienced such a situation can testify to this kind of experience and so constitute a very viable field of study for neurobiologists. Much information was collected by the hospitals' specialized services where these people were observed when they were in a coma. An important characteristic appeared in the plotting of their electroencephalograms (EEG): during this period, there is an analogy between the cerebral activity of a person who is near death and that of a person in a situation of epileptic fit.

In this moment of great intellectual confusion the nervous influx does not travel its usual roads any more. It connects usually independent zones between them, in particular the temporal lobes and the two underlying structures that are the amygdala and the hippocampus. These disorders are brought to light through the analysis of the EEG that presents anomalies in the range of the frequencies close to 40 hertz. The subject is then under the impression that he is losing his solitude and that he is connected to an inward visitor. The experience of god appears to be an extreme example of the meeting with this virtual visitor, especially for those who already believed in an omnipotent immaterial god.

Persons who meditate regularly or are in a mystical state of ecstasy (Buddhist monks) also indicate this same particular EEG profile. Thus, the states of spiritual contemplation cause a change in cerebral activity and this paradoxical situation appears in a predominantly natural way in each one of us through meditation or religious experience. And so we might say that "mystical" experiences are products of the brain when this brain is stimulated by religious rites.

Two researchers from the University of Pennsylvania, Eugene d'Aquili and Andrew Newberg, have even created a new academic discipline: "neurotheology". They reveal the results of their work in a provocative book, "Why God Won't Go Away". Between 1996 and 1998, they studied the cerebral functions and the blood flow of eight Tibetan Buddhist monks during their meditations. Many Franciscan monks also went through the same tests while they were praying. These researchers used markers to differentiate the parts of the brain that are activated by mental processes or physical actions.

They studied brains immersed in those mystical states with the help of images provided by proton emitting tomography. On depictions of horizontal sections of the brain, the left and right posterior superior parietal lobes display clearly lower luminance than usual. Meditation would thus dim some cerebral functions.

The zones affected correspond, according to scientists, to the feeling of the dichotomy of our personality, i.e., they correspond to our ability to distinguish ourselves from others and from our environment. The shutting down of this function explains the sensations that overwhelm us during these times; feelings of absolute plenitude, of transcendental communion

386

with humanity, animals, plants, trees and even all the universe. Sensations of this kind are generally associated with a divine manifestation. A similar process also explains the trances generated by certain "frenzied" dances. The action on other cerebral zones would produce the feeling of channelling all the cosmic energy.

A great number of the scientists in neurobiology thus build a splendid bridge between scientific reasoning and "mystical" perception and their works shed new light on the nature of the human consciousness and the basis of the religious phenomenon.

In short, "God" purely happens in the head of the individual, by no means from outside his head, where no immaterial, omnipotent, invisible god exists and cannot exist! Outside of our heads, outside of ourselves, there are only gods, physical and as "material" as we are ourselves!

Yes, let us dance and sing for them for they are our creators! Yes, let us praise them and thank them! Yes, let us send them our Love and our recognition, with consciousness, with full consciousness of what they really are... physical human beings of flesh and blood.

Our consciousness makes us similar to them and close to them and it is what they like to find in us. "Son of man stand upright on your legs,» they are telling us in the true Bible (the TORAH) which means «Do not kneel stupidly before us. It is not what we want!» It is time for all of us to understand that the time of blind faith by docility is over. We are now in the "Age of Aquarius". Science and, therefore, Comprehension are showered upon us. It is up to us to receive them.

It is also very important to note that the so-called Holy Trinity (the Father, the Son and the Holy Spirit) does not exist. It is a dogma issued by the Catholic Church. It is an invention of men, of these same men who adulterated the scriptures. Moreover, Elohim, our creators, had commissioned Mohammed the Prophet to set this subject right, to put in order that which the Church had deformed. He came to remind us, particularly the Jews and Christians, who had altered the truth (Koran actually means "reminder"). Here are some passages of the Koran that illustrate this very well:

"[...] so believe in Allah and His apostles. Say not: «Trinity": desist: it will be better for you: for Allah is one Allah [...] (Surah 4:171)
"They do blaspheme who say: Allah is one of three in a Trinity: for there is no god except One Allah. [...]" (Surah 5:73)

> *"Christ the son of Mary was no more than an apostle; many were the apostles that passed away before him. [...]" (Surah 5:75)*
> *"We sent after them Jesus the son of Mary, and bestowed on him the Gospel; and We ordained in the hearts of those who followed him Compassion and Mercy. But the Monasticism which they invented for themselves, We did not prescribe for them: (We commanded) only the seeking for the Good Pleasure of Allah; but that they did not foster as they should have done. Yet We bestowed, on those among them who believed, their (due) reward, but many of them are rebellious trans-gressors". (Surah 57:27)*

«We» in this last Surah stands for the word "Elohim" of the original Hebrew Bible and cannot thus concern a singular God!

So let us understand. The dogmas of Christianity are absurd and revolting; original sin, Holy Trinity, glorification of suffering, contempt of the body and pleasure, to name just a few. All these dogmas are only shameless and degrading inventions!

Let us now speak more on the subject of contempt of the body and pleasure. It is the subject of the following chapter.

WHITE POISON

33. The miserable "Christian" sexuality and nudity.

To begin this chapter, let us recall the fact that the Gods are human and physical and that they indeed proved it by having carnal, sensual and sexual contacts with humans whom they created on Earth. On this subject, and to open this chapter, let us look at a superb passage from Genesis, that I so much enjoy sharing with you:

> "And it came to pass, when men began to multiply on the face of the earth, and daughters were born unto them, that the sons of Elohim saw the daughters of men that they were fair; and they took them wives of all which they chose.[...] There were giants in the earth in those days; and also after that, when the sons of Elohim came in unto the daughters of men, and they bare children to them, the same became mighty men which were of old, men of renown".

(Genesis 6 - 1, 2 and 4)

We should also note that Greek mythology relates that many great heroes were born of sexual relations with gods and mortals. In this same Greece, the beauty of the body and nudity were much appreciated and bisexuality was accepted. Pederasty formed an integral part of the education system where teenagers were entrusted to a tutor who had the responsibility to initiate them sexually, among other things. This rite is all so familiar to me. I think of the initiatory places, secret places where our ancestors initiated young men to prepare them for their admission in the community of adults and for marriage. Among initiations in "the sacred woods" or the "sacred forest" was sexual initiation performed by adults on young men about to enter the circle of adults. Remember this, my brothers and sisters!

We can easily deduce from all this that the Gods delight in sensuality and sex and that, consequently, they must certainly not be ashamed of their bodies. They are "Gods" who have blossomed. But let us ask ourselves the right questions to know and understand how can it be that Christendom and Catholicism are so modest, so restrictive about nudity and sexuality? What are the origins of these enormous "Christian" taboos? From where do they come? One can surely expect to find as answer that it is, once again, an invention, a fraud of the Church!

Indeed, for what reason would the creators who made man in their image and their resemblance desire that man be ashamed of his body and his

nudity, that he be ashamed of his sexual libido, that he be afraid to mas-
turbate, that he fear mere discussion of sexuality on the simplest and
most natural levels. The creators would have never wanted that; to some
extent, this would have been a contradiction of who they are.

We are talking, once again, about one of these abominable conditionings
carried out by the Church in order to control humans. More importantly,
this conditioning indeed helps political leaders whose powers are based on
the oppression of the masses, because a sexually liberated individual who
is not ashamed neither of his body nor of his nudity cannot be controlled
easily; he is himself and thinks by himself. He is free; it is him who decides
how to make use of his body and his spirit.

For more on this problem, let us return to the history of Christian Europe.
Did our Europe always consider sexuality to be taboo, to be a Puritanism,
or a conservatism such as that which is inflicted upon it today? Not at all!

Let us look at the history of sexuality over the centuries as it pertains to
Christianity in general and Catholicism in particular. We will realize to
what extent they have maintained woman, man and child in ignorance and
guilt by developing in them a feeling of revulsion and a series of taboos.

In ancient Greece the poetess Sapho, on the island of Lesbos addressed her
works to young girls (from where the etymological roots of the words "les-
bian" and "saphism" come). Legislators, recognizing the danger of sexual
passion to the social structure of the time, imprisoned women who seemed likely to disturb the law and regulated prostitution. The "courtesans"
were prostitutes of great prestige, beautiful, intelligent and cultivated
who accompanied famous men. The doctors of the time believed that vagi-
nal secretions were as important as sperm for fecundation and concluded
about the need for women to have pleasure. Customarily, women practiced anal coitus as contraception.

Moving forward to Romans, we see that homosexuality was very widespread. In fact, the Emperor Caesar is reported to have claimed that he was
the lover of all women and the mistress of all men. At that time pederasty
was a luxury reserved for fortunate Masters that had harems of young slaves called "pedagogia" at their disposal. It is at the time of the Romans
that prostitution extended beyond the walls of the temples to become a
profit-making venture. Rich Roman matrons exerted a great influence over
their husbands and their sons, playing an indirect political role and treated
themselves to the sexual services of slaves and gladiators.

Just as the Greeks had, Romans accepted contraception and pleasure. And they provided a rich vocabulary in this field: masturbation, fellatio, prostitution, cunnilingus/cunnilinctus (from the verb "cunare", to insert, and from "lingua", tongue, or "linctus", the act of licking.)

I can imagine certain uptight Christians saying to themselves, "Okay, sure, that was the Greeks and the Romans... bunch of perverts"! To further validate these people, let us visit the Jews, the people of the Book, holder of the Torah - Scriptures relating the Genesis of Man - the people who had in the past a special Alliance with Yahwelohim.

Well, for Jews, polygamy was frequent (I Kings 11, Verse 3):

> "And he (King Solomon) had seven hundred wives, princesses, and three hundred concubines [...]"

It is only during the exile to Babylon around 550 B.C. that an extremely severe sexual code was established. For reasons of survival of their people, procreation was essential. Consequently, sexuality was exclusively for reproductive purposes ("Go forth and multiply"). Virginity and marriage had become the guarantee to a Jewish descent (one is Jewish from the mother).

Another Jewish custom of the time, marriage, was a trade agreement (the man bought a woman). We enter then the Judeo-Christian era which will make sexuality and nudity something "dirty", "cheap", "bestial", "impure", "horrible", "dreadful", and tutti quanti. Masturbation will become a fault (that of Onan); homosexuality would become a crime, and both would be punishable by law.

But a greater misfortune still awaited humanity at the beginnings of Christianity. Following the death of Jesus, the first Christians rejected Roman culture and retained the most austere currents of Judaism: procreation, the family, superiority of the spirit over the body.

And of course, once again, we will find Paul, "the man of the lie", at the root of this new problem. It is Paul who attaches the concept of sin to matters of the body. Then nudity, by itself, will be particularly associated with the "original sin". Moreover, this famous and omnipresent Paul, the so-called "Saint", would seriously worsen the manner of human relation. He would associate man to reason and to virtue, woman to matter and sin; ultimately, he would go as far as to make chastity an ideal!

One can say that this "Saint Paul", who was far from being a saint, rather quite the opposite, was really the great architect of an exacerbated sexism and machismo. These wounds continue to cause so much suffering on Earth today. For this, we thank you "Saint" Paul! As examples:

a. *New Testament, Paul, Romans 8, Verse 3: "For what the law could not do, in that it was weak through the flesh, God sending his own Son in the likeness of sinful flesh, and for sin, condemned sin in the flesh"; Verse 5 AND 6: "For they that are after the flesh do mind the things of the flesh; but they that are after the Spirit the things of the Spirit. For to be carnally minded is death; but to be spiritually minded is life and peace".*

b. *New Testament, Paul, 1 Corinthians 7, Verse 1: "[...] it is good for a man not to touch a woman". Verses 28 and 29: "But and if thou marry, thou hast not sinned; and if a virgin marry, she hath not sinned. Nevertheless such shall have trouble in the flesh: but I spare you. But this I say, brethren [...] that both they that have wives be as though they had none".*

And let us glance at other great ridiculous and notoriously silly ideals that arose from Christendom. Another "Saint", Saint Augustine, (354-430 A.D.) again, for whom nothing saintly can be assigned, emerging from a stormy youth (as his biographers discreetly write) he would become one of the principal theologians of the Occident and oppose the virtue of chastity as to the sin of sex. Already he expressed his dislike for the body by stressing that we are born between feces and urine. Here are two examples of the deep doctrines of this "Doctor of the Church":

a. *"Nothing lowers more man than the caresses of a woman and the pressures of the bodies".*

b. *According to him, the original sin would be a sin of flesh perpetrated from generation to generation since procreation inevitably happens through a sexual act.*

We should note, by the way, that it would be in the 11th century that Pope Gregory VII would impose vows of celibacy upon priests, the question of celibacy never having been raised prior to Pope Gregory's appointment to

394

"Holy Father".. From this point forward, Christians would be subjected to the feeling of a quasi permanent culpability because, paradoxically, sexuality reinforces its status of sin but procreation is imposed in the homes as a need, which intensifies culpability and leads to a complete state of mental confusion.

This becomes easier to understand when we recall that several decades ago Roman Catholic priests consecrated marriage by saying to the wedding couple, "As from tomorrow you will be entitled to the "allowed sin". It will be your duty to connect yourselves to pass life on to the future generations". Plainly, the infamous "marital duty".

Going back a bit further in time, we see that Christendom extended its prohibition by preventing sexual intercourse from taking place during certain Church-designated periods; Sundays, Lent, the Holy Week. These were attempts to force abstinence. As a result of these rules, in the 8th century there were only 185 days on which devout Christians could enter marital sexuality.

At this same period of time, when superstition was in vogue, Christendom attributed epilepsy to the "fact" that parents had not respected the periods of chastity imposed by the Church.

But the spirits not yet sufficiently traumatized, the "good fathers" and "Doctors of the Church" imposed further sanctions, maybe even with a certain sadistic delight. They "ruled" that non-reproductive sexual practices were the cause of epidemics of plague and, consequently, were to be regarded as faults worse than murder.

Consummately, let us specify that in relationships (marital, obviously, as all others were absolutely prohibited!) only the "missionary position" could be practiced to avoid condemnation for "bestiality". What happiness Hindus and Buddhists enjoyed long ago when they practiced Kama Sutra and Tantrism! But for Christians, under the authority of Rome, what a miserable product of their religion it is, these Christian Morals, that offers nothing but displeasure, guilt, non-living; all these evils as the precursor for boundless psychological and physical imbalances!

In the Middle Ages Christendom starts to accept nudity in the bed and in the bath! Bravo!

However, it is during this period that a "good Christian" named Thomas

395

Aquinas (1225-1274), who would also later be canonized (you suspected this, I am sure) wrote his "Summa Theologica" in which he specified Christian morals. In this work, for which he would receive, in addition to his canonization, the title of "Doctor of the Church", he described all non-reproductive sexual activities as "sin against nature". And to embellish on the "fine words" of Paul, "The woman needs the male not only to breed as with animals, but also to control themselves, because the male is more perfect by virtue of his reason and stronger in virtue". Yet another serious "Christian" reinforcement of sexism and machismo!

We should also note that in the 13th century getting married in the church became common practice, creating the norms for the only "respectable" and thus "acceptable" couple, exclusive and permanent. It is also at this same time that emerges an absolutely inane practice, one that will still have a terrible effect today on the spirits of young girls and women indoctrinated in the Judeo-Christian culture. And here I will address the advent of "courtly love".

It was, and still is to a great extent, the wonderful dream of almost all the fair sex of mankind, that these "ladies" or "demoiselles" have at their whimsy a "prince charming" who loves them for everything. Besides their bodies and curves which trouble them, these women and girls will test their wiles to ensnare the "troubadour of their heart", seducing them permanently, bending them into countless pieces, endearing them to follow them forever.

These notions occurred to them unwittingly from the ideal and idyllic worship of the very Holy "Virgin Mary" whom they called upon each day in their prayers and whom their descendants will call a few centuries later "Notre Dame of the Immaculate Conception", as doctrine obliges!

This myth, where the valiant knight maintained a non physical love relationship with an inaccessible lady (despite the fact that this myth has been the subject of countless novels) the fact remains that it is pure aberration, pure fiction. And once more, these unfulfilled dreams, myth passing for reality, continue to claim an incalculable number of victims. What abominable foolishness!

And then came the horrible Inquisition, the Catholic, Christian Inquisition made worse by the Protestant involvement, the Church further ratifying their ideas into law and made enforceable by the States.

Sex, this time will be associated with heresy; witches would be accused of having sexual intercourse with the devil. The privileged targets of these "Great Inquisitors", all men, it goes without saying, were young girls whose beauty captivated them, and poor old women who were excluded.

The body became the perfect object of sin, but the very powerful inquisitors to whom the so-called "divine" law supposedly exempted to enjoy, as much their own body as that of others, in sexual relationships, and capitalizing on their positions of power, took delight in unscrupulously torturing the very women with whom they would have their way. This, of course, would take place after these women would be interrogated by their tribunals.

Here, going back to this same period (idyllic, some claim!), we present some typical examples of lessons that were given by Christian teachers to the parents in order that their children be raised according to "good Christian precepts'":

a.Honest civility for the education of the children (1714):
"Stand up with so much circumspection that no part of your body appears naked even when you would be alone in the room. Do that for the respect of a God who looks at you".

b.Berthold De Ratisbonne (13th Century):
"If he remains in bed and that the devil turns and turns over the pin, he often devotes himself to the most serious of sins, that which one commits on oneself, without man or woman ". "You must separate the boys and the girls when they start to wake up and to become malicious". [the meaning of the word "malicious" was then "who is devoted to evil"]

c.The bishop of Saint Brieuc (1507) prohibited:
"Brothers and sisters or other parents of different sex to sleep together after the age of 7" [a habit that could] "give rise to an infinite number of horrible sins".

d.Martin Luther (1483-1546):
"If the woman becomes tired and finally dies of having given birth,

> *that matters little, she is there for that". "There is nothing better on Earth than the love of a woman"!*

Can you understand anything about what Martin Luther said? Personally, I really do not see where one can find Love in such remarks!
Now let us analyze the disastrous consequences of such rambling:

a. *The body is completely forgotten, nudity taboo and hygiene non-existent.*

b. *The last public baths, Roman relics, were closed because they were regarded as "pagan places".*

c. *One recognized Muslims as people with clean hands and feet. In order to avoid arrest, a good Christian was to remain dirty.*

d. *Right away at birth, the baby was immediately covered in order to protect it from worms. He was regarded as not finished, he was not washed, his clothing and his filth formed like a cocoon.*

e. *The majority of people spent their life without ever being naked or washing themselves.*

f. *A woman who bathed every day in a brook had preserved her beauty, simply because she was clean. The villagers believed that it was a source of youth; they threw themselves in the water and drank some. Seeing that they had not rejuvenated, they concluded from it that this woman had made a pact with the devil and condemned her to the stake.*

g. *Though the laws were of unremitting severity toward people of modest means, the clergy closed the eyes on the exactions of the nobility and of its own members. The courtesans were refined and cultivated prostitutes who profited from a true teaching of sexual pleasures. The kings, Popes, and clergy surrounded themselves with courtesans who bore illegitimate children. The Pope Alexander VI, alias Rodrigo Borgia (1492-1503) remained famous for his sexual excesses.*

Under the reign of Louis XIV in France, abbots such as Guiburg, Davot, Sebault, Lepreux and Monsignor Manette, the Episcopal Vicar of Paris, regularly celebrated black ("satanic") masses at the request and attention of France's nobility. During these "ceremonies", thousands of children were sacrificed, their throats cut, as numerous police reports and chronicles of the time attest.

John XII, Pope at eighteen years old (955-964), born of an incestuous relationship between Pope Sergius III (904-911) with his thirteen year old daughter, Marozia, was himself the lover of this same Marozia... his own mother. The Popes Jules II (1503-1513) and Leon X (1513-1521) were struck by syphilis (sexually transmitted and often fatal disease, very widespread among nobility and the clergy).

Sixte IV (1471-1484), designer of the Sistine Chapel, was bisexual. He was a great pederast and a notorious sodomite, to such a degree that, according to the writings of the Chancellor of Infessura, many people received from him the purple cardinalice as rewards for the sexual favours that they had granted him. And he too was afflicted with syphilis.

It is actually this same Pope Sixte IV who authorized organized prostitution within his "Holy Institution". With this intention he formed brothels that his Church would oversee. However overstepping the decree of his pontificate, this organization would last for a very long period.

The brothels instituted by the Church totalled hundreds throughout the Christian world. They were inexhaustible sources of profits. The Popes assigned them to the dioceses as a base of subsistence that the bishops shared in their turn with the parishes, giving to each one of them a prostitute. The latter, having become "property of the Church", remanded the profit of her work to her priest on every fortnight.

But among all these brothels, the largest was, without question, "the Vatican" itself. There, on a nightly basis, homosexuals and women disguised as men entered. Together these shady characters, conducted orgies with the clergy and the noble Romans. In the 15th and 16th centuries, some estimates indicate that approximately fifty percent of the population of Rome was comprised of bastards coming either from convents or brothels. And many of these were born of the sexual relationships with priests, as those frequently disposed of a high number of concubines!

Thus Rome came to be seen and known as "the capital of bastards"! These examples could be multiplied over time, lending credence to the notion that the Vatican seldom practiced what it preached. We could devote an entire chapter to this subject.

Inside this "high place", thanks to the initiative of Constantine, you recall, the bloodthirsty, self-proclaimed "Emperor of divine right" of the 4th century, belied sumptuous and opulent décor and works of art by famed artists. Indeed, behind this State border – thanks to Italian fascist Mussolini – the "practice" in the Vatican seldom conformed to the "teaching" promulgated by the Vatican institution itself.

But, as we know, this teaching is traditionally and exclusively reserved for "vulgars" (from the Latin "vulgus" which means "multitude"), that is to say, for the people, the masses. It is important to know that among these characters that designate themselves as "high prelates" or "oursignors", bishops, and other "eminences", this form of behaviour must certainly persist today.

They condemn homosexuality while knowing that the majority of their priests are homosexual. They collapse under the scandals of pedophilias and of sexual abuse towards religious sisters but continue to outwardly convey an image of "purity" and to present to the world sexual abstinence as an "ideal of virtue". This is designed to ridicule with impunity "those at the bottom", (the vulgars) you, the simple people!

Actually, these severe rules that they intend to impose with regard to sexuality are in place only to serve their power. These dishonest people, though many scholars, know fully that it is very difficult to control a sexually liberated spirit. It is very difficult to condition somebody who is "a free being" at the sexual level because this being thinks by himself and has no intention of allowing himself to be "standardized" by anyone!!!

In the 19th century, the State and the Church, whose powers had been largely shaken by the revolution and libertinage, adopted once again more severe rules. In terror, as the government sent its opponents to the guillotine, the Church took the opportunity to lock up the libertines, the prostitutes, the degraded and sodomites with an aim of protecting the family, the institution (so invaluable for its interests, that goes without saying!) Noting the influence of the philosophers and the search for reason among the middle-class population, the Church called upon scientists and doctors to support its morals. Thus, with Tissot, the pope's physician, sex having once been a sin now became a disease. One also saw change the perception of the woman, in the image of the Virgin Mary, pure and asexual, guardian of the low impulses of her husband.

Many women were to sleep with long night dresses; they could not be naked in bed. It was necessary for them to cover their body with a long dress bearing only a small slit at the height of their vagina allowing for the sexual act with the husband. Often on the dress near this opening would be found the inscription, "God wants it"!

In order to eradicate sexuality at the base, moralists attacked masturbation above all else. The wasting of sperm and vital energy was regarded as a threat to health (it is said that one drop of sperm = 50 drops of blood). It was claimed that the insane arrived in asylums "of their own hands". Masturbation was the cause for the softening of the brain, the Christian moralists claiming that cerebral liquid escaped with sperm at the time of orgasm. And on order of the Pope, for scientific reasons as we can suspect, they attributed acne, blindness, deafness, degeneration, tiredness, and many other afflictions on to masturbation. And the list is not exhaustive; Christian moralists also claimed that if one spread his semen on the hands, one was likely to see hair grow there! All that was of a very high medical value... as you can imagine.

Some signed remarks of Baden-Powell (the inventor of scouting):

> "Masturbation prevents the seed from strengthening in you the virile man. You throw to the wind the seed that was entrusted to you for later producing a son. "

He also recommended "keeping the clean organ in cold baths". I readily quote this nonsense from Baden-Powell, hoping to demonstrate my lack of appreciation for this manifestly racist character.

Christian doctors recommended burning with red iron or nitrate, castration, a method not widespread among boys as it was feared there would an insufficient number of heirs. Clitoridectomy (excision of the clitoris) was practiced in France until the 1930s and in the United States until the 1950s. Those who made love only for pleasure were regarded as degenerates, behind time on human evolution. Prostitution, very widespread, was tolerated as a regrettable need preserving married women from the horror of the animal impulses of their husband. To protect the children from the misdeeds of masturbation, they were tied down in bed, their pockets sewn closed in their pants.

The civilized man was to give up the primitive behaviour induced by the body. Thus, there were for men apparatus to install around their genitals to prevent night erections.

In spite of the fact that syphilis had become widespread, the manufacturers of condoms (or contraceptives) were prosecuted if they advertised them and the pharmacists imprisoned if they displayed them in their windows. The Christian doctors claimed that women with large breasts were stupid because blood stagnated inside; therefore they had brains with less irrigation. If a woman was victimized by rape, she was the one who bore the guilt... of seduction!

Some final anomalies concerning sexuality occurred at the beginning of the 20th century. In 1909, the wearing of pants by a woman was no longer an offence, provided she holds the handlebar of a bicycle or the reins of a horse. We note that in 1908, the first on-screen kiss in the history of cinema was regarded as a huge monstrosity by the Christian moralists. How did the Vatican then react? It created the Catholic Legion for Decency. The darkness of rooms was alone an invitation to sin. Viewing a film was a mortal sin exposing one to eternal damnation.

Later, after having supported France during the Second World War, the catch phrase of Marshal Pétain, "Work, Family, Fatherland", would become the pretext for the Church to benefit from the post-war social condition and organize a return to morals.

Couples separated for a long time did not reunite without tensions. There were claims of adultery and illegitimate children. The Church takes advantage of this discord to massively spread its concepts of the "Christian couple". As a result, during the 50s and 60s, the image of the woman became that of an asexual person for whom happiness depends only on a well-equipped kitchen.

Then there was a sexual liberation on all levels starting with the sexual revolution of the end of the Sixties and the beginning of the Seventies. But now Christianity, the Church again tries to restore, in part, at least, the power that it had before and tries to maintain today by reconnecting:

a. with a recrudescence of marriage;
b. with the fact that sex is associated with violence in the media;
c. with campaigns that support a rising birth rate (family benefits, retirements);
d. with a return to decency (disappearance of naked breasts at the swimming pool);
e. with the fact that the young people are still afraid of sex. The cour-

ses of information on sexuality do not address pleasure, but only the anatomical and reproductive aspects with warnings against sexually transmitted diseases;

f. with the growing lack of respect towards women in the suburbs and/ or the very popular districts of the Western cities;

g. with new legislations against prostitution;

h. with a new fear of science which pushes the governments to vote laws against research on reproductive and therapeutic cloning and other positive results of scientific advances;

i. with the fact that the Church reinforces, in the public spirit, the concepts of fidelity and abstinence and even intends to impose them, all over the world, to the whole of "its faithful".

Here, for confirmation on the matter, two beautiful quotations of John-Paul II:

-"The man does adultery in his heart not only when he looks at, in a certain way, a woman who is not his... but precisely because he looks at a woman in this way. Even if it were his own wife whom he looked at this, it would make adultery".

(Speech of October 8, 1980 Saint Peter Square)

- [With contraception...] "Husbands attribute themselves a power which belongs only to God".

The Vatican still refuses to allow its priests the right to marry, continues to deny couples the right to divorce; continues to prohibit women from sacerdotal ordination; prohibits abortion for any reason (including cases when a woman is raped or impregnated in "religious" acts of genocide; alas, too common).

But most fortunately, the Church begins to be seriously shaken by the scandals of its paedophile priests and its financial-gangsters, Licio Gelli, grand master of the P2 loge, to name one, but other examples to follow.

And here are two more recent facts:

a. At this beginning of the 21st century in France, a priest from For-bach in Lorraine, refused to celebrate the marriage of a couple be-cause neither partner wished to have children. The bishop of Metz *(diocese city of this area of the East of France), Mr. Pierre Raffin (because I couldn't, in any case, attribute to him the title of "my" Lord) supported this position as being in conformity with the ideology of the Church.*

b.A man of this same town of Metz was denied the sacrament of baptism for his two children because they were conceived by in vitro fertilization!

Let us see now what are, nowadays, the harmful consequences of sexism and machismo of the "Judeo-Christian" spirit initiated by "Saint" Paul, as we saw earlier, then passing, among others, through "Saint" Augustine and "Saint" Thomas Aquinas.

Let us look also at the consequences of all the other imbecilities that we enumerated in this chapter!

Here, once more, is a more non-exhaustive list:

a.A man who has multiple conquests is a "Don Juan", if it is a woman who acts in the same manner she is "a bitch".
b.It is still generally thought that happiness can only be found in couple life and family life.
c.One still makes women believe they will not have an accomplished life if they did not bring children into the world.
d.One voluntarily maintains the concept of "woman object" and the thought that any sexual intercourse should be accompanied by feelings of love.
e.Good manners regulate social behaviour ("the man proposes the woman lies out", etc). It is up to the man to go forward; the woman must refuse.
f.One conveys the thought that abortion would leave psychological after-effects, that divorce would perturb children, that jealousy would be a proof of love.
g.The parents monitor their daughters a lot more than their sons.
h.Being "single" is still a "little suspect".
i.One generally seeks to have a behaviour that sticks with sexual standards of our environment.

j.Sexual intercourse must obligatorily concern Olympic performance.

k.When one is a boy it is necessary to be "well endowed".

l.Sex shops often have their windows painted in black but not arms stores. The sale of weapons need not be concealed; would it be less dangerous?

m.In the cinema, on TV, violence is more trivial and more standardized than love.

n.The age difference in a couple is badly perceived.

o.The old people are no longer entitled to sexuality.

p.One speaks more easily about sexual relations than about masturbation.

q.In a couple, masturbation is a form of infidelity; one must obligatorily be sufficient unto the other.

So there, a wide array of harmful consequences brought by Christendom, by the Judeo-Christian Poison, a "White Poison", a string of consequences that Christendom exported with much success to Africa, contaminating her further after having already made her undergo "slavery", "spiritual colonization", "economic colonization", and "political colonization", as if all that could not be enough once and for all!

Not such a long time ago, we black Africans were not ashamed of our bodies. Our parents walked naked or nearly naked, the body expression and sensuality were part of education and were great ingredients of life. We lost all of it because of Christian colonization and consequently, we have even become more puritan than the whites! It is terrible! Today there are beaches for nudists in Occident, there are campsites for naturists in Occident, but there are none, or none any longer, in Africa!

It is funny, it is sadly comic, because our ancestors, those who preceded the Christian whites and before Christian colonization arrived, did not have problems with polygamy (even with polyandry practiced in many tribes), with sensuality, with sex, with homosexuality, (which is genetic and not a disease or a perversion) with nudity, with the concept of pleasure related to sensuality. All this was naturally integrated into their life.

All this disappeared because of Christendom. Christendom does not bring or teach anything good in this field. In this matter one may find it very beneficial to eradicate its concepts. For the nth time, "Every man becomes brutish without knowledge" (Jeremiah X, 14). But modern science,

thanks to its researchers and their accomplishments, completely invalida-
tes what the Christian doctrines teach with regard to sexuality, sensuality
and pleasure. On the other hand, it indeed reaffirms what our ancestors,
who were in the truth entirely, knew to be right. It is absolutely necessary
to find again our roots and our beautiful traditions, those that connect us
to our creators who are "in the Heavens" to be able to benefit fully from
the teachings that they bequeathed to our Ancestors, teachings based on
Self-love, the Love of others, the acceptance of one's body, the Love of
one's body, the use of all one's organs without exception, and all this in
the pleasure, with the pleasure and for the pleasure!

Nowadays, science has demonstrated that masturbation not only did not
present the dangers which Christian oracles of the Middle Ages proclaimed
but, moreover, it is essential so that an individual develops harmoniously
during the critical period of self-discovery. It is time to denounce the guilt-
induced stupidity that Christendom has hawked from the West to Africa.

What could be more disappointing for our creators than to see human
beings that they created naked with much love saying that nudity is something evil! Nudity, the image of what they did, of who they are! We should
never be ashamed of our body or our nudity because nothing displeases
more our creators than to see those whom they created ashamed of the
aspect that they gave them. Shame rather on colonizing and soul-des-
troying Christendom for having misled Humanity, and in particular Africa,
out of the way of the Truth, out of the just, in this matter so important for
the happiness of each one. Shame on it for that too!

It is necessary to love all of one's body and especially the part that is able
to give us the most pleasure, and to learn how to discover and to improve
one's knowledge of this organ, of one's organs, in order to increase the
quality of the pleasures which we can draw from them. We must especially not listen to the guilt-inducing Christian Church on this subject; the
concept of pleasure is fundamental for the balance of a human being,
whether he is man or woman. Each human being is a garden that should
not be left uncultivated; a life without sensual and/or sexual pleasure is
a human garden that is not cultivated, pleasure being one of best ferti-
lizers there is to open the mind. A being must center his existence on an
improvement of the quality of perception of his pleasure by increasing the
sensitivity of his senses.

Christian teaching is extremely restrictive about sensuality, sexuality and
pleasure. It can, because of that, lead to deep imbalances. It is now well

406

established scientifically: people who have difficulty on the sexual level often present physical and psychological disorders. Thus, a considerable number of catholic priests who respect their vow of chastity have serious psychological problems (See Chartrand L. (1990), "Sex and Clergy: the Church in the dock", l'Actualite, 15 (3):20-24, Canada). To the contrary, scientific studies have established clearly that an active sexual life is one of the most important ingredients for good psychic and physical health.

Contrary to what the Church preaches, aided by doctors and "obliging" even "accomplice" authors, masturbation is not an unnatural act. The Church can say what it wants, in all times humans have always masturbated and they will continue to do it as long as mankind will exist in the universe. There was never any modern scientific study that concluded that masturbation was harmful. Quite to the contrary! All the serious studies arrive at the conclusion that masturbation has only advantages both on the psychological and physical plans (there is, for example, when one is a man, much less risk in developing cancer of the prostate if one masturbates regularly). Masturbation forms an integral part, and of sexual blossoming in particular, and of human balance in general.

All these teachings from so many monotheist religions about sexuality still and always have harmful consequences nowadays. We should say it, yes, let's quote, for example, this incident that happened at the Athens Airport in Greece, in 2004. A 40-year-old British traveller departing for London triggered the alarms when passing through their gantry of metal detection. What could be the cause? Well, quite simply, but after much searching, the police force at the airport discovered that she was carrying a chastity belt! According to the Greek newspaper "To Vima", the woman had explained to the police officers that her husband had forced her to carry a chastity belt to ensure that she would not engage in extra-marital affairs during her short stay abroad! Not too beautiful, all that, is it, as one would say in England! (source: www.freemetro.be, February 9, 2004 - n° 725).

Shame on Christendom and other monotheist religions for the voluntarily programmed propagation of so many stupid things about sexuality and nudity! Shame on them.

May Africa be able to distance itself completely from all these horrors conveyed by these Western monotheist religions and may it again bathe in the purity of what it was before being soiled by these "great" moral principles, which are actually more "cretin" than "Christian".

WHITE POISON

34. The danger of monotheistic religions such as "Christianity and Islam"

"All big religious buildings (of Christendom) have crime as foundation, injustice and fraud as masonry and human blood as cement".

– HENRI FRÉDÉRIC AMIEL, Swiss writer (1821-1881) –

All you have to do is open a history book, watch the news on television, listen to the radio, read newspapers, to realize that monotheistic religions are indeed dangerous for mankind, and that they have been responsible for some of the greatest drama that mankind has ever known over many centuries and including the present time.

We cannot fail to observe this if we have a minimum of this very useful commodity that allows us to live more fully, "intelligence" (from Latin intelligere: to link together), in other words, if we know how to create links between the different events that "make" or "break" our lives and the ideas advocated and implemented by them.

In actuality, the attack of September 11, 2001 in New York created an emotional shock of such an intensity that the whole planet now lives (in an almost permanent way) in a state of insecurity, of alert, of wars, of conflicts, of hostility. In short, we live under the constant threat of becoming the next victim of one of those violent acts that the media outlets feed us day after day.

But how did we arrive at this point, we, the inhabitants of a small blue planet, so pretty to look at from the sky, as told by space travelers who were lucky enough to be able to admire this sight?

If we want to find out how human beings managed to get themselves into such a state of tension, it is necessary to examine the root of this evil. We have arrived at a point of mutual misunderstanding, where violence seems the only possible means of communication (knowing fully that violence never solved anything and never will). We see this everyday, violence breeding more violence. No act of violence ever brought peace. How did we arrive here?

Why are men so inclined to commit all these acts of violence and even of "barbarism?" Why is it that we seemed "predisposed" to an automatic vengeance and, at first glance, violent? Where is the fundamental root of this problem and what is it? For instance, how can anyone commit suicide with the goal of dragging along into death thousands of innocent people? In this precise case, what do we see? On one side, deranged people in full mystical delirium hurling a plane against a populated building while shouting "God is great", "God is with us", and "in the name of God"!

But which god are they talking about? Which god are they talking to?

Which one is it? Where is this famous "GOD" invoked to justify the death of several thousands of innocent people? Those are the questions we can ask ourselves when seeing these "mad mystics" disguised as "pirate pilots".

If we asked this question to these "criminals" (because actually, it is what they are, these so-called "martyrs;" any human being killing another human being is "a criminal", nothing more!), undoubtedly, in their answer, they would tell us that it is about the "good" God, because it is the "good God" who is with them and the "bad God" is necessarily with the others!

But then on the other side, what do we see?

Well, on the other side, to take comfort, the victims' people pray to their own "good" God. You know which one it is; the one whom the assassins of their close relatives estimate to be "the evil God". It is also about that one, good or evil - I cannot tell, because for me he doesn't exist – but in any case, it is indeed that god that their President speaks to them about in his interventions, punctuating all of his speeches with "God bless America".

Most of his fellow citizens appreciate this kind of ending, driven by the daily sight of their dollars where it is written "in God we trust", still the same trust that the SS and other Nazi torturers of World War II had, since on their belt it was written "und Gott mit uns" (and God [is] with us). And the same trust, of course, the Moslem kamikazes have in their "good God"!

Therefore on both sides we are going to claim that God is with us, and we will ask Him in procession to bless incendiary bombs that will burn civilians of all ages. Nothing but delirium for those "believers" who are devoted until death, their own deliberate death, but also the one of others who were only asking to live with or without God because, obviously, all this happens in the name of an eternal, immaterial, unique and almighty "God".

But really, can any Christian (since most of the Americans believe in the Christian God) tell me where their "good" God was at the time of the September 11th drama? Where is He, what is He doing when "believers" from New York or anywhere else pray to this unique, immaterial and almighty God in order to try to forget the pain that they have just suffered? Please tell me, me who thinks that he is entirely imaginary, that he is, in a way, a "virtual God". Whoever believes that I am mistaken, please explain to me. Where is He, this so-called "Good God", each time that a similar atrocity falls on the back of the poor mankind!

It seems more than obvious to me that the great danger rests squarely in this belief in a unique, immaterial and almighty God, because, very clearly, a lot of greatly "indoctrinated" populations rely on "Him", even if He doesn't do anything, either for, or against man. It suffices to look at the reality of the world to be aware of that; his absence is manifest and his silence...eloquent!

This so-called God is nowhere to be found. He is not on the side of those who shout "Allah Akbar" and he is not on the side of those who follow President Bush setting in motion his vengeance and telling his people: "We are on a new crusade"! What a speech!

With such a speech we go back to the Middle Ages, diving again headlong into the horrors of the past, in the abominations of wars of religions, in a violent repression of the crimes of "nasty face" as much as those of "blasphemy", a repression that intensifies more and more in many countries under the deceptive pretext of obligatory struggles against "insecurity" and/or "terrorism"!

Actually, here is the truth: this belief in a unique God is itself the cause of the biggest dramas that mankind has known since its beginnings. To us Africans, this belief has been imposed by strength, by means of colonization. Unfortunately, Africa accepted this situation, estimating herself too weak to resist. With the large majority of her inhabitants, she submitted; she adopted the Religion of her colonizers and delivered herself to her dominators, "body and soul", according to one of their favourite expressions, so proud that they are of this so-called "soul", another of their inventions especially made to better lull the mind of populations.

We could say that Christian monotheism has made its fortune by invading Africa while Africa herself has become "stained" by this Christian monotheistic "conquest". Let us hope that this "stain" will not be indelible in the mind of the African people and that they will be able to expunge it for good. Otherwise it would be a great pity for Africa and the generations to come.

Africa "stained" herself with this Christian monotheism without becoming aware of all the pain that monotheism caused and continues to cause on Earth. It is especially regrettable since her ancestors were in the truth, while honouring "polytheism", an "unstained" belief based on the pluralism of worlds in the universe, the pluralism of "humanized" gods that came from the sky. Her belief is not founded on a unique and immaterial God, as the Western one, in the name of whom the Christians, guided by their hierarchy, feel authorized to commit the worse atrocities to all of humanity. This, even if one finds, in the part of the gospels accepted by their Churches, the commandments in which Jesus brings the answer on how to be "good"; for example:

« ...thou shalt do no murder ... Thou shalt love thy neighbour as thyself. » (MATTHEW XIX, 18-19)

Africans, my sisters, Africans, my brothers, it is, above all, to you that I speak: Open your eyes, you only have to see; open your ears, you only have to hear.

From the time of Europe's colonization by the Muslims, the Christian crusades, the wars of religion, the Catholic inquisition, Nazism just the day before yesterday, Rwanda yesterday, and again today, conflicts in Ireland, those between Pakistan and India, Kosovo wars, those in the Middle East, it is always and everywhere in the name of a unique God, immaterial and almighty, that we kill each other. Everywhere we virtually tear each other apart in the name of that totally "virtual" being that no one ever saw and will ever see since he is, according to the Christian thesis, immaterial and, according to the atheists' thesis, nonexistent. For me, it is a pure invention, or rather, a very "impure" invention of the human mind.

The perfect instrument to embark people on such a "hell" and lead them where we want them to go is obviously mind manipulation. To achieve this conditioning, we take scriptures as a basis; scriptures that have been distorted over time by men who acted on their prejudices and voluntarily introduced in these so-called "holy" texts lies chosen by them, according to their own interests.

Now, all these altered scriptures, essentially the Bible, the gospels and the

412

Koran, have as their common goal to spread hatred, intolerance and very often encouragement to violence, or even to barbarism. And, we continue, at all costs, teaching these monotheistic theses to our children. The consequences of this teaching are costly, - in human lives, in suffering, and in money - yet, it is in this type of education that our children bathe. We even create schools specialized in that! We see, once more, that Jesus was right in saying: "Father, forgive them, for they don't know what they are doing". But, honestly, after 2,000 years, not much has changed! Now, it is time for a change!

« Eye for eye, tooth for tooth », from the beginning monotheism really set things in motion. But such examples are innumerable. Let us start with this one: Jewish scriptures recommend to those who belong to this community not to wed non-Jews. Another case that follows in the same direction: Today you will have the Israeli nationality automatically if you are Jewish, but it will be refused to you if you are not. Unfortunately, it leads insidiously to the practice of "ethnic cleansing", perpetuated against Palestinians in this actual case.

To change, let's take another example, in Muslim scriptures; those very clearly encourage discrimination. First:

> *"O ye who believe! Take not the Jews and the Christians for your friends [...]" (THE KORAN, Surah 5:51)*
> *Then to violence towards the non Moslem:*
> *« [...] slay the pagans wherever ye find them [...] » (THE KORAN, Surah 9:5)*

And on another plan, they encourage racism and devote themselves to conjugal violence:

> *"Men are the protectors and maintainers of women, because Allah has given the one more (strength) than the other [...] refuse to share their beds, beat them [...]" (THE KORAN, Surah 4 :34)*

All this proves that monotheism clearly encourages actions contrary to Human Rights and to the laws of Democracies.

All these abominable things have never been dictated or wished for by our creators who are in Heaven... Never!

413

It is high time that Africa escapes this swamp and recovers her beautiful religious traditions and humanized gods, to be again in the Truth.

At the dawn of this new era where science moves forward rapidly and at an ever faster pace, Africa must abandon monotheistic Christianity and embrace new technologies that are going to revolutionize her lifestyle: heal all illnesses, nourish all her population, increase the quality of life of her inhabitants.

It is high time for Africa to evacuate the colonizer's "false" Christian monotheism and to put back in their place, that is to say, in the minds and in the hearts, these humanized "gods who came from the sky" who were venerated by her ancestors.

It is also time for her to understand that Science should become her first religion. Science is light, intelligence (let's recall its meaning: knowing how to create links). Christian monotheism is obscurity, lies, stupidity, obscurantism. Science and Polytheism, the belief in several human gods, do not kill. On the contrary, both of them "save". Monotheism, by itself, kills...often and repeatedly.

If Africa really wants to prepare the future mankind, if she really wants to show the example and make this planet more human, she must decrease the negative influence of monotheism. She must do it and she can do it! How? Simply by leaving the colonizer's Religion, by apostatizing, by de-christianizing.

It is not surprising that the Taliban of Afghanistan forbade television, newspapers and the Internet, because the more people are educated the less they submit to monotheism. This book has for its goal to instruct the Africans in that direction, so that they succeed in their blossoming by breaking this submissiveness to monotheistic Christianity that, until today still, continues to transform all of them - or nearly all – in "colonized"... (in) "jailed".

The monotheism of the usurping and lying colonizer is dangerous: it is responsible for the highest number of deaths and sufferings perpetrated during the whole history of Mankind. We must say it over and over, and above all, it must stop... finally! It is only by giving up the colonizer's religion that Africa will be able to hope to enter in an era of peace, science, liberty, and universal happiness. It is what I wish for her, from the deepest of my being.

414

34. The danger of monotheistic religions such as "Christianity and Islam"

WHITE POISON

35. Conclusion

In the United States (the "1st Country of the world" as its inhabitants like to proclaim it!), the Christian population increased only by 23% during the last 20 years, whereas, during the same time in Africa, the mass of Catholics doubled. It thus increased by 100%, exceeding, as of the 3rd year of the 2nd millennium A.D., a record number of 100 million individuals!

Now the fief, the bastion of Catholicism in the world is Africa. Never, in all its history in Black Africa, has Catholicism known such an exponential growth! Africa offers today to the Seat of the Vatican approximately 400 catholic bishops, the greatest majority being African blacks!

In 2003 in the Vatican, it is estimated that 18,000 African black men were undergoing studies to enter the priesthood, up significantly from 4,000 in 1978.

This report is only an assessment. But if we look at the reality hidden behind these figures, the assessment is very sad; it is deplorable. It is high time that Africans - all Africans - must examine their consciences deeply especially "Christian Africans" who are, in large part, responsible for Africa maintaining its connection to misfortune. Africa still today is saddled with the burden of triple colonialism, spiritual, economical, and political, like a ball and chain, dragging heavy at its feet.

For the simple fact that they are not aware of the terrible dichotomy that these two words represent, "Christian" and "African", it is the people who define themselves as African Christians and do so with pride and conviction who are the biggest "enemies of Africa" today. Others may identify in this way unwittingly. Whether this is a conscious choice or not it is indeed "real" and too often "cruel" for those who have to suffer the consequences.

How can these Christian blacks, these catholic blacks, knowingly and with clear conscience approve and tolerate the unsavoury actions of the Roman Catholic Church in Africa? According to many highly reliable international sources, the Church is the principle recipient of outlandish sums of "dirty" Italian money, coming from the Mafias and other criminal networks. Do they even know that the Vatican ranks 8th in the world's money laundering destinations, this according to extensive studies done on the matter of classifying money laundering. The Vatican ranks better than the popular tax havens of the Bahamas, Switzerland, and Liechtenstein. Fortunately, the media has become more forthcoming in disclosing this information to the general public.

Investigations by the "London Telegraph" and by the "Inside Fraud Bulletin" nail the City of the Vatican as being one of the principal States... tax havens. Vatican City compares in size to Macao, Mauritius or Nauru, a tiny atoll populated with 8,000 inhabitants and situated in the Pacific Ocean between the islands of Hawaii and Australia (We should also point out that the number of inhabitants of Vatican City, while a deeply guarded state secret, is estimated to be between 2,000 and 3,000 people. David Yallop provides a credible estimate).

In fact, these financial investigations establish clearly that this tiny State of the Vatican is a State whose particular banking legislation makes it impossible to trace bank deposits. In this, their banking activity will remain sheltered from the inquisitive eyes of all the police forces of the world, "ad vitam aeternam" (for eternal life), as would say some "Monsignor" of the place.

There is however a notable difference between the other "vulgar" fiscal paradises and that of the "Saint" City of the Vatican. And let us recall that it owes its very existence to the "goodness" of Italian fascist dictator... Mussolini himself. Their status has not changed since 1929. In the Vatican, money laundering is not operated by private banks but by the Central Bank of this State, an institution named "Instituto per le opere di religione" which is recognized by another international banking institution, "the Bank of International Settlements"!

Certain people, surviving Serbs and Jewish of the Shoah [Holocaust perpetrated by the Nazis at the beginning of the Forties] endeavoured to file complaints against the Vatican with the federal court of San Francisco in the United States. These legal actions were intended to obligate the Bank of the Vatican to give an account of funds despoiled at the time of the Second World War. While some of these actions were successful with the restitution of funds by Swiss Banks, it is unclear whether the same will apply to the official Bank of the Vatican or not. Only the future will tell, but we do know that this fight is far from being won in advance!

On their side, the clergy dares to claim and even affirms publicly that... [the] "fundamental reason of being [of the Bank of the Vatican] is to promote acts of piety". Oh! Really? We should be astonished by this claim since we know that these people have already been accused of housing funds despoiled by the Nazis and that today they are held in suspicion for maintaining links with the world of organized crime!

The evidence continues to mount as time passes and continues to demonstrate plainly that the activities of the Vatican, of the Church and of Christendom in general, are connected more with criminality, Mafiosi, acts of piracy, and organized crime than with "Holy" works of piety. Admittedly works of piety are deployed on the ground, but this is nothing more than a smoke screen for the "believers" naïve enough to be duped. There is only hypocrisy in this, "make believe", to conceal another sordid and unmentionable reality.

It was always like that, from the beginning of Christianity with "Saint" Paul until the false Pope, the Pontiff Benedict XVI. Yes, I do mean "false" Pope as well as "false" Pontiff. Looking closely at the origin of the words, "pope" comes from the Greek "pappas" which means "father", and "pontiff" comes from the Latin "pontifex" which has the same root as "pont" (bridge in French), that which connects two points together (two banks of a river, two points on the planet, a planet to another planet in the cosmos).

The usurper of Rome is in no case the "father" of the African nations, of the African people. And he is much less, and never will be, the one who connects the men and the women of the Earth to their "human" creators who live elsewhere in the universe. No Pope since the beginning of the history of papacy has been mandated by the Heaven to speak in the name of our creators, in the name of Yahweh, in the name of Moses or Jesus. None! There is no mandate for this. It is an attribute they gave to themselves, misleading voluntarily and successively whole generations of earthlings, Christians and non-Christians.

The Africans must find their roots again, their own culture, and cast off these inferiority complexes promulgated by the whites, complexes that they have been cultivating for such a long time, but without reason. Africa is a continent that has the advantage of not being crippled by its culture. It has to its advantage the preservation of an extraordinary purity. Westerners cannot avail themselves of this favourable condition as they are handicapped by centuries of indoctrination by their Christian/catholic religion, so strongly sullied with so many crimes.

Maintaining our purity is a formidable asset. Let us seize this moment, the fortunate consequence of the foresight and wisdom we held in the face of so much adversity and aggression.

Yes, let us take the opportunity to understand through the preservation of purity that the mightiest enemy facing Africa is our sense of inferiority to the whites. Each time that an African claims this inferiority, again without reason, he opens wide the door of his spirit... to colonization, whether it is political, economical, cultural or religious, or all of these combined!

Africans are not inferior to whites. If we convince ourselves of this condition, we fall deeper into error! Let us remember that we have this purity that the whites have lost, precisely because of their culture and the crimes that their ancestors and themselves have committed, and still commit. These crimes began with the slave system and colonization directed, supported, and promoted by their Religion, this perverse "Christianity", wretched and more deformed with time, and was maintained through the fatal economic crimes of the current neo-colonialism.

The blacks were victims, the Christian colonizers the culprits. When people and their Religion become instigators of crimes as these colonizers were, they lose their purity, their freshness, they turn sour, become increasingly unpleasant, and lack love. Bit by bit, their civilization fades and withers away.

Let us Africans be conscious of that. We Africans never want to say, "Ah, the whites have discovered everything, and us, poor Africans, we did nothing. We are cursed, social degenerates". That would be false, completely false!

Those who would be afraid to succumb to this desire understand this well. There are certain whites that are geniuses, certainly. They are at the origin of inventions and discoveries. But with a beautiful unconsciousness, the rest of the white population deludes itself into thinking that they have only themselves to thank for their achievements and that geniuses were born among them. In truth, the great masses of Westerners are uncultivated, narrow-minded...and impolite too! Africa has no reason to develop a complex in this regard, none whatsoever!

It is true that there are also absolutely brilliant people among the whites, but those never came to colonize us, never committed crimes, neither against our people, nor against Africa, never. Those who came are invaders, usurpers, stupid colonizers who exploited things that they themselves had not invented, such as powder (invented since antiquity by Chinese), weapons (guns), planes, etc.

They used all of these materials invented by others than them, to conquer us and dominate politically and culturally all of Africa in order to abuse it as they liked.

To better "domesticate" us – one could just as well say, "to tame us" – they forced us to forget our ancestors and abandon our authentic religious traditions. They then forcibly imposed on us their Religion, Christianity, transforming us into "colonized" people, completely moronic, without proper identity, cut from their roots and their traditions. We became a people praying and lamenting before the white God, the white Jesus, the white Virgin and venerating a white Pope. Although we were not aware of it at the time, the reality is that this white Pope was already involved in orchestrating the miseries of our poor people!

No African who has respect for himself can call himself Christian! Let the Christians remain in Europe; they are at home in Rome! Their home, it is "over there", not in Africa where our ancestors were converted by theirs, with blows of whips and gun fire, and at the same time treated in mass like cattle to be sold. To be Christian when one is African is to betray all our African ancestors. It is to betray the whole of Africa itself. It is to insult our ancestors who suffered, who were converted by force, and whose children were brutally taken away and placed them in Christian schools.

But then, how is it that Africans who know about all these horrors of the past agree nevertheless to be Christian? Well, the explanation is this one: a great number among us are subjugated by this idea that the whites are superior to us! Here is how it is possible. The serious problem is that it is absolutely false: this so-called superiority is only an invention created piece by piece and masterfully insinuated into our heads by those who wanted, and still want, to dominate us and to exploit us as much as possible!

We, who are Africans, let's understand that we can and we must be ourselves. Let us stand up, let us be proud, and let us be ourselves and not "Christians", for to be Christian is not compatible with anything and it contradicts everything that we are!

Africans, there were in our past cultures many local religions. But the

421

Christian colonizers utilized, in addition to weapons (guns), the weapon of the absolute contempt of our cultures: they destroyed them and persecuted their followers in order to place these authentic religions into oblivion. However, these religions were much more beautiful than Christianity and they were directly connected to our humanized gods coming from the sky, therefore to Yahweh and the angels, to Yahweh and the remainder of the members of his people who live in the heavens; in other words, on their planet, distinct from ours.

Our old gods were called by names in African terms according to the regions, tribes, languages, etc. These gods are Yahweh, Lucifer, Satan, Gabriel, Michael, Azael, Uriel, Gadrael, and all the other angels of the original Hebrew Bible, where all together their people are called in plural "Adonaï" (etymologically: Masters or Lords) or "Elohim" (etymologically: those who came from the sky).

Africans, find them again! Find your roots while keeping in mind the pride of sciences of the future that will render us not only equal but superior than the former colonizers.

The religion of the colonizer whether we call it "Christianity" or that of "Catholicism", it is still an abomination. Give it up! Abjure it! Apostatize today!

There is no lesson, no model to learn from the Christians, from Western Catholics. None. On the contrary, what they are for us is "anti-models". The Vatican is a high place of crimes and offences, from its origin to our days. It is the smallest state of the world and yet it shows one of the highest rates of offences and infringements on the planet. Does that astonish you? If you read with attention all that was exposed in this book, that should not astonish you at all anymore. According to reports emanating from the seat of the court of the pontifical State, theft, illicit appropriations, swindles and insults to civil or ministerial officers were, in this order, the offences most frequently committed in 2002.

The majority of these offences are thefts of which the millions of tourists who come to visit Saint-Peter's Basilica and the museums of the Vatican are victims; 90% of these offences are never elucidated. With the passing of years, more than one thousand lawsuits, civil (397) and penal (608), have accumulated pending judgment. The equivalent of cases per capita is more than twenty times greater than that of its neighbour Italy! In 2002, the magistrates of the pope had to intervene in a record figure of 239 cases, as 110 cases lingered with no verdict yet returned.

The Vatican Justice was faced between 1998 and 2001 with an average of 118 lawsuits per annum; between 1972 and 1992 this average rose to 138 lawsuits, and this number increased to 239 in 2002. Having read these figures, it should not be astonishing that Picardi, the prosecutor, warned of "alarming symptoms" threatening "implosion" of the legal system of the small State. Not astonishing at all. All that, to practice dishonesty with others really does not lead to honesty at home!

(source: HTTP://www.alsapresse.com/aujourdhui/IGF/article_5.html)

Moreover there is reason to believe that the Catholic Church, the Vatican, will know as of the end of 2004, the Christian calendar, the beginning of its great financial collapse. It will inevitably realize how serious its financial problems are. Initially in the Archdiocese of Boston, it will be forced to pay 70 million US dollars of allowances to the victims of the sexual abuse done by priests. It may also be forced to reimburse survivors of the Holocaust who currently have suits against the Bank of the Vatican and the Franciscan Order for diversion and money laundering pertaining to the victims of the Nazi concentration camps.

But the biggest case that awaits it and that the Vatican tries to hide, to choke at all costs, is a case introduced before the Court of Mississippi by five States claiming together a sum of 750 million US dollars stolen by the gangster criminal Martin Frankel with the assistance of the Bank of the Vatican and three Cardinals ranking high in the Vatican hierarchy. One of them is the Secretary of State of the Vatican; the two others are Papal ex-Nonces in the USA. Two of these cardinals who conspired with Frankel to steal these hundreds of millions of US dollars from the American insurance industry were mentioned as "popable", that is, likely to succeed Pope John-Paul II upon his death.

(source: HTTP://www.vaticanbankclaims.com).

We will not speak about other cases, like the complaints filed in 1999, always against the Bank of the Vatican by survivors of the Holocaust of Ukrainian, Serb and Jewish origin!

Whether you like it or not, the Vatican, the Christian Catholic Church is a criminal, usurping institution. The African blacks wearing cassocks that belong to this institution are puppets, clowns, and marionettes. Perhaps they believed they were doing good. But in actuality, they do wrong to the whole of Africa, it is them who are our biggest traitors, and it is them who are the biggest enemies of Africa. For you who were not conscious of it

423

until now, it is surely unpleasant to learn, I agree, but it is essential that you know it, that we all know it: those "cassocked people" are the worst of the "colonized" blacks!

And now all of us, Africans, conscious of having been abused for such a long time and who continue to be mistreated by this dishonest, perverse and unceasingly perverted institution and to be duped by it still today, we must leave it without delay. Let us apostatize immediately! Let us abjure this religion that, by taste of the lie, claims itself as "holy". It is not ours.

Rather let us rediscover the "healthy" religions of our ancestors in order to renew contact with our "humanized gods". They, from "the skies" where they reign and live in joy and peace, wait patiently and tirelessly for us and continue to love us. They are ready to forgive us for the fact that for so many years their love was not reciprocated. We must end this spoiled cycle immediately...not tomorrow, but today!

Before concluding this book, I will dedicate my thoughts to the great and majestic people whom I will name for the last time because they have especially worked for the emancipation of the black race, for the pride of its negritude, for the beauty of its traditions, for the release and the decolonization of this splendid part of the creation which is "the black race" in all its nobility. I want to quote the Prophet Osiris, the Prophetess Kimpa Vita, the Prophet Simao Toko, and the Prophet Simon Kimbangu.

Farther from them in time and closer to us in space, my thoughts crown today "the one who brings the light of the Elohim", "the Messiah" announced by all the religions. Blessed be his name: "Nkua Tulendo" (expressed in Kikongo), such as he was announced by the Great African Prophet Simon Kimbangu.

Indeed, thanks to the "prophecies" of Simon Kimbangu, we know this to be true: there will be a hard and heroic conquest of a second Independence ("Dipanda Dianzole") for the black people and it will be led - that is what the Great Envoy Kimbangu said - by a powerful Man who will spiritually be invested in a high mission which will transform him into a Great Political, Religious and Scientific Leader simultaneously. This powerful Leader is called in Kikongo, "Nkua Tulendo".

This Leader who is at the same time King, experienced Politician and Prophet, will restore the broken link between Yahwelohim (our creators) and

424

the black people. He will restore true Peace and Harmony. He will come with a powerful message which will initially be rejected but which will ultimately be accepted by all.

Kimbangu announced the arrival of this Great King of divine lineage of the house of the Elohim and he asked his people (all the black people) to await his arrival and to follow him as soon as he arrives.

However, I said it to you: He is here! **RAËL**, my spiritual guide. You are free to get information, to document yourself, if you wish, far from the Western media-liars who defame him and ridicule him (www.rael.org).

Our distant African ancestors, in Ancient Egypt, called the "God of Gods" or the "Supreme God", the Chief or President of the creator-gods, i.e., **"RA"** which is the equivalent of **"Yhwh"** [Yahweh in Hebrew]. Our African ancestors in Ancient Egypt called him the "God Sun" the "God light" that traveled in a solar disc (oval-shaped spaceship)...and ironically, RAEL means in ancient Hebrew "the one who brings the light of the Elohim" or **"light of the Elohim"** and his name can be found in the word **Israel**! The true "Israel" of today is where anyone recognizes the Messiah and follows his teachings. The House of Israel is within that person and nowhere else. The Hebrew State on Earth today that bears the name of "Israel" does not have the celestial right or legitimacy to bear this name as long as it does not officially recognize **The Messiah RAEL**. To this day, they have rejected him and the Elohim of the ancient original Hebrew Bible are judged on Earth because, to many in Rome, Jerusalem, and elsewhere, the system has become more important than the fundamental truth!

In fact, one day a very good friend of mine in Paris, Jean-Pierre S., convinced of the existence of our creators (plural), met with a Jewish Rabbi and began talking to him about the Elohim who came from the sky...and this is what the Rabbi coldly said: "Listen Mr. S., we know today that "God" does not exist. We today have supreme power on Earth and we plan on keeping it. So may the Elohim not even bother to come here and even if they did come one day, they will have to give us an account of some of the things that our people had to live and endure and that we did not agree with. The planet is ours today and we have the supreme power. So I say to you again, if they come they will have to explain themselves...but the truth is that we don't want them here"!

May the black African people and particularly the disciples of Prophet Simon Kimbangu not reason the same way by judging our celestial creators and their Messiah. May we in Africa do everything in our power to welcome them with this beautiful human warmth so characteristic of our people. My African brothers and sisters, Kimbangists and others, our cultures, ancient traditions, and our bond to our ancestors do not entitle us to judge or criticize our creators and the Messiah for it would be a profound betrayal, similar to denying them. For certain people and western leaders to feel this way, it is their business and their consciousness. But here in Africa, we know what it means to welcome a Prophet sent by Yahweh the Eternal. Our culture must be such that we will only judge him by what he 'says' and nothing else. We must not allow ourselves to be influenced by certain media, lying leaders, and slanderers from the West who try to maintain their fief by opposing the Messiah.

As for me, his Nlongi (instructor, teacher) I say to you, my brothers and sisters of African extraction, wherever you may be on Earth:

""Alea Jacta Est" as the Latin said long ago, "fate is in your hands".In French today one says "the die more readily are thrown". In any case now, it is up to you; it is up to us all; it is up to the whole of Africa to play. "Amen"! Yes, "So be it"! That those who have ears hear and that those who have eyes see".

The history of Christianity is a big fraud!
The only possible spiritual decolonization for the Christian blacks:

APOSTATIZE!

To apostatize is not to disavow Jesus. It is precisely to recognize him by rejecting the Church of those who betrayed him, who speak on his behalf without having been mandated to do so.

36. Bibliography

Books

Psychiatrists – the men behind Hitler, the architects of horror –,
Röder, Kubillus and Burwell, Freedom Publishing Los Angeles

The first Christians,
by Maurice Chatelain, La Caravelle éditions, San Diego, 1990

"Mirage of the age"
by Andrew Thomas, Exposition Press New York, 1983

"La vie secrète de Saint Paul" et
"Jésus ou le mortel secret des Templiers"
by Robert Ambelain, Editions Robert Laffont, 1972 and 1970

"La Révélation des Templiers –
les gardiens secrets de la véritable identité du Christ",
by Lynn Picknett & Clive Prince, aux éditions J'ai Lu

ELOHIM,
une autre lecture de la Bible, RogerVigneron, Editions La vague à l'âme,
1993

Les mythes hébreux,
par Robert Graves et Raphaël Pataï, éditions Fayard, 1987

Inventeurs et savants noirs,
Yves Antoine, Editions l'Harmattan, 1998

Hommage à la femme noire,
Simone Schwarz-Bart, Editions Consulaires, 1988

Les racines africaines de la civilisation européenne,
J.P. Omotunde,Editions Menaibuc

A history of the Jews in America,
A.Karp, 1977

Les Dieux d'Israël, la vraie nature du dieu de la Bible,
André Cherpillod, Edition de l'auteur, F-72570 Courgenard

La Bible Ancien Testament, Tomes I & II,
Direction Edouard Dhorme, "Bibliothèque de la Pléiade", Editions Gallimard, 1985

La Bible Nouveau Testament, "Bibliothèque de la Pléiade",
Editions Gallimard, 1986
> *(For English translations of the Bible, we quoted from the King James Version on "www.crosswalk.com – online study bible"). Please note: the words "God" and "Lord" quoted in the King James Version were changed to the words "Elohim" and "Yahweh" where applicable to correspond with the words quoted in the French version above).*

Le Coran, Traduction et Notes:
M. Ksimirski Editeur : I.P. Verlagsgesellschaft, München, 1990
> *(For English translations of the Koran, http://www.muslimaccess. com/quraan/translations/index.asp was used).*
Diffuseur de la version française : J. Lazarus, Paris.

Les derniers rois mages du Rwanda,
Paul del Perugia, Editions Phébus, Paris, 1978

Au nom de Dieu,
de David Yallop, Editeur Christian Bourgeois, Paris, 1989

Dieu a t'il peur des femmes ?,
Editions Mouvement Jeunes femmes Nudité et pudeur, Duerr,
Editions Maison des Sciences de l'Homme

La sexualité regard actuels,
Germain et Langis, Editions Etudes Vivantes

Les combats des femmes,
Goldmann, Editions Castermann

L'inquisition,
Que sais je, Editions Presses Universitaires de France

Un siècle d'amour charnel, Hickman, Editions Blanche

Rich Dad, Poor Dad
by Robert T. Kiyosaki & Sharon L. Lechter, published by Techpress, Inc.,
Arizona, USA

Conséquences politiques, sociales et économiques de la fixation des fron-
tières de l'Etat Indépendant du Congo,
par Edouard Makumbuila, Université Libre de Bruxelles, Faculté des
Sciences Sociales, Politiques et Economiques, mémoire juin 1972

Media organizations

Journal "Solidaire", "400 ans de traite d'esclaves africains", N° 21, 20 mai
1998, (page 9)

Golias Magazine, "Rwanda : l'honneur perdu des missionnaires", N°
48/49, 1996

Magazine "Actuel", article "Grands Rois", N° 133-134, juillet-août 1990

Web sites - Pages to check out -

http://www.ne-kongo.net/communaute/mythekimbangu.html
http://www.secularhumanism.org/library/fi/paul_23_4.html
(the great scandal: Christianity,s role in the rise of the Nazis)
http://news.bbc.co.uk/2/hi/health/3176982.stm
http://www.katinkahesselink.net/his/messiah2.html
http://www.deboutcongolais.info/mulele_3.html
http://www.reseauvoltaire.net/article7605.html
http://www.vaticanbankclaims.com
http://atheisme.free.fr http://www.emeagwali.com
http://www.cultural-expressions.com/thesis/saide.htm
http://maliba.8m.com/Histoire/anciens.htm
http://perso.wanadoo.fr/d-d.natanson/devenus.htm
http://perso.wanadoo.fr/fidylle/docs/dogons.html
http://www.africamaat.com/article.php3?id_article=133
http://www.africamaat.com/article.php3?id_article=18
http://www.marie-madeleine.com/maryam.html
http://www.diegocuoghi.com
http://www.ufoartwork.com/
http://www.ankhonline.com/egypte1.htm
http://anti-religion.monblogue.com/main.php
http://www.tlfq.ulaval.ca/axl/amsudant/guyanefr1685.htm
(the 60 articles of the "Black Code")

January 2007

ISBN: 2-9600478-0-X

LEO
KHALEED
MUHAMAD

Printed in Great Britain
by Amazon